WITNESS

THE STORY OF A SEARCH

Witness: The Story of a Search
Author: J.G. Bennett

First published Hodder & Stoughton Ltd, London 1962
Second edition: Omen Press, 1974
Third edition Bennett Books 1997
Fourth edition Bennett Books 2005

This edition published by The J.G. Bennett Foundation
© The Estate of J.G. Bennett and Elizabeth Bennett 2017
All rights reserved

ISBN-13: 978-1545300237

ISBN-10: 1545300232

WITNESS

THE STORY OF A SEARCH

By

JOHN GODOLPHIN BENNETT

Contents

REVISED FOREWORD TO THE 1997 EDITION

In this re-issue of "Witness", we have reverted to J.G. Bennett's original subtitle, 'The Story of a Search', in place of 'The Autobiography of John Bennett', because the subject of the book - unusual for an autobiography - is not the writer himself but his 'aim'. Anyone with a cursory acquaintance with the ideas of G.I. Gurdjieff - Bennett's first teacher - will recognise that having an aim is seen as an essential prerequisite of transformation. Few of us, however, are able to keep that aim in front of ourselves throughout our lives, but Bennett was one of those who could, and this book is the story of the consequences.

"Witness" works on various levels. First of all, it remains a gripping account of an unusually diverse life. Secondly, it serves as an introduction to the ideas of, among others, Gurdjieff, the Shivapuri Baba, Pak Subuh and J.G. Bennett himself, and thirdly, it is an honest account of the spiritual life of an extraordinary man. As a life story it seems episodic: there's no career path, no obvious external continuity. In his spiritual life, Bennett seems to have moved from one teacher to another: Gurdjieff, Ouspensky, Madame Ouspensky, Gurdjieff again, Mohammad 'Pak' Subuh, the Shivapuri Baba, in a way which some colleagues and friends viewed as anything from frivolity to betrayal. Beneath these changes however, was an unusual continuity of purpose: Bennett's search for Absolute Liberation, which he talks of - and then merely in hints - only in the final pages of this book.

Just because "Witness" is 'the story of a search', there are many things it leaves unsaid that would appear in an ordinary autobiography. Bennett's involvement in worldly affairs is mainly described as an adjunct to his inner life. There is minimal name-dropping, and although interesting historical figures make an appearance, many more whom Bennett knew are not mentioned. Even close members of his family have only walk-on parts. His sister Winifred - two years younger than Bennett and herself a remarkable woman - noted, acerbically, that this life story begins when he was twenty-one, as if his childhood didn't matter. In fact, knowing them both, it was clear how alike they were in temperament and spiritual outlook - almost certainly products of an upbringing that Bennett hardly mentions. Such details, which, after all, include the writers of this introduction, may appear in a later biography, but they don't concern Bennett's own account. The last four chapters of this edition of Witness were written and published in 1972, as part of a revision of the original edition that had appeared ten years earlier. They were written in a hurry, but they still give a flavour of the extraordinary experiences in the last few years of his life.

That this book was revised rapidly was nothing new. Bennett always wrote at great speed - by hand - and, though he occasionally managed to take two or three weeks off to complete a book, his writing was usually fitted into an already overcrowded schedule which, by the end of his life, had reached almost lunatic complexity, even for a man half his age.

At the time "Witness" was revised and republished, Bennett was conducting courses at Sherborne House in Gloucestershire, England, which he describes in the final chapter of this book, entitled 'Life Begins at Seventy'. These courses involved around one hundred students at a time and lasted ten months, during which time Bennett attempted to pass on the fruits of his lifelong search, covering nearly sixty years. The students at Sherborne were people of all nationalities and ages, but mainly Americans in their twenties, whom he hoped would be able to use his teaching as part of a continuous process of transformation. As if Sherborne wasn't enough to occupy him, Bennett also put a great deal of energy, in his final years, into building bridges to other spiritual movements, including those followers of Gurdjieff from whom he and his own students had been estranged. He was a speaker at the conference to inaugurate Auroville in honour of Sri Aurobindo in India; he invited the Venerable Bhante Dharmawara to teach meditation at Sherborne; he maintained close contacts with the neighboring Beshara Sufi organisation; and he frequently visited Madame Jeanne de Salzmann in Paris to expedite the publication of Gurdjieff's Third Series. As part of these last discussions, he brokered an agreement between the Gurdjieff Foundation and Gurdjieff's family which allowed the film 'Meetings With Remarkable Men' to be made. And in his last years, Bennett kept in close and regular contact with Hasan Shushud, the last major spiritual influence in his life, and certainly the least known.

Those who knew Bennett at the time - even those, like us, who were scarcely more than children - could see that in the last years of his life he changed profoundly, though he took some care to conceal it. He gives some clues to the extent of this transformation in the final pages of this revised edition, but they are only hints.

During the Sherborne courses, Bennett lectured almost daily to his students, and many of his later talks are available in audio form. Some have formed the basis for books published posthumously, and one of the most remarkable - though not recorded at the time - formed the core of his last book, *The Masters of Wisdom*. This was the fulfillment of a prophesy of Gurdjieff, that Bennett would one day give a lecture on the role of Judas Iscariot for which people would be very thankful.

Hasan Shushud at first disapproved of the Sherborne experiment, insofar as it distracted Bennett from his own destiny, but it was entirely characteristic that Bennett should put his students, the publication of The Third Series - indeed almost anyone else's convenience - ahead of his own needs. And it is a measure of the importance that he attached to teaching people at Sherborne that he effectively killed himself in his efforts to maintain the courses.

Few of us noticed those efforts; we simply took his powers for granted. Looking at photographs of Bennett in the last year of his life it is now surprising to see an old man. At the time, we saw someone powerful and full of vitality, even if, on the physical level at least, this was an illusion that he himself projected. When Bennett died, he left many of his students with a strong sense of mission to continue his work, and over the years many have worked effectively in groups and communities with what they learned from him. For some former students, this has also involved experimenting with quite varied influences and ideas, while retaining the essentials of his teaching, perhaps only now beginning to see its real significance.

Such experimentation was certainly a characteristic of Bennett's own work. Throughout his life he was always prepared to try something new, if he thought it would advance his aim, almost always at the price of being shunned by his former colleagues. The day after he died, his wife Elizabeth told his pupils at Sherborne: "Remember him as an example of how much can be achieved in this lifetime." Witness is worth reading to see just how much that can be; but it also gives some idea of the price one must be prepared to pay.

George Bennett
Ben Bennett
Massachusetts, December 2012

John Godolphin Bennett

Sherborne House 1974

(Photograph: Annette Green)

PREFACE

The first edition of this book brought my life's search to the year 1961. So much has happened in the past twelve years that I needed this chance to make a fresh appraisal and I am grateful to Omen Press for giving me the opportunity. The last four chapters of the present edition are new and they bring the story of my search up to the present year. During this time, my concern has become more and more directed to the world situation and the future of mankind. In the last volume of *The Dramatic Universe*, published in 1965, I gave my reasons for believing that we are in the early stages of the *Parousia*, the Second Coming of Christ which heralds the end of the present world. I am often asked if this is intended to be taken literally, and if so, whether I still hold the same conviction. The answer to both questions is that I am no less convinced than I was ten years ago, and indeed discern growing evidence that the great event is in progress. We have to separate fact from fantasy, figurative representation of real signs from interpretations made a thousand or two thousand years before the time of change arrived. The facts are plain: the old world is disintegrating and before the end of this century will have disappeared. An immense destructive power is at work and it can be combated only upon the invisible planes of understanding and love. There is also unmistakably a creative counter-action that does not originate in the human mind. The influences that enter our ordinary human experience from these planes of spirituality never cease to flow: they find a home wherever they are willingly admitted and responded to. At the present time, the counter-action is growing more powerful and millions of men and women, especially those born after the last great war, are aware of it. All who are touched - even half-consciously - by the realization that a Great Work is in progress, feel drawn to take part in it. This creates the movements of enquiry and search which characterise our time.

We witness the accelerated changes that are occurring in our science and technology. Knowledge doubles every ten years. New discoveries such as jet propulsion, atomic energy, and satellite communication have changed our lives completely in the short space of one generation since the last war. We see the threat to our civilization from the population explosion and the failure of food supplies. We see governments and great corporations growing on the one hand more and more powerless to control the course of events and on the other more and more determined to concentrate power in the hands of small despotic groups.

From year to year, the probability increases that the social structure of the world will break down before the end of the present century. I believe we must reckon with a period of panic during which it will become evident to all that existing institutions are helpless to prevent catastrophe. Only the immense inertia and built-in resistance to change will keep things going for another thirty or forty years. After that an entirely new social system will have to take over. It will be neither capitalist nor communist, neither national nor international but consist of largely self-supporting experimental settlements learning to help one another to survive. The big cities will slowly be depopulated and fall into decay. National governments will be replaced by agencies, whose main function will be to maintain the distribution of vital supplies. Life will simplify.

For three thousand years and more, the world has lived by expansion and complexification. This trend has reached saturation. We must now turn again towards concentration and simplification. This does not mean throwing away the discoveries of science and technology that have real value, but it does mean abandoning all the results that threaten destruction. We shall have to give up the use of the automobile for private transport, the mass production of mechanical and electronic devices that are not necessary for life, the expenditure of vast resources on 'education' and 'defence'. I have put these last words in quotation marks for they stand for two of the great frauds of our time. 'Education' does not educate and 'defence' does not defend. An enormous simplification of life, and with it a great increase in human happiness and prospect of survival, will come when mankind begins to base life upon the principle of satisfying needs rather than that of gratifying the lust for more and more and more.

If these changes are to come without major disruption it will be necessary for the true situation of the world to be revealed. We are kept in ignorance of the reality, not so much by deliberate suppression as by the inability to see and think upon a large enough scale. We observe recurrent crises followed by encouraging signs of progress and prosperity.

The overall trend towards disintegration which must be seen over a period of at least a century is disguised by the ebb and flow of political and economic activity. The need is for more people who can see how things are going and work for the future of the human race. The real situation is that man unaided is powerless to prevent catastrophe. The sole hope is in cooperation with the Higher Powers that are acting in their own way and their own time. This is the Great Work in which all are called to take part who are able to do so. For this they must be trained to perceive, to understand and to withstand the strains of the world process. The training must be directed to man himself and all his powers bodily, mental and spiritual. We need people who can make the conscious, stable decision to dedicate themselves to serve the future.

In 1970, I became aware that I must do what I could to show that this training is possible. Fifty years of search had convinced me that Gurdjieff's method brought up to date and completed from other sources was the best available technique for giving just the training that the world needs. In October 1971, the International Academy for Continuous Education started its first course and now the second has been completed. The results show that the method works for those who can commit themselves to an all-out effort. I have described the enterprise in the last chapter.

All over the world people are aware of the need to prepare for the new age. Thousands of experimental communities, urban and rural, are searching for a new way of life. This search has in the 1970s replaced the political activism of the 1960s. Another feature of this decade is the proliferation of spiritual mass movements that offer some form of instant salvation. These trends sometimes combine in the form of spiritual communities that live with apocalyptic fervour awaiting the end of the world. There are also many realistic 'this worldly' settlements that aim only at survival.

These activities carry a significant foretaste of the new society, but they are not complete and most of them will fail before the end of the decade. By 1985 new factors will have entered the life of people throughout the world. Among these will be the actual taste of privation among those who have never been deprived and the hoarding of resources by those who control them. We can already see these attitudes forming and hardening, but they do not directly and obviously touch the lives of all the people of the world. When this happens a great change will come. People will look seriously for a different way of living and the new age will begin.

But if it is to begin aright, and if much suffering is to be avoided, the 'different way of living' must be there for all to see. That is why settlements or groups on the lines I have indicated must be created without delay. These cannot be done by human enterprise alone, nor can it come about by blind, unreasoning faith in Providence. It will require cooperation between man and the spiritual forces that are higher and more intelligent than himself. In a very real sense, these spiritual forces are the manifestation of Christ in the world. But it must be understood that spiritual forces are never coercive, overriding human will. Man will be saved in so far as he allows himself to be saved and cooperates in his salvation.

This is why I have called the coming age, the Synergic Epoch. Arrogance must give place to humility, selfishness to service and belief in expansion for its own sake must be replaced by the acceptance of the quality that simplicity alone can give. It is ideas and attitudes that change the world. We need a completely new attitude towards our mother the earth and all that lives on her generous bosom. Today we use our powers to despoil and destroy; we must be shown how to use them to cherish and preserve. Our future depends upon those who see and can help others to see. The older generations, with few exceptions, are blind. Hope lies with the young; but they too must put short-term selfish aims aside and work for the future.

1: NEAR-DEATH AND MARRIAGE

This is the story of my life, but it does not start with birth and childhood, nor with my early memories. The real beginning of life came to me with the taste of death, on the morning of 21 March 1918. There is a world of difference between seeing death nearby, but outside, and seeing death from the inside. Several times in my life, under very different conditions, I have known what it is like to be dead. This book is about the connection between life and death as, during the past forty-five years, it has gradually become clearer to me and more assured.

As every beginning has antecedents, I shall start from a bitter cold morning early in March 1918, when I climbed down into the chalk caverns of Roeux, leaving behind the mud and the trenches, the occasional rattle of machine guns, the barrages and raids that make the dull, obvious routine of trench warfare. Cave warfare was neither dull nor obvious. The chalk caverns of Roeux stretch for many miles from France into Belgium, from our front line as it was then, deep into the German sector. In the darkness, lights were precursors of trouble and in the dim glow to which one's eyes slowly became accustomed, a stalagmite could be a German sentinel; drops of water from the chalk roof could be the tapping of a pickaxe.

I have no idea how many hundreds of British and German troops sheltered and stalked one another in the caverns. I was there on a special mission, which I had brought on myself through a weakness that has always led me into difficulties. This consists in volunteering to undertake tasks for which I am less than half qualified and finding myself obliged to compensate, by an excessive effort, for my lack of skill and experience. We had in the Roeux caves a newly developed instrument to amplify weak currents of electricity passing through the earth and could, in this way, listen in to conversations on the German field telephones. To use the instrument, one had both to understand German and have some knowledge of thermionic valves. I was Guards Divisional Wireless Officer, and the interception instrument was operated by the Army Corps Intelligence, and thus no affair of mine. But the Intelligence Officer had been caught in a barrage on his way to the front line and was either dead or seriously wounded. We had been asked at Guards' Divisional H.Q. for a volunteer and I had offered, although I should have known that my school German would be inadequate for listening to faint German voices.

Once I reached Roeux caves there was no going back, for no one else there could either use the instrument or understand German. At that time, all the talk was of a great German attack impending, and any hint picked up from an indiscreet talk over the field telephone could save thousands of lives. So I sat in the darkness listening tensely and occasionally hearing tantalizing fragments of conversation that might mean much or nothing.

The hours passed. No one came to relieve me. Messengers came every hour to take away the notes I had made. During this time, by a strange freak, I tuned in to hear the letters S.O.S. signalled. I was then a trained signaller and could follow the message and its drama. A ship had just been torpedoed in the North Sea and was sinking. Writing after more than forty years, I can still feel again the stab of painful awareness of our common stake in death. I was here, under the earth in the deep chalk caverns, knowing that any day the fiercest battle of the war might kill me and a hundred thousand more like me. And out there were the ship and its crew, soon to perish in the bitter North Sea waters. The only bond between us was the prospect of an early death.

The ship's signals suddenly ceased and I tuned in again to the harsh, indistinct voices of German officers. The shock had filled me with new energy and I had lost the wish to sleep. When I was relieved, I was astonished to learn that two nights and two days had passed and that I had neither slept nor stopped listening. The way out of the caves led behind the high embankment of the Marne et Oise Canal to the shelter where I had left my motor-bicycle. Only when I mounted to ride back to Headquarters did fatigue overtake me. I fell asleep in the saddle and awoke several hours later half buried in the mud, feeling very, very cold and weak.

I returned to my own task of ensuring wireless contact with Guards Division front line, until the ominous quiet was broken by the expected artillery barrage and the great German attack had begun. My state was that strange condition known to all who have experienced extreme fatigue. The physical sensation is of a kind of disembodiment. There is a headache that is painful and even frightening, but with it a sense of being set free from the limitations of ordinary existence.

Under favourable circumstances, this state can pass into one of complete clarity in which the ordinary self is aware of the presence of a consciousness higher than its own.

From these last days before the beginning of my life story, one incident has left a vivid picture in my memory. With my trusted Corporal Jenkins, who knew in practice all that I had learned in theory, I went out one moonless night to erect a wireless aerial on a disused telegraph post.

I put on the signaller's climbing irons and clambered up as noiselessly as possible until I could rest my weight on the iron bars. Some sound alerted the Germans - only half a mile away - and a fierce machine-gun fire started to sweep the ground below me. Corporal Jenkins sheltered in a hollow, but I could not come down, for the machine-gun bullets were passing not far below my feet. I felt completely detached from my bodily state and the thought came to me: "How strange it would be to die hanging like Christ on a tree." I cannot tell how long the firing lasted, but just as my arms were beginning to tire, it stopped and after waiting a few minutes, I clambered down. Corporal Jenkins and I were astonished to find one another unscathed.

Three days later, I was wounded. I have lost all memory of what happened. I was riding on a motor-bicycle through Monchy-le-Preux, then quite deserted after a terrible battering from the German artillery. The German advance had started that morning and my job was done for the moment. The last thought I remember was of surprise that I was not afraid. The firing was still pretty heavy and I had not acquired the old soldier's indifference. I remember saying: "If I get through Monchy, I shall be all right."

My next memory is of waking up - not inside, but outside my own body. I knew I was not dead. I could see nothing and hear nothing, and yet I perceived that my body was lying on a white bed. I gradually became aware that there were other men present, and somehow I was seeing what they saw and even feeling what they felt. I am quite sure that my eyes did not open and that I had no sensation of my own body. Yet I was aware that stretcher after stretcher was being carried in and that there was no place for them all. Stretchers were placed on each side of my bed. I knew there were wounded and dying men, but heard no sound. I knew that we were being bombarded - not because I could hear the shells - but because I could feel the shock with which the people present reacted to them.

One very clear memory is of a man in a nearby bed. I knew he was an army padre and I knew that he was afraid of dying. I knew that in some way he was stuck to his body and I was not stuck. Some thought passed through me like: "How strange - he doesn't know that it will not hurt him if his body is destroyed!"

At that moment, it was perfectly clear to me that being dead is quite unlike being very ill or very weak or helpless. So far as I was concerned, there was no fear at all. And yet I have never been a brave man and was certainly still afraid of heavy gun-fire. I was cognizant of my complete indifference toward my own body.

Yet I was not totally disconnected from it. When my body was taken to the operating theatre, I went with it. I must have been unconscious during the operation - indeed, later I was told that I remained in a coma for six days. Yet I heard a voice saying: "Fine, please," and a woman's voice answer: "There is only coarse left." Several days later, when I returned to consciousness and the stitches were taken out of my head, the nurse said: "I wonder why they used coarse hair." I said: "They had no fine left." She seemed surprised: "However do you know that? You were unconscious."

Together with such trivial memories, there remains with me something that is not memory as when one remembers past events. It is the awareness that I entered some realm of experience where all perceptions are changed and our physical bodies are not required. I often tried later to recapture the certainty that made me say: "If my body is destroyed, what does it matter?" but there was no bridge by which I could pass from this world to that. Death supremely justifies the Chinese saying: "He who has not tasted does not know." But I would go further and say: "He who has not the taste of being dead present in his awareness cannot know death." Nearly every other experience can be preserved in our memory, but it seems well established that those who have died and returned to life can never recapture the taste of dying.

We also forget the taste of birth, but this seems natural, for a new-born child seems to have nothing to remember with. Yet perhaps he also knows what it is like to be without the need to have a physical body, but cannot keep the taste once he is well and truly fixed in the body that is to accompany him through this earthly life. My own belief is that birth and death have much in common. My experience on 21st March 1918, was as much a birth as a death - though I did not realize until much later that I had indeed died and been born again.

After a few weeks, I was transferred by hospital ship to England. I was taken to the First Military General Hospital in Cambridge. My mother came to see me as soon as I arrived. She had received a War Office telegram to say I was dangerously wounded, but had not felt that I would die. I was partially paralysed on my right side; I had a severe head wound, but the skull was not fractured. I was peppered with shrapnel - some fragments did not work out of my body for years. But compared with most of the men in my ward - severe surgical cases in the true sense of the word - I had little to worry about. Gradually I regained the use of my right arm and leg and could walk again. But I myself was no longer the same. The youth who had left England in 1917 was no longer living in my body. And yet I was living his life - the life of a stranger. Even though I could remember his thoughts, I could not feel his feelings.

A new life began in Cambridge. Among visitors to the hospital came Sir Arthur Shipley, Master of Christ's and then Vice-Chancellor of the University. He asked me if I wanted any books. Then I found that even if I were changed, my weaknesses were still present. Out of vanity or bravado, I asked for the works of Benedetto Croce in Italian. Shipley was delighted at the unexpectedness of my reply and soon after obtained permission of the hospital to take me to the Master's Lodge to convalesce. He introduced me everywhere as his 'wounded officer who reads Benedetto Croce in Italian'. Fortunately for me, as my Italian was strictly of the nursery variety, I had to content myself with Ainslie's translation, and I must confess that I could not make much of it.

Shipley was the kindest of men and was deeply distressed at the wholesale destruction of the young men of my generation. He made a great fuss of the little group of wounded officers he managed to collect at his Lodge, and seeing that my interest in philosophy and mathematics was not wholly insincere, he arranged meetings with the most famous men in Cambridge. So I had private talks with Sir Joseph Thompson about electrons and relativity; with Sir Joseph Larmor about the tensor calculus suddenly made famous by Einstein; and, above all, with Prof. J.A. Hobson, the Sadleirian Professor of Mathematics, about the geometry of higher dimensions. I had already begun to suspect that there might be a connection between geometrical higher space and the world without bodies, of which evidence had been shown me on 21st March. Hobson encouraged me by saying that a theorem I discovered about rotations in a space of five dimensions was worth publishing. It was an exciting time for a young man whose life had been lived in the obscurity of a London suburb.

One day, we were joined at lunch by General (later Field Marshal) Sir William Robertson and General Smuts, who had come to Cambridge to receive honorary degrees. Shipley made them speak to me and I was asked to give my impressions of the German attack of 21st March. I was astonished at their interest in what I said. Only much later did I realize that Robertson had been dropped by Lloyd George and that Smuts had stood by him in his quite unmerited disgrace. Smuts told me to visit him if ever I came to South Africa. Just thirty years later I took him at his word.

The war was still raging. I learned that my successor as Guards Divisional Wireless Officer had been killed within two days, and his successor also had been fatally wounded in the same terrible battle: the last great German effort of the war. Death was too close to be forgotten. A new question began to trouble me. Why was I still alive? So many of my schoolfellows and fellow cadets at the Shop had been killed and not I. Why not?

Whether from such thoughts, or from my head wound, or from a convalescence too exciting for my still weak body, I collapsed and was sent to Craiglochart Military Hospital near Edinburgh. Either there or somewhere else - I have forgotten - I began to walk in my sleep and once tried to jump out of the window. This time I again felt separated from myself. My body was walking and behaving foolishly: but I was not concerned - why should I be? This condition soon passed and I was allowed to go into Edinburgh for lessons in German, which had taken my fancy. My German teacher introduced me to Professor Henri Bergson, who was giving a lecture at the University on Emotion and Sensation, if I remember rightly. Something he said made me feel that he would understand my experience of *dédoublement*. He listened kindly, but not attentively, and I realised that his interest was more in ideas than in people. That was the first, and for a very long time the only, attempt I made to speak of my inner experience.

Early in September 1918, while at Craiglochart, I and all officers then convalescent in Great Britain received a War Office circular inviting applications for courses in Turkish and Arabic. No doubt hundreds, bored with the thought of months to be spent in a depot far from any war excitement, sent in the forms. I did so - but with a clear conviction that I was bound to go to Turkey. I heard nothing myself, but another officer was called to London for interview. Something had gone wrong. I suspected that my Medical Board grading 'Unfit for Foreign Service' was the reason. Somehow, I persuaded the Commandant to give me another Medical Board urgently, got a higher grading and rushed to London. I ought to make it clear that I was, at that time, neither a linguist nor interested in languages. I prided myself on being a mathematician, and my only linguistic exploit had been my German vigil in the chalk caverns of Roeux.

I reported at the War Office and was told that I had been rejected, not for health reasons, but because there had been so many applications that only those with some previous knowledge of Turkish or Arabic were being considered. Here, for once, my weakness proved a strength. I said boldly that I knew a little Turkish. The Staff Officer interviewing candidates, who was evidently tired of arguing, told me to wait and take a Turkish test. My claim to know a little Turkish could not have been weaker – I knew one word: *bilmem* meaning 'I don't know!' I naturally expected to fail in the test, but after three hours' wait, I was called and told it was too late, I was to return on Wednesday - two days later. I felt this to be a sign that I must succeed. I hurried to the nearest Berlitz School and was lucky enough to find an Armenian who taught Turkish. To my dismay, he told me I had to learn a new alphabet and a vocabulary quite unlike any European language. He assured me that even a smattering of Turkish could not be learned in less than six months. Two days was a mad joke.

However, I persuaded him and we set to work from morning till night.

When I returned to the War Office, I blushed at the absurdity of the undertaking. I went in for my interview and found myself facing Mr. G. Fitzmaurice, former Chief Dragoman at the Sublime Porte and an old friend of my father. I remembered that he was a famous connoisseur of oriental rugs, and, hoping to cover my ignorance, asked him if it was wise to buy rugs in Turkey. The ruse worked better than I dared to hope. For half an hour he lectured me on the folly of inexperienced amateurs expecting to outwit the carpet dealers of Galata. Then suddenly realizing the time had passed, he said: "By the way, I have not examined your Turkish. I suppose you learned it from your father. Anyhow, you had better try your luck with the course." Such is our ingratitude to the Divinity that shapes our ends that my only thought was: "Two days' work and five pounds of my good money gone to waste!"

So I found myself in an officers' course at the School of Oriental Studies with a really talented teacher, Ali Riza Bey. The Turkish language, with its syntax so different from that of any European language, fascinated me and I worked at it with an enthusiasm I had never before given to any task. I paid for private lessons every night with Ali Riza Bey and all day long between the regular classes learned Turkish poetry by heart. It is hardly surprising that I passed first over others who had started with a fair knowledge of colloquial Turkish, but no interest in the fine points of the language.

From that course, I began to see how all our thinking is dominated by our linguistic forms. Europeans and Turks could not possibly think in the same way. The subject-predicate form of our language makes a subject-predicate logic seem inevitable. In the Turanian root language, from which Turkish is derived, there is no predicate form. There are not even sentences as we understand them, but rather a single word complex that expresses the speaker's attitude or feeling towards a situation. There is in Turkish a natural, easily recognised, distinction between statements of fact, statements of opinion and expressions of feeling. We have in English to make these distinctions artificially and often omit to do so. In interpreting between Europeans and Turks, it is necessary to be sure that a clearly expressed uncertainty in Turkish is not rendered as a statement of fact. Accusations of bad faith against Turks and other Asiatics are often due to this kind of mistranslation. Even when a Turk speaks a European language, his forms of thought remain Turkish.

All this, and much more, I learned from Ali Riza Bey, and when I went to Turkey it enabled me to gain the confidence of the Turks with whom I had dealings; but I must add also that the Turkish modes of thought seemed nearer to my own inner needs than the subject-predicate logic I had learned at school. Less than three years had passed since I had discovered and made a hero of Aristotle. Now I was becoming aware that logic can be a great deceiver.

I was more and more drawn towards the East. It had not meant very much to me as a boy. Though my father had been a great traveller, Africa and South America had excited him more than Asia. I was being drawn towards Asia in spite of myself The war had ended, and the sensible course would have been to resign my commission and return to Oxford where my scholarships awaited me and where I had the prospect of a good degree. This course was the more obviously sensible inasmuch as I was about to marry. What I actually did was neither sensible nor consistent. I made every effort to get to Turkey as quickly as possible and yet I got married knowing that I must leave my wife behind.

This first marriage was a strange affair. Before going to France in 1917, I had engaged myself to marry the elder sister of a school friend. Evelyn McNeill was a tall, beautiful girl with large green eyes that had seemed to a sixteen-year-old schoolboy all that the world could offer of feminine tenderness. Certainly, I had been flattered to notice that she preferred my company to that of men of her own age. But the bond between us was more than the vanity and possessiveness that are elements in nearly all human relationships. She was my first love and I did not look to right or left. I had not yet awakened to my own male nature, and neither as a schoolboy nor as a military cadet had women meant much to me. My engagement had surprised me: I had not intended to propose marriage, but heard my own voice doing so during a weekend leave from the R.M.A., Woolwich.

When I returned wounded from France, all that had happened to me before was like a dream. Evelyn came to visit me in hospital and I was pleased to see her. But of my inner experience I could not say a word. One attempt to do so had so distressed her that I realized that she was afraid that my head injury had affected my brain.

As my body grew stronger after my convalescence, I began to feel, also, sexual impulses that I had not known as a boy. Everything seemed to point to an early marriage. My mother had brought me up so strictly that any sexual outlet except marriage seemed unthinkable. And yet she herself was deeply grieved at my intention to marry. Many years later, I saw a letter she wrote to Evelyn's father saying that she was convinced that the marriage must be a failure and begging him to intervene with his daughter. All this passed over my head. I was not one man, but two or even three. The youth who was committing himself week by week more helplessly to the marriage was like a wraith of my former self in strange alliance with my newly awakening man's body. The man who was to go to Turkey seemed to be living in a deeper and truer stratum of my consciousness. Behind both of them was that self - neither youth nor man - that had known the taste of death and immortality. I had not reached the point of asking myself the question: "In all this, who am I?" Nor did I realize that in everything I thought and did, the same unchanging defects of character were always present. My proposal of marriage was just another instance of my proneness to undertake a task for which I was not qualified. I was drifting into a situation that both frightened and fascinated me and that was at the same time quite unreal - for I was aware all the time that I was to find my real life in Turkey.

If I had had any capacity for introspection I might have seen that I had changed inwardly, and this might have given me the courage to change the direction my life was taking outwardly. But I was, and always have been, slow to see the obvious.

From Armistice Day, 11th November 1918, to 20th December, the day of my wedding, my life was tense to breaking point. At least ten hours a day were spent in learning Turkish. Meanwhile my father's illness was taking a deadly serious turn. He had been invalided out of the Army with blackwater fever contracted in Central Africa. Incurably optimistic, he was convinced he would get well and was constantly making plans for new journeys and new undertakings to make us all rich.

My father and mother loved each other deeply, but my mother's puritanical New England upbringing made her incapable of accepting my father's inability to behave properly either in sexual or in financial matters. For fear lest we children might be contaminated, she had sent my father away from home, but continued to meet him secretly. I could tell many stories of the stoic or Spartan attitude she had towards life - and, indeed, in which she took the utmost pride. When my father was dying, she went only once to visit him in a dingy boarding-house bedroom near Kennington Oval, to which he had been driven by poverty.

I was so unobservant that I understood very little of what was happening. I went often to see my father, whose body was visibly rotting away with the ravages of the fever. I can scarcely bear now to recall the picture the last time I helped him out of bed. I had not realized that a human body could be so devastated and yet live. And with it all, he spoke of a great plan for going to Sicily and reorganising the sulphur mines there.

The author's father, Basil Wilfred Bennett,
Boulogne, 1915.

The next morning he was dead. It was the day of my wedding. Early in the morning I went to Brixton; had my first dealing with undertakers, learned that I must register the death and give instructions about the funeral. My mother insisted that he should be buried as a pauper and that none of us should know where or by whom he was buried. She also insisted that no one should be told of his death until after the marriage. With her lips tight and her blue eyes like sparks, she said, "I do not approve of this marriage and I would have stopped it if I could. But now it is too late. You must go through with it." She added, with characteristic practicality: "You have a three days' leave for your honeymoon, and who knows when you will get another."

It seems as if every minute of that day has etched a picture on my heart. I can follow my footsteps to the Registrar of Births and Deaths. The bus ride to Waterloo and the train to Wimbledon. Changing into my hired morning coat. The walk to my grandmother's house on the way to the church. My grandmother was a majestic lady, reputed to turn the scale at twenty stone, but no one had ever dared suggest that she should be weighed. She disapproved of my mother, ostensibly because she was American, but really because she had stolen her beloved youngest son, her Benjamin, whom she had always adored and spoiled. For no other reason than that my mother was against the marriage, my grandmother approved it and gave me her blessing.

Then came the final walk up the steep hill and across Wimbledon Common to St. Mary's Church. Time did not exist - in spite of all I had done, I was early but I did not even know it. I felt again as I had nine months earlier - disengaged from my body. But this time my body was alive and walking to its doom. The word 'doom' is an absurdity, for I loved Evelyn and really wanted to marry her. I had no feeling that my mother was right in saying that we were hopelessly unsuited. The feeling of doom was quite without emotional content. Nor was it the result of thinking. On the contrary, my thoughts were helplessly observing all that was going on.

Why could I not turn round and walk away from the church? It was all wrong for me to be married - especially on that day and under those conditions. Was my father's body cold yet?

I reached the church and walked up the aisle. I suppose there were many people, but I saw no one. 'Now only an earthquake could stop it.' My bride came in and stood beside me. 'What would happen if I were struck dumb?'

Outwardly, I suppose, there was no sign of my inner disturbance. My body moved and spoke, but it was an automaton. I had nothing to do with its actions and had no power at all to influence them. Our honeymoon in Brighton was an agonizing experience. I had only the vaguest idea of what was required of a husband. I had never slept with a woman before and had been far too timid to ask questions. I had no sense of remoteness or of being out of tune with my wife. The overriding feeling was one of guilt; but I was too much exhausted in my emotions to experience anything very strongly.

We came home to a service flat in Temple Chambers near the Strand. I began to feel at ease with my wife, but the sense of unreality persisted. Nearly every evening I was out late for my private Turkish lessons with Ali Riza Bey. One night, I came home unexpectedly early and found a fellow officer, since dead. He and my wife seemed strangely embarrassed. I felt myself guilty for disturbing them. Neither then nor later did it occur to me that there was anything wrong, and yet I remember how the thought passed quickly through my mind: "Now I have an excuse for running away."

This was really ludicrous, for I loved Evelyn and she loved me. I wanted her to be happy, but at that time Turkey and the Turkish language were such an obsession with me that she and I were seldom together. She was very patient with me, though I believe I had begun to disappoint her.

Within two months of our marriage, the Turkish course finished. Having passed out first, I became the senior officer of the batch and was posted to Salonika to join the Army of Occupation in Turkey. My wife cried when I left, but my mother was happy. I knew even less about life and about people than most young men of my age. But I did know that life and death are far more interesting than most people suppose.

2: THE INTELLIGENCE SERVICE

It was February 1919. Communications in Europe were still irregular and hazardous. The Mediterranean had not yet been cleared of German mines and the Aegean was regarded as unsafe for transports. When we reached Boulogne, I learned that we seven officers were to share a railway wagon, bearing the familiar legend *hommes quarante - chevaux huit*. The journey from Boulogne to Tarento took us twelve days. For me personally, this was the first of many really uncomfortable journeys I have made. Reacting, no doubt, from the ten tense months since I was wounded, I caught some kind of influenza with acute diarrhea and shivering. We passed through the Alps in bitter cold, and every time the train stopped - which was mercifully very often - I had to jump out, there being no sanitation in the truck. I must have been a miserable companion for the others, but when we reached Calabria we ran into fine warm weather and found Italian peasants selling local Vermouth at every station. I arrived in Tarento helplessly drunk - but my illness was cured. After five days' waiting in the bewildering rest camp outside Tarento, where no one seemed to know his destination, we took ship for Itea in the Gulf of Corinth. From Itea to Bralo in Thessaly was a mountain road built by German prisoners of war. At one moment, the driver said casually: "Up there on the right is Delphi."

It is hard to reproduce unthought thoughts, but I remember the shock of excitement: "This is history and I belong to it. Next time I will stay there." That is as near as I can get to the experience of my state of mind. Throughout the journey my body was going to strange and unvisited lands, but I myself was coming back to familiar ground with which I had some intimate connection. Even today, I cannot explain such experiences. Some would say that they are fleeting glimpses of some past life, but I am very reluctant to believe in reincarnation, at least in any of its popular forms. I am, however, inclined to believe in premonitions, and that we have some connection with the future that influences our lives more than we are aware.

We spent a week in Salonika. There was a completely different feeling in the Army from what I had known in France. It had been another kind of war. Disease and bad food had been worse enemies than the Bulgars. The war was over, but there was no sense of peace. I had my first glimpses of the bitter quarrels between the victorious allies that were soon to disfigure the political landscape.

The railway from Salonika to Constantinople had recently been reopened, but our train crawled slowly from village to village. We amused ourselves by trading bully beef for roasted chicken and bottles of resinated wine and cigarettes from the finest leaf in the world. It seemed a poor bargain for the peasants, but they would run a hundred yards beside the train rather than lose a deal. Everywhere Turkish was understood, although it was already eight years since Macedonia had been ceded to Greece.

Finally, after nearly a month's journey from England, we arrived at Sirkeci Station in Istanbul. It was crowded with returning Turkish soldiers, with refugees from Russia trying to get away, no matter where, with Greeks, Armenians, Jews, and not a few Germans returning belatedly home.

The next day we reported to G.H.Q., the British Army of the Black Sea, where I, being the senior of my batch, was offered the one choice post - that of Assistant Liaison Officer at the Turkish War Office.

The others were assigned to the censorship - miserable, dull work that drives men to drink.

My work at the War Office required me to read, write and speak Turkish all day long and I made rapid progress. The only other British officer - the chief Liaison Officer - in the immense establishment was Major van M. He was at that time engaged in a tumultuous love affair with a Russian lady who demanded his constant presence. So I was left alone to deal with full generals, lieutenant generals and staff officers of all ranks, to give permits to staff officers to leave the restricted area of Istanbul, to translate and transmit instructions from the British G.H.Q. and - most ridiculous of all - to send in weekly reports on the 'Progress of demobilization of the Turkish Army'. What could I do but translate and sign whatever reports the Turkish General Staff might choose to give me?

As neither the French nor the Italian liaison officers could speak much Turkish, my office was constantly crowded with officers wanting problems settled - including many that had to be referred to our Allies. Within a few weeks I had a host of friends - mostly old enough to be my father.

Unwittingly, I became for a day an instrument of destiny. On 15th May, the Greek forces landed in Smyrna and met with unexpected resistance. The Sultan agreed with the Allied High Commissioners to send a mission under General Mustafa Kemal, the hero of Gallipoli, to make sure that the Turkish army kept out of the conflict. On 8th

June[1] - by a strange coincidence my twenty-second birthday - a Turkish staff officer came into my room and asked for visas for Mustafa Kemal Pasha and his mission. When I read the list I recognized the names of thirty-five of the most active generals and staff colonels in the Turkish Army. I did not like to give the visas. Major van M. was, as usual, away on private business. I decided to take the list to G.H.Q. and ask for instructions. I said to the staff officer on duty that it looked to me more like a war-making than a peace-making mission. I was told to wait while the British High Commission was consulted. After about an hour I was called in and instructed to go back and give the visas. "Mustafa Kemal Pasha," I was told, "has the complete confidence of the Sultan."

Just five weeks later Mustafa Kemal Pasha was outlawed by the Sultan. He had proclaimed war against the Greeks and was rallying the remnants of the Turkish army with the help of the very staff officers I had been ordered to send into Asia Minor. This episode was my first contact with high politics and it was the beginning of disillusionment with the wisdom of the great.

Meanwhile, all was going well with me at the War Office. One morning in June, chatting over cups of Turkish coffee and a dish of *muhallebi*, a senior officer spoke of their regret that so few spoke English, having been trained in Germany. On the spur of the moment, he asked if I would agree to give English lessons to some of the staff officers. After all, it would help to pass the time, as most of them had little or nothing to do. Without reflecting on the possible consequences, I agreed. The request seemed harmless enough, and to accept was in keeping with my instructions to make friends with the Turkish staff officers.

Unfortunately, my English classes were too successful. Having noticed that Turkish boys, even in high school, were still taught to learn their lessons by heart and to chant them aloud, I used the same method. First I gave a talk based on what I had learned from Ali Riza Bey and then produced a series of rhyming sentences in subject predicate form.

My first class had sixty officers, the second three hundred and the third more than four hundred. The great Staff Lecture Theatre seated a thousand and threatened to be filled within a few weeks. The staff officers were bored to extinction and they sincerely wished to make friends with Britain. Turkey and Britain had been friends for generations and everyone could see - *ba'ad al harab al Basra* - 'after the sack of Basra', as the Arab proverb says - that the Turks had made a big blunder in

---

1   [This is historically inaccurate. Gen. Mustafa Kemal is known to have arrived in Samsun on May 19, 1919. Ed.]

allowing themselves to be drawn into war against us. Neither the British Government nor the British Missions in Turkey understood the strength and sincerity of Turkish friendliness towards us until it was too late.

Our allies, and especially the French, knew and resented it. They could not believe that we were not equally aware and ready to exploit it to our advantage. Consequently, when news got round of English classes for hundreds of Senior Staff Officers conducted in the War Office itself, there was a vehement outcry. Instead of complaining to the British G.H.Q. and getting the classes stopped overnight, the French and Italian Governments made an official protest at the Supreme Allied Council in Paris. This happened at a moment when the Syrian question, the Sykes-Picot agreement about zones of influence, was causing acute embarrassment to several Governments. Everyone was on edge and my English lessons were worked up into an 'incident'.

The result was that I was summoned to British G.H.Q. to report to General (later Field Marshal) Sir George Milne, with the French and Italian Commanders-in-Chief and the representatives of the three High Commissioners, all sitting behind a black marble table of immense size and forbidding coldness. I was reprimanded for my unauthorized initiative. I was to be withdrawn at once from the Turkish War Office. An apology had been made to the French and Italian Commanders-in-Chief.

It was a strange experience, for I felt quite detached from the impressive scene. I was witnessing the childish behaviour of States and I was learning a lesson. I saluted and marched out - rather surprised that I was not under arrest! I was told to wait in the C.-in-C.'s anteroom. I expected to be relegated to the dull work of postal censorship.

An hour later, when all the Allied notables had left G.H.Q., I was called into the C.-in-C.'s private office - not, this time, the great Conference Hall taken over from the Turks. General Milne had with him the Deputy Director of Military Intelligence, a staff officer so grand that I had previously not even known of his existence. I was told to sit down and tell my own story. Made bold by a gleam in General Milne's eye, I spoke of my belief that the Turkish army sincerely wanted to turn to the British in friendship and forget their alliance with Germany. The D.D.M.I. put questions about certain officers whom he named and whom I happened to know fairly well. The C.-in-C. listened in silence and suddenly interrupted in the brusque tone for which he was famous: "I have to take an Allied Mission to Smyrna. We have to try to make some sense out of this trouble between the Greeks and the Turks. Would you like to come as my personal Intelligence Officer?"

I accepted silently, though I felt near to tears of gratitude for his kindness. Not a word was said about the War Office, but I believe that secretly the C.-in-C. had been annoyed with the French for making a mountain out of such a molehill. Besides, even I knew that no love was lost between him and General Franchet d'Esperey. The French C.-in-C. had blatantly dedicated a hospital bearing his own name to the city of Constantinople and did everything possible to build up French prestige against ours and the other Allies. Moreover, the French had allowed the Turks to retain in Cilicia large quantities of rifle ammunition that should have been destroyed, hoping in this way to be called upon to intervene in the frontier dispute. In comparison with this, my English classes could hardly be counted as a dangerous intervention.

At that time, I had little grasp of the bitter rivalries between Allied Governments and even between the different services, diplomatic, military and naval within the Governments themselves. The world about me, that seemed like an incomprehensible dream, was in truth a nightmare of human vanity and love of power. The seeds being sown had the word 'Peace' labelled on the packet, but they were the seeds of inevitable war.

The unexpected turn of fortune that took me to Smyrna seemed as unreal as everything else. I had been hoping to get my wife to Turkey as soon as the Allied Governments became aware that it was and always had been perfectly safe for women. The Mission to Smyrna was so exciting that I forgot everything. I had to interpret for the C.-in-C. at all his meetings. He could not or would not speak French, so I had to translate both into French and Turkish. I can say that I was not an ordinary interpreter. I had become deeply aware of the different use of language by Asiatic and European people. The interpreter who renders a statement, purposely couched in an indefinite form, by what might appear to be a positive pronouncement, can be the cause of perilous misunderstandings.

As personal interpreter first to General Milne and later to General Hare, I began to see quite a new side of human life. It happened that between 1919 and 1921, I met several famous men and became aware that they are moved by the same mean and trivial forces as everyone else. Human nature is the same everywhere. It does not change because a man happens to be very clever or able to impose himself successfully on others. It does not even change if he is a sincere patriot or humanitarian.

In Smyrna, I met for the first time a really clever politician. He was Mr. Sterghiadis, the Greek High Commissioner, a close personal friend of Mr. Venizelos and chosen no doubt as the man best fitted to realise, through the annexation of the western provinces of Anatolia, the Greek dream of Megali Hellas. There was no doubt that the Greeks had behaved badly. They had advanced deep into the hinterland of Smyrna and had driven the Turks to armed resistance by many small acts of provocation. We had almost daily meetings of the Allied Mission, at which Mr. Sterghiadis was called upon to explain this or that act of provocation. I could not but admire the dexterity with which he would turn every question. Sometimes he would talk without a pause for half-an-hour until the others - all fine soldiers but no match for his diplomacy - had forgotten their own question. Sometimes, I contrived in translating for the Turkish representative to remind General Milne of the real point at issue, and he would stick to it like a bulldog. But from start to finish Sterghiadis never conceded a single point that could have been used against his country at the Supreme War Council. Whereas all the others were concerned in the truth or otherwise of various accusations and counter-accusations, Sterghiadis seemed to be aware at every moment of the way the report of the proceedings would read in Paris. Yet for all his quick wit it was only too obvious that Mr. Sterghiadis was a slave to the common failings of the human race. Behind everything were the same vanity, the same fears and the same desire for power that moves all human beings great or small. The question: 'Why are people like this?' was beginning to form in me, but I was far too busy to wait for an answer.

My duties in Smyrna were not confined to interpreting. I had also to analyse Intelligence Reports about the situation in Anatolia. Here I had an undeserved success which made my reputation as an Intelligence Officer and earned me a mention in the C.-in-C.'s dispatches. I was faced with a mass of intelligence reports about the strength of the Turkish 'bands', as the Greeks insisted on calling them, that were resisting the Greek Army of Occupation. The Supreme War Council had called urgently for a report on the true situation. Allied officers were not allowed into the interior and we had nothing but these reports to go on. They were mostly wild guesses or the rankest of propaganda. The numbers in a given area were variously stated at a few score and several thousand. I was to prepare a map showing the strength and distribution of the Turkish forces. I could only judge by the tone of each report which way the writer was likely to be biased and, by his way of writing, the extent to which he was likely to exaggerate. I prepared a fine-looking map, which was sent by special messenger to Paris.

Almost immediately after it was gone, the Turks offered safe conduct for Allied officers to go and see for themselves. When these eye-witness reports came in they agreed, to an almost absurd degree of accuracy, with my estimates.

The Smyrna Mission taught me a lesson about atrocity stories that I have never forgotten. A particularly gruesome report was submitted by the Turkish representative, who asserted that there was clear evidence that a Greek detachment had murdered thirty-seven Turks - men and women - in a certain village and had thrust the bodies down a well. The pollution of the well seemed to be regarded as particularly atrocious.

Mr. Sterghiadis, as I then thought to gain time, proposed an enquiry. General Hare agreed and suggested that I should go to the place with a French and an Italian representative, so that we should not have to depend upon interpreters, I being the only staff officer in the combined mission who could speak Turkish.

The Smyrna-Aydin railway had been out of action since the war, but the permanent way was reputed intact. We set out in a dressaine - that is a small open truck with a petrol engine - with a guard of four armed men. I think they were Bengal Lancers, part of the C.-in-C.'s guard.

The journey took us through the ruins of Ephesus rising out of a green sea of liquorice plant. At the end of the line we found horses and went on towards the scene of the atrocity, making enquiries at each village. Everyone knew the story, but it changed from mouth to mouth. As we drew nearer, the accounts were far more confused and hesitant than they had been in Smyrna. All that people were sure of was that a well had been polluted. When finally we reached the scene of the atrocity we quickly pieced together the true story. A sheep had fallen into the well. People had heard its cries and thought it was murder, and did not dare to look for several days. By then the well was indeed polluted, for it was mid-August and putrefaction sets in quickly. Although it had been cleaned ten days before we arrived the stench was such that no one could drink the water.

I believe that many, if not most of the atrocities reported in war time are of this kind. There is some truth somewhere, but wild imagination and fixed ideas build from the facts some gruesome story.

On the way back from Aydin, I was asked by some Turks to visit the village of Sukie where help was desperately needed. I left my companions, intending to return to Smyrna the next day. They had some enquiries of their own to make.

Sukie is in the Meander Valley, now one of the richest valleys of Anatolia, but at that time virtually uninhabitable from malaria. I have never seen such a spectacle as met us as we came over the low watershed. The valley of the Meander River is perhaps twenty miles wide and was covered with a pale blue haze of mosquitoes. I could not believe it until we rode through the liquorice fields. Indeed there was little or no cultivation at that time, but liquorice root was collected in the winter when the mosquitoes are dormant. At one time there had been a brisk trade with America for chewing tobacco, but it seems that Mr. Wrigley with his gum had unwittingly impoverished the whole countryside.

When I reached Sukie I was taken to see the corpses of two men who had died of cholera. It was a sight hard to endure. No one dared to go near to bury them and the stench was unspeakable. I advised heaping lime on them. This had not been done evidently because the villagers felt that someone ought to see them first. However my presence seemed to reassure them. I had never before seen the ravages of diseases like cholera and malaria, and I confess that I was frightened. However, I stayed in the village for two nights while a messenger went to Smyrna to bring back a doctor.

My two nights in Sukie were my only experience of a genuine caravanserai. It had been for centuries a camel post for caravans going right from the Mediterranean to Persia and Turkestan. At that time there were still many camel caravans. The sound of camel bells and the smell of camels dominated everything. Within a few years all this was to disappear.

The world was changing fast in 1919, and at least as fast in Asia as it was in Europe.

When I returned to Smyrna I fell ill. It might have been anything, but turned out to be amoebic dysentery. There were no British doctors in Smyrna. Besides I do not think anyone on the mission realized quite how ill I was. I was too weak to stand and could only crawl to and from the stool. One day, the C.-in-C.'s aide-de-camp came to visit me and was horrified to see the condition of filth in which I was living. I was hastily evacuated to Constantinople and soon got well. But the dysentery left its traces from which I did not fully recover for forty years.

Meanwhile, my fate was being directed into a new channel. As soon as I recovered - it was then September 1919 – I was summoned to the D.D.M.I.'s office and told that there were two jobs open to me, and that I could choose. One was as British Control Officer at Baku on the Caspian Sea and the other was head of the Military Intelligence 'B' office in Constantinople. Both jobs were normally staff-colonel appointments, but both needed a good knowledge of languages and no one else was available. I was given twenty-four hours to decide.

It seemed strange that I should be given the choice. Later I realized that the Baku post was considered dangerous, and indeed the man who did go there was caught by the Bolsheviks and spent two or three years in a Communist prison. Baku did not draw me, except as the gateway to the Transcaspian region and beyond. I had begun in Sukie to dream of a caravan journey to China by way of Persia, Turkestan and the Gobi Desert. Constantinople, on the other hand, had immediate attractions, and I disregarded the friendly warnings of the G.S.I. Mess that I was taking on a very sticky job.

Thus began one of the strangest and most exciting periods of my life. I had felt out of place in England; but I was quite at home among the Turks, Circassians and Kurds, Greeks, Armenians, Jews and the whole medley of Levantine races, with whom I now had to work.

When I went to my new offices in Hagopian Han, discreetly hidden in a block of flats near the old Galata Tunnel railway, I found why there had been such a hurry to fill the post. Nearly all the officers were leaving immediately to return to their normal work in the Near East Consular Service, from which they had been seconded. There were no officers of the regular army who could speak, read and write Turkish well enough to do the job.

I took over at an awkward moment. The Greek invasion of Asia Minor had exasperated the Turkish population - quite resigned to British and French occupation, but bitterly resentful of the Greeks. Another and more immediate cause of discontent was the indiscriminate requisitioning by each of the Allied Commands of houses and offices in an already overcrowded city. Also there was a flood of travelers from Central Asia going on pilgrimage to Mecca, and it had been reported that there were many Bolshevik agents among them sent to undertake Pan-Islamic propaganda, and thus, by occupying the attention of the Allies, leave the Russians free to invade the Caucasus. Add to this that the Armenian population was excited over a succession of murders of Armenians suspected of collaborating with the Young Turks, and that the White Russian refugees from the Crimea and Ukraine were pouring into Constantinople by the thousand, and some idea can be formed of the work which fell upon the Political Branch of Military Intelligence in Constantinople.

No kind of instructions or advice was given me, except to pick up the threads from my predecessor. In a week, I had to learn the workings of secret service agents, the way to prepare reports, the extent to which officers were allowed to make their own enquiries, our relations with the Allied Military Police and so on and so on.

Somehow it all worked. I began to get good results, chiefly because so many people would drop in to gossip and enable me to get a good feeling of the day-to-day changes in the temper of the great sprawling city, with its population of one and a quarter million and its half-dozen races and four religious groups. The intensity with which I worked can be gauged from the fact that at the end of twelve months the numbered reports personally written by me were well over a thousand. The night hours were devoted to seeing very secret agents, morning and evening to reading and writing reports, and odd hours to hearing valuable gossip.

I received permission to bring out my wife. My chief recreation was Rugby football which was played by the Army at the Sweet Waters of Europe near the head of the Golden Horn. I had little time to spare for home life, and my wife did not easily make friends with the very few officers' wives who were allowed in Turkey. Nevertheless, the chief purpose of her coming was realised. Soon after her arrival a child was conceived - though we were both so ignorant that it was four months before we realized what had happened. Then she took fright and said that she must return to England to be properly cared for. I could not blame her. She had far too little place in my life. It seemed to me then, and has become even clearer since, that the true reason for our marriage was that she was destined to bear a child and I to be the father. That was the only real link between us. It is a very powerful link and I believe that neither life nor death can break it.

When Evelyn returned to England, I wrote regularly two or three times a week. These letters were kept and reading them now, I see how selfish and uncomprehending I was. They are a series of moans about my own fatigue and preoccupation with my task. Many protestations of love and sympathy - but no understanding at all of what a woman goes through when she bears her first child. Our daughter was born on 18th August, 1920. Almost immediately, I found myself unable to write home any more. England, my family, my own wife and daughter belonged to one world and I belonged to another. My letters were few and forced.

After much hesitation and very timidly, I had a love affair with an Armenian girl. I began also to drink -sometimes quite heavily. All that I really cared for was my work, and my Saturday games of Rugby became few and finally ceased. I was driving myself too hard and had no idea where I was heading.

To illustrate the pressure under which I lived, I will describe the events of 20th March, 1920. My wife had but recently left for England and I had moved my bed into my office so as to be able to work at night.

At that time the Turkish Chamber of Deputies, elected under Allied supervision with the transparent aim of giving weight to the iniquitous Treaty of Sèvres, was meeting in Constantinople. Mustafa Kemal Pasha was building up an effective armed force, but the Allies were still far from realizing his strength. A prodigious mistake was made at this point. The Chamber of Deputies was beginning to feel its feet and openly to criticize the Government of Damad Ferid Pasha and his cringing attitude towards the Greek invasion in Asia Minor and Eastern Thrace. These debates were in reality a most needed outlet for the outraged feelings of the Turks, and with wise handling the Chamber of Deputies could have supplied a bridge between the Sultan and his Government in Constantinople and Mustafa Kemal and his army.

Instead of this, in a moment of panic, the decision was taken to arrest all the deputies and intern them in Malta. I received a very secret notice of this decision, which was to be carried out, not by the Allied Police, but by Army detachments in uniform. All the houses of members of parliament were to be surrounded, and at four a.m. on 20th March mandates of arrest were to be presented at the door.

The absurdity of this procedure was obvious to me, if to no one else. I reported to the Intelligence Staff that the very construction of Turkish houses, with their Selamlik and Haremlik, would make it easy for every deputy to walk quietly out by the secret entrance with which every harem is provided and leave the Army looking foolish. I should mention here that under the arrangement by which the British were responsible for Pera, Galata and the north shores of the Bosphorus, the French for Istanbul and the Marmara Coast, and the Italians for the Asiatic side, we had to bear the main brunt of the operation, as most of the deputies lived in our zone.

The only concession to my warnings was an instruction to have the houses watched secretly by plain clothes agents as well as by the Army. I had no more than ten reliable agents and there were a hundred and twenty deputies. The impossible riddle was solved by the offer of my most reliable agent, a very brave and loyal Armenian gentleman, whom I will call Mr. P., to place at my disposal the resources of an Armenian Secret Society, the dreaded Dashnak Zutiun. At least three hundred members of the Dashnak must have been mobilized, for every Turkish deputy was kept under observation, from the morning of 20th March.

I stayed up all night in my office, and from four a.m. I began getting reports from my agents that the operation had been a complete fiasco. Eight deputies who had voluntarily surrendered had been arrested; all the rest had gone into hiding. I sat tight and did nothing. At eight a.m. came an urgent summons to H.Q. Could I take over the arrests, as unfortunately several had got away? I asked how many were actually under arrest and I was told: "About a dozen." I asked for the co-operation of the Allied Police to make the actual arrests. I knew well that my friend Bernard Rickatson-Hatt had trained a small but highly disciplined force with several good interpreters.

In the outcome, by nightfall, eighty-five deputies were under lock and key and our face had been saved. I was sent for to H.Q. and congratulated. I was told that I might even get a decoration - but I believe everyone wanted to forget the episode as quickly as possible. I myself felt very badly about it all. The entire move had been a tragic mistake. The forty-odd deputies who avoided arrest went straight to Ankara, and set up a provisional Turkish Parliament which disowned the Sultan and his Government and set the Allies a problem that was to be solved only at the cost of no little humiliation.

I expected that all my Turkish friends would turn against me for my part in the affair. But it seems that the true story was known everywhere, and even my strenuous but vain protest against the entire proceeding had got round the bazaars. Moreover, I was able to get a number of Deputies released on compassionate grounds and not sent to Malta. The result was that I was supposed to have far more authority than was the case, and my office was besieged from morning till night by the relatives of political prisoners. Every kind of bribery was tried on me. It was quite usual to arrive in my office and find a goat tethered to my desk and a couple of geese squawking on the floor.

One unexpected bird came home to roost. I owed a debt to the members of the Dashnak Zutiun who had made possible my success of 20th March. The Dashnak, about whom I knew almost nothing, had been founded in Russia as a revolutionary secret society to liberate Armenia from Czarist Russia. During the war, it had given much help to the Allies against the Turks. Now it had become an instrument of Armenian revenge against all who had taken part in the deportations and massacres of Armenians. The Dashnak was believed to be responsible for the assassination of Talat Pasha in Berlin, or Mahmoud Pasha in Milan and perhaps even of Enver Pasha in faraway Turkestan. They had now begun to assassinate prominent Armenians in Turkey who had collaborated with the Young Turkish Government.

The murders were planned and carried out with exquisite precision. They were done in broad daylight in the crowded streets. A shot was fired. A man would fall. The crowd contained scores if not hundreds of Armenians among whom the assassin would disappear. The police had no chance of penetrating the surging mass of people, shouting and gesticulating to distract attention, until it was too late. If a dozen of the crowd were arrested and interrogated, they knew nothing. Most indeed knew nothing at all, and even those who were involved probably knew only that they had to be at a certain place at a particular hour. In any case, there was no one brave enough to breathe a word that might get them into trouble with the dreaded Dashnak.

After the third or fourth assassination which completely baffled both the Turkish and the Allied Police, I was instructed to make enquiries. I guessed that the Dashnak was behind it, and asked Mr. P. point blank if it were not true that there was an organized plot. He did not deny it, but asked me to put myself in their place. He then proceeded to tell me one case history after another where the perfidy of Armenians had led to the death of hundreds of their own race and religion. The culprits could not be brought to justice by the ordinary legal channels, but the Armenian secret societies - he denied that the Dashnak was acting alone - weighed each case. I said we all owed a debt to the Dashnak. I knew what they had done in bringing messages in and out of Kut-el-Amara when General Townsend was besieged there, and in helping British prisoners to escape from Turkey. There was my own personal obligation after the events of 21st March. But I could not connive at political assassination.

The trouble was that no one had any idea who were the leaders and the committee of the Dashnak. Mr. P. himself was a trusted British agent and there was not the slightest evidence that he was personally involved. I decided to make a report to H.Q. and ask for advice. Evidently no one liked to act. I was told that this was a matter for the regular police and I had better leave it alone and forget what I had heard.

The next assassination caused a sensation because its victim was an immensely rich Armenian, killed in the Orient Express, probably as he was fleeing the country. The corpse was brought back to Turkey and a gruesome situation arose. It seems that this man had promised and failed to pay a very large sum to the Armenian funds. The body was seized at Sirkeci Station and held to ransom. For weeks the family bargained, but finally paid up; a magnificent funeral was held in the Armenian Cathedral.

I tackled Mr. P. about this affair. He assured me that the Dashnak was not involved in this assassination, but admitted that there were others in the air. I had by now a clue to some of the active members of the Society and threatened to take action. He asked for time and came back next day with an astonishing proposal. It seems that the Dashnak Committee had agreed that in future I should be the judge and that - without mentioning names - they would let Mr. P. lay all the facts before me, and if I was not forced to admit that the man deserved to die, they would spare him. This offer was made on the understanding that I would not speak to anyone - even at British G.H.Q. - of what was happening. I thought it best to agree, as I knew very well that no overt action could possibly help.

Only one case was brought before me. It proved impossible to get a clear picture without disclosure of names and places, and I refused to adjudicate. In the sequel, no more assassinations of Armenians occurred. I do not know to this day if my intervention had anything to do with it, but it was for me a peculiarly sharp experience to find myself offered powers of life and death. I had been forgetting about death in the in the midst of all my pre-occupation with the strangeness of life.

My life at that time was really very strange. I had inherited from my predecessor an enormous Mercedes car which had belonged to the German Commander-in-Chief, Liman von Sanders Pasha. I used to drive almost daily through Pera, Galata and Stambul, and had got to know so many faces, and the stories behind them, that I was able to follow the political life of the city merely by seeing people in the streets. I was credited by the Turks with knowledge and influence far beyond the reality. The British G.H.Q. took little notice of what I was doing except constantly to extend the area for which I was responsible. At first it was just Constantinople and its suburbs. Then in May 1920 it was decided to withdraw all British Control Officers from Asia Minor and to rely on the secret services. I was informed that the monthly sum at my disposal was to be increased five-fold, and that I was to cover all Asia Minor as far as the Russian frontier. Later the territory was extended again and again, until my obscure office in Pera was responsible for reporting on an area as large as Europe - stretching from the Dalmatian coast to the frontiers of Persia and Egypt. I had some genuine successes, but I also made many mistakes. I was utterly inexperienced, and yet I had a far more intimate knowledge of what was going on in the Near East than most of my seniors.

One example may be permitted. The disarmament of the Turkish Army in Asia Minor was supposed to be complete by the middle of 1919. All rifles and ammunition had been collected and removed. For some reason, it had been thought impractical to transport heavy guns, but the artillery experts had agreed that they would be rendered completely useless if the breech blocks were removed, since these could not be fabricated except in specialized workshops.

In June 1920, I received a report that breech-blocks were being fabricated at the railway workshops at Eskişehir, a big railway junction between Constantinople and Ankara. When I submitted my report I did not realize what delicate ground I was treading on, for it seems that a certain very senior Artillery officer had overridden the views of his own experts, who had not considered the removal of breech-blocks a sufficient precaution. My report was returned to me as unsubstantiated guess-work.

When I told the agent concerned - an Albanian former flying officer in the Turkish Army, and a real soldier of fortune - he was furious at having his word doubted. He went back to Anatolia and brought back obviously authentic photographs of workshops where the breech blocks were being fabricated. Soon afterwards our liaison officers with the Greek Army reported that the Turks were using heavy artillery which the French were suspected of supplying. A captured gun was found to have a breech block locally fabricated.

The explosion that occurred can be imagined. Fortunately for me the Commander-in-Chief had been among those who doubted the wisdom of leaving the guns in position. I consequently received a second mention in C.-in-C.'s dispatches and was recommended for accelerated promotion.

This and other successes went to my head and I began to believe I could do what I liked. I was only twenty-three years old, and men old enough to be my grandfathers would come and seriously ask my advice on high matters of state. I was daily meeting Turkish Cabinet Ministers, eunuchs and chamberlains from Yıldız - the Sultan's palace - spies and informers, political intriguers and gossips, and all regarded me as a high authority with a great influence in London. I afterwards learned that the story had gone round that I was connected - Heaven knows why or how - with our Royal Family. When this myth reached me, my denials, whether serious or jocular, only served to encourage the rumours.

For about nine months, from June 1920 to March 1921, I was in the thick of Turkish politics. I was entrusted with every kind of secret and consulted about the highest Government appointments. Since then several books have been written in Turkey about those Armistice years, and my name often figures as that of a sinister unaccountable figure. Nevertheless, my most treasured description was in an American newspaper, whose correspondent in Turkey referred to me as a 'notorious British gum-shoe operative'.

I was consulted by Turkish cabinet ministers on almost every kind of question and, with the ignorance of youth, freely gave my advice. Once I was asked to recommend a new Chief of Police, and put forward my friend Tahsin Bey, an Albanian whose honesty, at least, I could trust. He later helped me in many ways, but I can say that no intention of making use of the appointment crossed my mind at the time. Tahsin introduced me to a circle of provincial hangers-on at the Turkish Ministries that I might never have known. Photographs I happened to preserve of a dinner given at the Prefecture of Police will tell more of them than any words.

H.E. Hassan Tahsin Bey, Director General of Police; Istanbul (on author's right); Jaques Bey Calderon (second from right). Dinner in Istanbul, 1920

Capt.R.M. Cunningham; H.E. Hassan Tahsin Bey, Capt. J.G. Bennett;

Lt. J Chaytor, Istanbul 1920

3: FIRST CONTACT WITH ISLAM

My first encounter with Islamic mysticism came in the course of duty. The pan-Islamic movement had greatly alarmed the Allies, especially Britain, with a hundred and fifty million Muslim subjects of the Crown in India, Malaya and Africa. The Holy War, the jihad proclaimed under German pressure by the Turkish Sultan and Caliph, had been a failure, but the reverberations remained.

When I arrived in Turkey, there was a widespread belief that the Bolsheviks intended to foment pan-Islamism in order to divert Allied attention from their own plans in the Caucasus and Persia. There was not yet a strong central government in Russia, but the old Russian secret service was still at work, with its implacable hostility to everything British. There was also the ever-present fear that, with our inadequate Army of Occupation, the Turks might attempt some coup in Constantinople under the pretext of a religious rising. We were at that time flirting with a proposal to establish an independent Kurdistan, against which the Turks would very probably have opposed an armed resistance.

It was therefore important to keep in touch with the religious as well as the political currents in Turkey. I was instructed to find out what the dervishes were doing. I learned that, for centuries, dervishes have traveled, on foot or with merchant caravans, from end to end of the Muslim world. Any dervish might be a secret agent in disguise, or he might be a fanatical missionary on behalf of some politico-religious fraternity. Another important factor was the dervish fraternities, of which the most influential was believed to be the Mevlevi Brotherhood. The late Sultan Mehmed Reshad V had been a devoted member of this order. During his long years of virtual imprisonment in the reign of Abdul Hamid, he had consoled himself with the practice of Sufi mysticism under the guidance of the chief of the Mevlevi order, Ahmed Çelebi of Konya.

So I was to investigate the Mevlevi order, and find out if it had ramifications outside Asia Minor. One of my Turkish friends found it very natural that I should wish to visit a Mevlevi *tekke*, or monastery. Most visitors to Constantinople went to see the 'whirling dervishes' at Galata Serai. I asked if I would see the real thing there. He replied: "Well, no. That is for sight-seers. The most important *tekke* is outside the Adrianople Gate. That is where Merhoum (i.e. 'entered into eternal rest') Sultan Reshad used to go every week" So I elected to go to the *tekke* outside the walls of the ancient city. It was built at the spot where, when Constantinople was conquered by the Turks in 1453, a Mevlevi dervish had led the assault against the Byzantines and had made the first breach in the ramparts.

It was Thursday evening, the night when the ritual of the fraternity is open to visitors. I was the only foreigner, but there were many Turks. The ritual is called the Mukabele or Meeting. My first impression was of sheer amazement. I had no idea that anything of the kind existed in the world. Having since witnessed it many times and received explanations of the mystical significance of each movement and gesture, I find it hard to recapture my first impression. Thought and curiosity were not there: only a sense of deep peace and joy, which everyone present seemed to share. The movements of the dervishes, first slow and then turning faster and faster, seemed to set them free from the cares of this world. The music was not less moving than the whirling of the dervishes themselves.

The Mukabele has three parts. It takes place in the *semahane*, which means literally Heavenly Mansion. When we entered, a few dervishes were sitting cross-legged or kneeling on the floor. They had short open jackets covering a white shirt; long, very full brown skirts and tall brimless hats worn slightly tilted on the head. Round the waist was a tightly wound sash. The ages ranged, I should say, from eighteen to eighty. All had beards.

Others entered, walking slowly with bowed heads and making a deep bow before sitting down. The sheikh, the head of the brotherhood, came in, followed closely by two others, and stood below the musicians' gallery. The musicians began a gay melody evoking images of village life in ancient happy days. The dervishes rose, turned to the right and wound in slow procession round the hall. The floor was separated by a low rail from the raised platform on which we visitors were sitting on carpets or low stools. At one corner, the *Semahane* opened on to a space where there were three or four tombstones draped in embroidered cloths. These were the tombs of the founder of this *tekke* and of particularly saintly dervishes who had died there. As each dervish passed in front of the tombs he stopped and bowed deeply with arms folded across his heart.

This procession and the music symbolize earthly life. The melody changes several times, each new tune evoking forgotten memories of a free and natural life on earth. The halt at the tombs is a reminder that in life we must be mindful of death. As he bows, the dervish places his left foot over his right big toe. This reminds him there must be no reserve in his faith and trust in God. To understand this one needs to know the legends that surround the foundation of the order by the great saint and mystic, Jalal ad-Din Rumi, in A.D. 1246. He was called the Mevlana, which means 'our lord', and is venerated by his followers as second only to the Prophet of Islam. He had a cook, Atesh Baz, who was celebrated for his piety. One day, wood for the fire ran out, and rather than delay the Mevlana's pilav, he put his own right leg into the flames. He had not been burned except for the big toe. Realizing that this was a sign that his faith was not perfect, he had hidden it under his left foot when announcing that the meal was ready. The Mevlana, whose mystical insight revealed to him the whole story, called the dervishes together and said: "Few on earth have such faith as Atesh Baz. In future, all our dervishes will copy him, to remind them what faith really means."

In the Mukabele, the music is played on a reed flute called the ney. It is accompanied by drums and sometimes cymbal and kemal, a kind of violin. Unexpectedly, there is a clash of sound, a strident note on the ney. And all the dervishes stop still. This symbolizes the moment of death. The music starts again, now with a strong flowing rhythm accompanied by a steady even beat. The dervishes bow deeply three times and begin to turn round on the right foot, propelling themselves with the left. The young dervishes whirl rapidly; the very old turn quite slowly. The sheikh stands still with his hands clasped over his navel. There is a pattern in the movement that makes the whole group of some twenty dancers slowly gyrate. The whole gives an impression of exact order and yet of complete freedom. The dervishes have their eyes closed, or look through lowered lashes at the ground. They take no notice of one another but there are no collisions, even when the movements become rapid. There is absolutely no sense of excitement or ecstasy. On the contrary, a deep peace pervades the hall.

This is the Mevlevi zikr, or pointing of the soul towards God. It symbolizes the paradisal state of the soul when it leaves the body and enters the world of the perfected man, the Insan-i-Kamil. Later I learned how to perform the zikr myself, and could verify the state of beatitude, quite devoid of excitement, which it engenders.

The zikr was repeated three times. For the third and last time, the music changed into a strong and stately rhythm - much less dramatic than before. This time the Sheikh himself took part. For no reason that I could understand, I began to weep. I noticed that most of the others looking on were sobbing too. Nothing new seemed to have happened, but everything had changed. All too soon, the zikr ended and the dervishes instantly stopped, bowed three times towards the sheikh, who had resumed his position, and slowly filed out. I watched each face as they went by and it seemed to me that never before had I seen such serenity.

The ceremony made such a deep impression on me that I asked to go again and was told that I could come by myself, if I wished, any Thursday evening, but that they did not wish to encourage European visitors, who could go to Galatasaray, where the music was much better - and after all it was only five minutes from the Grande Rue de Péra.

The explanations of the ritual that I have given only came slowly. They were in no hurry to speak of it, but they also seemed to have no wish to hold anything back. I did not yet understand that dervishes are not allowed to have secrets, and must answer any questions put to them. They must not volunteer information nor go beyond what is asked of them. As most people do not know how to ask questions, it often happens that travelers write about the dervishes as jealously guarding their secrets from all but a favoured few. When I became used to their way of dealing with questions, I asked one wise old dervish about my experience of 21 March 1918, when I was wounded in France. He listened very carefully, and asked me one or two questions which reminded me of features of the experience that I had forgotten. He said: "The Mukabele has the effect of bringing us into the same state where all fear of death disappears. We know that if we die at that moment we shall experience only bliss. That is why dervishes are always the bravest soldiers." My mind leapt to the Sudan War and the strange fate which decreed that the last war of religion should bring brave Gordon face to face with the courage of dervishes who were not afraid of death. But one must really know death in order to cease to fear it. Perhaps these dervishes had the secret.

My next experience with dervishes was very different. I had heard that there was a *Tekke* of Rufa'i, the so-called Howling Dervishes, on the Asiatic coast of the Bosphorus, and that it was frequently visited by pilgrims from Persia and Central Asia, and by the Tartars of the Volga and Crimea. When I made enquiries about going to see for myself, I learned that the moment was most opportune, for a well-known and much venerated sheikh from Turkestan was staying at the *tekke*, and that a special Mukabele in his honour was to be held on the Thursday evening.

The hall of this *tekke* was enclosed in high square wooden walls, unlike the octagonal *semahane* of the Mevlevis. The gallery was higher above the ground and approached from outer staircases. There was a gallery for women with a close grille through which nothing could be seen. When I reached the gallery and was given a front seat, I found that the ritual had already been in progress for some time, perhaps three hours. The Rufa'i dervishes do not dance, but kneel or sit on the floor swaying their bodies from side to side, while intoning one of the names of

Allah. The musical instruments are different from those of the Mevlevi; they are more varied and harsher. There are several forms of percussion. Their melodies are not evocative but stimulating. The dervishes respond by more and more violent swaying of the body. By the time I entered, there was already an atmosphere of intense excitement and expectancy.

Soon the swaying changed into an unrestrained dashing of the bodies from side to side while they began to beat their breasts, tear at their hair and beards. The name of Allah gave place to the invocation *Ya Hu* - which means O Thou! By now they were gasping rather than intoning.

After about half-an-hour a tall, lean man with no clothes but a loincloth rose from the ground. He bowed to the sheikh of the *tekke* and stood quite still in the centre. Assistants brought in steel spikes with heavy balls at one end, long, thin skewers and heavy chains. The dervishes without ceasing to sway and cry *Ya Hu* seized the various implements, beating themselves with the chains and thrusting the spikes and skewers through their cheeks, their breasts and their thighs. There was no apparent fear or pain. The old man standing in the centre remained perfectly still and seemed to be the only one present not in a state of wild excitement.

I did not wish to be the victim of some kind of hallucination or suggestion and slipped out of the hall on a pretext, returning a few minutes later feeling myself perfectly calm and detached from what was happening.

The climax of the event was approaching. Two dervishes brought in a great curved sword or scimitar and prostrated themselves towards the Kabbe, a niche in the wall that shows the direction of Mecca. The old man lay down quietly on his back on the wooden floor, took the scimitar, felt the blade with his finger and laid it with the sharp side across his belly and drew it deep into his lean flanks. There was a sudden deep silence and the sheikh of the monastery came forward and stood on the sword, holding the hands of two dervishes who were trembling from head to foot and muttering *Allah-u-Akbar* - God is the Greatest. It seemed that the body must be cut in two for the sword seemed to reach the floor.

In the quivering silence, the scene appeared to last for ever. Quietly the sheikh stepped down. The old man lifted the sword with both hands without moving his body. Then with his right thumb he drew a line over his body where the sword had been, stood up, and all could see that his body was unmarked.

Though everyone was shaking with an indescribable emotion, the complete silence continued. The sword was hung up in sight of us all.

The dervishes lined up for the last prayer of the Muslim Sacred Office. My Turkish friends went down and joined them. This last prayer is the longest of the day, having thirteen *rika'as* or double prostrations, and lasts about twenty minutes. There was a two-fold sense: of power and of peace. I remained alone in the gallery and thought my thoughts. After the ritual, the friend who had brought me called me down and invited me to examine the sword, which certainly had not been touched. There was no trace of blood on it and it was as sharp as a razor. I could by no means account for what I had seen. Since then, I have witnessed many such demonstrations, and have no doubt that it is possible, by exercises of a special kind, to acquire extraordinary powers over the human body.

The Muslim religion was beginning to interest me very much. As a boy, I had been revolted by the quarrels of the Christian Churches. At my school, we had two teachers of divinity, one very High and the other very Low Church of England. The High Churchman was a mild but inept old clergyman, but the Low Churchman was a ruthless fanatic. He spoke of the Roman Catholic Church in terms that no schoolboy should be allowed to hear. We had moreover a succession of missionary lecturers who spoke to us with such an accent of self-righteousness about the heathen and their miserable state, that I and many others wanted to become heathens on the spot. When I spoke to my parents, my mother, who hated hypocrisy, said: "Most Englishmen are hypocrites, especially English priests." My father said: "Religion would be all right if it were not for priests and missionaries; but missionaries are the worst." As a boy, he had been at Lancing College and had experienced a religious conversion. Afterwards he had reacted against institutional religion and had done his best to prevent us as children from acquiring any fixed beliefs against which we might afterwards revolt.

It is hardly surprising that I grew up with very little sense of the reality of the Christian profession. When I was prepared for confirmation, our vicar had signally failed to answer my questions about the conflict of the churches and the justification of missions. I experienced nothing in the Eucharist, and only went to church to please others. At that time, I had not met a single Christian, priest or layman, who appeared to me to have real faith in his profession.

It seemed different with the Muslims I met. They had the same faults of character as everyone else, but many of them really believed in God. Once I had to go across to Istanbul to see the Minister of Justice, who had a very fine reputation for honesty and courage, but whom I had never met. When I entered his great salon, ushered in by six gentlemen in frock coats, and had exchanged the courtesies then usual in Turkey,

I began to look at the Minister and was sure I had seen him before, not once but many times. He saw my bewilderment and laughed: "I saw you last Thursday at the Edirne Kapı *Tekke*." Suddenly I realized that he was a dervish, and that I had seen him turning in the Mevlevi ritual. We became friends, and I learned from him many things about the Muslim faith and Sufi mysticism.

Such a combination of mysticism and practicality was not rare in the Turkey of the Ottoman Sultans. I used to visit an old man, former Chamberlain of Sultan Abdul Hamid, who lived up the Bosphorus at Tchamlidja. He once said to me: "The difference between Asiatics and Europeans is that we do not believe that any situation can change in a hurry, whereas you believe that you can graft good fruit on an evil tree. We have a saying: *def i mefasid celb i menafiden evla dir*, which can be translated: 'Evil must be extirpated before good can come.' But you would say rather: 'Good must come so that evil can be extirpated.' There is truth in both viewpoints, but so long as we are not even aware that they are different, we cannot understand one another."

The month of fasting, Ramadan, fell in that year in July. I decided to try keeping the fast, which consists in not eating, drinking or smoking between sunrise and sunset. I kept it up for a week, but found that my work was suffering. I grew tired and irritable before the day was half done. I observed that although most Turks kept the fast, they ate copiously at nightfall and before daybreak. I saw that they became even more irritable than I did - especially from not smoking. It was, however, an undeniable fact that the whole life of Constantinople was changed during Ramadan. I had never seen anything like it in any Christian city, and I was bound to admit that, on the whole, Muslims took their religion far more seriously than the majority of Christians. It was quite usual to see shops closed at midday because the keeper had gone to the Mosque for the midday prayer.

The twenty-seventh night of the fast of Ramadan is called the Leyl-ul-Kadir, or the Night of Power. According to Muslim tradition, in this night God sends the Archangel Gabriel to the earth to survey the souls of men. Whoever is found at that moment in sincere worship of God is saved, and his name is written in the books of those destined for Paradise.

I was invited to witness the prayers that night in Aya Sofia, one of the largest covered spaces in the world. I was told that more than ten thousand men were crowded on the floor. Women were in the immense galleries, except the West gallery, which was reserved for visitors. For two or three hours, men were wandering in and out, performing their prayers in private or sitting quietly in groups. At midnight the muezzin intoned loudly the call to prayer. All the men lined up touching shoulder to shoulder. When the cry Allah-u-Akbar went up it was like thunder. When ten thousand heads struck the floor in the prostration the great building was shaken. No one could be present and not feel wonder at the prodigious impact of such an act of concerted worship. In the night prayer there are seven prostrations made in unison and six more individually. The transition produced a strange sense of an inpouring of power. One might well believe that at that moment an Archangel had overshadowed the multitude. After the prayer they were slow in dispersing; most spent the night in the mosque, waiting for the dawn, when the fast was to end.

What could I make of it? The experience itself made a deep impression. But who was changed by it? Tomorrow they would all be as before - dominated by same passions and weaknesses as all other men. My mind went to Rome and same thunderous sound at Easter, when tens of thousands of throats shout "Tu es Petrus!" Men and women are bathed in tears and the heavens seemed to open. Was it not the same there also; did they not all return unchanged in character to the same life dominated by the same weaknesses?

I went out into the open air. All Istanbul was lit by oil lamps and candles festooned from minaret to minaret, from roof to roof everywhere. An incomparably beautiful city was dying. Soon there would be no Sultan living at Yıldız. I could not know how great the changes were to be, how soon the fez was to disappear with the women's veil. Soon the muezzin would call to prayer wearing a bowler hat, by the edict of a dictator of Jewish origin and a hater of religion. Soon the dervishes were to disappear from the streets, the *tekke*s to be closed and their leading men exiled.

I was witnessing the death of an Epoch, but I did not know it. I only knew that I was filled with a heart-breaking sadness. Where was I to go? I had just written to the warden of my college in Oxford to say that I would not take up my scholarships. I had been recommended for the Staff College, and yet I knew that an army career was impossible for me. I could not leave everything and become a dervish. The dervishes belonged to the dying world. They were a reminder that once men had known how to live to the full inwardly as well as outwardly. But it was only too obvious that the ancient fire had died.

There was no one to whom I could turn for advice. I found myself reciting a distich from a gazel of Fuzuli, the greatest of Turkish poets:

Dost bî-pervâ felek bî-rahm ü devran bî-sükûn
Derd çoh hem-derd yoh düşmen kavî tâli' zebûn

Sâye-i ümmîd zâ'il âfitâb-ı şevk germ
Rütbe-i idbâr âlî pâye-i tedbîr dûn

Friends do not share my feeling, the sky does not hear my plaint, the rolling spheres are never still.

My sorrows are many and none to share them, foes are mighty, fate daunts my will.

The shadow of hope for that sweet expected dawn grows longer, The rank of my aspiration is lofty; meagre and wretched, alas, my skill.

I wandered amongst the midnight crowds, down the street of the Sublime Porte, past the Kapalı Çarşı, the great bazaar of Istanbul, up by the mosque of Byazid to the Ministry of War. There I had started work fifteen months earlier, and foreseeing nothing of all that was to happen to me in that short time. My family was far away and I had almost forgotten their existence. I no longer had a home anywhere.

Turning north, I walked on until I reached the mosque of Suleimaniye. There are few buildings in all the world more impressive than this masterpiece of Sinan of Kayseri, architect of a thousand mosques and palaces. There, as nowhere else, the nearly impossible feat of blending a majestic dome with a group of minor structures is achieved. There is harmony, the indestructible majesty of a great work of art.

The question behind Fuzuli's lament began to haunt me. Where was my *rütbe-i idbâr* - the rank of my aspiration? What did I really wish to attain in my lifetime?

As these questions surged in me, I could feel my heart almost breaking with the anguish of emptiness. But soon my mind, with its inveterate habit of seeking for formulae, began to assert itself. There were some principles I could not doubt. I walked round and round the great almost empty, courtyards of Süleymaniye until I had put them into words.

First as regards myself, one thing certain was that I was an ordinary human being with the same deep faults as every other. I must never allow myself to feel different from other people or better than they were. I might differ from others, but why should I be right and they be wrong? Every human being I knew was self-centred. I must surely be self-centred also. I could therefore never trust my judgments about myself. Vanity and self-love seem to be the terrible enemies of mankind; at least I could try not to give way to them.

What help could I look for? What could religion give me? Everywhere I could see mutual exclusion, the denial of another's truth, the rejection of another's faith. I could not believe that any one religion could have the only truth and the whole truth. I could not turn for help to those who lived by the very exclusions that I wished to abolish in myself. Here again probability must be respected. Was it not infinitely improbable that a few hundred million people could possess the truth and four times as many be utterly bereft of it? This argument held equally for Christianity as for Islam, for the religions of the West as for those of the East. I vowed that I would never rest until I could find one Truth and one Faith in which all beliefs could be reconciled.

Then again there was the question of home. Where was I at home? In England, where I was born? In America, where my mother came from? In Turkey, where I felt at ease? Somewhere in Asia, where there might be a source of truth of which I knew nothing? Why was I proud to be an Englishman? All day long I was dealing with different races: English, French, Italian, Greek, Armenian, Turkish, Kurdish, Russian, Arab, Jews and people so mixed as to be no race at all. Each and every one was convinced of the superiority of his own people. How could anyone be right and all the rest wrong? It was nonsense. There could not be better and worse nations, nor favoured and unfavoured races. If I was to be a human being, I must put aside the feeling that I was British and therefore best. Here at least was a truth that I could accept without reserve: The human race is one and indivisible, and I must live my life as a human being before all else.

A sense of peace and accomplishment came over me. I had a *rütbe-i idbâr* - a goal to be achieved. I wished to be a man free from vanity and self-love, to find the source of all religion and the unity of mankind. As always, the reaction came at once. These were fine words and I could write them down and carry them about all my life. But neither I nor anyone else could do anything about it - we were all tarred with the same brush.

Were we after all? Might there not be someone, somewhere, who could help? For the first time in my life, the idea of search entered my consciousness. There was something that must be found, before there could be anything to be done. Dawn was approaching. I had men waiting for me in my office: secret agents who never appeared until after midnight. In a few hours I would be writing more reports. It was the day to prepare my weekly intelligence report-nicknamed by someone 'Bennett's Bright Bumf for Bored Blighters' - which went out to Control Officers and isolated posts all over the Near East.

I climbed into an *araba* - the open two-horse phaeton still at that time the principal conveyance in Turkish cities - and drove back to Hagopian Han. Nothing had happened, and yet everything had changed.

4: PRINCE SABAHEDDIN AND MRS. BEAUMONT

Whenever I could spare an hour or two, I took lessons in Turkish and Persian literature from Kurd Avni Bey. He was very proud of his descent from the great Bederhan; very tall, lean, poor and learned. He wrote poetry in Turkish and Persian, and even in the Kurdish language, which has scant literature of its own. He was a great admirer of the Turkish poet Fuzuli, a contemporary of William Shakespeare, and in his opinion no less a poet. I could not accept this assessment. Fuzuli, like all the great Islamic poets, was a mystic with little interest in the earthly elements of our human natures. His poetry depends so much on verbal subtlety as to be almost untranslatable. I tried my hand at the oft-quoted verse:

Canı cânân dilemiş vermemek olmaz ey dîl
Ne nîza eyleyelim ol ne senindir ne benim

The Soul of souls begged for my soul.
Say, heart, shall we our soul resign?
Why take we anguished thought and pine?
That soul is neither thine nor mine.

Avni Bey introduced me to the poets and writers of the day; but he particularly wanted me to encounter, before it disappeared for ever, the last flowering of the old Ottoman culture. He proposed to take me for the feast of Sheker Bayram, as the Turks call the Id-ul-Fitr, to the house of a rich Lazz merchant.

Our host was a Muslim of the old regime, with four wives and a rich establishment. Women were confined to the Haremlik and the party I met was all men, ranging from boys to greybeards. The old custom was followed of opening the door to all comers, and especially of inviting one or two beggars, as ragged and dirty as possible.

The meal was served by several men-servants and was eaten with the fingers in the old Turkish style. Round sheets of soft unleavened bread were before all the guests. Pieces torn off served to pick up food too soft or too liquid to be handled with the fingers. There was, of course, no alcohol of any kind, but several varieties of sherbet cooled with snow which had been buried since the winter.

As everyone knows who has travelled in these countries, meals have a disconcerting way of reaching an apparent end and then starting again. Pilafs with chicken, lamb, fish, various vegetable dishes, are followed by very sweet cakes and syrups, and the meal seems to be well rounded off. Then the servants bring in more pilaf, of a different colour perhaps, and the meal starts again. One must eat sparingly of the early courses, if one is not to commit an unpardonable breach of good manners by refusing the later dishes.

One of the beggars was a humorist - probably it was his profession to go from house to house and amuse the guests. He told stories of Mulla Nasrudin – the Turkish Til Eulenspiegel - and also racy gossip about well-known people in the city. The company did not always laugh; no one could be sure what would be repeated elsewhere, or how!

After the meal there was music. The best singers in Turkey were the muezzins, and those from the great mosques were much sought after. That evening the most famous of all, Nureddin Fahri from the Blue Mosque of Sultan Ahmad, was one of the guests. By that time, the charm of the traditional Turkish music had penetrated my defences, but I had never before witnessed the poetic and musical improvisation that was regarded as the highest form of art in the regions of Kurdistan, the Caucasus and northern Persia. I did not even know that it was to be met with in Constantinople.

Several well-known poets and musicians were present. The whole party had been discussing some rather abstract theme about the mystical content of certain Turkish poetry. Without any apparent change of tone, our host asked one of the poets to express what had been said in a poem. Without a word the musicians brought in their instruments. A few words were said about the mode appropriate for the theme and the muezzin began to chant the poem. The whole action, in its complete spontaneity, produced a most moving effect. But the response of the audience was exaggerated beyond measure. All were sighing or moaning. Half were sobbing. Some fell on the floor shaking, with loud cries of Maşallah, and other expressions of rapture.

When the singer ended there was a long silence broken only by deep sighs. The performance was repeated several times. Then the conversation returned to the original theme, which somehow the poems and music had clarified, for all were now agreed.

Music for Asiatic people is quite different from what it is for Europeans - at least for those Asiatics whose taste has not been changed by contacts with the West. It is an intimate ritual. Modern concert halls have destroyed this quality that our music formerly possessed until the nineteenth century. But it was not the music alone that made so deep an impression. The feast itself was a ritual act, and every part of it had a ritual character.

I spoke about this, and asked their opinion. One of those present said that Europeans approach every question through the mind and disregard the inward state of consciousness behind the question. "You have made far more progress in your social life than we have. We admire you for your technical achievements and your political institutions, but you know far less than we do about the inward life. You imagine that you know how to lie and that you understand joy and suffering, but you have no idea of the Hal (that is the psychic state) we come to when we hear such music as this." Another much older man praised French culture, and said that Turkey owed more to France than to any other nation. French culture was based upon a sense of fitness of which the British and Germans knew nothing. One young man, with an accent that I could not place, intervened and said: "The highest culture in the world is the Anglo-Saxon. No other people has ever achieved such respect for the individual combined with so sound a social conscience. We in Turkey should model our future social and political plans upon the British." His enthusiasm shattered the conversation and I lost the thread.

Before we left, the young man came up to me and said that I ought to meet his leader and friend Prince Sabaheddin, the hope of Turkish liberalism. Sabaheddin was the nephew of the reigning Sultan, and his father was the famous Turkish reformer, Damad Mahmoud Pasha, who had been exiled for his opposition to the despotism of Sultan Abdul Hamid.

I did not follow up the young man's suggestion, nor did I learn his name. But when an event is predestined, the fates have more than one shot in their locker. Within a few weeks I heard the name of Prince Sabaheddin again, this time from Satvet Lutfi Bey, a well-known friend of the Allies, who had come to see me about a deputy who had been arrested in error. Lutfi Bey's insistence that I ought to meet the Prince overcame my lack of interest and it was arranged that he should take me to dinner the following Wednesday.

Events that look like trivial accidents may appear later as evidence that there is a pattern that shapes our lives. The following Wednesday, I was very busy and nearly forgot my appointment to dine with the Prince. I was preparing a report aimed at convincing British G.H.Q. that the effective strength of the Turkish Army in Anatolia had been grossly underestimated, and I had just received the photographs of the railway workshops in Eskişehir which I have already mentioned. When Satvet Lutfi Bey came to call for me, some inner necessity took charge. I put everything aside and drove to Kuru Cheshme. Satvet Lutfi Bey told me that he had been a friend of Prince Sabaheddin since before 1908, when as a law student he had joined in the revolution against Sultan Abdul Hamid. He had later been imprisoned by the Young Turks, but had escaped to France. The Prince had strenuously opposed the war, but had refused to take part in any plots against the Unionist Government of Talaat Pasha. Nevertheless, Satvet Lutfi had unwittingly found himself entangled in several plots and had narrowly escaped with his life, having been twice condemned to death. He was a Bozniak, that is a Serbian Muslim, a race famous for their courage and their loyalty. He was then, and still is, one of the most handsome men I have met.

Kuru Cheshme was not really a palace, but a large villa overhanging the Bosphorus. It has since been destroyed to make way for oil-storage tanks. We were received by a footman in a frock-coat, but there was an air of poverty that was more felt than seen. We were shown into a typical Turkish drawing-room with faded Empire furniture. After a few minutes a diminutive figure entered. Sabaheddin was one of the smallest and slenderest men I have ever seen, but with such an immense dignity and so grand a manner that I knew at once that this was no ordinary minor princeling. He spoke perfect French and preferred it to Turkish. He wore the customary frock-coat which goes well with the fez. His courtly manner made me apprehensive of an evening spent in listening to platitudes in the grand style.

The Prince was himself a vegetarian, but, unlike most Muslims at that time, drank wine with his meals. He had ordered for me a famous Turkish delicacy: *cerkez tavugu*, that is, chicken breast served with a sauce of ground walnuts.

Sabaheddin was by no means the pompous grandee I had feared. He probably knew from Satvet Lutfi the work I was doing, and was far too delicate to allow the conversation to touch on awkward subjects. We soon came to his hobby-horse: the importance of fostering Private Initiative in the Social Order. I heard for the first time of Frédéric le Play and Edmond Desmolins and of the School of Social Science. Sabaheddin was a wonderful expositor, and it was a delight to watch his delicate little hands illustrating some point in his thesis. The entire subject was new to me, but I could well see how hard it would be for the Turks, accustomed as they were to a rigidly centralized administration, to see the value of *teşebbüs-i-şahsi*, that is, personal initiative. It was not surprising that the Prince sat alone at Kuru Cheshme, surrounded by his books, and neglected equally by the Sublime Porte and by the Nationalist Government in Ankara. Nearly forty years were to pass before his countrymen were ready to listen to his advice and study his theories. By then, he had been dead ten years.

When I rose to go, the Prince invited me to come again soon. Seeing that he sincerely wished to see more of me, I agreed, and very soon our Wednesday evening dinners at Kuru Cheshme became a part of my life. I suppose that this was in October 1920. Many years later, Satvet Lutfi told me that the Prince had been reluctant to meet me, but after our first evening had said: "*Ce jeune homme est un génie; je n'ai jamais rencontré un esprit plus fin.*"

Sabaheddin took upon himself to fill gaps in my education. He gave me books to read - and moreover obliged me to read them by discussing them the following week. One of the first was Edouard Schuré's *Les Grands Initiés*, which astonished me by the suggestion that all religions are the same in their origin and that the contradictions between them are due only to our imperfect understanding. This agreed so closely with my own convictions that I wanted to know more. Sabaheddin spoke to me of Rudolph Steiner, who was his personal friend, and of the teachings of Theosophy and Anthroposophy. He also told me of seekers after initiation whom he had known in France, such as the occultist Charles Lancelin.

When I asked if any proof could be given of all these remarkable ideas, Sabaheddin told me of experiments he had witnessed in which hypnotism and auto-suggestion were used to enable people to explore the unseen world. He gave me the books of Colonel de Rochas, whom he had known in Paris fifteen years before.

My Wednesday evening meetings with Sabaheddin brought again to life the problems and the hopes that had been aroused by my experience in the Casualty Clearing Station on 21st March 1918. Nevertheless, my own work took so much of my time that I did not do much serious reading of the many books he lent me.

Kuru Cheshme was the scene of two events that completely changed the course of my life. They were my meetings with the lady who was to become my wife and companion for nearly forty years, and with Gurdjieff, whose ideas and teaching were to become the chief concern of my inner life.

One evening, the Prince said that he would like me to meet an English lady, Mrs. Winifred Beaumont, whom he had met in Switzerland during the war and who had come with him to Turkey as companion of his only child, the Princess Fethiye. The Princess was well known in Constantinople for her almost excessive emancipation from the manners of the Seraglio. I had never seen her, because she never came to her father's dinner parties; nor did I want to meet this Englishwoman. I was wholly immersed in Turkish affairs and had not mixed in the limited English society open to officers. I did not want to think about England. If my own family and my daughter, only a few months old, meant so little to me - why should I want to be reminded of England?

Winifred Alice Beaumont

With the Prince, one could not be ill-mannered. He evidently counted on my acceptance and so the following Wednesday I went to

Kuru Cheshme expecting to be embarrassed or irritated and hoping that one meeting would satisfy Sabaheddin. When I entered the drawing-room, she was already there. My first impression was that her dignity and poise matched that of the Prince. I felt gauche beside them. When she spoke, her voice restored my confidence. It was a voice that spoke within one and to one, not, as do so many people's, at one and from outside. It had a quality that aroused in those who heard her speak feelings of renewed life and hope. I began to notice her face. It was beautiful, but her eyes were sad. She had white hair, but a clear, young complexion. Her eyes were brown and warm and matched her voice. Although she spoke little that evening, her presence brought a new quality to our talk. Until then I had been curious and interested in all that the Prince had told me. That night, it began to matter to me; as if I were hearing from inside and not from outside. I was far from understanding what was happening to me. Later, the Prince told me that he called her *l'Allumeuse* - she who lights a fire - the word conveys that quality that I felt from our first meeting. She had no car, so I drove her to her flat in Matchka at the other end of the Grande Rue de Pera from Hagopian Han, where I was still living. She told me that she had first refused to meet me, as she wished to keep away from British officers and anything British. She had come to Turkey to forget England, though she did not say why. I did not feel timid with her as I did with most women. Indeed, it was as if it had all happened before and that we were meeting again.

During the week that followed, I could not forget her. I hoped she would be at the Prince's dinner, because it had not occurred to me to ask if I could visit her. All this may seem very natural, but it was strange to me that anything or anyone could distract me from the Intelligence work in which I was so passionately interested.

The following week we met again at Kuru Cheshme and this time Sabaheddin's usual reserve in speaking of his own private convictions lifted, and he spoke about Jesus Christ in a way no one had ever spoken to me before. He had, of course, been brought up as a Muslim. He had studied Eastern religions - especially Buddhism, but he had found no satisfaction except in the contemplation of Jesus Christ. His face lit up as he spoke of the love of Jesus for mankind. I could see that Divine Love was a reality for him, whereas it had been no reality for the Christian priest who had tried to teach me the meaning of the Christian faith. Mrs. Beaumont was obviously delighted to hear him speak in this way. She drew him on with the right interjections. He said that Islam was a great and noble religion and that he had never renounced its central dogma - that is, the Oneness and the complete Otherness of God. The Holy

Virgin was for him as much a living reality as Jesus the Son of God. Only it was necessary to remember that no man ever could or ever would understand the true meaning of the relationship 'Son of God'.

For me this talk was a marvelous experience. I had never until that evening taken religion seriously. The next day I remembered much of what he had said. But before the week was out, the impression had faded. It was not until much later that I realised that no one can transmit his faith to another. I had been deeply moved by what the Prince had said - but it had not entered the depth of me. Looking back after many years, I am even astonished to see that I can remember so much of what was said and that for many long years I had forgotten.

During the same week, I met Mrs. Beaumont again, but under quite different circumstances. These arose from my being detailed rather frequently to take care of distinguished visitors and groups who came to Constantinople on some mission of enquiry, or simply to satisfy their own curiosity. My knowledge of the city and the language, coupled with my own tendency always to undertake more than I could accomplish, made me the obvious target for unwanted jobs. Sometimes they proved very interesting, as when I acted as interpreter for the Dardanelles Commission that came to Turkey to report on the wisdom or otherwise of the landings in Gallipoli. This time, I was instructed to befriend a delegation from the Second Socialist International on its way to Tiflis to consult with the Social Democratic Government of Georgia.

The British Army had recently withdrawn from Batum, the main seaport of Georgia, an infantry brigade sent after the Armistice to guard the oil pipe-line from Baku to the sea. This was, in my youthful opinion, a text-book decision taken in London by a misguided C.I.G.S. out of touch with the realities of the situation. I was convinced that so long as a British brigade - even a battalion - remained in the Caucasus, the governments of the three key countries, Azerbaijan, Georgia and Armenia, would resist the pressure of Russian Communism, and preserve their independence. On 9th July 1920, the brigade was withdrawn, and within four weeks the Georgian Government informed the Allies that they were unable to counteract Bolshevik propaganda. At the same moment a strange proposal reached me through a reliable agent. The main threat to Georgian independence was the activity of the Bolshevik Commissar, an Armenian. An Armenian secret society was prepared to assassinate him to prevent Armenia falling into Russian hands, but needed our help in evacuating those concerned.

I sent in a report, and a few days later received a curt minute: 'His Majesty's Government will never connive at political assassination.'

Now a curious, almost comic, situation had arisen. The Second Socialist International, which during and even after the war had been branded as a pacifist and subversive body by most of the Allied Governments, was now cast for the role of saviour of the democratic republics of the Caucasus. At its convention in Berne in February 1919, it had passed resolutions condemning Bolshevism and had agreed to send a 'Commission of Enquiry' to Russia. A year and a half had gone by and now at the eleventh hour the Allied authorities found it convenient to give facilities for such a Commission to go to the Caucasus in the hope of stiffening the Georgian Government. But the taint of pacifism still remained, and I was given somewhat conflicting instructions to do all that I could to help the Commission, and yet to be on my guard.

I went to meet the ship on which the delegation was travelling. To my surprise I found Mrs. Beaumont in the tender, and learned that she had been closely associated with the Berne International, and knew most of the members of the delegation. These included Arthur Henderson, Camille Huysmans, Vandervelde, Philip and Mrs. Snowden, Bernstein and other well-known leaders of the Socialist Movement in Europe. They had to wait for a few days while formalities were completed, and I took them to see the usual sights. Most of them knew Prince Sabaheddin, and a private reception was held at Kuru Cheshme at which I was asked searching questions about Turkey and the Caucasus. I took a great liking to the members of the delegation. Camille Huysmans was the outstanding figure, and evidently he and his daughter Sarah, who was with the party, were warm friends of Mrs. Beaumont. I could not help feeling that these men and women, who were guided by principles in which they firmly believed, were more to be trusted than the Allied leaders, who seemed to be moved by narrow and selfish motives.

One consequence of these meetings was that I became more and more attracted to Mrs. Beaumont. I was deeply impressed by her ability to set fire to the enthusiasm of this delegation, which had arrived in Turkey somewhat bewildered and suspicious, and left for Batum with a renewed sense of the value of their mission.

Before long, I began to visit Mrs. Beaumont at her own flat, and it seemed the most natural thing in the world to ask if I might go and live there. I moved in with my Turkish batman Mevlud, the most faithful servant I have ever known. His only failing was greed for bread. We were supplied at the G.S.I. Mess with very coarse bread, which our mess president would not serve at our table. Thus five or six large loaves a day went spare, and Mevlud ate the lot. Turkish soldiers hardly knew what it meant to eat meat; but their endurance was such that they could fight cheerfully on what to us would be near starvation rations. When unlimited bread came their way, they did not know where to stop.

Mevlud would never allow me to go out at night alone, but would wait patiently outside a house in any weather and make sure no one was lurking to ambush me as I came out. He was convinced that I had enemies who wished to kill me. He may have saved my life: I certainly did receive threatening letters, but never took them seriously. He fully approved of Mrs. Beaumont, and, between them, they brought into my private life some order which had for many months been sadly lacking.

From our first meeting, I never doubted that our lives were joined. We could not marry until 1925, after many adventures. She and the Prince must have spoken seriously about me. It seems he called me *notre enfant genial* and was sure that I had some special *rôle* to play in the future. He hoped that she would sustain my interest in the search for a deeper reality and not allow me to be drawn blindly into the struggle for success.

Stimulated by her interest, I returned to my mathematical studies. I connected them with the problem of spiritual free will and material determinism. Looking back over the years, I cannot understand why this question so obsessed me at that time. My interest was certainly sustained by the awareness that we live in two worlds: one visible, measurable and knowable, and the other invisible, to be felt rather than known. As I belonged to both worlds, they must be compatible with one another and connected in some way - but I could not tell how. It seemed to me that people compromise too easily with the evidence before them. On the one side, the physical and biological sciences pointed towards a strictly mechanistic account in which there was no place for free will - except by some evasive subterfuge. On the other side, morality required freedom and responsibility, and religion went further and demanded belief in a mysterious world where freedom itself was not enough. Religion could only accept the conclusions of modern science by a subterfuge no less evasive than that which was offered from the other side. The trouble was that these questions and these contradictions were inside myself, and that was why I could not help being obsessed by the need to find a solution.

One day I happened to receive from England a batch of scientific papers, among which was a paper by Albert Einstein on the luminiferous ether. He discussed the hypothesis that the ether is some kind of material substance and demonstrated that if this were true it must have the apparently impossible property of travelling in every possible direction at once, and what is more, it must do so with the speed of light.

I was fascinated by this conclusion. Einstein took it as demonstrating that the luminiferous ether could not be material, but I was struck by its geometrical implications. How could such a state of affairs be represented geometrically?

The following evening, at dusk, I was walking back to my office to finish some reports and was passing the Franchet d'Esperey hospital when the solution struck me like an electric shock. In a moment of time, I saw a whole new world. The train of thought was too rapid for words, but it was something like this: 'If there is a fifth dimension not like space but like time, and if it is orthogonal to the space-time we know, then it would have the required property. Any matter existing in that direction would appear from our standpoint to be travelling with the speed of light. And moreover it would travel in all directions at once. This must be the solution of Einstein's riddle. If so, the fifth dimension must be as real as the space and time we know. But the extra degree of freedom given by the fifth dimension opens all kinds of possibilities. It means that time itself is not unique, and if there is more than one time, there is more than one future. If there are many times, there should be the possibility of choosing between them. In each line of time, there can be a strict causality, but by changing from one line to another we can be free. It is like a railway passenger: so long as he remains on one train his destination is decided in advance. But he can change trains at a junction and so change his destination.'

With these notions flashing through my mind, I saw that my own riddle of free will and determinism could be solved by the addition of a fifth dimension. I was uplifted and carried right out of myself by the excitement of these revelations; and then I saw, or rather became aware of, a vision. I saw a great sphere and knew that it was the whole universe in which we live - that is, the universe we can reach with our senses. Inside this sphere was greater and greater darkness, and outside it light and more light. I saw beings falling from the sphere of existence into the darkness. I also saw bright forms descending on to it from beyond. And I understood that this was a vision of eternity. It was a vision of freedom and determinism, and I could see that souls could fall towards a more fixed or frozen state than that of our visible universe, and also that they could rise towards a greater freedom and glory. It seemed also that the free souls could enter the universe and leave it again.

All this must have happened within less than a minute, for I had not reached the Rue de Pera before the vision vanished and had become a memory. I did not go to the office, but turned back, trembling under the impact of what I had experienced, and went home to tell Mrs. Beaumont.

I asked her to make me a picture as nearly as she could of my description. She took a board and quickly sketched my sphere of sense perception with its inner and outer regions as I had described then.

The next time we went to dine with Sabaheddin, we took the picture with us. The notion of the ether moving in all directions with the speed of light struck his imagination. We were all three in such a state of elation that our talk lasted half the night. Mevlud was patiently waiting as we came out. He seemed able, without a word, to share in our sense of wonder.

I tried to express what I had seen in mathematical terms, but found no way of relating the notion of a fifth dimension with anything that could be measured and therefore tested, to prove it or disprove it. More than thirty years were to pass before this step was made.

At that time, I speculated upon the possibility of 'exploring' the fifth dimension by inducing special states of consciousness. I had heard that smoking hashish would produce a state in which the passage of time seems to cease. I knew there were many hashish addicts in Turkey, and soon found someone who undertook to show me how the drug is taken. I found the first taste of hashish both unpleasant and alarming. It burned my throat, which grew more and more constricted until I began to suffocate. Suddenly, a release came and I had the sense of floating in the air. I was filled with an upsurge of freedom and well-being which lasted for some time. There was no kind of vision, nor was the floating sensation in any way 'outside' time and space. I tried a second and a third time at intervals of twenty-four hours, as my Turkish mentor had advised. The release came more easily and the experience was less unpleasant, but there was nothing to indicate that I was exploring the fifth dimension. All that happened was that the connection between my awareness of myself and my awareness of my body had been dissolved. The floating sensation was entirely different from the separation from the body that I had experienced in the state of coma two and a half years earlier.

I told the Prince of my experiments, and he said that it would probably be necessary to go very much further to get interesting results. He advised me not to pursue them. He had tried similar methods himself and had assiduously studied the literature on the subject. He was convinced that there was a serious risk of permanent injury to the 'astral body' of man. This he regarded as a quasi-material organ having a special sensitivity that enabled it to act as a link between the physical body and the higher parts of the self. Sabaheddin believed that is presence in man could be demonstrated experimentally, and that it can even survive for some time after contact with the physical body is ruptured by death.

I did not understand his explanations of the astral body, because at that time I thought in Cartesian terms of mind and matter. I could not accept the notion of a quasi-material organ; for me the astral body - if it existed - must either be matter or a state of consciousness, not something between the two. Nevertheless, I was glad to take the Prince's advice, for in truth I was afraid of drugs. I have never again experimented with narcotics, and am therefore not competent to say whether or not they can open the door to an authentic experience of any supra-normal state of consciousness.

My interest in the border region between mind and matter did not abate. From time to time I visited the dervishes, or met some man from the eastern provinces, or even from Central Asia, who was credited with extraordinary powers. However, I could never discover any kind of phenomenon that could be made the subject of controlled experiments. Then, towards the end of 1920, at a time when I was somewhat less occupied with my intelligence work, I happened to learn of a demonstration of hypnotic power given by a Pole who called himself Radwana de Praglowski. One of my colleagues invited him to our little G.S.I. Mess to give a private show and he performed several experiments which I could not explain. I was particularly impressed by his feat of bringing a British officer - openly incredulous beforehand - into a cataleptic state in which his body was so rigid that, when his head was put on one chair and his feet on another, a man could stand on his stomach. In a queer way, this reminded me of the old Rufa'i dervish and his scimitar.

I invited Radwana de Praglowski to our flat and, finding that he had studied the deeper states of hypnotic trance, asked him to give me lessons, which he readily agreed to do. He told me that simple experiments could be made with almost any subject, but that if I wished to make any kind of deeper research, it would be necessary to choose two or three subjects who proved to be particularly sensitive.

Mrs. Beaumont herself and a Russian girl, whom we had met through our interest in the refugees from Russia, agreed to try, and both proved exceptionally good subjects. We met once or twice a week and I repeated many of the experiments described in the books of Colonel de Rochas. Among others, I convincingly verified the effect called 'exteriorization of the sensitivity'. This is obtained by bringing a subject into hypnotic trance to the depth at which the skin becomes insensitive and the subject can only hear the voice of the hypnotist. Then an opaque screen is placed round the head so that the subject - whose eyes are closed - could not, in any case, see his own body. Then an object, such as a gold ring, hanging from a fine silk thread, is very quietly brought near some part of the body. The subject is told to report anything he feels. When the ring comes within a few centimetres of the skin, the subject cries out and says that he is being burned. By this means it is possible to map out zones of sensitivity over the surface of the body. These appear to take the form of a series of sheaths, the closest of which is a few millimetres and the outermost a metre from the skin.

These experiments convinced me that there must be some field of force surrounding the human body that is linked to the nervous system within the body. They forced me to revise my unfavourable opinion of Sabaheddin's description of the astral body of man. I began to surmise that there are probably states of matter which can not be detected by sight or touch, but which nevertheless have a kind of sensitivity similar to that of the animal nervous system.

When these experiments were reported to Prince Sabaheddin, he was delighted but urged me to turn my attention to the phenomenon called 'regression of the memory', in which a hypnotized subject, after passing through four distinct trance states, begins to live in his own past. He completely forgets recent events, and does not know where he is. He appears to be living at a definite moment in the past. The voice and manners change and become younger and younger as the regression proceeds.

Mrs. Beaumont, who was then forty-seven years old, went back to her childhood in India and spoke Hindustani fluently, whereas when awakened, she could not with all her efforts remember more than a few words. The Russian girl went further and passed through what was unmistakably the prenatal existence, curled up exactly like a five-months foetus. Going further back, she claimed to be floating in space.

I tried several times with both subjects to go back to some past life. In neither case were there the slightest indications of any memories prior to conception. The 'floating in space' could be interpreted as the gastrula stage of development.

Sabaheddin was not a little disappointed at these limited results. He was rather a hesitant believer in reincarnation, and was probably hoping that some evidence would be produced that would convince us all of the reality of 'former lives'. I must say that so far as my limited experiments in regression of the memory were able to take us, we found no confirmation whatever of the kind of claim made by Colonel de Rochas in his book, Les Vies Successives.

I found the hypnotic experiments tiring, and did not see how they could help me to explore the fifth dimension. My two subjects could make nothing whatever of my suggestions that they should look from one time to another. When either of them was living her life of five, ten or twenty years ago, she neither knew nor cared about any other time - past or future.

New and absorbing interests entered our lives about this time, and I soon abandoned my experiments in hypnotism.

5: GURDJIEFF AND OUSPENSKY

The second decisive event of my life, for which Kuru Cheshme set the scene, was my first meeting with George Ivanovitch Gurdjieff, one of the most remarkable men of our century. The pattern of my life must certainly have required this meeting, for three distinct threads were leading me towards it.

The story begins with Mikhail Alexandrovitch Lvow, former Colonel of the Imperial Horse Guards. He was a member of the highest Russian aristocracy, had been converted by Leo Nikolayevitch Tolstoy, retired from the Army and went to live at Yasnaya Polyana, where he was at the time of Tolstoy's death in 1910. He had learned shoemaking and, having given away all his property, supported himself by making shoes. Nevertheless, following Tolstoy in his condemnation of revolution he had been obliged to flee from Russia, and in 1920 was living in great poverty in Constantinople. He made his bed under the staircase in the Russky Mayak, a club for white Russians situated near the Tünel, that is, the upper station of the underground mountain railway that runs between Pera and Galata.

Mrs. Beaumont met him and was so touched by his humility and patience that she proposed to let him have a small spare room in her flat. He admitted that the lack of privacy at the Mayak was distressing and agreed to come, providing he was allowed to do his own housework and was not disturbed in his hours of meditation.

We were glad to welcome him, though neither of us was much at home. She was then working hard as a teacher of English in the Turkish girls' school of Bezm-i-Alem, of which her great friend, Sabiha Esen, was headmistress. She loved her Turkish pupils and worked late with those who wanted special tuition. I was also often at the office till late at night, so we would have seen little of Lvow, if I had not been so strongly impressed by his personal qualities.

I had never before met a man like Lvow. His humility and love of poverty were unquestionable. At no time did he seek anything for himself, nor did he ever volunteer advice or information on any subject. Unless spoken to, he would remain silent all day, mending boots for poor Russians, who usually could not pay him. I suppose he was then about fifty years old, but his gentle pale blue eyes, his lean erect figure and his clear complexion gave him an ageless appearance. He was never depressed, and I never heard him speak ill of anyone or anything. His own standards of self-discipline were rigorous, but he never expected others to follow him.

One day, Lvow, with great hesitation and many apologies, told us that a friend of his, Piotr Demianovitch Ouspensky, wanted to hold weekly meetings in Pera, but could not afford to hire a room. Mrs. Beaumont's drawing-room was large enough for his need, and not being in use during the afternoons, he thought that she might be willing to lend it. She readily agreed, though Lvow stipulated that, the meetings being private, we would be expected to refrain from listening to what was said. Learning that the talks were to be in Russian, we could assure him that we would not understand a word.

So I met Peter Ouspensky, who was to become my teacher, and whose influence was one of the chief factors in forming my attitude towards life. His meetings were held on Wednesday afternoons, but were so late in starting that both Mrs. Beaumont and I usually returned from work before they were over. The meetings sounded like pandemonium. Everyone was shouting at once and we wondered what could so excite this little group of Russians. Lvow had given us a formal assurance that there would be no mention of political questions, and we knew that his word was sacred. We liked Ouspensky himself and although his English was hard to understand, we tried to make friends. At that time, he was living on the Island of Prinkipo with his wife and family, and was earning a little money by teaching English to Russians and giving lessons in mathematics to children.

Once I asked him what was spoken of at his meetings. He replied: "The Transformation of Man." He added: "You suppose all men are on the same level, but in reality one man can be more different from another than a sheep is from a cabbage. There are seven different categories of men." He took a piece of paper and drew a simple diagram as shown below.

He explained that all the men that we can expect to know belong to one of the three lower categories - that is, they live by their instincts, by their emotions or by their minds. "If any man aspires to transformation," he said, "he must first acquire balance and harmony of his instincts, his emotions and his thoughts. This is the first condition for right transformation. The transformed man acquires powers that are incomprehensible to ordinary people. Even Man Number Five is for us a superman."

Instinct Man 1	Feeling Man 2	Thought Man 3	Perfected Man 7
			Conscious Man 6
			Integrated Man 5
			Transitional Man 4

This conversation imprinted itself with photographic clarity on my mind. I can remember just how I was sitting on Ouspensky's left on a settee under the window. I remember the abrupt stop with which he brought his explanation to an end, and the way he peered short-sightedly through his pince-nez. The whole scene is as clearly present to me now as then; but it stands in isolation. I felt no urge to pursue the enquiry further and I did not connect the notion of 'transformation' with myself

When I went to dine with Sabaheddin the same evening, I told him of what Ouspensky had said. He showed no particular interest and I confess that Ouspensky's scheme seemed to me artificial and unscientific. I secretly thought that my discovery of the fifth dimension was far more interesting, but felt no urge to speak of it - chiefly, I suppose, because I could produce no tangible evidence to support the theory.

Whether on account of my lack of response, or of his own reluctance to make another move, Ouspensky did not reopen the subject of the transformation of man. We remained friends, and I went sometimes to visit him and his family in Prinkipo.

The second thread came into my hands through my love of music. I was one of a small group of Allied officers who joined forces to organize concerts in Pera. Among the refugees from Russia, were many orchestral players and two well-known conductors: Boutnikov and Thomas de Hartmann. Each had his own following, but there was no place for two orchestras, so we persuaded them to join forces. This was not easy, for there was intense rivalry. One had with him the trombonist of the Kiev orchestra who had succeeded in bringing out of

Russian several trunks full of orchestral scores. The other was backed by the leader of the Moscow Orchestra. There was much scope for manoeuvre.

Of the two conductors, Thomas de Hartmann most attracted my attention. His wife Olga was a remarkably beautiful woman, a former Russian opera singer. Hartmann had been a close friend of Alexander Scriabin, who had died in Siberia during the war. He spoke to me of Scriabin's belief that man possesses higher faculties that are exercised outside his physical body, and that by music these faculties could be awakened and developed. Hartmann wished to perform the two symphonic poems and Prometheus. Although he was himself a composer, he did not press his own compositions.

Boutnikov was the more dynamic and probably more versatile chef d'orchestre, but Hartmann was more than a conductor. Mrs. Beaumont and I both felt that he had access to some secret knowledge, and supposed it had come from his association with Scriabin. It did not occur to us that he might know Ouspensky.

The parts of the puzzle fell into place soon after. The next thread came from Prince Sabaheddin. He disliked the telephone, which he regarded as a baleful instrument for intruding in other people's lives. I was therefore surprised to have a call from him asking my permission to invite an old acquaintance to our next Wednesday meeting. The proposed guest was a man whom he had not seen since 1912, but whom he regarded as unusually interesting. He mentioned a name, which I could not catch over the telephone, and said that he had recently come to Turkey from the Caspian region.

I had not abandoned the idea of making a caravan journey up the valley of the Oxus to Chinese Turkestan and China, and took every chance of meeting people from Central Asia. I had even taken advantage of meetings with Sart, Uzbek and Turkmen travelers through Turkey to learn some of the Turki dialects of the Transcaspian region and Turkestan. It was in expectation of learning about these lands of my dreams that I looked forward to the meeting.

Knowing the Prince's punctuality, I arrived at Kuru Cheshme at a few minutes to eight and was introduced directly into the small salon where we used to sit and talk after dinner. The Prince joined me immediately. I learned that the name of the guest was Gurdjieff, and that the Prince had first met him by chance when he was returning from Europe to Turkey after the Young Turk revolution of 1908.

He had met Gurdjieff only three or four times, but knew that he belonged to a group of occultists and explorers with whom he had travelled far and wide. The Prince regarded him as one of the very few men who had been able to penetrate into the hidden brotherhoods of Central Asia, and had always profited by the talks they had had together. He could not, or would not, tell me any more.

We turned to my experiments in hypnotism. He spoke of his belief in the Akashic Records, by which he meant that there is a fine substance, the akasha or ether, that pervades all existence and is both sensitive and imperishable. All events and all experience leave their traces upon this substance. People in a sensitive state can read these traces, and so connect themselves with events in the past. Within each individual, there is a similar record that connects him with all his past lives. I could not readily accept this theory, because it seemed to me that if we had really existed before, there should be some simpler way of knowing it than reading Akashic records which were accessible only to a few specially endowed individuals.

Time went by, but the Prince showed no sign of impatience. It must have been half-past nine before Gurdjieff appeared. He came in without a trace of embarrassment, greeting the Prince in Turkish with an accent that was a strange mixture of cultured Osmanli and some uncouth Eastern dialect. When we were introduced, I met the strangest eyes I have ever seen. The two eyes were so different that I wondered if the light had played some trick on me. But Mrs. Beaumont afterwards made the same remark, and added that the difference was in the expression and not in any kind of cast or defect in either eye. He had long, black moustaches fiercely curled upwards. He wore a kalpak, that is, an astrakhan cap common in the Eastern vilayets but rarely seen in the capital. It was only when he removed the kalpak after the meal that I saw that his head was shaved. He was short, but very powerfully built. I guessed that he was about fifty, but Mrs. Beaumont was sure that he was older. He told me later that he was born in 1866, but his own sister disputed this and affirmed that he was born in 1877. His age was as much of an enigma as everything else about him.

He could not speak French or English and so our conversation had to be in Turkish, which Mrs. Beaumont understood but could not speak. I felt quite at ease with him, but she told me afterwards that she felt uncomfortable, as if he knew some secret about us that we would prefer to keep hidden. All this was quite beyond me, and it was not until much later that I discovered that Gurdjieff had the peculiar property of appearing to be a different man to everyone who met him.

It seemed that he had already been in Constantinople for nearly two months. He had come from Tiflis, the capital of Georgia, where he had founded an Institute in order to make public the results of his own researches. He intended to go to Europe, where he had been invited by Jaques-Dalcroze, the founder of the system of Eurhythmics, who then had his headquarters at Hellerau in Germany.

With the evident wish to bring me into the conversation, Sabaheddin spoke about our interest in hypnotism, and asked me to describe the experiments I had been making. Gurdjieff listened attentively, and I felt that he was not so much following my words as participating directly in the experience. I had never before had the same feeling of being understood better than I understood myself.

When I had finished, Gurdjieff began a long explanation to which the Prince and I listened with admiration and pleasure. He spoke as a specialist to whom the theory and the practice of hypnotism were equally familiar. Afterwards, when I tried to translate his explanation to Mrs. Beaumont, I found to my dismay that I had forgotten nearly all he had said. Later, this experience was to repeat itself many times, and not for many years did I understand its true significance. In one state of consciousness we see, hear and understand with different faculties from those which are active in another state. When we pass from one state to another, memory does not provide a link, for the nature of memory is to confine our attention to one narrow stratum of our experience, that is, to one line of time.

Gurdjieff spoke about levels of experience in relation to hypnotism. He began by defining various substances or energies, the existence of which, he said, could be demonstrated, but which natural science had not yet discovered. There were yet other substances so fine as to be beyond detection by any physical means. Every possible action depended upon these substances. For example, if we are to think, we must use the substance of thought. If we are to have any kind of supranormal experience, this will be possible only in so far as the appropriate substance is available.

There are ways of separating and controlling the finer substances. One of these ways is what we call hypnotism. There are many varieties of hypnotism, differing according to the substances that are brought into action. Gurdjieff explained the regression of memory as the property of a particular substance present in all living beings and capable of being, as he put it, "crystallized in the form of a kind of finer body within the physical body." The Prince asked if this finer body could reincarnate on the earth in other human or animal forms. Gurdjieff denied this, but he would neither accept nor reject the Prince's claim that reincarnation could be demonstrated. He said simply: "Reincarnation has been so much misunderstood and misrepresented in the West that it is useless to speak of it."

He spoke of the experiments I had made with the exteriorization of the sensitivity and the different responses of a hypnotized subject to different metals. With every metal, a particular fine substance is associated. The same substances also exist in man, although they are on a lower level than the true human substance. Each substance has a definite psychic property. As a subject is brought into a state of deep hypnotic trance, the different substances begin to separate - like iron and brass filings under the action of a magnet. In this condition, the subject can respond to the influence of substances to which he is usually insensitive. So, one can use different metals to induce different psychic reactions such as anger, fear, love, gentleness and so on.

Here I lost the thread of the explanation and began to listen without hearing. It was evident that this man had specialized knowledge of a kind I had not met with before. I was sure that he was speaking of facts he had verified, and not the fantasies which occultist writers always seem to be borrowing from someone else. It would be hard to explain how Gurdjieff was different, say, from the Prince or from the dervishes with whom I had spoken. I was acutely aware of my own inadequacy. I was sure that he could answer my questions - but I did not know what questions to ask.

I wanted to speak of my own experiences when wounded, but could not bring myself to do so. I was afraid of appearing to look upon myself as being different from other people. I did not want to be dissected, in the way he had dissected the experiments with hypnotism. Instead, I spoke about my discovery of the fifth dimension and my belief that it was the region of free will.

Once again, Gurdjieff listened very seriously, and examined the diagram which I drew to indicate the 'upper' and 'lower' levels of existence outside of our space and time. He said: "Your guess is right. There are higher dimensions or higher worlds where the higher faculties of man have free play. But what is the use of studying these worlds theoretically? Suppose that you could prove mathematically that the fifth dimension really does exist, what use would that be to you so long as you remain here?" He pointed to the diagram and sphere representing the whole of space and time. "If you remain here you will have to go down. If you wish to ascend into the world of freedom, then you must do so in this present life. Afterwards, it will be too late."

He reminded me of what he had said about the crystallization of a finer body and added: "Even that is not enough, because that body also is under material laws. In order to be free from the laws of space and time, you yourself must change. This change depends on you, and it will not come about through study. You can know everything and yet remain where you are. It is like a man who knows all about money and the laws of banking, but has no money of his own in the bank. What does all his knowledge do for him?"

Here Gurdjieff suddenly changed his manner of speaking, and looking at me very directly he said: "You have the possibility of changing, but I must warn you that it will not be easy. You are still full of the idea that you can do what you like. In spite of all your study of free will and determinism, you have not yet understood that so long as you remain in this place, you can do nothing at all. Within this sphere there is no freedom. Neither your knowledge nor all your activity will give you freedom. This is because you have no . . ." Gurdjieff found it difficult to express what he wanted in Turkish. He used the word varlık, which means roughly the quality of being present. I thought he was referring to the experience of being separated from one's body.

Neither I nor the Prince could understand what Gurdjieff wished to convey. I felt sad, because his manner of speaking left me in no doubt that he was telling me something of great importance. I answered rather lamely, that I knew that knowledge was not enough. He did not answer me directly but, without giving any impression of ignoring me, began to speak to the Prince about Temple Dances and their importance for the study of ancient wisdom. He invited the three of us to see a demonstration of Temple Dances by a group of pupils whom he had brought with him from Tiflis.

We drove Gurdjieff back to the Grande Rue de Pera, where he said he had an appointment at midnight, which seemed odd. He repeated his invitation to Yemeneci Sokak for the following Saturday.

The Prince did not wish to go. Indeed, he never went out at night on any pretext. Mrs. Beaumont and I made our way to Yemeneci Sokak at nine p.m. as directed. When we arrived the only occupant of the long room was a tall man in a white costume and a yellow sash, who was standing in a corner with his back to the room and slowly nodding his head backwards and forwards. Others, both men and women, came into the room. All were wearing white costumes. Both men and women wore tunics buttoned up to the neck. The men had loose white trousers and the women white skirts over white pantaloons. No one spoke or took any notice of the others. Some sat cross-legged on the floor, others began to practise various postures and rhythms.

Chairs were arranged at one end, and two or three visitors entered and sat down. To our immense astonishment, we saw Ouspensky come into the room, looking neither right nor left and appearing not to recognize us. Soon afterwards Thomas de Hartmann came in and sat down at the piano. I had not suspected that either of them was connected with Gurdjieff.

Gurdjieff himself came in soon after. He was dressed in black. As soon as he entered, all the performers stood up and arranged themselves in six lines. They wore different coloured sashes, and I expected to see them arranged according to the colours of the spectrum, but for some reason the red was in the wrong place.

Hartmann began playing. The first dance was accompanied by a magnificent slow theme that was more like a Greek anthem than an Eastern temple dance. The dance itself was very simple - almost like Swedish gymnastics. Each dance lasted only one or two minutes. The action grew more and more intense. After a time, the straight lines were broken up and the performers placed themselves in some intricate pattern. Before the dance began, one of the men said in English: "The exercise that will follow represents the Initiation of a Priestess. It comes from a cave temple in the Hindu Kush." This was the most impressive and moving event of the evening. The exercise lasted much longer than the others. The part of the priestess, who scarcely moved at all, was taken by a tall and very beautiful woman. The expression of her face conveyed the feeling of complete withdrawal from the outer world. She seemed unaware of the complicated weaving movements of the men and women surrounding her. I had never before seen such a beautiful dance, or heard such strangely disturbing music.

After the Initiation of the Priestess, there were several exercises for men only. Then everyone lined up at the back of the room while Hartmann played a series of chords. Gurdjieff shouted an order in Russian and all the dancers jumped in the air and rushed at full speed towards the spectators. Suddenly Gurdjieff in a loud voice shouted "Stop!" and everyone froze in his tracks. Most of the dancers, being carried by the momentum of their rush, fell and rolled over and over on the floor. As they came to rest they became rigid like people in a cataleptic trance. There was a long silence. Gurdjieff gave another order and all quietly got up and resumed their places in the original ranks. The exercise was repeated two or three times, but the impact on us was no longer the same.

Described in cold blood, this strange charge may seem like an anticlimax, but it fitted somehow into the whole picture. Also it reminded me very strongly of the stop in the Mukabele of the Mevlevi Dervishes.

I wanted to ask Gurdjieff if this stop of his also represented the moment of death. But he quickly left the room, and the dancers dispersed one by one. Hartmann came over and greeted me and Mrs. Beaumont in a very friendly way. When we looked round for Ouspensky, he had already disappeared.

Piotr Demianovich Ouspensky

In spite of the intense interest aroused by Gurdjieff himself, by his conversation and by the work of his pupils, neither Mrs. Beaumont nor I felt drawn to find out more about him for ourselves. We received the impression of having met a closed circle - almost a secret society - whose members kept their own counsel and were not interested in outsiders. It may be that this impression came chiefly from our contacts with Ouspensky. It did not occur to us that we could ever have a place in Gurdjieff's circle. For one thing, the discipline required to produce the remarkable display of skill and endurance that we had witnessed seemed possible only for those who could devote their whole lives to the undertaking.

I cannot remember the dates exactly, but I believe Gurdjieff stayed nearly a year in Turkey, leaving for Germany in the autumn of 1921. I met him occasionally, chiefly in connection with difficulties he was meeting in getting visas for his party to travel to Europe. At that time, it was very hard for Russians to go anywhere. I helped as much as I could, but Russian refugees came under a section of the Allied Organization in Turkey with which I had little contact.

One day in 1921, Ouspensky came to visit me, bringing three copies of his book *Tertium Organum* in English, which he had just received from Claude Bragdon in New York. He had also received a cheque for royalties, which, he said, would enable him to go ahead with his plans for going to England. He had been learning English assiduously and already spoke it much better than when I first met him. He told me that he had friends in England connected with the Theosophical Society, and I advised him to write and ask for a formal invitation. He very kindly presented me with a copy of *Tertium Organum*, which I read with deep interest and admiration. This book opened my eyes for the first time to the possibility that mankind was about to pass through a great change, which would bring once again into active use faculties and powers latent in man but long buried under the weight of our logical thinking. I had scarcely finished reading *Tertium Organum* when Ouspensky came to see me again, this time with a telegram from Lady Rothermere, sent from New York, and saying: "Deeply impressed by your book *Tertium Organum* wish meet you New York or London will pay all expenses."

Ouspensky asked me what I knew about Lady Rothermere. I told him that her husband was generally believed to have great influence with the Prime Minister, Mr. Lloyd George, but that it was impossible to say whether she could arrange questions of visas and permits. These often proved a stumbling block even to very influential people. For some weeks nothing happened; money came for the journey, but that it was impossible to say whether she could arrange questions of visas and permits. These often proved a stumbling block even to very influential people. Ouspensky was evidently anxious to get to London as soon as possible. He accepted Lady Rothermere's invitation, explaining the visa difficulty. For some weeks nothing happened; money came for the journey, but no visa. My experience had taught me that attempts to arrange things 'from the top' usually meant delay, and I went myself to speak to the Russian Section. There being no objection whatever to Ouspensky and his family, the visas were soon given and they left for London.

Soon after, Gurdjieff and his party, including the Hartmanns, set off for Germany. I did not foresee the part that these meetings with Gurdjieff, Ouspensky and Hartmann were to play in my future life. My life was at that time too full and too interesting to leave place for so exacting a discipline as Gurdjieff was likely to demand.

6: POLITICS, HIGH AND LOW

The picture I have drawn in the last two chapters is one-sided. It might seem that I devoted a great part of my time and energy to the search for truth. In reality, I was engaged day and night in my Intelligence work, and my meetings with Prince Sabaheddin were more in the nature of a relaxation than a major interest. As I look back at those years in Turkey, I am distressed at my lack of feeling for the people with whom I had to deal. Mrs. Beaumont and the Prince watched me with affection, but could not understand my obsession with politics. The Prince said to her: *"Notre enfant génial a le coeur encore glacé."* Much was to happen before the ice melted.

I was hard upon myself and upon everyone near me. From August 1919 to January 1921, I drove myself unsparingly, never taking a rest. I had an insatiable thirst to know all that was happening in the Near East and why. The Turkish Nationalist Army was fighting on three fronts: in Smyrna, Cilicia and in Armenia. The French were fighting the Arabs in Syria. The Russians were advancing into the Caucasus. Venizelos had fallen from power, and a plebiscite recalled King Constantine of Greece. The Americans, under pressure of the great oil companies, were seeking a foothold in Mesopotamia. New governments were springing up in Armenia, Azerbaijan and Turkestan, and no one was very clear as to their likely affiliations.

Information was pouring into my office, and I wrote twenty or more reports every week. But my main concern was the unfortunate Turkish Government in Constantinople. The British Foreign Office insisted upon the *de jure* status of the Sultan's government, and did not wish to admit the de facto authority of the Nationalists. It seemed to me both necessary and possible to bring the two Governments together, especially after the fall of Venizelos had removed the main obstacle to an understanding with Greece. I had become a firm friend of the Crown Prince, Abdul Medjid Haidari Effendi, who, probably without much justification, believed that I had saved his life.

In May 1920, very early one morning my telephone rang, and when I answered, the Crown Prince in person spoke to me. This was so entirely contrary to protocol that I could scarcely answer. In a very agitated voice, he asked me to come at once to the Dolma Bahçe Palace, where he was in residence, to take a letter that he wished me to deliver personally to the British Commander-in-Chief. He added that the Sultan had imprisoned him, and that he was afraid he might be assassinated.

The big Mercedes car was always ready at short notice. My driver was a Russian who had driven armoured cars during the war, and often forgot that he was doing so no longer. Within a few minutes he arrived at my office, and when I explained what was wanted, he insisted that I should take a loaded gun-which I refused to do. When we reached the Dolma Bahçe, we found a cordon of Turkish sentries behind a barbed wire entanglement hastily thrown up round the palace. With a gleam in his eye, my driver turned and said that he could easily get through without damage to the car. The Turkish N.C.O. in charge of the guard shouted "Dur! Geçme!" (Stop, don't pass!), and his men rather hesitatingly lifted their rifles. With the dislike of being thwarted that was only too strong a feature of my character, I decided on the spur of the moment to go through. The Turkish soldiers evidently were not expecting a British officer in uniform and did nothing but shout. The next moment I was at the door of the palace and found the Crown Prince waiting for me with an enormous sealed envelope.

He told me that the previous day he had ordered his yacht to be put under steam so that he could take his baby daughter, the Princess Durr-i-Shehvaz, just recovering from bronchitis, for a trip in the Sea of Marmara. It appeared that the Sultan, who had been warned, suspected that his real intention was to cross over to Asia Minor and place himself at the head of the Nationalist Army, and had sent the Palace Guard to prevent him from leaving. He then spoke rather incoherently about poison, saying that they planned to kill him and then to announce that he had committed suicide-as had happened to his father, Sultan Abdul Aziz, forty years before.

I took the letter to British G.H.Q. and found a great state of excitement prevailing over a rumour that the Crown Prince was about to proclaim a holy war against the Allies. All this had come about because the Captain of the Port in the Golden Horn, under whose control the Turkish fleet had been placed, had reported that the Crown Prince had ordered his yacht and was leaving for 'an unknown destination'. The letter I brought explained the situation, and within a couple of days all had calmed down. Abdul Medjid remained convinced to the last that his cousin the Sultan had plotted to have him assassinated and always spoke of me as his saviour. He presented me with a magnificent gold watch with a picture in enamel of the Dolmabahçe Palace and a small coil of the barbed wire as a keepsake.

Seven months later, the situation had greatly changed. The Allies would perhaps have been thankful if they could have found in Prince Abdul Mejid Effendi an intermediary with Mustafa Kemal Pasha. I became involved in complicated and secret negotiations to bring about a rapprochement. In the outcome, Marshal Izzet Pasha, the Minister of War, decided to go to Ankara. Once arrived there, he refused to return until the allies consented to revise the more odious clauses of the Treaty of Sèvres. Before he crossed over, he invited me to his villa on the Asiatic side of the Bosphorus above Scutari. He asked me whether I sincerely believed that the British wished to be friends again with Turkey. If he could believe this, he would do all in his power to persuade Mustafa Kemal Pasha to meet the British Commander-in-Chief, and come to an agreement about the Greek evacuation of Asia Minor in a form that would safeguard their national susceptibilities. He believed that King Constantine, whom he had known during the war, was anxious to put an end to the hostilities, and would himself be ready to go to Athens and meet him.

This was for me an agonizing meeting. I desperately wanted to give the assurance he asked for, but I suspected that the Foreign Office out-bourboned the Bourbons in their inability to forget and to learn. Lloyd George and Curzon might leave the political scene, but the machine of government would go on grinding out the same prejudices and the same stubborn policies as before. I could only say to Izzet Pasha that all who came in contact with the Turks soon grew to like and trust them, and that given time I was sure that real friendliness between our peoples would develop. But I could not speak for the policy of His Majesty's Government. He shook his head sadly and said: "Even in a democratic country like yours, it is the government that counts. For more than a century the British have sustained the Ottoman Sultanate, and by doing so have stabilized politics in a vital quarter of the world. You are now destroying your most useful ally in the Muslim world. One day you will have to retrace your steps and once again build your policy on a strong Turkey. Meanwhile we shall have to take care of ourselves."

A few days later, he went to Ankara as the official representative of the Sultan. When he arrived there with his mission, he issued a statement that the reunion of Turkey under the Sultan depended upon the Allies. Until they were ready to cancel those provisions of the Treaty of Sèvres which made an independent Turkey impossible, he would remain in Ankara.

I put in a report about this meeting which had unexpected consequences. I was called to G.H.Q. to give fuller details of the conversation and was told that although the information I had obtained was valuable, I had gone too far in expressing an opinion on the policy of H.M. Government. By this time, I was past caring much for the views of higher authority. I felt singularly ill, and did not realize that my trouble was mainly fatigue and strain.

I do not remember what I said, but I must have given the impression of an overtired and irascible young man, for I was told a few days later that I had been given leave to England and should take a complete rest for a few weeks. I left Constantinople on the day that Mustafa Kemal Pasha notified the Sublime Porte that it was no longer the seat of government. Meanwhile, the Allied Governments, at the suggestion of Lord Curzon, had decided to invite the Greek and Turkish Governments to meet in London. This encounter was called 'The Conference for the Pacification of the Near East'. I knew nothing of this proposal at the time.

My departure from Constantinople was a peculiar scene. The platform was crowded with people to see me off. Neither the Commander-in-Chief nor the British High Commissioner would have been given such a send-off, and yet who was I? A junior officer of no importance, travelling home with no idea whether he would ever return.

Mrs. Beaumont sat with me in the narrow sleeping car compartment loaded from floor to ceiling with bouquets of flowers, boxes of Turkish delight and other gifts from my Turkish friends. The platform was crowded. I was distressed to see men in tears. I could not feel towards them as they did towards me. Although exhausted and disheartened, I was burning with an inward fire of life that I did not understand.

I cannot and will not attempt to write of my relation with Mrs. Beaumont. It seems to me that the unity of man and woman should concern no one but themselves. I said to her repeatedly: "I will never leave you" - and I knew that I was speaking more truly than in my marriage vow taken two short years before.

I had been living with Mrs. Beaumont for four months. It was only when I verified the dates that I became aware that our time together had been so short. Mrs. Beaumont had become for me 'Polly', the name by which I called her for nearly forty years. She was to become my wife, and to share all the joys and sufferings of my mature life. I was then twenty-four years old, the age at which man enters the first phase of maturity. I had learned much about human nature, but very little about people. I had been living in my head, and my heart was an empty shell. I could not understand myself. Why was I so sure that the link with Mrs. Beaumont would never be broken? It seems to me now - looking back forty years - that my certainty came neither from my head nor from my heart, nor was it connected with my body. It had much more the character of a premonition, a seeing ahead into the future, which had nothing to do with my thoughts or my wishes.

Later, when I returned to her in Constantinople, Mrs. Beaumont told me that, for her part, she had been convinced that she would not see me again, and that I would remain with my wife and child and forget her. Indeed, when I said "I will never leave you", her reply was "Quien sabe? You must remember that I am old enough to be your mother, and you must now find your own life and your own way." Quien sabe? (who knows?) was the motto she had chosen for herself. Her writing paper bore a blue *fleur de lys* and *Quien sabe?* below.

The time for departure came. I went out on the platform and clasped many hands. I was unable to understand this demonstration of affection. I was ashamed that I could not feel as they did, but I did not know for certain that I would return to Turkey. There was something more, but hard to define; I was aware that my life would follow a pattern which had nothing to do with my own will, and that in that pattern Turkey and the Turks would have a significant place.

As the train drew out of Sirkeci Station, I had the same feeling of unreality that had come to me at each of the critical moments of my life. I was an unimportant person, and I knew it I had not intentionally deceived anyone, and yet I had been treated by the Turks as if I wielded an influence equal to that of the High Commissioner or the Commander-in-Chief. I was filled with a intense sadness. I did not wish to lead an unreal life, and yet my actions led me again and again into false situations.

I reached London on 4 February 1921, and saw my daughter Ann for the first time. She was not quite six months old. I looked at her in astonishment, unable to take in the fact that I was really a father. For two days I was never alone with her. On the third, I took her for a walk in her pram, going up the hill to Wimbledon Common, past my old school. I spoke to her quietly, for it seemed that even if she did not understand the words, some kind of communication was yet possible between us. At one moment she looked into my eyes and it seemed that she knew me. That one moment was our only real contact for nearly twenty years. With my wife, I could feel no contact at all. She welcomed me with sincere affection. We slept in one room, but I could not bring myself to treat her as my wife. My memory of those days has so far faded that I cannot remember anything that we said, nor even whether she was distressed or surprised at my aloofness. Before I could settle down to enjoy or fail to enjoy my leave, a fresh surprise changed everything.

When I was leaving Constantinople, my chief, Colonel Gribben, gave me a letter of introduction to Ormsby-Gore, then a junior member of the Government, and suggested that I should see him and tell him of my talk with Izzet Pasha. It happened that on the day I met Ormsby-Gore, the Nationalist Government had announced its intention of sending a delegation to the London Conference. This news must have caused dismay to some and amusement to others. Ankara held the keys to most of the problems requiring solution, but no one wished to admit it.

To my surprise, Ormsby-Gore took my story very seriously, and sent me to see Robert Vansittart, then Lord Curzon's private secretary. He made me repeat my conversation with Izzet Pasha and give him my own version of the strength and organization of the Nationalist Government. He then telephoned to someone - I believe it was Ormsby-Gore - and said in my presence: "We should try to arrange for this man Bennett to have breakfast with the P.M. He has been asking for a first-hand account of the situation in Turkey, and here is someone who can give it. Will you try to arrange it with Philip Kerr?" I did not even know the name of Lloyd George's Private Secretary, soon to succeed his father as Lord Lothian and later to be our Ambassador in the United States during the Second World War. Vansittart turned to me and said: "The Prime Minister likes to get ideas over the breakfast table. If he agrees to see you, speak to him just as you have spoken to me."

He then spoke to me about the delegation sent by the Nationalist Government from Ankara and asked if I knew anything about its head, Bekir Sami Bey. I said that he was a Circassian landowner from the Trebizond area, and was going on to speak of the various groups who were influential in the councils of the Nationalist Government when he interrupted me and said abruptly: "Ormsby-Gore tells me that you are here on leave. If I can get the War Office to agree, would you like to act as our unofficial liaison officer with the Ankara Delegation? As we do not recognize their Government, we cannot appoint anyone from the Foreign Office to look after them, but they are the power in Turkey and we must reckon with them." As I listened, I experienced that strange state of unreality which came over me whenever I saw that some future action was inevitable, and that my own will was powerless to influence the course of events. I had returned to England on sick leave and really needed a rest - I could have said this and got out of the whole thing. I felt that it was wrong for me to be concerned once again in Turkish politics. I should have refused, and yet I knew before he had finished speaking that I would accept.

Vansittart took my agreement for granted, telephoned the War Office and told me that a room would be reserved for me at the Savoy Hotel where the two Turkish Delegations were to stay. He said I should wear a morning coat, which I did not have. I went from the Foreign Office to Scholte's - the only Savile Row tailor I knew - and they undertook to fit me out in three days. I bought a top hat, a gold-topped malacca cane, yellow gloves, and found myself transformed from an officer in an untidy uniform into a creditable imitation of a diplomat.

I went to see Philip Kerr, but what I said did not seem to interest him, and my breakfast with the Prime Minister was shelved. I did not know that he had just written to Mr. Lloyd George asking to be released from his post as Private Secretary. Vansittart told me that I should meet the Turkish Delegation and do everything I could to make them feel at home. He wanted me to go every morning to the Foreign Office and report their reactions to the proceedings of the Conference. My morning coat arrived just in time for me to meet the Orient Express on 18th February, only three weeks after my own arrival.

The next ten days were an experience and an education. I met and listened to the great war leaders. Curzon was elected President of the Conference, but Lloyd George attended most of the sessions and from the start seemed to gather all the reins into his own hands. Aristide Briand made the most favourable impression on me. He was then Prime Minister of France, but had a very different attitude from other Frenchmen I had met. He sincerely, passionately believed that the hope for the world lay in creating a United States of Europe. His political vision was so far in advance of his time that after forty years his countrymen have scarcely yet caught up with it, Count Sforza, the Italian Foreign Minister, Colonel Edward House, the personal representative of President Wilson, and a very intelligent Japanese were the other leaders. These were names that for two years had meant for me the Supreme Allied Council and its strange decisions, which had been the direct cause of so many of our troubles in Turkey.

I saw for myself that famous people are moved by the same petty motives as the rest of us. I could not but admire Lloyd George, in spite of his almost frivolous indifference to facts. He was so quick-witted that he could come into the Conference quite ignorant of the subject at issue, and within half an hour see the weak points in some position and turn the whole discussion into the channel that happened to suit him. But I never heard him bring forward any constructive ideas. Briand struck me by his obvious anxiety to reach agreement, so much at variance with the belligerence of the French representatives I had known in Turkey.

I was troubled by the futile misunderstandings. It seemed clear to me that both the Greeks and the Turks were sick of the fighting. The Greeks were not nearly so confident as they made out and as the British Government supposed them to be. Their ill-trained, nervous army was holding down a hostile population over an area in Asia Minor the size of Greece itself. In Europe, they were threatened by their Slav neighbours - Serbs and Bulgars. They had not received from the Allies the help they had expected, but Constantine's Government dared not surrender what the hated Venizelos had gained. The Turks for their part were very weary of war. They had been mobilized for twelve years and had fought five wars.

The procedure of the Conference was farcical. The Turkish Delegations were staying at the Savoy Hotel and the Greeks at Claridge's. The Greeks refused to meet the Ankara Turks, so sessions were held alternately with the two Turkish delegations, and of course the conference got nowhere. I had been drawn in as interpreter and sat through all the sessions. Lloyd George was not making things easier by his ignorance of the basic facts of history and geography. One day, reference was made to alleged Turkish massacres of Armenians at Hadjin. He asked where this was, and when told that it was in Cilicia, he said that he had not been aware that Turkish forces were in Silesia. To cover our embarrassment when one of the Delegates slyly exposed the mistake, Mr. Lloyd George proposed that an unofficial Armenian delegation should be invited to give evidence. This suited no one, and Lord Curzon abruptly adjourned the session.

I went out with the British Delegation, and Lloyd George said: "We must get away from the conference atmosphere. I am going to invite the Turks to tea. Does anyone know what they are like at home?" Vansittart motioned to me to speak, and I took the chance of saying: "These men are mostly from the West country. Bekir Sami Bey is a Circassian. He is an enthusiastic farmer, and has asked me where he can get English pedigree rams to take home." This was enough for Lloyd George, and, fascinated, I watched him at his best. Before the tea party was over, he had captivated Bekir Sami Bey by assuring him that he held farming to be far more important than politics and by offering to put at his disposal the best English experts on sheep-breeding. The next day Bekir Sami made a conciliatory speech at a joint session of the three Delegations. The Allies were able to agree to leave the situation to be negotiated between Greece and Turkey, and the Conference was wound up with the appearance of agreement. In reality nothing had been accomplished, and everyone knew it. Moreover, the French and Italians had been hard at work negotiating secret agreements with the Nationalist Delegation. Yet this Conference was probably the beginning of the long slow movement of reconciliation between Britain and Turkey, which led ultimately to the present balance of power in the Near East. The French, for all their cleverness, failed to win Turkish acceptance of their plan for the partition of Cilicia, and within a few days of Bekir Sami's return to Ankara, fighting broke out between the Turks and the French.

At the end of the Conference I was confronted with a choice. It was clear that the War Office did not intend to send me back to Turkey, and they were quite right. I had been recommended for the Staff College. I had no impulse to return to Oxford. And I felt miserably out of place in Wimbledon with my wife and her family.

After a month's separation, I became more fully aware of the strength of the bond which linked my fate with that of Winifred Beaumont. I resigned my commission. In order to get my papers through quickly, I went in person to the R.E. Headquarters depot at Chatham. I hired a car and drove down. As I sat alone in the big Daimler car and passed through Woolwich, where little more than three years earlier I had been a Prize Cadet at the Shop, and remembering one by one the places where I had done training exercises, it seemed impossible to believe that I was the same person. But it seemed equally impossible to believe in my present self. Who was I to be driving in a big, expensive car? Why had I not gone, as anyone else in my position would have done, to Chatham by train? I was cutting myself away completely from the life I had entered when I came away from Oxford to enter the Army. Nothing was real.

I walked into the Officers' Mess at the R.E. Depot and lunched for the last time as a sapper and a soldier. I knew no one, and no one knew me. Soon I was driving back to London. My papers were in order, and my resignation would soon be gazetted. I had nothing to rely upon except my own wits. I was determined to take no help from my wife's family, and my mother would soon be needing help from me. As I drove back through the Kentish fields skirting the suburbs of London, I looked towards the future. There was no longer any doubt that I would return to Turkey, and I knew that I was going because I had to learn to live. I was nearly twenty-four years old, and it seemed to me that the next six or seven years of my life would bring me the experience I needed. I wanted to know all about life, and I knew with an uncomfortable clarity that I was going to do many foolish things before finding my own destiny.

At last the journey ended. When I reached Wimbledon, I told Evelyn that I was returning to Turkey. I did not invite her to come with me, and she did not ask me why. I was going out of my own life with the feeling that I was a stranger in it. The facts were unchanged: I was still a son and a brother, a husband and a father. I was even still senior mathematical postmaster at Merton College, Oxford, where the long-suffering Warden was holding my scholarship open. But all my values had changed. I was beginning to learn that we live by values in the timeless eternity of my fifth dimension, and not by facts in the time of clocks and calendars which cannot adapt themselves to the hide-and-seek of Value. Life as we live it flows in more than one track of time. The tracks are separated by our different states of consciousness, and our memory tends to run back along one track to the exclusion of the others. In this way, we lose touch with a great part of our past life, especially those events which contained experiences alien to our present mood. This is not to be wondered at, since values are what we care about and respond to, whereas facts are indifferent. It is probable that we scarcely ever remember the facts of our past life, unless they happen to be connected with some value. Not all values please, but all do matter to us in one way or another. One result is that life in retrospect usually seems interesting to us, though our story of it may seem quite uninteresting to others.

Another consequence of the 'one-track' character of memory is that it is quite impossible to be completely honest and sincere in our attempts to reconstruct the past. The tantalizing, though not surprising, conclusion is that the greater the significance of an experience, the less are we capable, even if we wish to do so, of telling the whole truth about it.

7: THE HEIRS OF SULTAN HAMID

The Snowdens had been particularly friendly when I met them as members of the Socialist Commission to the Caucasus. As they had warmly invited me to visit them when I came to London, I had done so soon after my arrival. They introduced me to Ramsay MacDonald, who wanted first hand news of the situation in Armenia. He had been out of sympathy with British support for the Greek adventure in Asia Minor, and was distressed at the reports of Turks being massacred. I sensed in him a capacity for sincere feeling that was different from the intellectual fervour that I had noticed in the other Socialists I had met. I could speak with him about my personal problems, and he advised me to take up politics and interest myself in Near Eastern questions.

It happened that after the close of the Conference, MacDonald was fighting a by-election at Woolwich. On an impulse, I offered to go and canvass for him. I was allotted to a middle-class ward, and as I went from door to door I learned something of the unreasoning prejudices that war can instill into reasonable people. They really believed that to have worked for peace was a betrayal of England and that the Socialists had been ready to hand the country over to foreign domination. I was insulted in terms I had never known, and this had the effect of making me feel strangely remote from what was happening round me. The election was a disaster for MacDonald. I believe he lost his deposit. Hysterical enthusiasm surged in the crowd about the Town Hall when the results were announced. I was grieved and angry. To enhance the absurdity of the experience, my pocket was picked for the first and only time in my life. I had just drawn forty pounds from the bank, and this was for me then a considerable sum. It was a sad and rebellious young man who made his way back to Wimbledon that night.

The next day at breakfast my father-in-law, David McNeil, was jubilant over the Woolwich result. Like MacDonald, he was a Scot from Lossiemouth in Morayshire, and he spoke of him personally as a man, and of Socialism in general, with what seemed to me a bigoted narrow-mindedness. I said to myself that I would leave England and not return for a long time. I looked at my wife; she had been patient, without understanding, and kind, without opening her heart. She had tried to adapt herself to the many new friends I had made, but at no time during the six weeks that I had spent in London had there been any reality in our life together. I looked at my daughter Ann sitting in a high chair at the breakfast table. I felt quite unfit to be a father, and said to myself that she would be better off without me. Yet even as I was saying these words to myself, I knew that they were not true. I knew that I would go away, not because of my father-in-law, not because I could not be a husband and a father, not because I was disgusted with politics, not even because of Mrs. Beaumont or some mystical call of the East, but simply because I had to. I had no power to choose.

By one of those coincidences that mean more than our carefully planned actions, I went that afternoon to visit Ouspensky, then living at a hotel in Russell Square. It was our first meeting since he had left Turkey several months earlier, and he told me of the success he had met with in London and of lectures he was giving to a group of theosophists and psychologists. I told him that I had decided to leave England and return to Turkey, but said that I would like to hear some of his lectures. He said: "Come if you like. But you cannot decide. If you go to Turkey, it is not because you decide. You have no power to choose. No one has power to choose."

His words, echoing my thoughts of the morning, and the deep seriousness with which he declared that man is not the master of his fate, impressed me strangely. They threw a new light on all that I had seen and heard during the past year. I was convinced that he was right, and that the foolishness of men was not wilful or intentional, but the consequence of the inability to choose. The memory of this talk remained with me, and eventually drew me back to London to study and work with him.

And so, inevitably and helplessly, I returned to Turkey. My wife sadly watched me go. She seemed to know even better than I did that our marriage was ended, but she could do nothing about it. As I turned the corner of Cambridge Road, I looked back and saw her standing at the gate of her father's house holding our daughter in her arms. I was walking out of a life that had never existed, but this did not prevent me from feeling wretched and guilty. Through all these weeks my mother had looked on, saying nothing. She had been enormously interested in the Peace Conference, for she loved history. She approved my return to Turkey – it is hard to say why, for she would have been still happier if I had entered politics, for which she believed me to be particularly suited.

The journey from Calais to Constantinople by the Orient Express then took four and a half days. I had plenty of time to contemplate my life and my future. Many possibilities had become might-have-beens, but I felt no regret. I was going to Turkey, where I had no place and no prospects, and yet I was full of confidence that all would be well.

When the train drew into Sirkeci Station, I was amazed to see a crowd of familiar faces on the platform. So much had happened to me that I had forgotten how short was the time - barely two months - since I had left. I was treated as if I had not gone away. I was no longer in uniform, but it was taken for granted, in spite of my denials, that I was still connected with the Secret Service. The agents who should have been reporting to my successor insisted on coming and recounting the most exciting news to me. Turkish politicians, to whom it should by now have been obvious that I did not speak for His Majesty's Government, believed an even more preposterous story that I was working for His Majesty King George V in person. It must be remembered that the tradition of the Mabeyn, the body of unofficial go-betweens employed by the Sultan, still dominated the thoughts of everyone connected with Turkish politics. I had observed that the Turks could not grasp at all the working of a constitutional monarchy, and were convinced that Buckingham Palace must be the centre of a spider's web of intrigue like that which surrounded Yıldız. I could deny and ridicule as much as I pleased the suggestion that I was a member of the Mabeyn of Buckingham Palace, or that I had any kind of mission in Turkey; all I could evoke in response was a knowing look and the assurance that my wish for discretion would be respected. New rumours about me emanated from Ankara. Bekir Sami Bey seems to have returned with a story that Lloyd George had been influenced by secret instructions from the Palace to avoid trouble with Turkey, and that I had been the intermediary. This completely imaginary version of Lloyd George's tea-party brought me an invitation to go to Trebizond and visit Bekir Sami Bey and the other Nationalist leaders.

The height of absurdity was reached when my friend Tahsin Bey, still Chief of Police, asked me to receive a deputation of Albanians, sent to see me on an important mission. They arrived, and after assuring me at great length that the Albanians were a proud people and wished to strengthen their ties with England, told me that they were looking for a king of Albania, and asked me if I was prepared to be a candidate for the throne. As I knew that the Albanians had been canvassing most unlikely prospects, I could not resist the temptation of telling them solemnly that I was descended from Neville, Earl of Warwick, the King-maker, and that my ancestors had always declined offers of a throne. I quickly realized that to be obscurely facetious was unwise, for they invited me to go back with the Deputation to Tirana and meet members of their Government. I tried to make my position clear without giving offence; but Tahsin Bey told me after the meeting that I had made a good impression because the Albanians wanted a tall king! When, later, Zog was made king, I could not help reflecting that I would have cut a better figure.

During the same few weeks after my return to Turkey, an old friend came to see me. He was Jacques Bey Calderon, one of the real Mabeyn of Sultan Abdul Hamid, who knew everyone and, strangely enough, was universally liked and trusted. He told me that Abbas Hilmi Pasha, the ex-Khedive of Egypt, had been greatly impressed by my understanding of Near Eastern affairs, and asked me to accept a gift of a thousand gold sovereigns. He added that the ex-Khedive would like to meet me to discuss Egyptian affairs. I told Jaques Bey to take back a message to say that I would be pleased to meet His Highness, but he should know I had no influence whatever in British politics. A few days later the visit was arranged, and I was ceremoniously received at the ex-Khedive's palace on the Bosphorus. I listened to a brilliant analysis of British policy in the Orient, and heard the reasons why a strong pro-British ruler in Egypt was essential. He explained how the misunderstanding had arisen which had led to his being deposed. An attempt had been made to assassinate him in Constantinople. He had gone to Switzerland to recuperate. False reports from his enemies had led the British to believe that he was in league with the Turks. He was willing to accept the British protectorate, and even now could offer a counter-weight to Zagloul Pasha and the Wafd. He asked me if I would act for him as a go-between with the British Government. I told him quite plainly that I had no standing, nor was I likely soon to return to London. He said that he quite understood and hoped that we might meet again.

The next day, Jaques Calderon came with a suitcase full of sovereigns, and said that the Khedive wished me to accept them even if, for the present I could do nothing for him. He added that he hoped I would not refuse, as he himself was in desperate need of money and thought that I might let him keep half for himself. I agreed, and took five hundred sovereigns. This was a dishonest transaction, because evidently Abbas Hilmi Pasha believed that he was buying my support in his intrigues to regain the throne of Egypt. At the time I felt little compunction, because I knew that Abbas Hilmi was immensely rich and frequently gave such presents to people he thought might help him. As time went on, the memory of this affair grew more and more distasteful, and it became a factor in making me understand that we carry the consequences of our actions within ourselves for years after the external results have disappeared. I came to realize that we can be free from the past only when we have so changed ourselves as to be no longer the same person who performed the action. A dishonest man does not become honest simply by ceasing to act dishonestly, but by an inward change that makes it impossible for him to act dishonestly. It was, however, many long years before the real meaning of 'inward change' became clear to me.

I used the ex-Khedive's money to participate in a commercial venture exporting figs from Asia Minor to London, where they were very scarce that year. I made a good profit in a few weeks simply because I happened to know the right people. I was next offered, by an old Turkish friend, a share in a brown coal mine. This had been worked during the war, and was said to be near the Asiatic coast of the Dardanelles and to have its own harbour. Mrs. Beaumont and I set out to visit the mine, though I knew nothing whatever about mining or about coal. We went by a small coastal steamer to Lapseki and thence we drove along the coast in an old Ford tender. The roads were almost impassable, and we were devoured by bugs wherever we stopped for the night. We went through territory supposedly occupied by dangerous brigands; but found only villages where Turks and Greeks were still living together in amity, less than sixty miles from Balikeşir where the Greek and Turkish armies were fighting out their unnecessary war. My indignation against the legislators of Sèvres and Neuilly was reawakened as I saw how the seeds of future war had been sown throughout the Balkans and the Orient. The Territories of the Ottoman Empire had immense natural resources. The races which occupied them, Turks, Arabs, Kurds, Armenians, Greeks, each had good qualities lacking in the others. There was no hatred between the races except what was stirred up by professional agitators and politicians.

I spoke of all this to the head man of a village far off the main routes, a place where the last visit of a European was remembered only by the old people. I was astonished at his grasp of the situation. He said: "We have no quarrel with the Greeks. For centuries we have lived together and have learned to trust each other. I will prove this to you. We Turks have the land and we have the fruit trees, but we have no capital, and we don't know how to sell our fruit. Every spring the Greek merchants come to our villages, and together we make an estimate of the crop. They then lend us the money to pay for collecting and packing the fruit, and for our own needs. In the autumn we send the fruit to Smyrna, or Panderma. It never happens that a Turk will sell his crop to any merchant but the one who lent him the money, and it never happens that the merchant fails to send us back the balance of the sale price of our fruit. If we can trust each other in this way, why can't our political leaders trust each other too? We need the Greeks and they need us. Both of us are being ruined by these foolish wars." All this was said without bitterness, as if he rather pitied than condemned the politicians who could not see that the price of harmony is worth paying.

I found the mine, and realized that I could neither evaluate nor work it. So far as I was concerned, it was a hole in the side of a hill, almost overgrown with rampant vegetation. A flimsy railway track and half a dozen tiny wagons were the entire equipment. The guide who had brought us to the mine offered to find me the ustabaci, or foreman, who had worked it. He turned out to be a dervish, a pious Muslim and ready to take whatever came to him as an indication of God's Will. He offered to get some workmen together and send the coal by boat to Panderma, where there was a good market for brick and tile making. I stayed there a week, during which time I made a plane-table survey, left the ustabaci enough money to pay a month's wages, and returned to Constantinople feeling very foolish. I was part owner of a coal mine; it was actually working and producing coal - but I myself had done nothing, and there was nothing I could do. Worked as it was, the venture was too small to be of any use to me; to develop it properly was beyond my resources and my knowledge. I brought back a plan and samples, and put up a sign over our apartment reading: "The Dardanelles Mining Company" By a lucky chance, I sold the mine to a Levantine for enough to satisfy my pride and the needs of my Turkish partner.

During this time, the weekly meetings with Prince Sabaheddin had been resumed, but there was no longer the same sense of detachment. I discovered that Sabaheddin was heavily in debt, and that the Government had failed to return certain family properties that had been confiscated when he and his father were exiled. He was already disheartened at the lack of response to his proposals for reform of the Turkish economy. Mrs. Beaumont was always with us and did her best to restore the Prince's courage.

I remember one talk about destiny. I told the Prince of my talk with Ouspensky whom he had met and liked - though regarding him as less interesting than Gurdjieff. He would not admit that Ouspensky could be right in asserting that we have no power to choose what we will do. Mrs. Beaumont said that she was inclined to accept this, but that she was certain that everything that happens to us is the consequence of our own actions. She said: "I have often been made to suffer, and often it has looked like injustice on the part of someone else. But I have always seen clearly that whatever suffering I have had to bear, it has always been my own fault." She said this with tears in her eyes. I knew that before coming to Turkey she had been on the verge of ending her own life, and that she had been very cruelly treated. The Prince was as moved as I was, and we sat in an unaccustomed silence which drew the three of us very close together. It seemed to me that fate was a mystery which none of us could understand and that no formula could express.

The next day I was very restless, and in the afternoon I went off by myself across the Bosphorus to Scutari. I walked up the hill to the old Turkish cemetery that stretches for a mile or more over the hills. The scene was indescribably beautiful. Spring had come. The Isles of the Princes and the profile of Istanbul, with its domes and minarets, stood out from the intense blue of the Sea of Marmora. The rapid stream of the Bosphorus swirled round Leander's Tower below me. With reminders of death about me, I mused idly on the legend of Hero and the tradition of heroic suicide. I asked myself why people choose to die. The question returned as an echo. Why rather do we choose to live? About me were the slender cypresses of the cemetery and the worn tombstones, with their carved turbans and inscriptions in beautiful Persian script. I sat and watched the scene changing as the sun sank quietly into the sea. Slowly my attention turned inwards, and I was aware that my own life was spreading out before me. I could not doubt that I was being shown the future, but even though I did not doubt, I also did not believe what I saw.

It seems to me that I heard a voice speaking inside me, but I am not sure if it was a voice, or only the soundless echo of a voice. I was to be given seven years to prepare, and then my life would begin. I was to perform some great task, but not until I was sixty would I know what the task was to be. Then at the last faint echo, something told me that I would not know my true destiny until I was seventy years old. Then the voice - if it was a voice - said to me: "You must first learn to live. You are still ignorant of this world and all that is in it. This you must learn before you can understand your destiny."

Described in this way, the experience seems unconvincing and fanciful, even to myself, who remember the whole scene so vividly as to feel myself again sitting on the tombstone and distractedly reading the inscriptions, while listening to what was being said within me. It can have little reality for another, and yet this memory has returned to me again and again at moments when my life seemed to have lost all direction and purpose, and it has helped me to live through long years of dry despair.

The next day I awoke with a violent toothache. I was recommended to Sami Bey Gunsberg, the Sultan's own dentist. I went to his apartment, a few minutes from where we lived. A crowd was waiting in to or three salons furnished in Empire style, with a profusion of photographs of Sultans, princes and pashas, dedicated to their friend Sami Bey Gunsberg. Ignoring the waiting crowd, Sami Bey called me in and seated me in the chair. After one look at my mouth, he said: "You have a very bad abscess - the simplest thing is to drain it at once, but it will be painful." With no idea of what was in store for me, and with the bravado of ignorance I told him to go ahead. With no anaesthetic or other such foolery, he drilled straight into my tooth. Writing after nearly forty years, I wince at the memory. Dying a thousand deaths would be a mild description of the intensity of the pain. But it was soon over, and I realized that I was in the hands of a true artist. He insisted on giving me a thorough examination and, as I had completely neglected my teeth since losing a front one when I was wounded in France, there was much to be done.

I then discovered what a marvellous weapon dentistry can be when allied to politics. Having me safely in his chair with my mouth propped open, he discoursed for ten or fifteen minutes on his pet hobby: the injustices suffered by the Imperial House of Osman. His devotion to the princes of the Osmanli blood was complete. I learned afterwards that all his very considerable earnings as a dentist went, regardless of deserts, to one or another of the princes or princesses.

He told me tales of the vast wealth that had been illegally confiscated by the Young Turks. How, single-handed, he had brought a suit before the Supreme Religious Tribunal, which had declared the confiscation null and void. He descanted upon the Mosul oil fields. With uncanny foresight, the Sultan had seen, long before the hunger for oil had aroused the cupidity of great nations, that unlimited wealth lay beneath the sands of Iraq and Arabia. He had wished to preserve this treasure for his own descendants, and from his private fortune had paid for surveys and had taken out exclusive concessions in their name.

Sami then disclosed his great plan. The Imperial Family knew and trusted me, and he was sure that he could persuade them to give me a power of attorney to represent their interests before the British Government at the Peace Conference, which was to meet and revise the Treaty of Sèvres. I suppose that I was sitting in his chair for two hours while his unfortunate patients were kept waiting in the gilded salons.

A few days later, Sami telephoned to say that I was to expect a confidential visitor at eleven p.m., to admit him myself, and make sure no one saw him. This kind of procedure was familiar enough, but I was not prepared to open the door to the Sultan's Chief Eunuch, of whom I had heard, but whom I had never met. The eunuchs were already a vanishing race - they were mostly Berbers castrated in childhood and sold as slaves to the Palace. In Abdul Hamid's time, the Chief Eunuch had been one of the chief members of the Mabeyn, and even under the timid Mehmed Vahideddin, they still counted in court affairs. The Chief Eunuch was everything one would picture a palace eunuch to be. Tall and with a large paunch, he had the familiar high-pitched voice that usually speaks in whispers. Whatever he might be saying or doing, he conveyed the impression that some portentous secret was being revealed. All that he had come for was to let me know that the Sultan had heard that I was to represent his nephews and nieces, and to make me understand that although the Sultan himself had no direct part in his brother's inheritance, his *himet* - protection - would be forthcoming if his legitimate interests were somehow safeguarded. Everyone knew that I was so clever that I would find a way of arranging this.

It was useless to protest that I had barely heard of the Abdul Hamid heritage and that I had not even discussed it with any of the heirs. Such denials are a customary part of Asiatic negotiations, and the Eunuch clearly assumed that I understood the procedure, and said that he would like to visit me again. It was also customary to talk at length upon any subject except the one at issue, so I was able to hear some interesting court gossip before we parted.

The next move was an invitation to dinner with one of the princes. This time, I had the good fortune to participate in what must surely have been one of the last social functions of the old regime of the Ottoman Empire. There were Turkish musicians, and a dinner of at least fifteen courses. After dinner we listened to Chopin played beautifully by the Princess, sitting at the piano out of sight in another room. There were also five or six court dwarfs present to amuse the guests. Each of them had a brightly coloured toy balloon floating from his fez. They mixed and joked equally with the guests and the frock-coated footmen. Not a word was said about the famous inheritance, nor was I asked any awkward questions.

The next day a go-between came to call, and said that the princes had been favourably impressed by my demeanour and my understanding of the sad plight of the Imperial Family, and they would be glad to make me their representative if I would help them to raise some money on their expectations.

I was both intrigued and flattered by these proposals, but I had not the slightest idea how to follow them up. I told the whole story to Mrs. Beaumont, who, while expressing considerable misgivings, suggested that she should put me in touch with a man who was accustomed to international negotiations and who, if he were interested, could help the princes out of their financial difficulties. His name was John de Kay, and although both she and Prince Sabaheddin had previously spoken of him, I had not been curious to learn more about him. She wrote to him about the proposals and received a long and enthusiastic cable in reply, inviting us both to meet him in Berlin. Mrs. Beaumont, after first refusing, finally decided to come with me. Sabaheddin referred to John de Kay as his *ami providentiel*. I learned that he had given the Prince the money for his journey back to Turkey.

I did not feel the need for any documents, but Sami Gunsberg insisted that I should be given an official status, and a power of attorney was drawn up and signed by four or five of the heirs. These preparations occupied several weeks, and during this time an unusual disaster occurred to me. From eating some Bulgarian cheese, I contracted foot and mouth disease. It seems that it is exceedingly rare for this to attack a human being, and at first the British Army doctors who came to see me could make nothing of it. When one of them made the correct diagnosis, I became a medical curiosity, and I think scores of doctors must have come to examine me.

The disease in human beings attacks the membranes of the mouth and throat, which swell alarmingly, covered with painful ulcers. For days I could swallow nothing, and lay in the most painful discomfort, thankful to be able to breathe. No treatment was known, except rinsing the mouth with disinfectants, which only made the pain worse. My wretched state was not helped by the knowledge that none of the doctors had much idea of how it might end. The acute condition must have lasted about a week, and then one night, soon after midnight, all the ulcers burst together. For several hours, I had a haemorrhage that literally poured blood from my mouth and throat. When it was over, I knew that I was cured, but I was terribly weak. Nevertheless, about ten days later, I was able to travel, and started upon an adventure from which I gained very much experience, but little else.

An incident on the journey confirmed my feeling of the general absurdity of life in these early years after the war. We reached Szabadka, recently annexed from Hungary and renamed Subotitza by the Yugoslavs. A King's Messenger travelling in the next compartment warned us that this frontier station was notorious for pilfering, and advised us not to take our eyes off our baggage. It happened that Mrs. Beaumont had some valuable old lace and good furs, and I noticed that the customs officer fingered them rather knowingly. However, the luggage was all piled back into the van under our eyes, and we returned to our carriage. It was very hot and I took off my jacket. As a last precaution, I looked out of the window as the train began to move, and saw the cabin trunk being pulled out on to the platform.

On the spur of the moment, I jumped out of the carriage and seized the trunk. The train went off across the frontier. I soon realized that I had no money, no passport, no means of identifying myself, and I could not even speak Serbian. When I tried German, they either did not or would not understand a word I said. I asked for the station-master, and having handed over the trunk to him, went into the town to find, if possible, the British Consulate.

It so happened that on that very day there was a general round-up of Communists in Serbia. I was hatless and coatless, travel-stained, and worst of all, I tried Russian in the hope of making myself understood. Very naturally, I was arrested and taken to the nearest police post.

In the end, I found someone who could speak French, and my situation began to look brighter. By this time, it was mid-afternoon. I had been standing in the torrid heat for hours with no food and no means of buying even a cup of coffee. When I was finally released by the police it was dusk. I learned that there was no British Consulate or other representative in the town, and I went to a hotel with the doubtful hope of getting a room on credit.

However, I had not reckoned with Mrs. Beaumont's resourcefulness. On the advice of the King's Messenger, she had left the train at the Hungarian frontier station, returned with all our luggage to Subotitza, found the trunk with the stationmaster, and guessed that I must eventually go to a hotel. So when I arrived I found her in the foyer with my jacket and passport, and two days later, when the next express passed, we travelled on to Budapest and Prague.

During my stay in Subotitza I met some Hungarians, and learned that the town and surrounding country was almost exclusively inhabited by people of the Magyar race. Some private wire-pulling at the Peace Treaty had enabled the Yugoslavs to bring Szabadka into their territory, but the whole region was seething with ill-feeling. The so called 'round-up of Communists' had been made as an excuse for arresting many who were passively resisting the Yugoslav occupation. I was told that four thousand people had been arrested, and that the entire life of the town had been thrown into chaos.

Knowing well that similar absurd but dangerous incidents were happening all over Europe, I was invaded by gloomy forebodings for the future. If the leaders of mankind were so lacking in responsibility and understanding, and the masses so passive and inarticulate, what could the future bring but new and more terrible wars? When I arrived in Berlin, it happened to be early morning, and I watched the crowd of workers streaming out of the Charlottenburg Station. The pinched faces that I saw everywhere made a miserable impression on me. Seeing obvious war profiteers in magnificent cars thrusting their way through the crowds, I was affronted in my deepest feelings. I had forgotten that there were people who make a business of war.

A few days later, an incident occurred on the road between Berlin and Warsaw that, when I recall it, seems too apt to be authentic, and yet really did happen to me. The cities were starving, chiefly, because the farmers, not trusting the currency, were holding back their crops. There was much talk of a general strike to force the Government to secure more food for the workers. I was being driven to Berlin, and we stopped to give a lift to a very wretched-looking but powerfully built working man. We spoke about the strike, and he said that it had been forbidden, so there was nothing that they could do. They had been prepared to starve, if only they could hope to get food for their children afterwards. I said: "But if it goes on like this, is there no danger of revolution?" He looked quite upset and said: "Oh, no! Revolution is *polizeilich verboten*." I then began to understand the terrible readiness of the German people to let themselves be dominated by authority. My memory of that time is filled with similar pictures, all of which disposed me towards the doctrine of human impotence expounded by Ouspensky, which, when I first heard it, had made so little impression.

Meanwhile a new unexplored world was about to open for me.

8: JOHN DE KAY

John de Kay, when I met him in Berlin in May 1921, was a magnificent figure. He had a flowing crown of grey-white hair, a large mouth tightly expressing a formidable self-will, pale but brilliant blue eyes. He was not tall, but very broad, and he had singularly beautiful hands. He had known and sat for Rodin, and the heads of John de Kay in the Tate Gallery and the Rodin Museum in Paris show what the sculptor loved in his subject.

He was born in 1872 in North Dakota and his family had been ranchers and cowboys. His own ambition was to write. He began to sell newspapers at the age of twelve, was an editor at nineteen and owner of three newspapers at twenty-two. His mother was a religious maniac, who killed herself on his twenty-first birthday. He himself was fired with revivalist fervour, but humanitarian rather than religious. He had followed with growing enthusiasm the career of William Jennings Bryan - that not uncommon blend of religious mania, political opportunism and gross ignorance - and thrown all the weight of his journals into the Cross of Gold campaign of 1896. Twenty-five years later, with tears running down his cheeks, he used to quote Bryan's: "You shall not crucify the common man upon your Cross of Gold." Relatively few newspapers supported the campaign, so de Kay's eloquent and well-documented attacks upon the Chicago slaughterhouses attracted wide notice.

When his hero was routed by McKinley, he became disgusted with politics, sold his papers to a rival, and went off to Mexico to find Porfirio Diaz, whom he pictured as the hero-ruler who had led his people out of chaos into prosperity. The young zealot and the old dictator were admirably matched and became friends at once. De Kay conceived the bold plan of establishing in Mexico City a meat-packing business to compete with Chicago. He fired Diaz with his dream of clean, humane slaughterhouses and a business built upon good working conditions - all that Chicago claimed to be and was not. Diaz granted him an exclusive concession for fifty years. Failing to get support in New York, where his campaign against the meat trusts still rankled, he had gone to London with little besides his concessions, his charm and the compelling eloquence of a man with a mission.

Dressed in mid-western costume, packing a six-shooter and flourishing a Stetson, he had made his way into the partners' room of one of the great merchant bankers of Lombard Street. Mexico under Diaz was an Eldorado for foreign capital, and John de Kay obtained his finance, designed and built a model meat-packing factory, and by 1910 had become - at least on paper - a multi-millionaire.

John de Kay, from a newspaper engraving.

He had the presence and the joy of life to play the part of cowboy philosopher turned millionaire. Meeting Winifred Beaumont, he swept her away with him to Mexico, where she acted as his secretary and hostess, communicating some of her own fire to Diaz and his ministers, and painting in her spare time pictures of Mexico and its people. De Kay wrote a play which Sarah Bernhardt, who had with him one of her many tempestuous love affairs, took to America and produced in her repertoire. He published at his own expense books of poetry and aphorisms, believing that he was a true stoic, destined to become a second Marcus Aurelius.

He claimed descent from the Sieurs de Coucy; made a contract to buy the Château de Coucy, one of the finest Norman castles in France, and dreamed of re-establishing his line there after five hundred years.

Meanwhile, affairs in Mexico were not going well. The meat business was flourishing, exports were mounting, but the aging Diaz was losing his grasp and finally withdrew. John de Kay gave his allegiance to his nephew, Feliz Diaz, and that soldier of fortune General Huerta, as the legitimate successors of his friend and patron. In consequence, he had fallen foul of the redoubtable H.L. Wilson, United States Ambassador to Mexico, who had formed a bitter personal enmity against Huerta, and had supported the rebel forces under Madero. When the United States Government began supplying arms to Madero, John de Kay, outraged by what he saw as American imperialism, undertook to buy arms in Europe for the legitimate government. Selling Mexican Government Bonds in London and Paris, he placed large orders with a famous French armament firm. The collapse of Huerta's Government and the outbreak of the European War made the shipment both useless and impossible. John de Kay exercised an option he had astutely obtained from Huerta, resold the arms to the French Government, and took the purchase price in settlement of his claims to the meat concession. The German advance to the Marne in August 1914 overtook him and Mrs. Beaumont at the Château de Coucy, and they drove in his car through both German and Allied lines to Paris. The shock of direct contact with war converted him into a militant pacifist, and he lavished money upon various peace movements. The enmity of Washington, due to his support of their bugbear Huerta, overtook him in London where, in 1919, he was arrested on an extradition warrant on a charge of fraud in connection with the issue of Mexican bonds. He was imprisoned in Brixton prison and, as is usual in such situations, his friends deserted him with the exception of Mrs. Beaumont. Fighting almost single-handed, with lawyers apathetic, and amidst the passions of war, she obtained the evidence necessary to enable the extradition warrant to be refused. They went to Switzerland, where de Kay became interested in the peace programme of the Second Socialist International. He poured out money to enable meetings to be organized; first the Conference of February 1919, then the Amsterdam Conference three months later, where they met and made friends with many of the Socialist leaders of Europe.

At this point, Mrs. Beaumont discovered that John de Kay - whose sexual morality had never been impeccable - was the father of two children by a mutual friend. She decided to withdraw from his life, and not wishing to return to England, went to Switzerland. There she met Prince Sabaheddin, whose work for a separate peace between Turkey and the Allies had been helped by John de Kay's money. He invited her to return with him to Constantinople, with the sequel already recounted.

Haunted by memories of the past, and with many misgivings, Mrs. Beaumont brought me to Wannsee, then an outer suburb of Berlin, where John de Kay and his new family were living in the house of Humperdinck, the composer of *Hansel und Gretel*. She wanted me to learn about life, and she was not disappointed. De Kay was fired with his old enthusiasm over the injustices suffered by the Turkish princes, worked out in a few days a plan for defending their rights, and sent me to London with an introduction to his old banking friends. So great had been the impression he had made twenty years earlier that they took the proposals seriously, and I began an adventure which would have astonished me more, had I realized how far removed it was from the customary dealings in Lombard Street.

Mrs. Beaumont and I were not long in London, but during that time we saw a great deal more of Ouspensky. I began to attend his meetings, which had now been transferred to Earl's Court, at 38 Warwick Gardens, where they continued without intermission for seventeen years. Ouspensky had made great progress with his English, and his lectures were attended by well-known psychologists and writers.

Ouspensky set himself to destroy in his listeners the illusions by which modern, civilized man is pleased to live. He would repeat: "You think you know who and what you are, but you do not know either what slaves you now are, or how free you might become. Man can do nothing; he is a machine controlled by external influences, not by his own will, which is an illusion. He is asleep. He has no permanent self that he can call 'I'. Because he is not one but many, his moods, his impulses, his very sense of his own existence are no more than a constant flux. You need not believe what I tell you, but if you will observe yourselves you will verify its truth. Make the experiment of trying to remember your own existence and you will find that you cannot remember yourselves even for two minutes. How can man, who cannot remember who and what he is, who does not know the forces that move him to action, pretend that he can do anything? No. The first truth that must be grasped is that you and I and all men are nothing but machines. Man has no power to direct his own private affairs, and he is equally helpless in his social and political life."

This assertion aroused violent opposition. Many were confident

that the war had been no more than an unhappy incident in the great
march forward of mankind to universal peace and justice. I was aghast
as I listened to the optimistic arguments. All that I had seen, both in my
own private life and in the political arena, had convinced me that no one
either does what he intends, or knows what he is doing. Ouspensky's
thesis was unanswerable in the face of all experience. And yet people
still believed that man had free will and could control his own destiny.

Probably my intellectual conviction that all that Ouspensky said
was obviously true prevented me from feeling the tremendous impact of
his teaching, as did others, such as A.R. Orage and Maurice Nicoll. Nor
could I understand those who protested that his analysis was cold and
heartless. I was among those who found it amusing to hear A.E. Waite, a
well-known author, rise to his feet and say: "Mr. Ouspensky, there is no
love in your system," and walk solemnly out of a meeting.

Mrs. Beaumont felt otherwise. What Ouspensky said was only too
dreadfully right; but she had experienced the reality of human helplessness and wanted to be shown a way out. We were not much together
at this time, because having found her mother much aged and not
well, she went to stay with her. We were regular in our attendance at
Ouspensky's meetings and I made a point of getting to know some of
the pupils, especially the psychologists. I only saw my wife two or three
times during our stay in London. My mother met Mrs. Beaumont, and a
warm friendship quickly sprang up between the two women, whose ages
were only separated by six years. My mother prided herself, perhaps to
excess, on not being able to suffer fools gladly, and enjoyed the sparkling
conversation that delighted all Mrs. Beaumont's friends.

In July 1921, we returned to Turkey. I was now armed with a
power of attorney, financial guarantees and a draft contract drawn up
by John de Kay that seemed to me eminently fair - though it did not
offer the Princes any cash until their rights had been substantiated by
some independent authority. We travelled by the Orient Express through
Serbia and Bulgaria. We reached Sofia just as a general strike had been
declared in Greece. We found a dozen trains bound for Greece and
Turkey waiting in the station. We could sleep in our compartments, but
no food was available.

To pass the time, we went out to the races. I watched horse racing
for the first and only time in my life. I found it tedious, but when the
horses were paraded for the second race, Mrs. Beaumont pointed to one
and said "Number so-and-so will win." It did so. She did the same for
the next race, and again her choice won. I felt that we should bet on the
next race, but I had no idea how it was done, and we again watched her

chosen number win. She did this four or five times, if I remember rightly.

For some reason, this incident impressed upon me the notion that gambling is a wrong activity for man. It was not a moral notion, but rather that there was a hidden danger which one would be foolish to incur.

Discovering that the strike might last for weeks, we followed the advice of a Turkish traveller and took the next train to Burgas. This was then a small port serving Bulgarian trade in the Black Sea. It was notorious for the lawlessness of the sailors and brigands, who met to exchange contraband and drugs and who terrorized the police. There was no hotel, and we were advised to go for the night to a han near the quay. These hans had remained from the time when Bulgaria was Turkish. They were built on the Asiatic plan: a great courtyard, in which pack animals were collected, surrounded by a three-storied wooden building with rooms giving on to open verandahs. Most of the rooms were occupied by several people, men and women being separated. In the centre of the courtyard was a fountain, the only means of washing. We arrived in an araba with our luggage, which was piled in the centre of the courtyard. I had to go and get our tickets for the steamer, and as we dared not leave the luggage unguarded, Mrs. Beaumont stayed with it. When I reached the office of the shipping company, the agent, giving me our two tickets, asked me where the lady was. When I told him she had stayed with the luggage in the han, he gave a shout of horror: "She will be murdered - go back to her at once! No woman would be safe there alone!" I hurried back in the growing darkness and arrived in the han, dimly lit by oil lamps and candles, to see Mrs. Beaumont with two villainous-looking Bulgars and no luggage. It seems that she had not liked their looks, and so had ordered them to take the luggage up to our room. They were evidently stunned by her onslaught and complete lack of fear and were following her about like sheep. She was glad to see me, not because she felt nervous, but because the overpowering odour of unwashed human bodies was making her sick, and she wanted to get out into the fresh air.

The next morning we boarded the steamer, to find it being loaded with goats. This cargo was not just a few goats, but, as we soon learned, more than two thousand. There were goats everywhere, even on the captain's bridge, which was so crowded that he had to clamber over the goats' backs to reach the wheel. The journey lasted only ten hours, but the weather was very hot, and the smell of goat grew stronger and stronger until we felt we should never get it out of our nostrils.

When we reached Constantinople, we learned that there were

rivals in the field. Two mining engineers had secured the backing of two or three of the heirs, and we were faced with an awkward situation, because it was necessary to disabuse the Princes of the illusion that their rights could easily be established. Seeing competition for the honour of representing them, they naturally opened their mouths and began to demand cash advances.

The next nine months were for me intensely instructive. For the first time in my life, I had to stand alone. Up till then I had always been part of some large machine, such as the Army, and even if I had been independent to the verge of insubordination, I had never been alone. Now I was in a situation where no one could help me. John de Kay was far away and knew nothing of Turkey and the Turks. Our financial supporters in London had made it clear that they would do nothing, and not even allow their names to be mentioned, until a contract was signed.

In six months I had made little progress, and there was every likelihood that the Treaty of Sèvres would come up for revision with no representation of the Princes. Mrs. Beaumont and I went again to Berlin in December 1921. The Wannsee was frozen over, and the young people skating, or sailing incredibly rapid ice-boats, made a pleasing contrast to the fat Berliners we had seen basking in the sun during our previous visit six months before.

John de Kay was not in the least dismayed by the difficulties I had encountered, nor by our growing shortage of money. He changed the entire plan. Since we could not get a power of attorney to represent the Princes who wanted to sell their properties outright, we would offer to buy them for shares in an American company, which he proceeded to organize by cable. Within a week, the Abdul Hamid Estates Incorporated had been registered in the state of Delaware with a capital of $150,000,000, the estimated value of the Princes' estates. I was to go back to Constantinople and offer shares, reserving for ourselves a commission of ten percent. Another company was to undertake to liberate the properties and organize and finance their development.

I sent cables off to Sami Bey Gunsberg and the lawyers to say that I was bringing new and important proposals, and asked for an early meeting. It was then Friday. Mrs. Beaumont and I travelled back by way of Budapest and Bucharest. This journey has remained as such a vivid memory that I must describe two or three incidents. We reached Bucharest early on Sunday morning. My meeting with the Princes was on the following Thursday, and we were booked on the Lloyd Trestino mail boat due to reach Constantinople on Monday afternoon. We were the only through passengers, and our luggage had to pass the customs in Bucharest station. There was no customs officer on duty. A French passenger assured us with a sardonic grin that we should have to bribe every Romanian official we met, and quite a number who were not officials. An old porter at the station who spoke Turkish offered to go and fetch the customs officer. An hour passed, and he returned to say that the officer had to go to church and would come later. After four hours we sent our emissary again, and he returned to say that the customs officer would come after lunch. As this would mean missing the express train to Constanza, I became impatient and asked if we could offer a present. The porter brightened and said that he would come for a thousand lei (about three pounds). This was an outrageous sum, and I offered two hundred. After more bargaining, five hundred lei was agreed, but the customs officer would not be hurried. We missed the express and had to travel by the night train conventionnel. We dined in the city and returned half an hour before the train was due to leave. The ticket collector would not let us go on to the platform, and I began to wonder if he too would need a bribe. However, this time I insisted, and, protesting, he let us through. We then discerned the reason for his reluctance. The train was composed of ancient third and fourth-class carriages, and we had first class tickets. To meet the situation, one of the porters was engaged in painting a Roman l over the III on the door of a compartment, for all the world like the gardeners in Alice. We were thankful for the hard wooden seats, for any upholstery would have been alive with bugs.

At that time, the Cernavoda Bridge over the Danube, destroyed by the Germans, had not been rebuilt, and we had to detrain and go by cart over a bridge of boats. When we reached Constanza, the Lloyd Trestino mail boat had already sailed. I went to a shipping agency, and was told that this was the only service of the week; the Greek steamers which normally plied between the Black Sea ports having been requisitioned for the war with Turkey.

I said that we would go by the very first craft leaving Constanza. Mrs. Beaumont and I went off to try the famous mud baths. When we returned and called the agency, the man said that there was no prospect of a steamer for the rest of the week. The only craft expected to leave the harbour was a tug towing a schlep (a large lighter). We could travel on the tug, and Mrs. Beaumont could have the captain's cabin, but he warned us that it would be terribly uncomfortable. As the journey was only about two hundred nautical miles and the tug could do six knots, we should arrive within a day and a half - in time for my meeting. I decided to go. My reason for giving the calculation is that it illustrates a recurrent weakness of mine: I could never bring myself to allow for contingencies and the unlikelihood of events going according to plan.

Anyway, we went down to the quay on Tuesday night. The prediction of the French traveller was fulfilled, for although our passes were in perfect order, we had to bribe the sentry on duty to let us on to the quay. From the moment of entering Romania to that of leaving, I had been compelled to bribe every official and unofficial person with whom I had to deal.

The tug was far worse even than the agent had led us to expect. After a minutes, Mrs. Beaumont came out of the captain's cabin with a scream. Not only the bunk, but the walls and floor were literally erupting bugs. There was only one hammock, which was slung for her on the deck. We sailed before dawn, and seemed to be going well, but within a few hours we ran into one of the notorious Black Sea storms that take toll of scores of fishermen's lives every year. These storms come so suddenly that even large fishing vessels are overturned. The powerful tug towing an eighty-foot lighter reacted to the storm with a motion that is indescribable. Pitching violently, the propeller would come out of the water, the lighter would drift on, and as the tug again went forward there would be a violent crash as the hawser tightened. No one could stand upright and we seemed bound every minute to capsize.

After four or five hours the captain made his way to my side where I was sitting on deck, clinging to a rope. He said he must put into Burgas, as he was afraid of the hawser parting. Mrs. Beaumont had a flask of brandy for the journey which she handed to him without a word. Swallowing it without drawing breath, he cheered up and said he would keep to his course.

Conditions more miserable would be hard to imagine. We were all soaked to the skin. Our hamper of food was ruined by sea-water and inedible. There was no water to drink. For twenty-four hours we were subjected to a buffeting that would have turned a fish's stomach. On Friday the storm abated, and we steamed through the moonless night under the brilliant starlight - quite unable to get dry and beginning to feel very hungry and weak. On Saturday morning as the sun rose behind us we saw the menacing black rocks that guard the northern entrance of the Bosphorus - the ancient Symplegades through which the Argonauts returned bearing the Golden Fleece.

As we steamed into the Bosphorus, a small pinnace with a very young British naval officer in immaculate uniform bustled alongside and hailed us. We were grimy, sodden and soot-covered, and he must have been astonished to hear us answer in English. With a gallant salute, he offered to take us off. We shook hands with the captain and his crew of two and shot away to Therapia, where we had the most welcome bath of our lives.

We had missed our meeting, but we learned that the rival group had withdrawn and the Princes were in a very docile frame of mind. The new proposals were much too complicated for them to understand, but one of the Princes, being convinced that he could borrow money on the American shares, persuaded the rest to sign.

Several weeks were lost because of three recalcitrants, but finally on 22nd April 1922, I signed a contract by which nineteen out of twenty-two heirs vested all their rights in the Abdul Hamid Estates, Inc., and received share certificates in exchange. The transfer was only to become definitive when they had received a substantial advance. The incidents that occurred during the negotiations, my personal relationships with the Princes and Princesses and widows of the Red Sultan, the behaviour of the various authorized and unauthorized intermediaries would make a story in itself. I learned a great deal about Asiatic people that has enabled me to feel at home whenever I have had to deal with them, but it would throw this account out of balance if I were to put down all that I can remember.

9: STRANGE NEGOTIATIONS

As soon as the contract was signed, we packed up or sold all that we had in Turkey. Our money had nearly run out, but we were able to return to London by way of Berlin. My hardest parting was from Sabaheddin. He was the first man who had been able to evoke in me a sense of a spiritual reality. He was deeply disappointed and wounded by the failure of his countrymen to take serious notice of his plans for social reform. Our weekly meetings had been a great solace to him, but we believed that we should return and be able to help both him and his plans. As it turned out, I did not return to Turkey for thirty-three years, by which time Sabaheddin had died in Switzerland. He took to drink and died in great poverty. I never saw him again, though we continued to correspond at rare intervals until the end of his life.

Our journey to Berlin was uneventful. We found John de Kay full of plans for carrying out the contract. He was in touch with big American oil companies interested in the Mosul Concessions. He had made friends with a family of very rich Jews, who wanted to buy land in Palestine and knew that Abdul Hamid had bought great tracts from the Arabs, with the intention of re-selling them to Jewish settlers. He had heard that the Abdul Hamid olive groves at Benghazi in Tripoli produced a grade of oil excellent for soap making, and wanted to set up a factory to make a very fine toilet soap for export to America. All these and many other ideas had come to him from the reports I had been sending him about the Princes' claims in different countries. He coached me carefully in the presentation of the various projects in England, and hoped that we might get the support of the British Government for Anglo-American cooperation in the development of the Near East. I tried to persuade him to come to England, but he said that his name would antagonize the American Government and that he preferred to remain in the background.

When I finally reached London just before my twenty-fifth birthday, the eighth of June 1922, I went to the Foreign Office to enquire about the policy of H.M. Government towards our plans. My friends there were noncommittal, and advised me to wait until the fate of the Treaty of Sèvres was settled. The Government was gaining strength from month to month. Allied dissensions were playing havoc with our policy. Lloyd George, against all expert advice was pinning his hopes upon the Greek Army. It was the wrong moment raise the question of the Princes' rights at a time when the Middle East was like volcano on the point of eruption.

When I reached London, I was still under the influence of de Kay's magnificent dreams of world betterment; but, seeing that I would have to spend some time in England, I felt free to devote myself wholeheartedly to Ouspensky's teaching.

At that time, many people were filled with high ideals - or rather dreams - of helping humanity. John de Kay had spent the past two years in working out the Constitution of an International Institute, to be called *Intellectus et Labor*, that would provide the means for realizing the programme of the Second Socialist International. He believed that nothing less than a great crusade for the rights of the common man, as against all the powerful organizations of State, religion, finance and industry, would secure peace and progress for mankind. He believed that the Mind and the Hand of man were natural partners, and that Intellect and Labour should cooperate to overcome the lust for power that threatened the modern world. He wanted to make a great deal of money quickly, in order to launch his great scheme in all the countries in the world.

John de Kay's enthusiasm and eloquence could not win me over to his ideas, for I was more deeply impressed by the dangers that stem from man's helplessness and ignorance than by the threat of power-seeking oligarchies. I was strongly drawn to Gurdjieff's ideas as they were presented by Ouspensky. But I also believed that money could help, and soon after we arrived in London, Gurdjieff came over to expound his own plans for a great Institute for the Harmonious Development of Man. These plans needed money. Gurdjieff's plans were no less grandiose than those of John de Kay. He also spoke of his Institute as destined to spread all over the world and to regenerate mankind.

My own dreams were not unduly modest. I conceived world-wide research to establish the reality of the unseen world of the fifth dimension, bringing in, on the one hand, the social ideals of de Kay and, on the other, the psychological methods of Gurdjieff. All this was to be financed from the riches of the East in the form of the Abdul Hamid lands and concessions.

When we came to England, John de Kay had promised to put ample money at our disposal, and Mrs. Beaumont and I took a service flat in Queen Anne's Mansions. There we happened to meet the American biologist T.H. Morgan, who had just arrived with a collection of his famous fruit-fly, Drosophila melanogaster, with which he had demonstrated the reality of the genes and their mutations. Through him, I met a group of biologists, Julian Huxley, J.B.S. Haldane, R.A. Fisher and others, to whom I spoke of John de Kay's Intellectus et Labor and of my own plan for a Research Institute independent of all governments. The plans were animatedly discussed. Morgan spoke of the immense vistas that were opened by the possibility of directing the future of life on the earth through artificially induced mutations. Each had his own private dream.

All the time I felt deeply the unreality of what we were saying. Somehow I knew already that nothing would come of the Abdul Hamid Estates or of the various Institutes for human betterment.

Within a few weeks, we heard from John de Kay that he had been unable to arrange the promised funds. As we had very little money left, Mrs. Beaumont and I hastened to remove ourselves from Queen Anne's Mansions into cheap lodgings in Bloomsbury.

We began to go regularly to Ouspensky's meetings at 38 Warwick Gardens and to small groups organized in different people's houses. Because I was quick in picking up ideas, I was invited to repeat and explain the explanations given by Ouspensky. The 'System', as he developed it week by week, made an immense impression on the forty or fifty people who came regularly. I was fascinated by Gurdjieff's cosmology, with its broad sweep of worlds beyond worlds, that carried us right out of the limitations of the geocentric and anthropomorphic notions that weighed down on the philosophy and theology of our time. On the other hand, the penetrating psychological analysis was an antidote to the tendency towards unverifiable speculation that so greatly marred the teachings of theosophy and anthroposophy.

The inevitable long delays in the negotiations for the Princes' properties ceased to disturb me, and I was thankful to be able to devote nearly all my time, by day and night, to the 'Work', as the study and practice of Gurdjieff's method was called by his followers.

At this time, I was chiefly interested in the problem of 'Self-remembering', which Ouspensky regarded as the keystone of any valid theory of human nature. He encouraged us to make every possible effort to remember ourselves, and to report the results at the weekly meetings. None of us had a very clear idea of what self-remembering ought to be, but we soon realized that we were quite unable to remember ourselves voluntarily for more than a minute or two at a time. I struggled desperately hard. This was my first experience of 'work on myself', and it opened a new world for me. I began to see for the first time what Gurdjieff had meant when he said at our first talk that it was not enough to know, but that one also had to be. I was convinced that self-remembering and the power of choice are intimately linked. Ouspensky said: "How can you speak of power of choice in relation to a man who is asleep, who has no permanent I and who cannot remember himself?" I answered this question for myself: "I am and shall continue to be the helpless plaything of every chance influence until I can remember myself. Everything else is a waste of time."

Once Ouspensky said: "You cannot remember yourself without a reminding factor - something that will act as an alarm clock to wake you up whenever you fall asleep. The simplest reminding factors are your habits. If you will deny yourselves and struggle with your habits, they will act as alarm clocks." We all tried this. The following week one man reported a result that taught me so much that I have never forgotten it. He said: "I set myself to stop smoking. For a day or two this was a wonderful alarm clock; but then it became easy. Tonight as I was coming here, sitting in the tube train, I was saying to myself that to give up smoking is far easier than I imagined, and little use as a reminding factor. As I was chatting contentedly to myself in this way, I happened to glance at my right hand and saw a half-smoked cigarette between my fingers. This was such a shock that I realized for the first time what it means that we are all asleep."

After several weeks, it became clear to us that struggling with habits could only serve as a reminding factor for a short time. Then Ouspensky said: "It is necessary to sacrifice. Without sacrifice nothing can be gained. Try to sacrifice something that you find precious; then you will understand why it is so hard to remember yourselves." The following week one woman began to speak in a state of deep emotion. She said: "I have a tea service that belonged to my great-grandmother. We have kept it for four generations without breaking a cup. I always wash it myself, because I can trust no one with it. I said to myself: 'If I can break one cup, I shall remember myself'; But I could not bring myself to do it. This has upset me so much that I have not been able to sleep all night and I tremble whenever I think of the tea service. Whatever am I to do?" Ouspensky answered coldly: "If one cup is more important to you than remembering yourself, what do you imagine you can do? You can do nothing."

For weeks afterwards the unbroken teacup haunted our meetings. I knew myself so little that I supposed that I would have broken a teacup. Not until long, long afterwards did I realize that we all have our particular attachments that we are powerless to break. Nevertheless, this incident and dozens of others like it made me understand that we cannot remember ourselves, chiefly because we are too much attached to all the things that keep us asleep.

The psychological studies were supplemented by a remarkable exposition of Gurdjieff's idea of the universe and the laws that govern it. Ouspensky encouraged us to look for precedents and parallels to the ideas he was expounding. This led me to the study of oriental religions and languages. I was sure that there was an immense fund of wisdom in the sacred books of the Hindus and the Buddhists, but soon became convinced that no one could grasp the original meaning of the Sacred Books of the East through translations or commentaries. I set myself to learn at least enough to study the original text. I studied Sanskrit and Pali at the School of Oriental Studies. By great good fortune I found a real teacher in M.H. Kanhere, a Sama Veda Brahmin from Benares. He was a saintly man and a fine musician. Though an orthodox Hindu, he had left his caste in order to come to England and teach. He was convinced that it was his duty to help in bringing about closer understanding between Christians and Hindus.

I learned something of the Asiatic attitude towards holy men when Mrs. Beaumont and I brought him to meet the Maharaja Gaekwar of Baroda. Her father, known as Elliot of Baroda, had been the Gaekwar's tutor and later his adviser, and the old man greatly respected his memory. He was staying at the Hyde Park Hotel, where he and his suite occupied an entire floor. Much interested to hear that I was learning Sanskrit, he asked to meet my teacher. A few days later we brought Kanhere, who lived very poorly in lodgings in Putney, to see him. When Kanhere came into the room, the Gaekwar knelt down and asked his blessing. With the unconcern that only modesty and dignity can bestow, the Brahmin blessed him.

As well as Sanskrit, I studied Pali with Mrs. Rhys Davids who, with her husband, had been a pioneer in bringing the early Pali Buddhist texts to the knowledge of European scholars. I used to go weekly to her house in the Surrey hills. She would talk for hours about her belief that the true original teaching of the Buddha had been grievously distorted by the monkish scribes and commentators. She did not believe that Gautama Buddha had really taught that man had no soul, or that there is no Supreme Being. She believed firmly in reincarnation, and told me of experiences that had convinced her that she had lived in the time of Buddha as the nun Dhammadinna, one of the most famous of Gautama's women disciples.

Mrs. Rhys Davids helped me to understand the psychology of the Buddhist religious experience. Our long discussions, regarding the true significance of words referring to various psychic states, were an important factor in convincing me that there is one underlying pattern common to all religious experience, quite irrespective of the forms of religious belief and worship.

My interest in Asia was not confined to language and religion. I felt a close contact with all that was happening in the East. I joined the Central Asian Society and spoke at its meetings whenever the Near and Middle East were in question. I believe that Sir Valentine Chirol was the President that year. He disliked me and usually swept aside my comments with some reference to the unchanging Turk. My chief ally was that strange mixture of ardour and inconsequence, Commander Kenworthy, later Lord Strabolgi.

Ouspensky's meetings occupied three or four evenings every week, and during the day I worked either at the School of Oriental Studies or at the British Museum Library. I became one of those silent figures that wait for the library to open, collect an enormous pile of books that have been reserved overnight, and settle down for the day to read and make notes.

At that time Mrs. Beaumont and I were living on a shoestring in Bloomsbury. John de Kay was supposed to send money through his American company, but for some time none reached us. We sold what we could and Mrs. Beaumont pawned her jewels, until finally we had nothing left. Neither of us could contemplate the thought of asking our families for help.

Our bill at the lodging house was unpaid, but we could still get one meal a day. We knew hunger, and were thankful for this experience, which I regard as essential for the understanding of human nature. Once day Dr. Mizzi, a rich Maltese lawyer who was involved in John de Kay's plans asked us to go with him to the London Zoo - which he had never seen. It was August 1922, and the summer was very hot. Mrs. Beaumont said to me: "At least we shall get a lunch", but when he arrived, he announced that he had lunched early so as to have time for a good visit. We walked round and round the zoo until tea-time. By now our hopes had dwindled to the expectation of a good cup of tea. Evidently he had no idea of our plight, and at 4:30 he took himself off, delighted to have done the zoo properly. We were both so tired that we could scarcely make our way home - we did not even have money for a cup of tea.

That evening, looking through our trunks, I found thirty-five Turkish liras and changed them the next day for five or six pounds of English money. We felt ourselves rich, and a few days later a remittance arrived from Germany. There is a difference between going hungry for want of means to buy food and voluntary fasting. Later, I became interested in the use of fasting as a means of influencing the relationship between mind and body. It certainly has great value; though, even when I practised it regularly, I never became used to it and always dreaded the return of Sunday evening, when I was to go without all food until Tuesday morning. There is a serious disadvantage in voluntary fasting that I have observed in myself and other people. This comes from the inner sense of superiority that it engenders. When I discovered that I was beginning to pride myself upon fasting, and that I liked other people to notice and even speak about my austerities, I left them altogether. I believe that a man needs to be very free from self-love before he can safely allow himself to practise austerities. It is not enough to hide them from other people, for even this adds to the inner feeling of superiority which is a fault more deadly to the soul than greed.

Involuntary hunger from real poverty has a different effect. It is a state we share with hundreds of millions of our fellow-men. For this very reason it does not isolate us from others, but engenders a sense of kinship. Moreover, such suffering as one learns in this way is always accompanied by the awareness that millions suffer far worse than we do, with little or no hope of relief. Voluntary fasting is good only when it is practised by an entire community, as in Islam. The fast of Ramadan is an obligation, the fulfilment of which confers no special merit. It was instituted to enable the rich to participate in the feelings of the poor and understand the need for sharing their wealth.

While living through these experiences, and, at the same time, hearing Ouspensky week after week expound his doctrine of the cosmic insignificance of man, and of our own ineptitude as individuals, I received one day an invitation to lunch with Ramsay MacDonald at the Athenaeum. He was now leader of the Opposition, and a power to be reckoned with. The meeting has left a vivid memory, for I made a decision in which I felt that I was guided by the vision of the future that had been shown to me in the cemetery at Scutari nearly a year before. After lunch we went up the great stairs and sat on the landing under the gilded Apollo to drink coffee. MacDonald said that he was convinced that the future of the world lay with the moderate socialism represented by the Second International. The Labour Party would come to power, but they needed young men with varied experience. There was a special need for men with knowledge of Foreign Affairs. He remembered that I had canvassed for him at the tragic by-election of January 1921, and he thought I would prove an acceptable Labour candidate at the next general election. He had heard that I spoke well at meetings of the recently formed Institute for International Affairs. If I got into Parliament and made a good impression, I could be sure that he would keep his eye on me.

All that he said was reasonable. I felt myself in sympathy with him and the Snowdens, and I had no ties that prevented me from accepting the proposal. But as we sat and watched the grave, elderly members of the club passing up and down the staircase - many greeting MacDonald and eyeing me without curiosity - I knew that all this did not fit the pattern of my life. At that time, and for long years afterwards, I had the very common human weakness of finding it very hard to say no. I made the excuse that I did not have enough money to fight an election, but that I might be better placed soon. He told me to come and see him as soon as I had made up my mind.

The choice presented itself in an unexpected form within a few days of this meeting. Ouspensky announced that he was going to have a special series of meetings on Wednesday evenings. This happened to be the same night as the meetings of the Institute for International Affairs. If I gave up the latter, I should soon lose the place I was gaining as an authority on Near Eastern affairs. I had a stimulating talk with Arnold Toynbee, who amazed me by his intimate knowledge of the inner history of the Ottoman Dynasty that I had learned mostly at first hand, but which he must have acquired by reading. His suggestion that I should write articles on the Middle East, combined with Ramsay MacDonald's proposals, opened up vistas that were attractive and exciting.

I talked it over with Mrs. Beaumont. She refused to influence me, but I felt that she thought I should enter politics. She herself had many connections that could have helped me, with leaders of the old Liberal Party opposed to Lloyd George. I went on the Wednesday night to Ouspensky's meeting and entered into a foolish argument with him about organic evolution, the reality of which he denied. Armed with the facts I had learned from T.H. Morgan, I talked about mutations - a word Ouspensky did not or would not recognize.

I could hear my own voice and the tone of arrogance, disguised as humility, with which I pressed my objections. There were forty or fifty people present, and I could sense their antagonism. Nearly forty years later, a Scottish lady told me that she had really hated me that evening and had never quite forgiven me for disputing with our Teacher.

That evening I walked out of Warwick Gardens alone. I was angry with myself because my stupid cleverness had got the better of me. I said to myself: "It is all a waste of time. I will give up Ouspensky's meetings and devote myself to foreign affairs.' As I spoke the words, another consciousness deeper within myself was aware of what would really happen. I was going to resign from the Institute of International Affairs. I would write to Ramsay MacDonald and say that it was impossible for me to enter politics. I was going to drop everything in order to follow

Gurdjieff and Ouspensky.

All my plans were upset by the announcement that a new treaty of peace with Turkey was to be negotiated in Lausanne. John de Kay had secured the interest of the most famous lawyer in America, Samuel Untermyer, to act as the representative of the Turkish heirs. or the time being, all other interests were swallowed up in the excitement of my first contact with International Big Business and High Finance.

It had been arranged that I should meet Untermyer in Munich, and answer the questions he had prepared. I left by the first train, but when I reached Munich, I found that Untermyer was about to leave for Paris in his private railway coach, and he took me with him. He travelled in splendour, and I met for the first time the strange phenomenon of American wealth. It was very different from the spontaneous lavishness of the Gaekwar of Baroda - probably a far richer man. Between Munich and Paris, Untermyer assimilated the whole story. He made me start with the history and geography of the Ottoman Empire and go through the relationships of the Dynasty, the story of Abdul Hamid's dealings in lands and concessions, the policies and relationships of the Allied Governments. He read for himself the decision of the Supreme Religious Tribunal declaring that the confiscation of Abdul Hamid's properties by the Young Turks was illegal and of no effect.

By the time we reached Paris, his mind was made up. He said: "There is no tribunal to try this case except the public opinion of the world. I am going to appeal direct to that tribunal." He called an International Press Conference - at that time something new and strange in Europe - and having collected scores of correspondents from the leading American and European newspapers, announced that the Heirs of Abdul Hamid had] retained him to represent them, and that the powerful American financial interests were prepared to develop their concessions for the benefit of all concerned. The potential wealth of the Near East was so vast as to be capable of redressing the economic balance of the world. I listened in wonderment to his magnificent restatement of my own dreams. Untermyer's name was then associated in people's minds with his tremendous cross-examination of John D. Rockefeller and Pierpoint Morgan in the anti-trust lawsuits, and the newspapers were ready to print any story that fell from his lips. Thus, overnight, the case of the Abdul Hamid Heirs became known all over the world.

Untermyer went on to London and I remained in Paris, to meet a no less redoubtable figure in Walter Teagle, president of the Standard Oil Company of New Jersey, who arrived in Paris a few days later and occupied a princely suite at the Ritz. Sam Untermyer had prepared the ground so well that Walter Teagle, without asking any questions, told me that the Standard Oil Company was prepared to pay one hundred thousand dollars in cash for an option on the Princes' concessions and a two and a half percent interest in the Company which would exploit the concessions. I said that in my opinion a compromise would have to be made, and he assured me that the Princes' share would be maintained even if other oil interests were to share in the exploitation.

I telephoned to John de Kay and told him all that had happened. At this point, he made the capital mistake of overrating the strength of our position, and demanded a million dollars in cash and a larger share in the Company. I expected that there would be some bargaining, but evidently the Standard Oil Company were prepared to pay just so much to have a bargaining counter, and were not prepared to have their hands forced. Walter Teagle said to me: "Tell your friend de Kay that he has missed his chance. And I advise you, young man, to learn that it does not pay to overcall your hand."

I followed Untermyer to London, but he was already interested in some other scheme. He said that there was nothing to be done until the peace conference was in session, and then he would bring pressure to bear on the State Department to support the interests of the American Abdul Hamid Company.

All this happened in October 1922. In November I was in Lausanne, and stayed with Mrs. Beaumont at the Beau Rivage Hotel. The discussions dragged on. There were great festivities at Christmas; all the delegations took part in a fancy dress ball, and I went dressed as a Bedouin, wearing a head-dress given me by the Sherif Ali Haidar. Haim Nahoum Effendi, the Chief Rabbi of Turkey, played an important part behind the scenes. The Turks had great confidence in his extraordinary knowledge of world affairs. I got to know and like him by the accident that he and I, with a Japanese baron, took dancing lessons together from a Russian lady. It was all absurd, but not more so than the conference itself. Ismet Pasha, the leader of the Turkish Delegation, had come with a definite mandate, and would not concede the smallest point. Lord Curzon, who presided, was furious at his own helplessness. Ismet Pasha was deaf, but his deafness varied according to what was said. On 4th February I went into the great ballroom to hear Curzon deliver his ultimatum: "A point has been reached where delay will produce no further change. All the Allied Delegations are agreed that they will accept no further discussion." I knew only too well that both the Italians and the French were already negotiating behind our backs, and Ismet Pasha knew it also. His deafness became complete. Curzon broke up the conference, and when he returned to England the Spectator wrote: "Disraeli in 1878 brought back peace without honour; Lord Curzon has brought back honour without peace."

During the three months, no progress had been made with such minor details as the status of the Imperial Estates; but there had been the most complicated intrigues and negotiations about the oil and other concessions. At one point I went to Paris to see Walter Teagle, who had shown a passing return of interest in the Abdul Hamid concessions. I took the opportunity of going for a week-end to Gurdjieff's Institute at Fontainebleau. An immense activity was in progress. The erection of the Study House for the practice of Gurdjieff's exercises had been completed, and it was to be opened the following week. This building was constructed from the framework of a war-time aeroplane hangar bought by Gurdjieff for a song. Many stories were told me of the extraordinary experiences of those who took part in its construction. There were many English people staying at the Prieuré under severe winter conditions. Katherine Mansfield was there; I met her, for the first and only time, a week before she died. I was told that Gurdjieff had cured her of tuberculosis, by making her sleep in a loft over the cow-byre. Orage, who was there on a short visit, told me that he had decided to sell the New Age and devote himself wholly to Gurdjieff's work.

There was an atmosphere of excitement and a glowing confidence that made a dramatic contrast with the miserable play-acting of Lausanne. I longed to get away from what I was doing and stay permanently with Gurdjieff. I only spoke to him for a few minutes. He introduced me to Katherine Mansfield saying: "He is friend of the Turkish Prince who is my friend." I was afraid she might speak of books, for I had not read a word she had written. Instead she said: "Why don't you bring your Turkish Prince here? He will find what he is looking for." Her voice had such a quality that I was filled with the resolve to do what she suggested. Gurdjieff invited me to stay another week and witness the opening of the Study House, for which, he said, a special ceremony had been arranged. I was obliged to return to Lausanne and so missed the dramatic moment when Katherine Mansfield died and the Study House came to life, nor did I succeed in bringing Prince Sabaheddin to the Prieuré. Somehow he and Katherine Mansfield have remained associated in my memory. They both gave an impression of a refinement that was too delicate for this earth.

As I was traveling back to Paris early on Monday morning, I said to myself: "This is your chief feature: always to be doing the thing that is less important and neglecting what matters to you most." I wanted to drop everything and go to live at the Prieuré. Unfortunately, I had no money at all, and I knew that those who were going to live at the Prieuré had made large financial contributions.

I returned to Lausanne to find that the American support we had hoped for was not likely to amount to more than an expression of hope that justice would be done. The conference wound up on the fifth of February, and I returned to England. I found that Bonar Law's Government was tottering. The Prime Minister resigned and was replaced by Stanley Baldwin. MacDonald's star was in the ascendant, but I had burned my boats. There were indications that British policy would become more constructive. I also learned that the Turkish and American Delegations at Lausanne had agreed to insist upon the maintenance of private rights, including those of the Imperial Family.

I went back to Lausanne on 22nd April, exactly a year after signing the contract with the Princes. This time there was a great change in the atmosphere. The State Department had secured the Chester Concession and was apparently inclined to let well alone. The initiative passed into the hands of the Italians. Signor Montagna, the Italian delegate, had made such a close friendship with Ismet Pasha that the other delegations were obliged to follow his lead. I had several meetings with Ismet Pasha, whose support was indispensable for our case. Unfortunately, the Turkish National Assembly in Ankara had just passed a law making it high treason to do any act favouring the restoration of the Sultanate. Ismet Pasha was little moved by my argument that it was better to secure the Princes' rights, than to send them away destitute to seek the protection of other powers.

As the American Delegation had lost their interest after securing the position of their own oil and railroad groups, I had little chance of getting a hearing. Nevertheless, with the help of an old friend who was a junior member of the Turkish Delegation, we succeeded in getting the disastrous article of the Treaty of Sèvres, which gave all imperial properties to the successor states, replaced by a neutral clause which said that the 'juridical nature of the properties and possessions registered in the name of the Civil List would not be modified.' This left us free to prove the Princes' title under the laws of Turkey and was the best we could hope for.

I left Lausanne as soon as the Peace Treaty was agreed on 8th July, and returned at once to London. John de Kay had financed our unofficial delegation, though he had not himself come to Lausanne. When we went back to London we had little money left, and I could not see how the means were to be found for fighting a number of lawsuits in half a dozen countries, from Tripoli and Greece to Iraq and Palestine. After eight months of political manoeuvring, I felt a terrible reaction against it all. I could see that, in this short time, the means had overshadowed the end. I had lost touch with the spiritual aims which I had imagined that all my efforts were to serve.

When I spoke to Ouspensky about my experiences, he advised me to go for a long visit to Gurdjieff's Institute in Fontainebleau.

10: WITH GURDJIEFF AT FONTAINEBLEAU

I went to Fontainebleau alone. Mrs. Beaumont did not come because she felt an obligation to go to Dax, near Biarritz, to join her mother who was taking a cure. As I wrote to her every day and she kept the letters, I am able to reconstruct my stay at the Prieuré more exactly than some other parts of my life. So very much happened to me that, if I had relied on my memory alone, I could not believe that I was there only thirty-three days.

The lime tree grove at the Prieuré

I arrived tired and timid. Many stories were current in the London group of the hardships of life at the Prieuré. Orage, the journalist and critic, the intellectual par excellence who had never used his hands for labour, had developed powerful muscles and the hard skin of the peasant or fisherman. Maurice Nicoll, the psychoanalyst, abandoning his admiring following in Harley Street, had turned into a labourer and his wife into a housemaid. Wealthy and titled members of Ouspensky's group had gone over, and had been astonished to find themselves enjoying work as scullery maids. I felt myself singularly unfitted for such a life, but I felt an absolute need to break out of the spiritual prison into which I had fallen.

The Prieuré had changed much in the eight months since my previous visit. The Study House had been completed, and work had been started on a Russian bath. The Study House had acquired an atmosphere that reminded me of the Mevlevi *Tekke* outside the Adrianople Gate of Istanbul. This was only the first impression; very soon one began to feel that it was Gurdjieff and nothing but Gurdjieff. About a hundred feet long and forty wide, it had a deep stage at one end and a low gallery, ten or twelve feet broad, surrounding a space where the pupils sat round on cushions on the earth floor. Facing the stage were two boxes partly hidden by curtains, in which Gurdjieff's wife, Madame Ostrowska, used to sit and watch the 'exercises'. At the corners were fountains, and the windows were painted by hand to imitate stained glass. All through, the building had an impromptu air about it - more like a stage set than a permanent structure. And yet its character was so strong and so distinctive that no one who entered could withstand its influence.

I arrived on a Saturday night, when the exercises were performed in the same white costumes I had seen in Constantinople, and visitors from Paris were allowed to watch the performance. The exercises consisted of the same rhythmic movements and ritual dances that I had seen before. There were also various demonstrations of telepathic communication that much impressed me at the time; later I was shown the tricks by which the results were obtained.

There were twenty-five or thirty Russians and about as many English visitors. There were no French or Americans at that time, and between the Russians and English there was very little contact - chiefly owing to difficulties of language.

I was fortunate in this respect. When I arrived, Madame de Hartmann received me in an elegant drawing-room on the ground floor of the château, and told me that Georgy Ivanitch - the name by which Gurdjieff was known among the Russians - would see me the same afternoon. Speaking Turkish, we had no need of an interpreter. He asked for news of Prince Sabaheddin, and went on almost at once to speak of the very same subject - the distinction of Being and Knowing - that we had left at our first talk at Kuru Cheshme, nearly two years before. I made notes of all the talks I had with him, and can therefore reproduce them fairly accurately after all these years. He said: "You have already too much knowledge. It will remain only theory unless you learn to understand not with mind but with heart and body. Now only your mind is awake; your heart and body are asleep. If you continue like this, soon your mind also will go to sleep, and you will never be able to think any new thoughts. You cannot awaken your own feelings, but you can awaken your body. If you can learn to master your body, you will begin to acquire Being.

"For this, you must look on your body as a servant. It must obey you. It is ignorant and lazy. You must teach it to work. If it refuses to work, you must have no mercy on it. Remember yourself as two - you and your body. When you are master of your body, your feelings will obey you. At present nothing obeys you – not your body, nor your feelings, nor your thoughts. You cannot start with thoughts, because you cannot yet separate yourself from your thoughts.

"This Institute exists to help people to work on themselves. You can work as much or as little as you wish. People came here for various reasons, and they get what they come for. If it is only curiosity, then we arrange things to astonish them. If they come to get knowledge, we have many scientific experiments that will instruct them. But if they come to get Being, then they must do the work themselves. No one else can do the work for them, but it is also true that they cannot create the conditions for themselves. Therefore, we create conditions."

I said that I was tired of being as I was and wanted to change. He replied: "You must begin at the beginning. You start as kitchen boy; then you will work in the garden, and so on until you have learned how to master your body." He asked me how long I could stay, and I said that I did not know, as it depended on the Peace Treaty with Turkey. He did not seem very interested and said: "It does not matter. You start now, and we shall see."

I was introduced to a middle-aged Russian, Dr. Tschernwal. He looked to me a little like Gurdjieff, except that he had a magnificent long beard, but a less impressive head. He showed me my room, a small cell in what had been the servants' quarters of the château. The room was scantily furnished and not at all clean. The first day I was left alone and wandered round the grounds. There was a formal garden with water lily pools behind the château. Beyond this was a narrow avenue of lime trees, with a broad path in the centre and rows of seats on each side facing the lawns. At the far end of the lime trees was a very large circular pool. To the right was the Study House, and to the left the stone quarry destined to become a Russian bath. There were small paddocks with cows, sheep, goats and a very large hen run, but no pigs. Behind the paddocks in the direction of the Seine, the grounds merged into the Forest of Fontaineb-leau, with large fir trees, beeches and oaks. A path led away through the wood to an enormous sawpit, where planks of timber were being cut.

On the third day I became kitchen boy. I guessed that Gurdjieff must have taken some of his ideas from the dervishes, for in the Mevlevi *Tekke* each future member of the Dedegian passes through twenty-one stages, in each of which he serves the community. The first task given to the neophyte is that of kitchen boy. I knew nothing about kitchens or indeed any kind of household work. My first task was to wash the stone floors of the kitchen and scullery. They were very dirty, and I lavished hot water on them, feeling very proud that the dirt was coming away so easily. I suddenly became aware that I had no idea how to remove the water that was flooding the floor. At that moment, Madame Ouspensky, a majestic figure dressed entirely in black, and with dark chestnut hair and flashing eyes, appeared standing in the doorway; a high step above the floor. I had not seen her since we had met on the Island of Prinkipo more than two years before. She laughed like a young girl, snatched up a couple of kitchen cloths and went down on her knees to mop up the water and squeeze it into a pail.

I felt very small and incompetent to have been ignorant of so simple a procedure, and at once imitated her action. Every day there were a dozen lessons of this simple kind, in which my practical ignorance and my mental arrogance were painfully knocked together. My kitchen boy duties included that of putting out the breakfast food before eight a.m., when the people came in from the early morning work. In the first three days I learned something about human nature that I had scarcely suspected. The food was scanty and everyone was hungry. The amount of bread, butter, jam and porridge that I was allowed to put out was enough to satisfy about two thirds of the people. There was also a particularly unpleasant drink called 'coffee', made, I believe, with roasted acorns prepared according to some recipe laid down by Gurdjieff himself.

People would come in from work early and take more than their share. Standing beside the tables to collect and wash plates and cutlery, I could watch and listen. I could scarcely believe that the selfishness, indifference and malevolence, usually so deeply hidden in people, could be so nakedly shown over the simple process of eating breakfast. I began to see what Gurdjieff meant when he said that everything at the Institute provided conditions for work on oneself.

One day, I was taken off the scrubbing to spend hours grinding cinnamon in a mortar. I was told that, at that time, Gurdjieff was eating nothing but sour cream and powdered cinnamon. Not a day passed without a variety of unexpected, often inexplicable happenings.

After a few days, I was transferred to the sawpit. I worked there under

Alexander de Salzmann. An immense two-handed saw, about twelve feet in length, was handled by one man on a precarious stage, with another deep in the pit. Tree trunks eighteen inches in diameter were sawn into planks three inches thick. It was gruelling work in the heat. If one was above, one had the whole weight of the saw to lift. If one was in the pit, sawdust poured down and stuck on one's sweating face. De Salzmann set the pace. He was so skillful in shifting the great logs with the woodsman's hooked tool that I asked one of the Russians where he had learned it. He replied, with perfect gravity: "He has lived all his life in the Caucasus forests, and was a forestry inspector before the war." In point of fact, he had been a famous stage designer in Moscow, and later an associate of Jacques-Dalcroze, and had never handled a saw until Gurdjieff had taught him a month before I came. Learning completely new skills in the shortest space of time was part of the training at Gurdjieff's Institute.

From the sawpit I went to the stone quarry, where the mercilessly hard limestone of Fontainebleau Forest was being quarried to build the Russian bath. A burly young Russian named Tchekhov Tchekhovitch was in charge of this work. The second day I was on this task a very large block of limestone broke away. Tchekhovitch said it was just what Gurdjieff wanted to make the lintel of the Russian bath. It was far too heavy for us to remove, and we tried to break it up with stone chisels and crowbars. After two hours, during which we had made no impression on the stone, Gurdjieff suddenly appeared in his town clothes. I learned later that he had just come from Paris, having been up all night. He did not say a word, but stood on the edge of the pit and watched us. We went on hacking away at the stone. Abruptly, he took off his coat and jumping into the pit, took a hammer and chisel from one of the Russian workers. He looked closely at the rock, placed the chisel carefully and tapped three or four times. He walked half round it and, after a careful examination, tapped again. I am sure he had not struck the rock more than a dozen times when a huge flake, weighing perhaps a hundred pounds, cracked off and fell away. He repeated the operation three or four times and behold, a slab remained less than half the size of the original. He said: "Lift." We put out all our strength and the rock came up, and we carried it over to the bath.

It was a telling exhibition of skill that has remained in my memory as vividly as when I saw it. But this is only half the story. More than twenty-five years later I was sitting beside Gurdjieff at dinner in his flat in Paris, and Tchekhovitch, now grey and almost bald, was standing facing us. Gurdjieff was talking about Ju-jitsu and saying that he had learned a far more advanced art in Central Asia than that of the Japanese.

It was called Fiz-lez-Lou, and he had thought of introducing it in Europe and was looking for someone to train as an instructor. As Tchekhovitch had been in his youth a champion wrestler, he had been the natural candidate. He then spoke to Tchekhovitch, and said: "Do you remember at the Prieuré when we were making the Russian bath, how you tried to break the rock for the door frame and could not? I watched you then and saw that you did not know how to look. I could see just where the rock would crack, but you could not see even when I showed you. So I gave up the idea of teaching Fiz-lez-Lou in Europe."

Tchekhovitch, who adored Gurdjieff as if he were a divine incarnation, stood motionless and said: "Yes, Georgy Ivanitch, I remember." Then tears began to roll down his cheek. I trembled in sympathy. This incident, which had taken twenty-six years to complete its cycle, was not only characteristic of human ineptitude, but terrifyingly applicable to my own condition.

The day's work began at six in the morning and continued until six at night, with breaks for breakfast and the midday meal. The food was meagre and unpalatable, except on Saturday nights when there was a rich feast and open house for visitors.

No one who worked at the Prieuré in 1923 will ever forget the sense of expectancy and wonder with which we awaited each new theme of work given out by Gurdjieff. All went at a breakneck pace. For a few weeks the theme was based on various kinds and degrees of fasting. Then it would change to psychological tests so penetrating that everyone seemed to be stripped spiritually naked.

One example connected with fasting will illustrate the delicacy with which Gurdjieff could give lessons if he chose. There was at the Prieuré a famous Russian lawyer named Rakhmilevich, who had formerly been the leader of the St. Petersburg bar before the war. He had joined Gurdjieff in 1911, and was inclined to lay down the law as the senior pupil. Once Gurdjieff came into the drawing-room as he was saying to another Russian: "I should know best what Georgy Ivanitch means, as I have been with him five years longer than you." Gurdjieff said quietly: "Rakhmil, if you are not ashamed to say that for yourself, be ashamed for my sake. You expose me as a bad teacher if after twelve years you have understood so little." Soon after this came the announcement that a course of intensive fasting was to begin. Rakhmilevich secretly hid some food in a tree. Several of us had seen him, but no one said a word. When the fast was due to begin, Gurdjieff told each one what his programme was to be. He left Rakhmilevich to the last, and then said: "Rakhmilevich need not fast; he already knows too much." I felt a great pang of sorrow as I heard this, for I saw how Rakhmilevich had sacrificed everything to follow Gurdjieff, but could not sacrifice himself. After the fasts, Gurdjieff turned to mental exercises to be combined with the manual labour in the grounds.

Gurdjieff's doctrine of 'Conscious Labour and Intentional Suffering' was often understood with that comic literalness that overtakes Europeans and Americans when they are confronted with Asiatic subtlety. When I arrived at the Prieuré, the mental exercises took the form of learning long lists of Tibetan words. The ladies - mostly middle-aged English women - were set to grub up the roots of large trees felled by the men. The task was manifestly impossible, except by digging deep holes or using a winch. The ladies sat in the shallow holes, digging away with small trowels, or even, owing to the endemic lack of tools, with tablespoons, throwing the earth behind them like fowls grubbing on a rubbish heap. Tucked under wrist-watches or bracelets were pieces of paper, pulled out surreptitiously every few minutes. The ladies, looking like anxious hens, were muttering the lists of words. I wondered, as I looked at them, what they had come to Fontainebleau to find. Of their sincerity there could be no doubt, but where had they left their common sense?

Gurdjieff had ruthless methods of getting rid of those whom he did not want. He seemed to invite and yet to detest a kind of stupid adoration which made his every word and gesture into symbols of some eternal truth. One lady was particularly foolish about him, and he played a cruel trick on her that showed me how we should take his warning to trust nothing and no one, and especially not himself.

Every Saturday after lunch, all work was put aside and preparations were made for the weekly feast and reception. In the afternoon, a formal English tea was on the terrace of the château. Once we had ice-cream prepared with fresh cream from the Prieuré cows. Gurdjieff walked round, with the strange effortless gait that marked him out from any other man. He came up to this lady's table and said: 'You not know how to get best taste from ice-cream. Should eat with mustard.' She dutifully got up and went into the house for a mustard pot. As she returned, Gurdjieff in a thundering voice pointed to her and said: "You see what is round idiot. She all the time idiot. Why you here?"

The poor woman went scarlet and burst into tears. She packed up her bags, went off and was never seen again.

Another time, a young American named Metz, who also suffered from uncritical adoration of Gurdjieff, had been told to put a new headlight on Gurdjieff's car. That night Gurdjieff had to go to Paris. When his car was taken out and he found the headlight had not been changed, he shouted at Metz to sit on the bumper and hold the light all the way to Paris. Metz meekly sat on the mudguard, until Gurdjieff contemptuously pushed him off with his favourite word: "Idiot!"

A concert pianist named Finch, with most beautiful hands, tenderly cared for as if they were priceless treasures, came to stay at the Prieuré. He was set to look after the hens. As the days passed he looked more and more anxious. Finally, he said to Gurdjieff that the hens were not laying so well since he took them over. Gurdjieff replied: "Of course not. Because you not love them. Hens here know people. They lay for people who love them. Must learn to love them."

The next day I passed the hen house and saw poor Finch gazing into the run, evidently bent upon loving the hens, but quite unable to guess how it was done. Every evening after dinner, a new life began. There was no hurry. Some walked in the garden. Others smoked. About nine o'clock we made our way alone or in twos and threes to the Study House. Outdoor shoes came off and soft shoes or mocassins were put on. We sat quietly, each on his or her own cushion, round the floor in the centre. Men sat on the right, women on the left; never together.

Some went straight on to the stage and began to practise the rhythmic exercises. On our first arrival, each of us had the right to choose his own teacher for the movements. I had chosen Vasili Ferapontoff, a young Russian, tall, with a sad studious face. He wore pince-nez, and looked the picture of the perpetual student, Trofimov, in *The Cherry Orchard*. He was a conscientious instructor, though not a brilliant performer. I came to value his friendship, which continued until his premature death ten years later. He told me in one of our first conversations that he expected to die young.

The exercises were much the same as those I had seen in Constantinople three years before. The new pupils, such as myself, began with the series called Six Obligatory Exercises. I found them immensely exciting and worked hard to master them quickly so that I could join in the work of the general class.

At that time, Gurdjieff was preparing a special class - composed almost exclusively of Russians - to give public demonstrations. The general class could learn any new exercises, but did not take part in the special training reserved for the demonstration class.

Gurdjieff's method of creating new exercises had a living spontaneity that was one secret of his success as a teacher. While the new pupils were practising on the stage, some of the Russians would gather round the piano, where Thomas de Hartmann sat with his bald head perked like a bird. Gurdjieff would begin to tap a rhythm on the piano top. When it was clear to all, he hummed a melody or played it with one hand on the piano and then walked away. Hartmann would develop a theme to fit the rhythm and the melody. If he went wrong, Gurdjieff would shout at him and Hartmann would shout furiously back.

Then the older class would line up in rows, and we would stand at the side and watch or go back to our places on the floor. Gurdjieff would teach the postures and gestures of the exercises partly by doing them himself; or, if they were complicated, involving different movements by different rows or positions, he would walk round and place each pupil in the desired posture. There would be vehement arguments. The stage became a chaos of dispute, gesticulation and shouting as the pupils tried to work out the sequence required. Suddenly, Gurdjieff would give a peremptory shout and there would be a dead silence. A few words of explanation, and Hartmann would begin to play the theme that by then he had worked out into a rich harmony. Sometimes the result was spectacular; a beautiful ensemble never seen before would appear as if by magic. At other times, the task was too difficult and the exercise broke down, to be worked over for hours during the succeeding days.

In addition to the set exercises, many hours were spent in performing rhythms with the feet to music improvised by Hartmann. Sometimes Gurdjieff also used his famous Stop Exercise. At any moment of the day or night, he might shout: "Stop!" when everyone within hearing had to arrest all movement. First the eyes were to fix upon the object of their gaze. The body was to remain motionless in the exact posture of the moment the word 'stop' was heard, and the thought present in the mind was to be held. In short, every voluntary movement was to be arrested and held. The Stop might last a few seconds, or five, ten minutes or more. The posture might be painful or even dangerous; but, if we were sincere and conscientious, we would do nothing to ease it. We had to wait until Gurdjieff shouted "Davay!" or, "Continue!" and then resume what we had been doing before.

The rhythmic exercises were often so complicated and unnatural that I despaired of learning them. And yet, again and again, a minor miracle occurred. After hours of fruitless and maddening struggle, the body would suddenly give way, and the impossible movement would be made. The work in the Study House always continued until midnight and often much later, so that we seldom had more than three or four hours' sleep before starting the morning's work. About midnight Gurdjieff would call out: "*Kto hochet spat, mojet itti spat,*" or "Who want sleep go sleep." One or two would get up and go out, but the great majority remained, knowing that often the most interesting explanations and demonstrations were given after the regular work was done.

Sometimes Gurdjieff gave lectures. These were very great events, for everyone was avid for a better understanding of all the strange things that were happening to us. I can repeat one lecture verbatim.

One evening Major Pinder, a former British Intelligence officer who had met Gurdjieff in Tiflis in 1919, and who, knowing Russian very well, acted as his interpreter, announced that there was to be a lecture. We all went to the Study House as usual, but instead of practising the exercises sat expectantly round the hall on our cushions. Time passed: ten o'clock, eleven o'clock, midnight. At last Gurdjieff arrived - evidently having driven out from Paris - accompanied by Madame Ostrowska, Madame Ouspensky and Major Pinder. He stood and looked at us all for a long time and said, in English: "Patience is the Mother of Will. If you have not a mother, how can you be born?" He then walked out of the Study House. This lecture made a very strong impression on me, because I knew that I was lacking equally in patience and in will. I can only record a few incidents, out of dozens, that happened every day and produced an extraordinary state of tension, in which people were stripped of all the psychological protections by which we live in our usual world. Some people went mad. There were even suicides. Many gave up in despair. Some were so lost in their private dreams that they scarcely noticed the extraordinary conditions in which we were living.

After about a fortnight of this life, I began to feel very ill, chiefly from a return of the dysentery from which I had suffered in Smyrna four years before. I took literally what Gurdjieff said about disregarding the objections of my body and forced myself to work even harder than the others. At that time, there was a prolonged drought, and every evening we all had to help in watering the kitchen garden upon which we depended for a good part of our food. I noticed an ample stream flowing only a hundred yards from the kitchen garden, and that the level of the water would allow it to be used for irrigation. I mentioned this to several of the pupils, who, without exception, were shocked at the very suggestion that we might devise something to lighten our work. One day Gurdjieff came up to the kitchen garden and, with considerable trepidation, I asked him if I could make irrigation canals of the kind used in Anatolia. He agreed without discussion. The next day, I built a dam and started cutting a canal, but as it had to pass over some higher ground, I saw that it would take me weeks to dig it in the little spare time I had after lunch. However, I reckoned without Gurdjieff. The same evening he came up to the kitchen garden and made a great scene about the stupidity of carrying water when a stream was so near. Everyone was set to digging canals, and the irrigation system was working the next day. Afterwards I heard Gurdjieff describe it as a special system that he had seen in Persia, and it became one of the marvels of the Prieuré, shown to visitors as an example of Gurdjieff's uncanny wisdom.

Each morning, it was harder and harder to get out of bed, and my body shrank from the heavy &work in the heat of the sun. The constant diarrhoea made me very weak, but somehow I kept going.

Finally, a day came when I simply could not stand up. I was shaking with fever and very wretched in myself, feeling that I had failed. Just as I was saying to myself "I will stay in bed today," I felt my body rising. I dressed and went to work as usual, but this time with a queer sense of being held together by a superior Will that was not my own.

We worked as usual all the morning. I could not eat lunch that day, but lay on the ground wondering if I was going to die. Gurdjieff had just introduced afternoon practice of the exercises, out-of-doors under the lime grove. When the pupils began to collect under the lime trees, I joined them. Gurdjieff and Hartmann came out together. The piano was carried out from the Study House by six men. I was one of them, and I stumbled, nearly bringing the others down. I was hot and miserable.

We started by working on a new exercise of incredible complexity that even the most experienced Russian pupils could not master. The structure of the exercises was drawn on the board in symbols, and head, feet, arms and torso had to follow independent sequences. It was a torture for all of us.

Gurdjieff pretended to be angry and stopped us, saying we must practice rhythms. Hartmann began to play one rhythm after another, which had to be followed with the feet. I felt very ill and weak. A deadly lassitude took possession of me, so that every movement became a supreme effort of will. One of the English pupils stopped and sat down. Then another and another. Soon I ceased to be aware of anything but the music and my own weakness. I kept saying to myself: "At the next change I will stop." Hartmann went on and on. One by one, all the English pupils fell out, and most of the Russian women. Only six or seven men and, I believe, Jeanne de Salzmann continued.

Gurdjieff stood watching intently. Time lost the quality of before and after. There was no past and no future, only the present agony of making my body move. Gradually, I became aware that Gurdjieff was putting all his attention on me. There was an unspoken demand that was at the same time an encouragement and a promise. I must not give up - if it killed me.

Suddenly, I was filled with the influx of an immense power. My body seemed to have turned into light. I could not feel its presence in the usual ways. There was no effort, no pain, no weariness, not even any sense of weight. I felt an intense gratitude towards Gurdjieff and Thomas de Hartmann, but they had quietly gone off, having dismissed the class, and leaving me quite alone. My own state was blissful beyond anything I had ever known. It was quite different from the ecstasy of sexual union, for it was altogether free and detached from the body. It was exultation in the faith that can move mountains.

All had gone into the house for tea, but I went in the opposite direction towards the kitchen garden, where I took a spade and began to dig. Digging in the earth is a searching test of our capacity for physical effort. A strong man can dig very fast for a short time or slowly for a long time, but no one can force his body to dig fast for a long time even if he has exceptional training. I felt the need to test the power that had entered me, and I began to dig in the fierce afternoon heat for more than an hour at a rate that I ordinarily could not sustain for two minutes. I felt no fatigue and no sense of effort. My weak, rebellious, suffering body had become strong and obedient. The diarrhoea had ceased and I no longer felt the gnawing abdominal pains that had been with me for days. Moreover, I experienced a clarity of thought that I had only known involuntarily and at rare moments, but which now was at my command. I returned in thought to the Grande Rue de Pera and discovered that I could be aware of the fifth dimension. The phrase 'in my mind's eye' took on a new meaning as I 'saw' the eternal pattern of each thing I looked at; the trees, the plants, the water flowing in the canal and even the spade, and, lastly, my own body. I recognized the changing relationship between 'myself' and 'my pattern'. As my state of consciousness changed, 'I' and my 'pattern' grew closer together or separated and lost touch. Time and Eternity were the conditions of our experience, and the Harmonious Development of Man towards which Gurdjieff was leading us was the secret of true freedom. I remember saying aloud: "Now I see why God hides himself from us." But even now I cannot recall the intuition behind this exclamation.

Gurdjieff had said to me, at our first meeting at Kuru Cheshme, that it is not enough to know that another world exists; one must be able to enter it at will. Now I was living in Eternity and yet I had not lost my hold on Time. I was aware that Life itself is infinitely richer and greater than all that our thinking mind can possibly know about it.

As the pupils began to return to the garden to begin the evening watering, I left my digging and wandered into the forest. I went past the stone quarry, past the saw-pit, along a path that led up the hill behind Avon. The great trees, the grey rocks, the cloudless sky and the murmur of evening insects all blended with my inner life. There was no distinction of outside and inside: everything was where it was and so was neither inside nor outside of anything else. I no longer wished to test anything or prove anything; I was satisfied to be just as I was.

Turning a bend in the path, where there was a big grey rock, I met Gurdjieff. Our meeting seemed inevitable, although I had never been in that part of the forest before. Without any preliminaries, he began to talk about the energies that work in man.

"There is a certain energy that is necessary for work on oneself. No man can make efforts unless he has a supply of this energy. We can call it the Higher Emotional Energy. Everyone, by a natural process, makes a small amount of this energy every day. If rightly used, it enables man to achieve much for his own self-perfecting. But he can only get to a certain point in this way. The real complete transformation of Being, that is indispensable for a man who wishes to fulfil the purpose of his existence, requires a very much greater concentration of Higher Emotional Energy than that which comes to him by nature.

"There are some people in the world, but they are very rare, who are connected to a Great Reservoir or Accumulator of this energy. This Reservoir has no limits. Those who can draw upon it can be a means of helping others. Suppose that a man needs a hundred units of this energy for his own transformation, but he only has ten units and cannot make more for himself He is helpless. But with the help of someone who can draw upon the Great Accumulator, he can borrow ninety more. Then his work can be effective."

He let all this sink in, and then stopped, and looking into my eyes said: "Those who have this quality belong to a special part of the highest caste of humanity. It may be that one day you will become such, but you will have to wait for many years. What you have received today is a taste of what is possible for you. Until now, you have only known about these things theoretically, but now you have experience. When a man has had experience of Reality, he is responsible for what he does with his life." He added that, in a day or two, he would speak to me about his plans for the future and tell me how I could find a place in them if I wished to do so. I felt no need to ask any questions. For the moment, I had lost all interest in knowing more and was content to live with the experience that had so wonderfully come to me. Gurdjieff went off, saying no more, and I continued to walk in the forest.

A lecture by Ouspensky came into my mind. He had spoken about the very narrow limits within which we can control our functions and added: "It is easy to verify that we have no control over our emotions. Some people imagine that they can be angry or pleased as they will, but anyone can verify that he cannot be astonished at will." As I recalled these words, I said to myself: "I will be astonished." Instantly, I was overwhelmed with amazement, not only at my own state, but at everything that I looked at or thought of. Each tree was so uniquely itself that I felt that I could walk in the forest for ever and never cease from wonderment. Then the thought of 'fear' came to me. At once I was shaking with terror. Unnamed horrors were menacing me on every side. I thought of 'joy', and I felt that my heart would burst from rapture. The word 'love' came to me, and I was pervaded with such fine shades of tenderness and compassion that I saw that I had not the remotest idea of the depth and the range of love. Love was everywhere and in everything. It was infinitely adaptable to every shade of need. After a time, it became too much for me. It seemed that if I plunged any more deeply into the mystery of love, I would cease to exist. I wanted to be free from this power to feel whatever I chose, and at once it left me. As it went, and I began to see again with my own eyes and think with my own thoughts, a distich of Blake's spoke itself in me:

> Grown old in love, from seven till seven times seven,
> I oft have wished for hell for change from heaven.

I realized that for Blake this was no mere trick of words, but the expression of a real experience. I knew that the world I had entered was one where there is no loneliness, because all who enter into that Eternal Source meet there as brothers. Everything had become quiet and clear, I was aware of my body, but it was completely 'outside'. I remembered perfectly clearly my experience in the casualty clearing station on 21st March 1918. I had just the same awareness that it would not in the least matter if my body were destroyed.

That evening, in the Study House, we worked at the same complicated exercise that had completely baffled me the same afternoon. I saw instantly how it should be done. One rhythm could be done by the intelligence present in my body. For another, I needed only to hear the music and let it guide me. There was a third that I could carry in my mind. The unity of the movement came from the state of feeling that it expressed. Because I was able to separate these different powers in myself, I could follow the whole pattern without effort. The pattern could not pass from the mind to the body, as I had been trying to make it do. I did not wish anyone to notice that I could do the exercise, and this interested me also, because I was well aware of the silly vanity which usually made me sensitive to my successes or failures in front of others.

Before long, Gurdjieff stopped the exercises and had the big blackboard placed in position for a lecture. He proceeded to draw an intricate diagram consisting of a schematic representation of the human body and the principal functions. To this he added a mechanism that looked like shafts and pulleys of various sizes. He then gave a lecture in Russian which Major Pinder translated. At that time, I found myself following all that he was saying and even noticing when Pinder made mistakes in translation. I understood that Gurdjieff was showing how our capacity for work depends upon the way we are connected with the sources of energy inside us and beyond us. All that he said illuminated my own experience. Gurdjieff's explanations reached me in a direct way as if they came from inside myself, rather than through his words and my hearing. The significance of what he was saying went far beyond by own situation; I saw a picture of all humanity thirsting for the energy that was flowing through me. Gurdjieff spoke of the Great Eternal Reservoirs, which are connected with Sacred Beings who have come to the earth to help mankind. He then passed to another diagram showing how the Will of God in creation acts through energies of different density of fineness. I could see that such sources of help are really present and was aware of the great mistake that we men have made in breaking the contact that we could have with them.

After the lecture, the pupils dispersed and went to bed. I went out into the garden. The air was still hot and the night was brilliant. Sleep was impossible. Once again, unexpectedly, Gurdjieff met me on the path. He said nothing but: "Now time go sleep", in English. I protested in Turkish that I could not sleep. He replied that I could, and that I would lose nothing by sleeping. I went to bed and slept immediately. The next morning, nothing was left of the experience but memory and the conviction that some day, somehow, I must not only taste, but make my own, the power to connect myself with the Great Accumulator that could endow man with such marvellous powers.

There was an interesting sequel to Gurdjieff's lecture, for the next day Maurice Nicoll and others came to me to say that they had not understood what Gurdjieff was driving at, but felt that somehow I had been able to follow him. When I tried to explain, I found myself quite unable to remember a word of his lecture or speak of what had happened to me the previous day. It had been the most extraordinary and important day of my whole life - but it could not be shared with others. I was able to reconstruct his diagram, which enabled me, in writing *The Dramatic Universe* thirty years later, to give an interpretation of the Creative Process that would otherwise have been quite beyond my understanding.

Two or three days after this great experience, Gurdjieff invited me one morning to drive with him to Melun, where he had business. On our return, he turned the car into a forest track and we came out in a clearing a hundred feet or more above the Chateau de Prieuré. He told me that this was his favourite view, and as we sat together on a seat, he spoke to me of his plan for buying more land and building an observatory. He said that there were many facts about the movements of the planets which astronomical science overlooked, and he wished to continue researches that he had started in Central Asia thirty years before. I had no idea how old he was and assumed that he might be sixty or seventy years old - though he looked much younger. He spoke of himself at one moment as an old man, and at another would boast of his youthfulness and virility. It was impossible to tell when he was speaking seriously and when he was trying one out with some flight of outrageous fancy.

Anyhow, I took his plans for an observatory and centre for scientific researches quite seriously. It fitted into my own dreams, and I did not ask myself if perhaps Gurdjieff were making a fool of me.

I returned to the Prieuré feeling very important because Gurdjieff had let me into his secret plans. A letter was waiting for me, giving news I had been hoping for - that Mrs. Beaumont was arriving in two days. I had been writing and urging her to come. Gurdjieff had asked about her and told me to assure her that she would be welcome, but for some reason that I could not understand, she had been hesitating. It transpired that the reason was very simple; I had painted such a picture of the strenuous life at the Prieuré that she felt she would not be strong enough to stand it and did not want to hold me back.

When she did arrive towards the end of August, Gurdjieff welcomed her personally and told her to stay as long as she wished. However, when she saw me she was alarmed. She was also shocked to see that the Russian doctor who was giving injections for dysentery had no care for the rudiments of hygiene, but would come straight from the cow-byre with dirty hands to use an unsterilized syringe. Indeed the whole state of the Prieuré horrified her. When she went into the kitchen and saw it black with flies, she went straight out to the village and bought dozens of fly-papers and hung them up herself.

The English visitors looked at her askance. It had been taken for granted that the flies in the kitchen were a 'test' with which we had to bear. She also antagonized the Russians by her apparent lack of respect for Gurdjieff. He himself was delighted and went out of his way to praise her for being sensible enough to fight with the flies.

Within a few days of the great experience, my dysentery had returned and I was feeling weaker than ever. Mrs. Beaumont insisted on taking me away to Paris for a rest. Within a day or two I felt much stronger and, having nothing to do, I decided to try out Gurdjieff's recipe for learning Russian. He had said at dinner one evening that the way he learned languages was to set himself to memorize two hundred words a day, making sure each morning that he had not forgotten the previous lists. At that time there were benches in the Champs Elysée, from the Rond Point up to the Étoile. When I saw that there were twenty, I decided to learn ten words on each bench and then pass on to the next. I chose two hundred words from Bondar's Russian Grammar and started. The first day, I learned the list in two hours. The second day, it took me six hours. On the third day, I had a violent headache and had to abandon the attempt, having learned five hundred words in all. However, I found to my surprise and delight that with this foundation I could now read Russian and understand what was said to me.

Meanwhile, I had a letter from John de Kay urging me to go to London as soon as possible, as he had heard that Lord Curzon was leaving the Foreign Office, and we might expect a more friendly attitude towards the Turkish claims. I went back to the Prieuré the next morning, feeling much better in health but very unsettled in spirit. I was suffering a reaction after the prodigious experiences of the week before. Gurdjieff saw me the next day. I told him about John de Kay and his hopes and added that if the claims of the Abdul Hamid heirs were recognized, I should have enough money to help him to build his observatory. In the meantime, I had nothing. Also, I needed to help my mother, for my father had died penniless, having lost her money as well as his own. I had other obligations, and it was necessary to make some money. I would have wished to stay at the Prieuré, where I had found what mattered to me most in life. He said to me: "So far you have come here as a trial. You have been given something. But if you come here to work, you must understand that nothing is given. If you wish to acquire something of your own, you must learn to steal. What I have to give cannot be paid for; it is priceless. Therefore, if you need it, you must steal it.

"You have the possibility of learning to work. The truth is, that very few people in the contemporary world have this possibility; for most people there are barriers that they cannot pass. Everyone has these barriers; they are in human nature. You have seen that it is possible to be directly connected with the Great Accumulator of Energy that is the source of all miracles. If you could be permanently connected with this source, you could pass all barriers. But you do not know how it is done, and you are not ready to be shown. Everything is still in front of you to be done, but you now have the proof that it is possible. It may take twenty, thirty or even forty years before you will be able to enter into possession of the power that was lent to you for a day. But what is a whole lifetime if such a thing is possible? Ever since I was a young boy, I have known of the existence of this power and of the barriers that separate man from it, and I searched until I found the way of breaking through them. This is the greatest secret that man can discover about human nature. Many people are convinced that they wish to be free and to know reality, but they do not know the barrier that prevents them from reaching reality. They come to me for help, but they are unwilling or unable to pay the price. It is not my fault if I cannot help them."

He spoke again about Being and Knowledge, and the danger for me of losing everything if I relied on knowledge alone. He said grimly: "With too much knowledge, the inner barrier may become insurmountable."

I said: "If I should stay with you, how much time would be needed?" In view of what he had just said, I expected him to tell me that it would take twenty years, but he replied: "If you will devote all your energies to the task, it may take two years before you can work alone. Until then you will need me - for you cannot create the conditions for yourself. But afterwards you will not need me anymore. But for those two years, you must be ready for anything."

When I reminded him that I had no money and that I could not stay without paying, he replied: "I am not interested in your money, but in your work. There are plenty of people who will give me money, but very few who will work. I will give you the money you need. I shall soon go to America, and, you can help me, if you will learn Russian and be my interpreter. Soon you will learn to give lectures in the way I require. At present you will have to take because you have nothing to give. Later you will be ready to give your last shirt to help the work - as I am ready to give mine."

Gurdjieff was facing me with a great decision, but I knew that I could not accept his offer. I told myself that I would go away and make money, and then I would return. He did not ask me to decide anything; having said what he was prepared to do, he seemed to lose all interest in me. I could not even find him to say goodbye. It was at the beginning of September 1923, that I walked, for the last time, up the hill to the station of Fontainebleau and took the train to Paris. A chapter had been closed, and nothing was to be written in it until I returned to him. I was very far from foreseeing that twenty-five years were to pass before I met Gurdjieff again. It was only after Gurdjieff reached the end of his life that I became aware that the pattern of his own life required him to drive away all those who could be most useful to him. He drove away from him P.D. Ouspensky, Alexander de Salzmann, and even his most devoted friend Thomas de Hartmann. He also drove away A.R. Orage, Maurice Nicoll, and many others. None of these were ever able to return - though several tried. I was most fortunate in being able to go back to Gurdjieff. This was certainly through no merit of my own, but probably because I was much younger than the others and, twenty-five years later, was still alive to take another chance.

11: CONFLICTING INFLUENCES

I returned to London ill and exhausted, but I soon recovered my strength. I went to see Ouspensky, who asked me what I had found. I wanted to tell him of my wonderful experience, but found myself quite unable to speak about it. The event had not happened to me as I then was, but as I might one day become. I felt ashamed to speak of it, as if I were pretending to be other than I really was. I told Ouspensky, as well as I could, of Gurdjieff's lecture on energies and the changes of speed. He was not greatly interested.

Mrs. Beaumont was distressed by her inability to make Gurdjieff out. She was accustomed to make definite and usually accurate judgments of people, but Gurdjieff eluded her. She went to Ouspensky and - as she told me the next day said to him: "I want you to tell me the truth about Gurdjieff. I know he is not an ordinary man, but I cannot tell if he is very good or very bad. I like him and I hated him. I did not want to come under his influence. Will you tell me sincerely what you believe?" Ouspensky had answered very simply and without reservation: "I can assure you that Gurdjieff is a good man. But Bennett was right to come away; he is not yet ready for that work."

During the autumn and winter of 1923, I went regularly to Ouspensky's meetings, and worked with small groups. We were greatly stirred by the magnificent sweep of Ouspensky's exposition. I worked hard to put into practice the basic psychological methods of self-observation, self-remembering and struggle with one's habits and features. In the small groups, we looked for connections between Gurdjieff's cosmological ideas and the discoveries of contemporary science. This work occupied nearly all my spare time. During the day, I kept going, singlehanded, the London office of the Sultan Abdul Hamid Estates. John de Kay had many irons in the fire, and there were people to be seen nearly every day. A group of London financiers was interested in the project, and I had to collect information from Turkey and elsewhere to reply to their questions.

On 22nd January 1924, the first Labour Government was formed, with Ramsay MacDonald as Prime Minister and Foreign Secretary. Arthur Henderson, Secretary of the Labour Party, was regarded as the all-powerful king-maker behind the scenes. Philip Snowden was Chancellor. John de Kay decided to come to England, believing that these friends, for whom he had done much at the time of the struggles of the Second Socialist International in Zurich and Amsterdam, would help him to secure arbitration on the Princes' claims in the British Mandated Territories of Mesopotamia, Arabia and Palestine.

He reckoned without his hosts. The Labour Government, new to office, allowed itself to be guided in all but major issues by the civil service. The Foreign Office had long been hostile to the Turkish Imperial Family, and MacDonald was advised to have nothing to do with the proposed arbitration. John de Kay was nothing if not tenacious and pressed his demands upon Arthur Henderson who was, by nature, ready to listen to a plea for the oppressed. The Turkish Imperial Family had recently been expelled from Turkey by the Nationalist Government, which had proclaimed a republic. Many were stranded, almost penniless, in one or another European capital. John de Kay excelled when crusading in the name of justice for the underdog. He had so convinced himself of the legality of the Princes' claims that he asked only for arbitration by any tribunal that the British Government might approve. By the middle of April 1924, progress seemed assured when the legal advisers of the Foreign Office drew attention to the fact that they were asked to deal, not directly with the heirs of Abdul Hamid, but with an American company. This brought in the State Department in Washington, which thus became aware of John de Kay's presence in England.

The old rancour over de Kay's espousing of General Huerta's cause in Mexico had not died. On the allegation of fraud against de Kay in connection with the sale of Mexican Government bonds, a new application for his extradition was made in London. He was arrested and taken to Brixton prison. I went at once to visit him. Mrs. Beaumont, who had strongly opposed his coming to England and already regretted that I had become involved in his tortuous transactions, showed her wonderful qualities of courage and resourcefulness. It was largely through her that he was at once released on bail, and we began a long and disheartening fight against his extradition. Sir John Campbell, the Chief Magistrate at Bow Street, was not unsympathetic, but de Kay did not help his cause by attacking the good faith of the American Embassy.

The case was, of course, based entirely upon documentary evidence. I threw myself into it, as if my own freedom were at stake. Until then I had not suspected the fascination of legal procedure. It was a new world to me, and I was determined to understand it. I spent hours with the lawyers, who had the extremely difficult task of showing that no prima facie case could be made out. I think we were all convinced - including the Chief Magistrate - that de Kay was innocent of intent to defraud, but it was also evident that his optimism had led him to take obligations upon himself that he was unable to fulfill. De Kay insisted that he was the victim of political persecution and counted upon help from MacDonald and his friends of the Second Socialist International.

Upon me fell the embarrassing task of importuning members of the Government to intervene and reject the extradition application without a hearing. In vain I explained to de Kay that this was impossible under British law. His position was equivocal, because President Huerta had ceased to be recognized by the British and American Governments at the time that de Kay had been acting as his agent. The case dragged on for four months. I learned many a bitter lesson about the cowardice of good people in front of embarrassing situations. Sir John Campbell was fair and patient, and was evidently troubled by the suspicion that political animus was not wholly absent from the American attitude towards the case. In the end, he decided to make the extradition order. John de Kay was rearrested and taken to the United States. I never saw him again. He was embittered by the course of events and had begun to drink brandy to excess. He did not trust American justice and was convinced that he would be railroaded, as he put it, into a long prison sentence. It turned out quite otherwise. Having got him back to America, the United States Department of Justice decided that the case could not be proved, and de Kay was acquitted after a short trial.

My association with John de Kay had lasted little more than two years. I had learned much from him, especially to look at every problem in a big way. He had a rare capacity for expressing what he wished to say in the simplest terms. More than anything, he taught me that in this life a man must rely upon himself if he is not to be a parasite in society. I was just twenty-seven years old when he was deported, and I had relied upon him too much. He was, in many ways, the opposite of myself. His heart was so far from icy that it took fire at every real or fancied injustice. But he had the almost fatal defect of believing that he was not an ordinary man. His weaknesses were terribly apparent to me in the light of what I learned from Ouspensky. Both Mrs. Beaumont and I wanted these two to meet. We succeeded in bringing them together, but little came of it. John de Kay was burning with the desire to help others, but could not see how much he needed help himself. Both Mrs. Beaumont and I wondered what Gurdjieff would have made of him, but by now Gurdjieff was beyond our reach. He had gone off to America with his Russian pupils.

One evening, Ouspensky invited me to a meeting at Ralph Philipson's flat in Portland Place. There were not more than ten of us at this meeting, and it was evidently not a usual occasion. Without preliminaries, Ouspensky began: "I have asked you to come because I must tell you that I have decided to break off all relations with Mr. Gurdjieff.

This means that you have to choose. Either you can go and work with him, or you can work with me; but if you remain with me, you must give an undertaking that you will not communicate in any way with Mr. Gurdjieff or his pupils."

Although I had been aware that something had gone wrong between Ouspensky and the Prieuré, this bald announcement stunned me. Most of us were so much in awe of Ouspensky that we dared not ask for the reason. Only Philipson, a blunt north-country man and, moreover, a very rich man on whom Ouspensky depended, asked the question we all were thinking. Ouspensky was evidently ready for this and, speaking very slowly and carefully, said: "Mr. Gurdjieff is a very extraordinary man. His possibilities are much greater than those of people like ourselves. But he also can go in the wrong way. I believe that he is now passing through a crisis, the outcome of which no one can foresee. Most people have many 'I's. If these 'I's are at war with one another it does not produce great harm, because they are all weak. But with Mr. Gurdjieff there are only two 'I's; one very good and one very bad. I believe that in the end the good 'I' will conquer. But meanwhile it is very dangerous to be near him. We cannot be of any help to him, and in his present condition he cannot be of any help to us. Therefore, I have decided to break off all contact. But this does not mean that I am against him, or that I consider that what he is doing is bad."

Someone said: "If it does go the wrong way, what could happen?"

Ouspensky answered: "He could go mad. Or else he could attract to himself some disaster in which all those round him would be involved."

So far as I can remember, I said nothing. I was much younger than the others who were present, and there was something I could not understand. I wanted desperately to be with Gurdjieff. He was unlike anyone I had known, and he had aroused in me a feeling of love that I had never felt before. I owed him the greatest experience of my life. And yet as my feelings were surging this way and that, I knew that I would not go to Gurdjieff. I was bound to continue to live just as I was living.

In later years, I was often asked why I had not followed Gurdjieff. I do not believe that I was influenced by Ouspensky's warning. It was much rather as if Gurdjieff himself had withdrawn from me and would not let me follow him. Much later, I learned that shortly before this time Gurdjieff had suffered a fearful accident, driving his car at high speed head-on into a tree, on the road from Paris to Fontainebleau. I have heard, from several of those who were living at the Prieuré at that time, of the prodigious spiritual impact upon them of this accident and of the days when Gurdjieff lay unconscious between life and death with such a terrible head injury that his survival seemed beyond possibility. He himself has described this accident, and the events that led up to it, in an autobiographical chapter of overwhelming power that forms part of his unpublished book Life is real only then when I Am. If this book is ever published it will reveal far more effectively than I could hope to do the intensity of the forces at work which destroyed, or at least deferred for many long years, the hopes that many had formed that Gurdjieff's system might change the course of human history.

During the year 1924, I saw a great deal of Ouspensky and helped him with the translation of his books from Russian into English. Although frequently absent from England, I took an active part in Ouspensky's study groups. I believed that this work meant more to me than anything else and that I was prepared to sacrifice anything to achieve the goal of conscious individuality that Ouspensky set before us. I also believed that by the practice of self-observation that I had been pursuing for the past two years I had come to know myself and my own weaknesses. Looking back after a third of a century has passed, I can see that I had not even begun to understand what it all signified.

My outward situation was not easy. John de Kay had left the scene. His American Corporation had failed to carry out its undertakings towards the Princes, and the contract had been formally terminated on their behalf. The project had either to be abandoned or started virtually from the beginning. I felt an obligation towards the Princes to make the attempt. For the first time I was really alone, in the sense that I had no one to whom I could turn for advice and support.

Through an old friend of Mrs. Beaumont, I met various people, and almost spontaneously there was formed a group of men who had made a great deal of money in the war and who wished to find, in new countries, outlets for their capital. I was entrusted with the task of getting a new contract with the Princes. For this I had to travel to Paris, Nice, Rome, Vienna and Budapest. I was generously provided with money for expenses to enable me to entertain the Princes and, where necessary, to make them small advances of money. The next six months were very successful outwardly but not good for my inner life. I went to cabarets and nightclubs in half a dozen cities. I drank too much and went out with women of the strange half-world I had never known. When finally the contracts were signed and I returned to England in triumph, I could only justify the way I had been living as a necessary part of my education. To this day, I do not know if this is true or not. We cannot understand what we have never experienced, but it is not at all certain that it is necessary to understand how those people live whose major incentive to action is the immediate satisfaction of their desires. I see no value in a public confession, but this account of my experiences would not be complete if I did not make it clear that between July 1924 and February 1925 my way of living was quite incompatible with the high ideals I had set before myself.

The contracts were completed at a propitious moment. The Treaty of Lausanne had been ratified and the way was open to negotiate settlements with the successor states. When I went to Budapest, one of the Princes introduced me to Mâitre Simos, a former Minister of Justice in Greece, who assured me that the Greek Government would recognize the private nature of the properties bought by the Sultan. He suggested that the simplest way of obtaining a settlement would be to submit an offer that British capital would be provided for the development of the properties, which included agricultural land, mineral rights and house property in the cities of Macedonia.

This was encouraging, and the thread that was drawing me towards Greece grew stronger when I met in Nice an old friend from Turkey. He was Mâitre Aristidi Georgiades, a Greek lawyer, formerly a member of Abdul Hamid's Mabeyn, and well known as a most able negotiator. He assured me that he could obtain from the Greek Government recognition of the Princes' claims on the basis proposed by Mâitre Simos, whom he knew personally. He referred us to the Greek Ambassador in London, who confirmed that he was persona grata with his Government, and my principals decided that we should make our first attempt at negotiating a settlement in Greece.

When they asked me to go out to conduct the negotiations, I was faced with a dilemma. During my travels I had never been away from London for more than a few weeks and had kept in close touch with Ouspensky's work. This time it meant going away for months, and perhaps years. I went to Ouspensky and asked his advice. Instead of giving a direct reply, he told me a story: "There is a Russian fairy tale of a knight who sets out on a great adventure. He arrives at a place where the road divides into three. Unable to decide which to choose, he sees an old man who tells him that if he goes to the right he will lose his horse, to the left he will lose himself, while if he takes the road in the centre, he will lose both himself and his horse. He reasons with himself that a knight without a horse is helpless, and a horse without a knight is useless, so he might as well risk losing both. He chooses the middle path, and after desperate adventures, in which the old man's prophecy is fulfilled, he finally reaches his goal." Ouspensky added: "You are now in that position. But I may as well tell you that if the knight had chosen either of the other two paths, it would have been the same in the end. Only it was necessary that he should persist and never give up. That is the only condition."

This conversation remains vividly in my memory. There were strong inducements to remain in England. Madame Ouspensky had just come to England, and I was teaching her English while she was teaching me Russian. Ouspensky was allowing me to take a greater part in his work, sharing with Dr. Maurice Nicoll the duty of answering questions at meetings when he himself was absent. I was immensely interested in his teaching and could see a hope of making a contribution of my own. But if I stayed in England, I would have no money to live on.

I said to Ouspensky: "I am sure that this work can lead to the attainment of Consciousness and Immortality, but I am not sure if I can reach it myself. The more I learn about myself, the less do I seem able to achieve anything. In fact, in the last year I have gone back rather than forward."

We were in his little sitting-room in Gwendwr Road, West Kensington. He stood with his back to the gas fire, peering at me as usual through his powerful pince-nez. He sighed deeply and said: "You say that you are sure that this work can lead to consciousness and immortality. I am not sure. I am sure of nothing. But I do know that we have nothing, and therefore we have nothing to lose. For me it is not a question of hope, but of being sure that there is no other way. I have tried too much and seen too much to believe in anything. But I will not give up the struggle. In principle, I believe that it is possible to attain what we seek-but I am not sure that we have yet found the way. But it is useless to wait. We know that we have something that has come from a Higher Source. It may be that something more will come from the same Source."

I was deeply stirred by this sincere confession that Ouspensky himself was still not sure of the way. It gave me far more confidence than any positive affirmation. When I returned and told Mrs. Beaumont, she said that she could not advise me, or even express any opinion. I must decide. If I went to Greece, she would stay behind until my position was clear.

This was a heroic proposal on her part, because I had just been divorced. The proceedings had been very painful to both of us, as my father-in-law had found letters from her in my room when I had last visited my wife and child, and these letters were read in court and widely published in the press. For my own part, I had no doubt at all that I wished to marry her and would do so at the first opportunity. Her own friends warned her against such a step, saying that a marriage with a man twenty-two years her junior could not possibly last. Strangely enough, my mother, though only six years older than Mrs. Beaumont, had become her close friend and was entirely in favour of our marrying.

The arguments and counter-arguments did not touch me. I knew that she was the woman with whom I was to share my life. I was also well aware that she would die before me and that I would be left alone. But I was quite certain that I would never leave her, and so in the event it proved.

So it came about that we set out together for Athens early in April 1925, intending to get married at the British Consulate as soon as we arrived.

12: GREECE - THE END OF A CYCLE

Our arrival in Greece was unusual. We ran into a railway strike, and our train was held up for several days in Larissa, where Mount Olympus looks over the Thessalian plain, across the Vale of Tempe towards Ossa and Pelion. Spring in Thessaly is a poet's dream, and for two days we wandered in the flower-covered foothills of Olympus, wishing that we could be sure of three days delay so that I might climb Olympus and look down upon Thermopylae. I was already beginning to live in the past, and savour the strange delight of hearing names and seeing places that had hitherto been little more than words.

When it became apparent that the strike might last for weeks, and trains ceased to come through from Salonika, I accepted an offer made to me by a Greek driver to take us to Athens by road. He had an old Fiat car, but it seemed solid enough, and we started out with our luggage strapped on the back.

Having no maps and finding my school Greek useless for conversation, I had no means of knowing where we were unless the driver volunteered the name of a town. Each ancient site or city was an unexpected discovery. On the second morning, we reached Lamia, the birthplace of Achilles. Our driver pointed to a great rock at least eighty feet high dominating the whole village and said: "Acropolis Lamia." As we rounded a corner, its sheer face stood boldly out, and even more boldly, painted in enormous letters, each at least ten feet high, was the word Ford! Time had taken its revenge on the Myrmidons.

The next day we passed the Lion of Chaeronea, standing lonely in a cypress grove. Passing through Thebes over Cithaeron, we reached Eleusis by late afternoon. As we rounded the bay of Salamis, the full moon was rising over the hills that hid Athens to the east. I said to Mrs. Beaumont: "I wonder how many moons will rise before we leave Greece?" At the moment I thought it might be four or five. Not fewer than fifty moons were to wax and wane before the Greek adventure ended.

Mrs. Beaumont and I were married the week after our arrival. I did not like to visit the Embassy, although we had friendly introductions, being embarrassed over the publicity that had accompanied my divorce. In the sequel this proved very foolish, as we had been expected and our failure to make ourselves known was misinterpreted as hostility towards our own Government. My task was hard enough without the need to alienate the sympathies of the British colony in Greece.

The difficulty of my situation was soon apparent. My only contact with the Greek Government was through Aristidi Bey, who had all the tortuous secretiveness of a true Mabeynji. He was a small man, with small keen eyes and a small tidy grey beard. He had never learned French or English and preferred Turkish to Greek. He was a perfect vicar of Bray, who had kept his place in the Palace through three reigns and had not lost it when the Dynasty was deposed. He had strings everywhere and, so far as I could see, everyone trusted him as a man who never broke his word. Aristidi understood negotiation as a tortuous game of intrigue. He played upon the need of the Greek Government to placate Turkey; upon the mutual jealousy of Government departments; upon the ambitions of ministers; and did not despise outright bribery. I was no more than a pawn in his game. When it suited his book, I was introduced to ministers or high civil servants; told what to say and when to stop. He did not reject the plan I had brought from England, of offering British capital for the development of the properties, so that the country would derive more benefit by handing them over than retaining them; but he was unwilling to bring it out into the open. He said, probably rightly, that it would only excite the greed of politicians, and we should be held to ransom if it were thought that British capitalists were ready to invest large sums in Greece. Therefore, the plan was kept a close secret to be revealed only to those in whom Aristidi had complete confidence.

He insisted that we must first of all secure formal recognition of the Princes' title and only afterwards bring forward development proposals as a weapon for securing a rapid settlement. When I reported his advice to London, my principals were wholly in agreement and decided that he should be retained as our lawyer to conduct the negotiations in cooperation with myself.

The years 1925 to 1927 were a period of great political instability in Greece. There were two revolutions, leading to the dictatorships of Generals Pangalos and Kondylis. The army was constantly shifting its support. Communist propaganda was powerful, especially among the quarter of a million refugees from Asia Minor who had come to Greece under the exchange of populations agreement, and were mostly living under conditions of miserable hardship. Negotiations that might have been completed in a few months with a stable government, dragged on for years.

An additional complication was introduced by John de Kay who, having won his acquittal in America, was seeking to revive his claims under the old contract. He found a moderately rich American, who was fascinated by the hope of founding a vast enterprise, and came to Athens as representative of the Abdul Hamid Estates Incorporated, whose contract had been annulled owing to failure to make payments promised to the heirs. John de Kay had by now turned implacably against me, and accused me of having stolen his rights. De Kay, who believed that press publicity was an invincible weapon, had prepared press statements promising great benefits to Greece from the investment of American capital. Thus the very great danger that Aristidi wished to avoid was thrust upon us from across the Atlantic. My wife was deeply distressed by de Kay's ingratitude. I could see the situation through his eyes and knew well enough that he was convinced of his own righteousness and my perfidy. I was beginning to learn that people nearly always judge situations without seeing any viewpoint but their own, and I did not want to fall into the same trap.

Although I could see the foolishness of making judgments of right and wrong, I let myself be drawn into a campaign which did harm to everyone and justified Aristidi in his policy of caution and secrecy. I saw for myself the uselessness of any kind of violence, but I was still far from having learned that one must be free from the causes of violence in oneself I disliked it, but I did not see that one must be ready to sacrifice the desire to be ahead of others, if one is not to be drawn into conflict with them.

Long months passed. In any other country the waiting might have been too much for my impatient nature, but in Greece there was an endless interest. My wife was a painter by profession. She had studied with Clausenaar in Brussels, and having won a Slade Scholarship at fifteen, worked with Henry Tonks and the other great Slade teachers of the eighties and nineties. She painted in the impressionist manner, with a rare power of handling bright sunlight effects. She had not painted since she was in Mexico in 1911, and it was with difficulty that I persuaded her to start again. Once launched, nothing would stop her. The light and the colours of Greece suited her style perfectly. She found as models two Greek sisters, fourteen and sixteen years old, of the purest classical beauty. During our stay in Greece she completed over a hundred pictures, some of which she sent to a one-man show at the Brook Street Galleries. They received most encouraging notices.

I myself studied ancient Greek and worked as an amateur assistant with the American School of Archaeology. For my own satisfaction, I made a very detailed survey of the Parthenon, in the hope of elucidating the geometry of the imperceptible curves introduced by the builders to enhance the massive impression made by the building.

We had many adventures during our four years in Greece. One happened soon after our arrival, probably in May, when I received a message from a friend that the volcano on the island of Santorini - the ancient Thyra - had erupted and that a ship was sailing in a few hours with anyone who wished to see it. We made up a party of twelve, with some friends from the French Embassy and several Greeks. We reached Santorini within twenty-four hours of the first eruption and were thus able to witness the rare spectacle of a new island emerging from the sea. In 196 B.C., the island of Thyra had been the scene of a terrifying catastrophe when the entire centre of the island had collapsed into the sea, leaving a narrow ring of island fragments. In 1860, a submarine eruption had brought some land to the surface. For sixty-five years the volcano had remained dormant but had now blown up again.

When we arrived, a billowing column of smoke and steam was rising from the new island in the centre of the bay - about fifteen miles across. The sea rushed into the crater, producing a vast pressure of steam which exploded, throwing high into the air great masses of magma - some as large as a house. A more terrifying natural spectacle can scarcely be imagined. By the time we had moored at the tiny harbour of Santorini beneath a sheer cliff nearly a thousand feet high, the volcano had ceased to erupt, and we hired two rowing boats to visit the new island.

The sea grew hotter and hotter, and a few hundred yards ahead we could see it boiling. Boiled fish were floating beside lumps of pumice stone and fragments of yellow sulphur, making an extraordinary pattern of death in life. One other man and I threw off our clothes and swam in the hot water. The boatman invited us to land on the island and take photographs. It was then several hundred yards across and perhaps half a mile long – newly thrust out of the water and still hot underfoot.

After taking our photographs, we re-embarked and rowed back. Only when we came near the shore, did we realize the foolish risk we had taken, for the island blew up, and where we had been standing twenty minutes earlier was a white hot stream of molten lava. The explosions started again and no one ventured to approach the island for several weeks.

We were not due to sail back till the following evening, so we decided the next morning to take mules and ride across the main island to see some volcanic rock formations described in the guide-book as fantastic beyond words. There were neither hotel nor restaurant on the island, and there was not enough food on board our ship for several hundred passengers. Before starting on our expedition, I took the precaution of bargaining with the owner of the only cafe for a meal for our party. All the hens in the town were being slaughtered, and I was promised roast chicken for twelve. Making, as I thought, sure of my bargain, I paid in advance, and we set out. We rode through miles of desolation where only prickly pear and bitter aloes were growing. The eastern coast of Santorini is more a nightmare than a fantasy. The soft volcanic rock cliff is cut into demonic shapes, and the sea shore is covered with a sulphurous slime. In spite of the torrid heat, none of us cared to bathe in the foetid water, and we returned to Santorini village as the sun was in its zenith - the temperature over 110 degrees in the shade.

Hopefully we entered the cafe, to meet an embarrassed host who had evidently forgotten us. However, he put on an air of sublime confidence and said that all the other travelers had eaten, but that our meal would be ready in a few minutes. We entered the guest-room to find twelve glasses of warm insect-laden water, twelve small slices of bread and twelve plates on which rested, variously curved, but equally repellent, the necks of twelve chickens.

We had many such adventures and learned to like the Greeks - especially the country people, who were hospitable, honest, and full of life and humour.

The autumn and winter of 1926 passed, and the dispute with John de Kay ended with the return of his emissary to America. In the spring of 1926, I was beginning to feel really desperate, when I had an unexpected visitor in the person of Nicholas Nicolopulos, a former secret service agent who had worked during the war for Compton Mackenzie, and is described under the pseudonym of Davy Jones in one of his war books. He had been the hero of extraordinary exploits in the Dardanelles campaign. Later, he had worked for me in Constantinople, where he had met my wife, then still Mrs. Beaumont, and a strange friendship had grown up between them. Both had a debonair disdain for danger and a joy of life that are rare in this century. Nico had been devoted to her and was beside himself with delight to learn that we were now married.

Nico was tall for a Greek, very handsome, with magnificent moustaches and flashing dark eyes. He spoke English well and had an endless fund of stories, many of which were true, about his own heroism and the part he had played in the Allied victory. He was an ardent Venizelist. In spite of his braggadocio, he inspired liking and confidence; but he was born out of his time, and after the war he could find few outlets for his adventurous spirit.

He arrived at our flat in Athens with his usual air of mystery, and prolonged the denouement as long as possible, finally produced with a flourish half a dozen title deeds of lands belonging to the Ottoman Civil List, duly certified by the Land Registry in Kavalla. He offered to act as my agent and undertook to produce all the title deeds if I would supply him with a list of the properties. This was a step which I had not expected to make before we received the recognition 'in principle' for which Aristidi was working. He asked a modest fee for his work, saying that he wished to settle down and hoped that if he proved his value he might be made manager of one of the estates.

When I consulted Aristidi, he was obviously piqued that I had found a valuable ally other than himself, but he could not deny that the title deeds would be a value, especially as the original books were not carefully guarded and might at any time be lost or destroyed. He drew attention to the fact that, notwithstanding the seizure of Abdul Hamid's properties by the Young Turks, none of the properties had been transferred to the Turkish Government or to Greece as the successor state.

It was no longer necessary for me to sit in Athens and wait for Aristidi's next move. I began to travel in Macedonia and Thrace to inspect the properties. My wife came with me on all these journeys, and found new scope for her painting.

One of the places we visited was the mountain of Golema Reka, southwest of Salonika. The name means in Bulgarian 'the Great Rift'. It is a region rarely visited, for it is not known to have any archaeological or historical interest, and being off the main routes is little known, even by the Greeks. We found a Bulgar village that had probably remained for centuries untouched by the political and economic changes of the surrounding world. The villagers spoke Bulgarian, but a few elders knew Turkish and did not seem to realize that the Ottoman Empire had ceased to exist. We saw women weaving on looms that might have been centuries old. The most vivid memory is of the episode during our return on mule-back down a very steep gorge. We met a Bulgar woman striding up the hill, carrying on her head a pile of brush-wood almost her own height, shepherding a flock of goats and at the same time spinning wool on a hand spindle. It was a picture of poise and confidence; every fibre in her body was perfectly in harmony with the movement of her hands and feet, and her eyes alone seemed to keep her flock in rhythm with her own stride. Not until twenty years later, when I watched Basuto villagers working in a remote valley of the Eastern Transvaal, did I see such a demonstration of the natural powers of the human body. No dancer, no acrobat or athlete could match that perfection of balanced movements. We have lost the sense of such physical perfection, and this is part of the heavy price we pay for civilization. Had that woman been obliged to sit in a mechanical vehicle or even perhaps upon one of our modern lavatory seats, she would have lost that unerring sense of balance that enabled her to carry a mass of brushwood weighing nearly a hundred pounds up the rocky slope, while delicately spinning a fine skein of wool without even looking at her hands.

In spite of these journeys, the strain of waiting was affecting me badly. I am by nature so impatient that any kind of waiting seems endless. Having changed considerably with age, I find it hard to recapture the sense of nervous tension with which I drove out two or three times a week for evening conferences with Aristidi, in his richly furnished villa in Kiphissia. But I do remember how I finally broke down and one night, while being driven back to Athens with my wife, began to scream and, when she tried to quieten me, turned and beat her with my fists.

This gave us both a shock, for we had never once quarreled since we met. I knew that I was stretched to breaking and agreed with her proposal to go away for two weeks. This was Easter 1926, just twelve months after my arrival in Greece. We stayed for Easter at Megaspelion, in Arcadia. The mountain railway from Platonos to Kalavryta in the Gulf of Corinth passes through tremendous scenery, past the waters of Lethe, and indeed, within twenty-four hours, I had forgotten my anxieties. We spent Easter in the monastery of Megaspelion, where we heard scandalous tales of the amours of the monks with peasant girls from a village across the valley. Megaspelion claimed to possess a miracle-working ikon of the Blessed Virgin painted by Saint Luke.

Another memory is of standing upon the battlements of Mycaenae and looking eastward over the plain. The essential history of the Greek legends is imperishable. I could see returning Agamemnon and his weary followers and sense the turbulent emotion of Clytemnestra far more vividly than in Aeschylus' presentation of the tragedy. In Greece, I first began to experience the undyingness of the past. I saw that history is more than fact, and that it cannot be known by the mind alone.

When we returned to Athens, I made up my mind to abandon the incessant meetings at which I tried to prod Aristidi into action and devote more of my time to the study of Greek antiquities. I went back again and again to the Acropolis of Athens. I wished to understand how such works of art could have been created. I can say that I studied the Acropolis stone by stone. I visited Mount Pentelikon and saw for myself how the blocks had been quarried; how many, that had fallen from the rollers, still lay on the sides of the hill. I examined the method of doweling with iron and lead and the unbelievable precision with which each stone had been placed in position and faced. Comparing the Parthenon with other Greek buildings of almost the same date, I became convinced that its builders had access to secrets that were already lost a generation later.

I was not less impressed by the archaic statuary then but recently discovered under the foundations of the pre-Periclean building to the east of the Parthenon. Comparing these seventh-century sculptures with those of the classical period, it seemed that I was witnessing a prodigious transition that could not be explained simply as a change of style. Just as the transitions from Solon to Pericles, from Hesiod to Euripides, are not accounted for in terms of mere fact, so also in Greek art the change is too great and too rapid to be explained as simple development.

On the northern slopes of Mount Pentelikon is a little known shrine of the Orpheic cult. Archaeologists believe that the site was abandoned before 500 B.C., when the Greek drama began to supplant the ancient rites. The esoteric cult belonged to the old Epoch. Sitting in the ruins of the shrine, I felt the power of a form of worship which demanded long preparations made in secret; but I realized how foreign to my own convictions was the belief that secrecy was a merit in itself, and that only a chosen few were entitled to participate in the divine mysteries. It is hard for us now to understand how great must have been the spiritual revolution that made all Athenian citizens equal in celebration of the cult in open theatres.

One small event that occurred at this time made a lasting impression upon me. One day, after torrential floods in Athens in which several people had been drowned, I was walking in the Omonia Street, when my gaze was attracted by a horrifying window display consisting of waxen figures representing people dead and dying of the plague. It had been set up to support a campaign to encourage prophylactic inoculation, but the repulsive figures aroused in me quite a different train of thought: 'Here am I with a strong healthy body, but what am I like inwardly? My inner state is as diseased and hideous as any of these figures, but it remains hidden from the outside. I am full of lust and malice, and I cannot change myself. What is the use of a healthy body, if one has a diseased soul? I must change, whatever it costs. I should have disregarded every other consideration and stayed with Gurdjieff. He at least has a method - but I have only theories. He spoke to me of Being the first and last times that I saw him. I know more and more, but I still am nothing. I must be free from all this and return to work upon myself.' This happened when I was just thirty years old. I thought to myself: 'Nearly ten years have passed since I began to search and I still have nothing to show for it. My situation is the same as that of nearly every other man on the earth. If only we could all see ourselves and one another from the inside, as I am seeing now, everything would be changed. Why can we not see? Or seeing, how can we forget?'

When I returned home, I spoke of this experience to my wife, and we agreed that we should try more seriously to put into practice what we had learned from Ouspensky and Gurdjieff. But, alas, the pressure of outer things was too strong for us. I was so deeply involved in what I was doing that there could be no escape, until a decision came one way or another.

My holding aloof from Aristidi had an unexpected result. He began to be alarmed. I saw my opportunity and hinted that my principals were tired of waiting and wanted me to go to another country. It so happened that a change of government brought a friend of Aristidi to a key position. From an almost hopeless situation I found myself, within a few weeks, being invited to attend a meeting at which the form of a recognition in principle of the Princes' rights was agreed and signed.

Since meanwhile Nico Nicolopulos had obtained certified copies of three-quarters of the title deeds, I was able to return to London with an impressive array of documents proving the Princes' title to several hundred large estates, totalling in value several million pounds and including some of the finest tobacco lands in western Thrace. My principals were delighted and offered me a contract as Managing Director of the Aegean Trust, with a salary of 5000 pounds a year and authority to set up an office in Athens to prepare a development project acceptable to the Greek Government, on a condition of giving us possession of the lands and buildings. At the age of thirty, it seemed that my dreams of an early retirement from business might be realized.

While in London I had several meetings with Ouspensky, who encouraged me to invite two of Gurdjieff's former pupils, Ferapontoff, my former instructor at the Prieuré, and Ivanoff, a young Russian accountant, to join my staff. Ferapontoff had emigrated to Australia but had failed to make the contacts hoped for and was anxious to return to Europe. I took out with me an English secretary, and agricultural experts were to follow as soon as the permission of the Greek Government was obtained. My mother came out to Athens to pay us a visit. I found that Aristidi was looking forward to another series of complicated negotiations and was quite unwilling to sponsor a direct official approach. The friendly attitude of the Greek Government turned to hostility under pressure of the refugees from Turkey, who had seized many of the unoccupied lands belonging to the Princes on the pretext - or perhaps rather the genuine belief - that they had been owned by Turks who had been repatriated to Asia Minor. I began to be acutely aware of my own inadequacy as a negotiator. Two and a half years of dependence upon Aristidi Georgiades had deprived me of the direct contact with Greek

Government officials that was now indispensable.

Nevertheless, by the beginning of March 1928, I had been able to secure a genuine response to a plan to combine the land development with an irrigation project, based upon utilization of the waters of Lake Edessa. On the morning of 21st March I went as usual to my office to find half a dozen Greek police in possession. They showed me a telegram from the Greek Juge d'Instruction - Examining Magistrate - in Kavalla, ordering my arrest on the charge of forging title deeds. I was taken to the police station without opportunity of speaking to anyone. My resourceful secretary, Miss Pearson, informed my wife, who notified Aristidi. He immediately took fright and refused to be concerned in the affair. She found another lawyer and began to fight for my release.

It was already very hot in Athens, and the cell in the police station had no furniture but a wooden bed and a chair. I can remember vividly my impressions. Knowing that Nico Nicolopulos was capable of anything, it was quite possible that, without my knowledge, he had been up to some unlawful business, and I would have no means of proving that I was ignorant of what he might have done. I might be found guilty and sent to prison, and I could not look to the British Government for help. The whole thing might be a plot of the Greek Government to discredit our claims, and, if so, all the evidence might be well prepared against me.

At that moment my state of consciousness changed, and I saw that all this had no importance. I had allowed myself to be drawn away from my real aim, and anything would be better for me, even prison, than continuing to engage in affairs that involved so much intrigue; affairs which, even if successful, would never give me any true freedom. I lay on the bed and went peacefully to sleep. When I awoke, I was told that I was to be taken to the Athens &Psychokinetcisprison to await the arrival of the Examining Magistrate from Kavalla.

The next few weeks were among the most interesting and valuable of my whole life. Those who have never been in prison, with complete uncertainty as to when they might be released, can never know the experiences of a prisoner. Certainly, the Athens prison of 1928 was unlike our modern ideas of a prison. There, murderers and brigands, drug addicts and prostitutes, political prisoners and men merely accused and awaiting trial were all thrown together in a community of several hundred. I was the only foreigner, but by that time I could speak Greek as easily as English and was soon made at home. The wildest rumours spread through the prison: I was an anarchist, a murderer, a forgerer, an incendiary, a British spy. None of this seemed to matter; the one certain fact was that I belonged to the fraternity of those who are behind bars.

The complete absence of privacy, the door locked upon one's cell at night, the ever-burning lights - all these make a world which thousands know, but which is none the less strange for one who enters it for the first time.

By day, those of us who were still only 'suspected persons' were free to wander through the prison and to receive our friends. There was no 'prison food', and prisoners had to pay for food that they received. Thus, a prisoner convicted of some small offence might find himself at the end of his sentence confronted with a bill he could not pay. Those who had no outside friends to help them might linger on for months, unless some richer prisoner would pay their debts. As any Englishman was regarded eo ipso as a rich man, I at once began to receive deputations asking for my help for such and such a one, with long pitiable details of his condition. Having nothing better to do, I set myself to examine each case, with a view to helping those in real need. Only then did I become aware of the extreme poverty that can exist in a country like Greece. Many steal literally from hunger, and on the whole they are leniently treated until the moment comes for leaving prison and paying the bill.

A fellow-feeling existed in the Athens prison that included the wardens and guards. Entering such a prison one loses one kind of freedom, but one gains another. So many of the things that matter in ordinary life do not touch one at all in a prison.

The condemned prisoners were confined to long, cavernous cellars, one end of which had a wall of iron bars from floor to roof and an iron door. One of these contained between fifty and sixty drug addicts and, if I remember rightly what I was told, men condemned for sexual offences. It was a filthy horror that vividly reminded me of the experience on Omonia Street a few months before. Here, at least, the revolting qualities that infect our human nature were visible on the surface. I went several times to stand before the iron grille and watch this foetid mass of human beings, mostly in rags. Sometimes a man would begin to scream and throw himself on the others, who beat him off until he fell exhausted upon one of the wooden racks that lined the wall. The mass was never still, producing the impression of some monster writhing in the slime, in which the traits of individual men disappeared. I was horror-struck but fascinated, for I had never previously seen for myself the degradation of human nature which can result from a material cause like drug-taking. The condition of the thieves and swindlers appeared to be much more normal, and yet, if one started to make a moral assessment, it was not easy to say that the unfortunate man who had slipped helplessly into the habit of taking drugs was morally worse than the swindler who, keeping his health, had perhaps ruined the lives of innocent people.

I myself suffered little hardship. My wife brought me food every day, prepared by a devoted and enthusiastic Greek cook who looked upon me as a hero, being convinced that I had been put in prison 'because of Venizelos'. My lawyer had gone to Kavalla and was satisfied that a simple mistake had been made. The Examining Magistrate was young and inexperienced and had acted upon a rumour that my agent, Nico Nicolopulos, was obtaining forged title deeds in order to evict the peasants from their tobacco fields. Nevertheless, the situation was extremely awkward. There had been so much publicity that to drop the case would be damaging to Greek prestige and, moreover, greatly strengthen our case, as it would imply admission that our title deeds were good. There had been no forgery or falsification of any kind, but the local registry offices should have reported that they were being asked to issue certified copies, and had they done so, would probably have been instructed to refuse. Nico had acted within the law, but he had persuaded the registrars to act incautiously.

Meanwhile I remained in prison, and my wife and mother came daily to visit me. My poor little mother was terribly distressed. She understood nothing of what had happened, and no one had time to explain it to her. One of my co-directors, Shirley H. Jenks, arrived from London to take charge of the Aegean Trust interests. He advised my mother to go straight back to England. She preferred to go to her sister in Florence, and he hustled her on to a ship before my wife could restore her confidence. She was not distressed by the event in itself, but by the fear that I had inherited my father's weakness and got myself into trouble, as he had so often done when we were children.

Various solutions were proposed to my lawyers and brought to me for approval. One was that the Greek Government should drop the case, if I would agree to leave the country. This was obviously unacceptable, as it would be equivalent to abandoning our claims with no valid reason. Another even more shocking suggestion was that poor Nico, who meanwhile was held prisoner in Kavalla, should be made a scapegoat and condemned for bribery and corruption, while I was declared innocent through ignorance of my agent's doings. As there was no evidence whatever that Nico had bribed any official in the course of his manoeuvres, it was manifestly unfair to fasten blame on him. Indeed, I am fairly confident that Nico's method consisted far more of cajolery over a flask or two of wine than of any illicit payment. He never had enough money from me to pay bribes.

It was then proposed that I should be released on bail. This seemed simple and obvious enough, but by now Aristidi Georgiades had re-entered the picture. Realizing that a mistake had been made, he changed completely round and was intent upon exploiting the Greek Government's embarrassment to force action upon the specific recognition of the disputed title deeds. He urged that we should insist upon my unconditional release. After several weeks of bickering, no solution had been found. My wife took the situation in hand. A Greek friend of hers, a Red Cross nurse, assured her that I could easily feign sickness, and the authorities would be alarmed and promptly release me. The method proposed proved to be very disagreeable for me personally. I was to be suspected of appendicitis, for which I had to describe certain symptoms and have a high temperature. The latter would come without any difficulty if I would drink a quantity of iodine an hour or two before I was examined by the doctor.

The only place where the iodine could be drunk secretly was in the latrines, which I would have preferred not to mention, for they were filthy beyond words. The prisoners were supposed to clean them, but they were never inspected, and it is really surprising that serious diseases were not contracted by those who used them. I confess that I was afraid. I had been warned that for a few minutes the effect would be unpleasant; and, notwithstanding the assurance that drinking iodine does no real harm, I had little confidence in the whole plan. However, I was committed to the attempt and at the first opportunity went down to the subterranean horror and drank the prescribed amount. The iodine seemed to burn the skin off my throat and I choked, hardly able to breathe for more than a minute. I began to shiver and could scarcely return to my cell, where I lay gasping on the bed with all the symptoms of acute fever. The doctor was due to visit me two hours later - but after I had waited for four hours, feeling really ill, a warder came and told me that he had been prevented from coming and would come the next day.

The thought of repeating the performance nearly made me lose courage and I must have looked very ill, for the warden became alarmed and offered to send for the prison doctor. As it had been arranged that an independent doctor should examine me, I had to refuse and passed a most unpleasant night. However, by morning the effect of the iodine had worn off, and by the time my wife came to visit me, I was able to go out and meet her. She was horrified by my appearance, but went off and returned later with another small flask of iodine - feeling that, at all costs, she must get me away from the prison.

It is difficult, in cold blood, to subject oneself to physical suffering - and I was still afraid that something might go wrong. Moreover I felt the utmost nausea at the very thought of returning to the latrines. But such disagreeable experiences also produce some degree of separation of the inner from the outer man. I was beginning to feel inwardly detached from the body that was being so unkindly treated, and, by this time, found myself able to go through the whole process as if it were happening to a stranger. The ruse succeeded. A certificate for medical treatment was given the same evening, and I was taken to a nursing home. My wife, who had herself been very ill with bronchitis during the critical weeks, had never missed a visit to the prison and had hidden her own sufferings from me, so that I knew nothing of her illness until after my release. My mother had already left for Florence, where she spent a few weeks with her sister at the Villa Lemmi.

Then began another long series of manoeuvres to bring the case to trial. The Greek authorities had every interest in allowing the proceedings to drag on. While they were pending, it was impossible to make headway with the negotiations, and although the Ministry of Public Works was favourably disposed towards the irrigation schemes, it could not move without appearing to prejudice the interests of the refugees who had squatted on some of the farms.

The Examining Magistrate completed his researches and found no evidence of forgery. Meanwhile, Nico Nicolopulos died in prison in Kavalla - the circumstances of his death were never clarified, but it was certified as a heart failure, which was perfectly possible. I felt very sad when I learned of Nico's death, for I could have obtained his release on bail and had allowed myself to be overruled by the lawyers, who had insisted that he would stand better before the court if he was presented as the victim of an injustice.

In order to put pressure on the Greek authorities, I was advised to go and live in Kavalla, where, strangely enough, the case should have been heard in a minor court. My wife and I spent six or eight weeks in this little Greek seaport. The Greeks have the capacity of dreaming of greatness, even when the facts proclaim weakness and poverty. This has been their strength, as when they were the first of the Sultan's subjects to throw off the Turkish yoke in the time of Byron. But it can also be ridiculous, as when my wife and I, walking past a small white-washed house in the outskirts of humble Kavalla, saw an immense notice-board on which were painted the words 'Pan-Cosmic School of Dancing'! In dealing with the Greeks one has always to take account of their Pan-Cosmic dreams, but also to remember not to take them too seriously.

While waiting in Kavalla, with quite literally nothing to do, I occupied myself by making a concordance of the Upanishads. I had with me the Sanskrit text and English translation of the six principal

Upanishads, and working for several hours a day, I made a concordance that I still have and use. I also began to see some of the psychological significance of the peculiar sequences of ideas. It seemed to me that Western students - who, following Schopenhauer, have valued the Upanishads as expressions of a lofty monism, or who have relied upon commentators like Shankaracharya who, writing a thousand years after they were composed, had lost touch with the psychological meaning of ritual - had missed much that could be learned from these ancient works.

Kavalla lies in a broad bay beyond which is the island of Thasos, with its great mountain peak that glows in the setting sun. Away to the southeast is the Holy Mountain of Athos, visible on most days in the clear Greek light. I wanted to visit Mount Athos, but from week to week put off making the journey, expecting that I would be in Kavalla until the cool weather of autumn. One day, a telegram arrived asking me to go to London for a conference with my principals. I left the next day with Mount Athos unvisited, enriched only by the lesson that we should take our chances when they present themselves and not wait for a more convenient 'tomorrow'.

When I reached London, I found an embarrassed group of men who clearly wanted to get rid of me. In truth, I felt my position acutely. I had done nothing either legally or morally wrong, and yet I had brought the whole project to the brink of disaster. I had recommended Nicolopulos, and Aristidi had not failed to remind us of his advice to leave the title deeds in abeyance until a settlement had been reached. It is a very common human characteristic that when we give contradictory advice, we tend to remember only that which proves to be right. I offered my resignation as Managing Director, and the Chairman agreed to buy the shares in the company which had been allotted to me. The company undertook to pay the costs of my defence. I remained in England for Christmas 1928, with the feeling that my entire life was suspended and with no idea what direction it would take next. I occupied my spare time playing games of chess, took part in the Hastings Christmas Congress and also played in matches for Kent. Playing on the second board, I had the opportunity of meeting many of the best players in England. This experience helped me to see better a serious defect of my nature. I could evaluate positions as well as really good players, but my impetuosity made me lose games that I should have won. Such I was, and such I have remained. It is not true to say that seeing one's defects is half-way to remedying them. Human beings in general do not learn from their own mistakes, any more than from those they see made by others. To a small degree, we are conditioned by experience - like Pavlov's dogs - but we do not learn from it.

This was the year 1929, when the economic systems of the world tottered. I could do nothing to earn my living, and my wife and I lived quietly in London. I had no contact with Ouspensky, for reasons to be described in the next chapter. My mother had returned and recovered her usual calm. During the months of waiting, I began to write, trying to express my conviction that the invisible world of eternal potentialities is continuously connected with the world of actual events. I was drawn, in this way, back to the study of mathematics that I had neglected for eight years.

Winter passed into spring, spring into summer, and at length I received a cable to say that the date of my trial had been fixed for 27th September, and that it was to be before the Court of Appeal in Salonika, the capital of Macedonia. My wife and I returned to Athens by the Orient Express, on which we had made so many journeys. The case lasted sixteen days, three of which I spent in the witness box. I decided - against the advice of my lawyers - to dispense with an interpreter. At that time, I could speak modern Greek really well, but they were afraid I might be trapped into some admission. It was clear from the opening of the prosecution that in all these months no evidence against me had been discovered and the only danger could come from myself. Yet I was obstinate, being quite sure that I could hold my own. My examination and cross-examination lasted many hours, and at the end, the Public Prosecutor, Mr. George Exarhopoulos, rose and said that he was unable to present any evidence of guilt and proposed our acquittal. The court awarded us costs against the Greek Government and the much publicized 'Affair of the Forged Deeds' ended as ineptly as it had begun.

One effect of the decision was to strengthen the Princes' claim. The group which was financing the Aegean Trust was feeling, like everyone else in the world, the onset of the Great Depression. The prospect of any large capital investment in Greece had disappeared. What might have been a glorious opportunity of providing work for tens of thousands of Greek refugees had been lost. The Greek Government itself was passing through a grave crisis, and when, at the end of the year, Venizelos returned to power with the hope of a stable government, there was little to be done.

Nevertheless, the Aegean Trust decided to continue the negotiations. It was obvious that I could no longer help and I was very grateful to receive generous compensation of the termination of my contract. I felt much worse about myself than others felt about me. A phase of my life that had lasted eight years had ended in failure. Since the age of twenty-four, I had been engaged in the affairs of the Abdul Hamid succession. I was now thirty-two and Ouspensky's prophecy that I would lose both my horse and myself had been fulfilled. It was not easy to make a fresh start, for the strain of the last twelve months had left its mark on me. I had grown very weak physically; the tuberculosis that was to invade my lungs four years later had probably already taken root and I had an emaciated appearance that alarmed my friends. I had lost confidence in myself, feeling that everything I touched must fail. I wanted very much to return to the work with Ouspensky, but I had no prospect of making a living in England.

13: BACK TO SCIENCE

The years from 1929 to 1933 were a period of great transitions in my life. During this time my close connection with the Near East, which had lasted for fourteen years, was broken. From being an international adventurer, I became a scientific worker engaged in a specialized field of industrial research. The change in my inner life is harder to describe, but no less definite. I had hitherto looked only for my own personal self-realization; I now began to feel myself responsible for the welfare of others.

According to an ancient tradition, a man's soul is ready to be born only when he reaches his thirty-third year. No doubt, this tradition is connected with the mystical participation in the death and resurrection of Christ; but I first learned of it from a Muslim source many years after the time of which I am writing. Nevertheless, as I look back, it seems to me that my bitter experiences in Athens were a kind of dying; and that when I returned to England, a new life began.

My own connection with Greece was not yet to end. During the trial in Salonika, I received a visit from a Greek engineer, a casual acquaintance from Athens named Dimitri Diamandopoulos. He told me that he was convinced that I had been the victim of an anti-Venizelist conspiracy and had been impressed during the trial by my exposition of our plans for the development of the Turkish Estates. He was the sole owner of a concession for the Vevi Brown Coal Mine, but having no financial connections could not develop it on a large scale. He offered me as a free gift a half share in the mine, if I would go and visit it before returning to London and would help him with its development.

Having no pressing reason for returning immediately, my wife and I decided to go. I confess that I was greatly heartened by this mark of confidence, so remote from my own inner attitude of distrust towards myself. I was also attracted by the idea that I might do something constructive for Greece, a country that, despite my tribulations, I had come to love.

When the trial was over, my wife and I went by train to Edessa, a town famous in early Church history, that lies in the foothills of the Albanian uplands. Here Diamandopoulos met us, and we went by car through the Vodena gorge up to Lake Ostrovo, which lies a hundred miles west of Salonika, at an altitude of two thousand feet above sea level. It is a remarkable geographical feature in many ways. About fifteen miles long and six miles across at its widest, it is enormously deep; in fact at that time its deepest waters had never been plumbed. Great catfish, up to two hundred pounds in weight, are sometimes caught in the depths. It has the remarkable property of changing its level by about thirty feet, in a cycle of about seventy years. This is explained by the presence of vast caves in the limestone mountain of Golema Reka, which I had previously visited from the east. By some kind of siphon action, these caves periodically empty and fill from the waters of Ostrovo, which has no direct outlet to the sea. When the railway to Tirnovo was built in 1880, the level had been low. By 1910 it had risen and submerged the line. When I was there in 1929 the level was again falling, and the old rails had just appeared.

To the north of Ostrovo we entered a wild, sparsely inhabited plateau containing close to the surface, great deposits of brown coal. We stayed at the village of Vevi, then a tiny hamlet with barely twenty houses, and were made welcome by a Greek village family. It was an immense relief to be for a time far from city life and from the people we knew.

At that time northwest Macedonia was a wild undeveloped country. The swamps round Ostrovo were a natural sanctuary for every kind of marsh bird. There were also mountain birds. On our first morning, we saw a pair of great white eagles flying down from the Albanian mountains twenty or thirty miles away. They were superb creatures, credited with the ability to carry off a full-grown sheep or goat. The villagers would not attempt to shoot them in spite of their depredations, believing that they brought good luck to the village.

The Vevi Brown Coal Mine consisted of a simple adit, or horizontal gallery, driven into the side of a steep gulley. The main seam was some forty feet in thickness and composed mainly of xylite or woody brown coal. Trunks of trees that covered Southern Europe ten million years ago were carried down in great floods and deposited. They can still be recognized, piled up against carbonized tree trunks still in situ. It was my first sight of a great deposit of coal, and it excited my interest beyond all expectations. The picture of intense reserves of energy preserved for millions of years under the soil, and waiting for man to come and use them, was a challenge of a kind I had never met before. I made up my mind to do what I could to help Diamandopoulos, and hurried back to England.

The only mining expert I knew was James Douglas-Henry, who had been one of my competitors in the negotiations with the Abdul Hamid heirs. We had become good friends, and he had met and instantly admired Ouspensky. While I was away in Greece, he and his wife had joined Ouspensky's circle.

My own relationship with Ouspensky had gone wrong. When I

finally returned to London in the autumn of 1929 and telephoned for an appointment with him, I met with a rude shock. Mr. Ouspensky would not see me and had forbidden his pupils to see or speak to me on any pretext. It was only in 1930 that I discovered the cause of my rejection. When I was arrested, Ouspensky had sent me a friendly telegram saying: 'Sympathy to Bennett under ninety-six laws.' This was a reference to Gurdjieff's doctrine that man lives on earth under forty-eight kinds of limitations or restrictions upon his freedom of action. By his own folly and weakness he can fall under more and more limitations. The limit is reached when he comes under ninety-six laws or restrictions, for then he loses all possibility of choosing what he will do.

I was only too well aware of the justice of the reproach implied in the telegram and did not feel myself in any way cut off. Ferapontoff and Ivanoff soon returned to England, and when I went back in the autumn of 1928, I had seen them, together with Ouspensky.

It transpired, however, that when the Greek police had perquisitioned my flat in March 1928, they had taken away all the letters they found. These had included two or three from Ouspensky which, seeing the Russian name, they had imagined might indicate some Communist affiliation. The letters had not been returned to me, but had been handed to the British Embassy in case they should have some political significance.

The result of this was that, while I was in Kavalla, Ouspensky had been called to the Home Office and questioned about his possible connection with Bolshevik Russia. He was quite fanatical in his hatred of Bolshevism, and the mere suggestion that he might have had some connection with Communism had so angered him that he could not easily forgive me. Moreover, his experience in Russia had made him deeply suspicious of the police, and he felt it would be safer to cut off all connection with anyone so lacking in caution as I evidently was.

At first I was dismayed. I thought of returning to Gurdjieff. Having an opportunity of going to Paris, I went out to the Prieuré and asked for him. The lodge keeper, a Frenchman, said that the Russians had gone away, but knew no more. I made enquiries in Paris and could learn nothing about him. Later, I heard that at that time he was in the United States and was entering a critical period in his own development. Having completed his writing, he was preparing himself for a fresh attempt to put into practice the psycho-cosmological system he had been evolving since his boyhood. He was not in touch with pupils in Europe. I was thus cut off from any source of help in my spiritual life.

My wife and I took very cheap lodgings in Pimlico, so that my small capital should not be wasted. In spite of the Depression - or perhaps because of it - I did not find it hard to get support for the brown coal project, which required little expenditure. Douglas-Henry introduced me to a Jewish financier, who assured me that he could produce all the capital required if we would submit good technical reports.

A few months later, my wife and I returned to Greece and went up to Vevi, this time with Douglas-Henry as the mining expert. He had to make some borings to prove the extent of the coal deposits. The seam being near to the surface, this did not take long. During this time I was collecting information about the market for brown coal, transport facilities, availability of labour and so on. The work delighted me because it had an objective quality that had been missing in the affair of the Abdul Hamid Succession.

While at Vevi, we witnessed an event that has no doubt often been described, but was new and deeply impressive for me. The Ostrovo swamps were, that summer, the rendezvous of storks from all over Europe. Storks are common in Macedonia, but they began arriving in flights of six, ten, twenty and more. This continued for four or five days, with an atmosphere of growing excitement in the swamps. There were trial flights of larger and larger flocks, and an unending clatter of stork voices. Then early one morning, we heard a great sound and hastened out of doors to see the entire swamp alive with birds rising. We were to the South of the swamps, which stretched northward for miles. The immense concourse of birds took shape as a great dense column, with single scouts flying at a distance of about a hundred yards from the main body. They flew straight overhead literally darkening the sky. I tried to count them, but when I reached six hundred I could count no more; the impression was too powerful to be expressed in numbers.

I could not doubt that I was in the presence of an intelligence that operates quite differently from the mind of man. Long after the birds had passed, I remained standing in astonishment. I had become aware of a collective consciousness that remembers and sees and knows the complex pattern of stork life, and yet neither thinks nor expresses itself in words. This collective consciousness must somehow hold, in unity of life and purpose, tens of thousands of storks, scattered through the summer over the house-tops of Europe. It draws its members together, and for a brief spell the great Stork Being becomes visible as an articulated whole and then disperses again along the riverbanks of Egypt and Ethiopia.

We know little of such societies and the collective consciousness in which they share. As I stood in the deep silence left by the great birds, I caught a glimpse of the future of mankind. One day, we shall become aware of the collective consciousness of humanity. It may take millions of year, but when it comes, it will be a power incomparably greater than that of any living species. In this vision, there was also a promise that the time was not so far distant when the human race would make a step forward and begin to look beyond the narrow loyalties of nation, race and religion, towards the distant goal of human unity.

What I saw engendered in me a state of exultation which lasted for several days. I spoke to my wife of what I had seen and of my wish when we returned to London to share my vision with others. It was a verification of much that I had learned from Gurdjieff and Ouspensky, and if I could no longer learn from them, I must begin to work with others. I was convinced that it is useless to attempt to work alone. She went further than I dared, saying: "You have been given this vision because you have your own task to do. You have relied too much on others. If Ouspensky has turned you out, it may be because he knows that you should be working on your own. You must gather your own people round you and make your own school. You make a mistake in not trusting yourself and your own powers."

I could not accept what she said. I was acutely aware of my own defects. I remembered also the vision that had come to me in Scutari eight years before, when I had been shown that the true significance of my life would not be visible until I was sixty years old. I was convinced that I was still being prepared and that I was far from ready to undertake any spiritual work on my own.

Nevertheless, the state of enhanced consciousness which had come upon me had one tangible result. The next day I went to the brown coal mine, and as I looked at a face freshly cut by Douglas-Henry, I saw that some of the wood had been turned into charcoal, evidently by forest fires millions of years ago.

As I looked, the thought occurred to me, 'Why should it not all be turned into charcoal, which is the main cooking fuel in all the Greek towns and villages? The forests are being devastated to supply charcoal. Here is a cheap and plentiful supply.'

As soon as I saw Douglas-Henry I told him of my thought, and we immediately made the experiment of charring some of the dried brown coal. The result was so startlingly like charcoal that we both became enthusiastic. Greece was at that time dependent upon imports of charcoal from Yugoslavia, and here was a chance not only of making her self-supporting, but of sending exports to all the Mediterranean countries which still largely use charcoal as fuel.

I returned to England with more samples of the brown coal and lignite, and took myself to a source of knowledge that had never failed me, the library of the British museum. I could find few books on coal, and none of these could tell me much about lignite. I decided to make my own experiments. Chemistry had been my best subject at school, although my heart was given to mathematics. I learned that the Northern Polytechnic Institute gave facilities for private research and inscribed myself as a research student in coal chemistry. My first experiments were disappointing; for although I could produce a charcoal, it burned with a most unpleasant smell and would be quite useless as a fuel for cooking in open braziers. The Head of the Department, who had become interested in what I was doing, advised me to consult the fuel Research Board and introduced me to the Director, the late Dr. C.H. Lander, a most kindly and unselfish man who went out of his way to help me.

I made a preliminary report, which was so well received that a company called the Grecian Mining and Development Company was formed; capital was subscribed and I was made managing director. I went and told my story to Sir John Stavridi, then chairman of the Ionian Bank and a close friend of Venizelos. He was most encouraging. Sir Sydney Lawford, a friend of Douglas-Henry, a retired general, became chairman of the company, and offices were opened near London Wall.

My wife and I moved into a comfortable flat near Bryanston Square and began to renew old friendships, in the hope that some of these people might be interested in studying and working with me. Nothing came of these plans, but two or three meetings, seemingly accidental, changed the picture. My wife went to Switzerland to see Prince Sabaheddin and take him a little money. In the train she met a young man, Lucien Myers, to whom she spoke about our ideas and so fired him with enthusiasm that he asked to join a study group. Soon after her return to London, on a Number 16 bus between Hyde Park Corner and Victoria, she met a woman, Mrs. Beeban Dobie, who responded eagerly to her proposals for study. I met a young and brilliant chemist at the Northern Polytechnic who wanted to find a wider world picture than science could offer. My wife's sister, an opera singer, had just come from Paris to live in England, and joined our circle with two of her musical friends.

In this way, at random and without plan, came into existence early in 1930 the first study group for which I took personal responsibility. We met at our flat for one or two preliminary meetings. When I saw that there was a serious wish to study, I pondered deeply upon my own situation. I did not feel that it was right for me to set myself up as an expositor of Gurdjieff's System without permission either from him or from Ouspensky. Finally, I decided that I would go forward but make a full report of each meeting and send it to Ouspensky. In sending the reports, I wrote to say that if he disapproved he had only to tell me, and I would stop.

For months, no word came. The group slowly grew. The meetings were a great stimulation for me personally. I began to make efforts to struggle with my own weaknesses and habits, such as I had not made for years. I have preserved copies of many of the reports I sent to Ouspensky at that time. What I said was right and often interesting; but it is painfully clear, reading them after nearly thirty years, that I was still devoid of true human feeling. I worked and I taught with my intellect only. My heart was cold, and not even the vision of human unity vouchsafed to me at Vevi could make me feel the warmth of human fellowship. I still merited the rebuke in my last report from school, when the headmaster wrote of me: 'He suffers from intellectual arrogance.'

I spoke convincingly about the distinction between knowing and being. I could remember how each of Gurdjieff's talks with me had been variations upon this theme. But I did not yet understand what I myself was saying. I did not grasp the simple truth that I had been given the taste of being, but not its substance. I was as weak and as riddled with inconsistencies as any other man, and as ignorant of myself.

The summer of 1930 passed. Real progress was being made with the brown coal project. I was beginning to recover the confidence I had lost in 1928. At the beginning of October, I received an unexpected telephone message from Ouspensky's secretary, Madame Kadloubovsky: "Mr. Ouspensky says that you and Mrs. Bennett with Mr. Myers, Mrs. Dobie, Mr. Binyon and Major Turner may come to a lecture at Warwick Gardens next Wednesday." This was the first and only indication that Ouspensky had ever read my reports.

The lecture was the first of a series called, as well as I can remember, 'The Search for Objective Consciousness'. They aroused great interest in London. Ouspensky had allowed nearly seven years to pass since his break with Gurdjieff. During that time he had continued to work with some forty or fifty pupils, under conditions of strict secrecy. He had decided that the time had now come to make his work more widely known. Without a word about the past, he not only allowed me to attend his meetings, but very soon gave me the task of reading the lectures aloud in his presence. Often the same lecture would have to be repeated two or three times in a week, so great was the influx of people interested or merely curious.

Ouspensky allowed me to go and visit him at Gwendwr Road, as I had done five years earlier. At one of these private talks he said to me:

"I waited for all these years because I wanted to see what Mr. Gurdjieff would do. His work has not given the results he hoped for. I am still as certain as ever that there is a Great Source from which our System has come. Mr. Gurdjieff must have had a contact with that Source, but I do not believe that it was a complete contact. Something is missing, and he has not been able to find it. If we cannot find it through him, then our only hope is to have a direct contact with the Source. But there is no chance for us to find it by looking, of that I have been convinced for nearly twenty years. It is much better hidden than people suppose. Therefore, our only hope is that the Source will seek us out. That is why I am giving these lectures in London. If those who have the real knowledge see that we can be useful to them, they may send someone. We can only show what we can do and wait. But we must understand that we cannot really do anything for ourselves. The essential secret is still missing. We can prepare ourselves, and we can prepare others, but we can do nothing positive."

Nearly twenty years were to pass before I began to grasp the significance of what Ouspensky said on this occasion. For my part, I was concerned with a much more personal problem: that of reconciling the acceptance of responsibility with the renunciation of self-will. I felt a desperate need to deepen my spiritual life. I was too easily distracted by worldly affairs, and it seemed to me that lack of persistence was my chief failing. I therefore decided to set myself the task of keeping a journal. I had never succeeded in keeping a diary; something in my nature objected to anything that would bind me to the past. As New Year's Day, 1931, approached, I thought deeply about my situation. It seemed that I might succeed within three years in gaining freedom from material cares, and I wanted to prepare to devote myself wholly to the spiritual work.

Finally, on 1st January, I took a vow with myself to begin in three days to keep a journal for a thousand days, and to write in it every single day what I had done to keep my spiritual work alive, and also where I had failed. On 1st October 1933, I wrote: "The period I set myself is ended and I have no tangible results to show for my work. Nevertheless, I have gained the minimum which I set for myself."

Many bitter lessons still awaited me, the first of which was to come through the Greek Lignite project. I was pleased and not a little proud that my own chemical researches had shown that the evil smell of the lignite charcoal came from small traces of sulphur compounds called mercaptans. I found that if the temperature of charring was raised above 900° C, these compounds were destroyed. The problem was to find a way of doing this on a commercial scale.

Dr. Lander introduced me to Dr. E.W Smith, then Technical Director of the Woodall-Duckham Company, the pioneers of gas manufacture in continuous vertical retorts. These gave just the conditions required for my process, and the City of Birmingham Gas Department most generously put their unique experimental retorts at our disposal. A trial run proving most successful, we decided upon a large-scale test lasting three days, for which forty tons of brown coal were brought from Greece.

Eleutherios Venezelos, Prime Minister of Greece with the author in Birmingham, 1933

It happened that Mr. Venizelos, then Prime Minister of Greece, was coming to England, and he came with the Greek minister in London to witness the tests. A civic luncheon, with a speech of welcome by Austen Chamberlain, was followed by a visit to Nechells' gas works in pouring rain. The demonstration was an outstanding success. Sir Sydney Lawford, who had joined the company with misgivings, was now delighted. Venizelos invited him to Greece as the guest of the Government.

I wrote up the results, together with a detailed survey of the needs and potentialities of Greece as a market for fuel. This was published with the title Problems of the Greek Fuel Industry. It was my first appearance in print, and I was very proud of it. The stage was set for a great scheme of development, which was to include cement works to use the fine charcoal unsuitable as domestic fuel and a power station to supply electricity to Salonika, in conjunction with a hydro-electric station using the Edessa waterfalls.

On one of my rare visits to Greece in connection with our industrial development project, Douglas-Henry told me that he had been urged to visit and report upon a reputed gold mine in the mountains east of Salonika. He suggested that we might take a few days off and see for ourselves. He had prospected for gold in Australia and could soon tell if there was anything in the claim.

It seems that a Greek who had emigrated to Colorado when young and had become a prospector for gold, having returned home to settle, felt the urge to search for gold in his native mountains. Finding ancient workings abandoned since the time of Philip of Macedon, he had explored and claimed to have hit upon a vein of gold-bearing quartz.

To this day, I cannot tell whether the whole business was a hoax. He showed samples of rich quartz, which might have come from Macedonia or indeed from many other places. When I returned to London, a little historical research showed that gold certainly had been worked in antiquity in the mountains north of Salonika; and there was just a possibility that veins might be found too poor to be worked by the ancients, but payable with modern methods. Douglas-Henry had experience of gold mining, and I agreed to join him in a prospecting expedition.

In a remote, uninhabited valley the sand-banks by the river looked promising, and Douglas-Henry gave me my first lesson in panning for gold. After many unsuccessful attempts, I finally succeeded in finding 'colour'. There is a special kind of excitement in finding gold that must be connected with the perennial quest of men for this enigmatic metal. As I gazed upon the tiny yellow grains, tears came into my eyes, and I felt an unreasoning urge to go on searching until I found real gold for myself. The mood passed almost instantly, but it reminded me that we must never judge of other men's impulses until we have experienced them ourselves. The lust for gold is an incommunicable experience, but none the less real for that.

Douglas-Henry decided that there must have been very rich gold deposits in these mountains, but that they had been worked out long ago. I returned to the planning of our own great scheme with growing enthusiasm and hope.

With catastrophic suddenness, the scene changed. Venizelos fell from power. The Tsaldaris Government which came to power was suspicious of anything British, especially if sponsored by Venizelos. Moreover, the extravagant accounts which had appeared in the Greek

Press of the success of the Birmingham trials had created the illusion that a vast fortune was there for the taking. As the government found that it could not touch our concessions, it placed a prohibitive tax on lignite and brown coal, twice as much as the actual cost of mining. For months we struggled on, losing more and more money. My own position grew more and more difficult. Douglas-Henry up at Vevi was trying to improve methods of production, but he could make no progress without capital. I sent him all I could, but I left myself without money. I believed in the enterprise. It was my first creative undertaking, and I loved it. I sustained the courage of my co-directors, when I should have admitted failure.

The winter of 1931 passed. Our manager on the spot, a sturdy Welshman called Evans, who had lived for many years in Greece and had a Greek wife and family, tried to sell enough brown coal to keep going, but endless vexations at the Department of Mines in Athens made his task impossible. Finally, in June 1932, some disgruntled workmen, whom Evans had been obliged to payoff, quite unjustly claimed that he had failed to pay their wages. He was arrested. In the same week came the final rejection of our plea for reduced taxation. On the seventeenth of June I wrote in my journal: "Today - or rather during two hours this afternoon - the whole weight of external difficulties fell on me. Evans' arrest, Green's refusal, Drossopoulos' procrastination - one blow after another fell on me and, as a background to it all, the realization that I have nothing to live on and no means of paying all this money due next week, except by selling some of our few remaining possessions.' I added: 'This afternoon, the suffering in my heart drowned all feeling of past and future. Yet, after all, it is still the future which is the source of pain.' Indeed, at this time my life began to enter a phase when I suffered in many ways. The satisfaction I had felt in working with my small group of pupils for more than a year since I had started in October 1929, gave place to the constant exposure of my deficiencies in my work with Ouspensky. I watched, with nostalgic memories of my own beginnings, the enthusiasm of the hundreds of newcomers to his groups. In ten long years, I had gained nothing but profound disillusionment. Many of those who had studied with Ouspensky since 1922 were in the same condition; and, no doubt to encourage us, he introduced various new themes of work. As my relationship with Ouspensky was the main theme of my inner life during the next few years, I will devote a chapter to the subject.

14: MR. AND MADAME OUSPENSKY

At this point Sophie Grigorevna Ouspensky re-enters the scene. She was, in every act, a great lady. Ouspensky was her second husband, and she had one daughter and a grandson, Leonide Savitzky. I first met all the family on the Island of Prinkipo in 1920. A granddaughter had been born at the Prieuré. Since my latest meeting with Madame Ouspensky was in 1959, she occupies a large part of my life. Her influence upon me has been one of the chief factors in my development, and it has been altogether good, so that I owe her an extraordinary debt of gratitude.

When Ouspensky separated from Gurdjieff in 1924, she had remained at the Prieuré. In a letter written at the time, which I quote from memory, she said something like this: "I do not pretend to understand Georgy Ivanovitch. For me he is X. All that I know is that he is my teacher and it is not right for me to judge him, nor is it necessary for me to understand him. No one knows who is the real Georgy Ivanovitch, for he hides himself from all of us. It is useless for us to try to know him, and I refuse to enter into any discussions about him." When in 1929 the Prieuré was closed and Gurdjieff went to America, Madame Ouspensky came to England. After feeling her way very cautiously, she decided to stay and work with some of Ouspensky's pupils. This led to a division of responsibilities that grew more marked as time went on. Madame Ouspensky set herself to create conditions for work, while her husband continued to be the teacher, lecturer and writer. He required no external facilities; for ten years he had been content to live in a modest flat at Gwendwr Road, West Kensington. He needed only a place where he could hold his meetings. If Madame Ouspensky was to do her work, she needed a house and grounds where people could live and work together, as they had done in Russia during the war, and as they had done in the Caucasus and Constantinople after the Revolution, and for nearly seven years at the Prieuré.

Madame Ouspensky had her own clear conception of her role. She insisted from start to finish that she was not a teacher and refused to be put in a false position. She could not work with many people and refused to undertake any task that she did not feel able to carry through. She began on a very small scale and only after two years agreed that a house should be taken on a long-term basis. This was Gadsden in Hayes, Kent, less than an hour by car from the centre of London. Gadsden was a large Victorian mansion standing in seven acres of land. Eight to ten English pupils went to live there and to work with Madame Ouspensky. I was not invited, nor could I have gone, for I had neither the leisure nor the means. I was, however, encouraged to go every Sunday to work and occasionally to stay for weekends.

This soon created an almost intolerable situation, because my wife, after one visit, was not permitted to go again. I have never understood the reason for this harsh decision. It meant that we could never be together on the only day of the week that I was free. Had it been for a few months we could have borne it, but this went on for nearly three years and caused my wife acute distress.

I could not reject the opportunity offered by Sunday work at Gadsden and later at Lyne Place, a far larger and more imposing house near Virginia Water, to which the Ouspenskys moved in 1934. The work was the nearest approach to what we had at the Prieuré: hard physical effort and disturbing psychological conditions. This alone might not have decided me to let my wife suffer. The overriding factor was the resolve I had taken to do, without question, anything that Ouspensky might ask of me. I had accepted him as my teacher, and I understood the first duty of a pupil to be implicit and unquestioning obedience.

There was something radically awry in my attitude at this time. I took for granted that I was being subjected to a test intentionally imposed and consciously carried through. I also assumed that Ouspensky knew everything, that he was the superman I myself aspired one day to become. I was completely blind to his limitations. If he required me to abandon my wife every week, then there must be a good reason for it, and it must eventually be for our good.

The years of self-study and struggle to overcome my defects and weaknesses had not been wholly without fruit. I had more than once known the taste of a higher state of consciousness, the attainment of which seemed worth any price. Moreover, the reiterated failure of my outward undertakings was evidence that, until I myself should change, my life would always go wrong. Mixed with these motives was, undoubtedly, a kind of spiritual ambition which made me long to become a superman. I believed firmly in Gurdjieff's assertion that we men have latent possibilities of attaining a higher level of being. My experience at the Prieuré had even shown me something of the powers that must accompany such an attainment.

Although I could see that I was far from the goal, I took for granted that Gurdjieff and Mr. and Madame Ouspensky, and possibly others also, had already reached it. Therefore they must be almost infallible in their judgments and their actions.

Long afterwards I realized the unwisdom of such an attitude, especially when I saw others show it towards myself. I had long before become convinced of the fallibility, often verging upon incompetence, of men who by usual standards were to be regarded as great, but I had excepted spiritual teachers from this judgment. When I found myself in the position of a spiritual teacher and saw that my most ill-considered suggestions were taken as inspired utterances, I became aware of the necessity for anyone who has the task of guiding others in spiritual matters to abstain from hiding his own defects and mistakes, and to make sure that no one shall look upon him as an 'authority' in his own right. In this respect, Gurdjieff was an example to us all; he set himself to shock and even to disgust those who came to him for teaching.

In Gurdjieff's first published and most controversial book, *The Herald of Coming Good*, he refers to Hvareno, the mysterious attribute of kingship, the belief in which was an article of faith in Babylonian Mithraism, and which we can recognize in the historical books of the Old Testament and the third temptation of Jesus. The man who has Hvareno and does not aim at external dominance, but at spiritual leadership, must do everything possible to hide it from others.

In 1931, I was still very far from understanding any of these things; and it seemed to me that if I wished to succeed in overcoming my own self-will, I must submit myself entirely and unquestioningly to my teacher. What Ouspensky said encouraged this attitude and, to some extent, his actions did also. I failed to see that he distinguished between himself as an ordinary man, and the role he had, from time to time, to assume as a teacher. Consequently, when he did unbend and try to treat me as a friend, I remained obsessed with the notion of implicit obedience.

One example will show what I mean. Ouspensky had the hobby of collecting old prints. He wanted, for his study, prints of St. Petersburg and Moscow and once asked me to find him a shop. I discovered Mr. Spencer in Oxford Street, who at that time had one of the largest and most varied collections in the world. When I told Ouspensky, he was delighted and asked me to go with him one afternoon at two p.m. It happened that I had that day to interview an important client. I took this as a test. I contrived to put off the client and spent the afternoon with Ouspensky. He thoroughly enjoyed himself, bought a number of prints, and said he would go again a week later. He invited me to tea, which he made with great care from special Chinese leaves he had personally selected at Twinings. I was ridiculously stiff, not realizing that Ouspensky was a human being who enjoyed human companionship.

In such ways, I created for myself a host of imaginary enemies. I struggled desperately with my conscience over submission. I could obey Ouspensky, but I could not submit. I felt guilty, and yet I knew that I would keep my own judgment, and that I continued and would continue inwardly to rebel.

This made me ask myself a very serious question: "If I cannot submit to a man, can I submit to God?" I saw that I had no idea of what such a question could mean, let alone how to answer it. That night I walked round and round Bryanston Square, wrestling with the problem and feeling lost and desperate. I could see no way out. On the one hand there was a refusal, far deeper than my own will, to submit myself to any man. On the other there was an inability, far deeper than my own understanding, to see what it could mean to submit myself to God.

When finally I went into the house, my wife was waiting. I felt like bursting into tears and weeping on her breast. But I could not give way. I could only tell her that I was desperate and hopeless. With womanly shrewdness she said: "You are upset because your business is going badly." I was outraged at this suggestion and in the same moment I saw that it was true. It was my own frustrated self-will that was suffering, not any authentic longing for unattainable perfection.

I could not bring myself to admit the truth, but my wife's loving warmth melted my feelings, and I turned towards her with gratitude. For all my involuntary neglect, she never turned away from me, nor failed to understand the turmoils through which I was passing.

By one of the coincidences that play so great a part in shaping our destiny, the next evening Ouspensky introduced a new theme that was to have a great influence on my life for the next twelve years. He spoke about methods used in esoteric schools throughout Asia and Eastern Europe for fixing the attention and preventing the mind from wandering in vain imaginings. These are based on the fact that memory can work only in a single track. If we remember one thing, we forget others. By exercising the memory, we exclude random thoughts. This can be done either by memorizing or by repetition.

This made sense to me because I had often asked myself why Hindus, Muslims and Christians continued to learn their sacred scriptures by heart, a thousand years after the need to preserve them orally had ceased to exist. My Sanskrit teacher, Kanhere, had shown me the method used by the Brahmins of India for memorizing the Vedas and Brahmanas. I had met Hafiz, that is, 'preservers', who knew the Qur'an by heart and could reproduce it with every grammatical error perpetrated by the Prophet.

MR. AND MADAME OUSPENSKY

In Greek Orthodox monasteries, monks set themselves to memorize the entire Bible, and indeed such undertakings were not uncommon in Western Christianity as late as the nineteenth century. They had always seemed to me a meaningless survival of the days when reading and writing were rare accomplishments, and the few manuscripts easily lost or mutilated. Now I saw that the practice of memorizing the scriptures was indeed a survival, not of an illiterate age, but of a time when men understood the danger of living too much in their thoughts.

Ouspensky went on to speak about repetition. He described the prayer of the heart - that is the constant repetition of the invocation: 'Lord Jesus Christ, Son of God, have Mercy upon me'. When this was introduced more than a thousand years ago into the monasteries of the Greek Orthodox Church, it had produced spectacular results, thousands of monks and nuns attaining to states of illumination by following literally the injunction of St. Paul to pray without ceasing. He said that the prayer of the heart in its original form is suitable only for monks, but a form of repetition less disturbing for the emotions might be useful for us.

He therefore suggested that some of us might undertake the task of learning by heart the Sermon on the Mount, or even all the Gospels. Others might try the constant repetition of the Lord's Prayer, but in this case he recommended learning it in Greek, as the English version did not reproduce the rhythm of the original.

He then went round the room telling each one present which exercise to do. He passed me over and at the end said: "This exercise is not suitable for Bennett." I was accustomed to such shocks, but this time I was really distressed because I was in great need of something to hold on to. I was tempted to learn the Sermon on the Mount and say nothing, but I had set myself to obey and, after a short struggle, did so. The following week when the others were describing their experience with the exercise, I sat quietly by and there came over me a great inward calm and gratitude. I became aware of how much better it is to bear deprivation than to enjoy possession. It may be that Ouspensky sensed my state; anyhow, at the end of the meeting he said: "Bennett, you can try repetition now if you wish."

From that day, for the next four or five years, I carried on the task of repeating, as often as possible during the day; the Lord's Prayer in Greek. Before long, I could repeat it while reading or speaking with others. After three years it united with my breathing and went on continuously even when I was unaware of it. My journals for the years 1931-5 are filled with references to the exercise of repetition. I learned,

175

for example, to repeat the prayer simultaneously in Greek and Latin at different rates and, even for a very brief spell, to add also the prayer in German or Russian. This produced a state of controlled dissociation; the usual connection between my intellectual, emotional and instinctive functions was suspended, and a link of a new kind - a condition of pure consciousness - held them together.

During this time, I also set myself to learn the Gospels by heart and have always been grateful for the intimate contact with these marvellous writings that I gained from this exercise.

Within a few weeks of introducing the exercises of memorizing and repetition, Ouspensky refused to discuss them at his meetings, saying that they had been misunderstood and, if persisted in, would give wrong results. As he did not specifically tell us to stop, I and several others continued. I regarded the exercise of repetition as something very intimate and personal and seldom spoke of it to anyone for nearly fifteen years.

Time and again, Ouspensky would introduce some such new theme that seemed full of promise, only to drop it, apparently having lost all interest, within a few weeks or months.

During this time, my own meetings - known as Bennett's Group - continued regularly. In 1931, at a time when the affairs of the Grecian Mining Company were going well, I introduced an experiment that has continued almost without a break ever since. This was to invite my group to join me for a period of intensive work and study. As large bungalows, in which a dozen people could sleep, were available cheap at Shoreham-by-Sea, we went there in August 1931. The following August, just after the Grecian Mining Company had gone into liquidation, I went again, this time with a group of twenty. My wife and I travelled down from London by bus; she was very tired after the strain of the preceding months. As I read my journal of the four weeks we spent at Shoreham that year, I was amazed that the others could bear with me. My own state was wretched, and I took a pride in my own wretchedness. If we had a beautiful day with a walk over the downs to Chanctonbury Ring, all that I could write was: 'There is something so revolting and humiliating in one's enjoyment of pleasant things, that one shudders away from oneself when a moment of awakening comes.' The next day I wrote: 'The task of escaping from this miserable world is no easier when things are painful than when they are pleasant.'

It would be tedious to continue the story of these years if it were all as wretched as my journal entries. There were, however, also times of illumination and the reawakening of hope. Once, at the height of a crisis in the affairs of the Grecian Mining Company, I went out at lunch-time to walk in Finsbury Square. My thoughts turned to the problem which had troubled me for twelve years, of finding some concrete interpretation of the fifth dimension. As had happened in June 1920, I began to 'see' the world in its five-dimensional form. As I entered the fifth dimension, time stopped but life went on. I saw life as energy or rather a quality of energy. Rising into the fifth dimension, the quality changed, growing finer and also more intense. Nothing was happening and yet everything was changing. I saw that there was no degradation of energy. In a flash, I realized that this was to be expected if time stood still. The formula took shape in words: 'In eternity the laws of thermodynamics are reversed. Within a closed system, entropy is eternally conserved, but energy itself has many values.'

I was overjoyed with this formula, so obvious to me at that moment that I could not understand how I had overlooked it for so many years. I saw how the eternal pattern of everything that exists has its own laws of development, only its unfolding is not in time; that is, it has not the property of succession. It is rather an intensification of existence itself. I remembered Gurdjieff's saying: "Two men may look outwardly the same, but one may have incomparably more Being than the other. You cannot see this because you are still blind to Being." I understood at last that this statement can be taken literally. 'To be more' means to stand upon a higher level in the scale of eternal energies.

The next day, at one of Ouspensky's weekly meetings, I tried to describe what I had seen and understood, but Ouspensky brushed it all aside, saying that it was 'formatory thinking', that is, the automatic working of the associative mechanism of the brain. I knew that in attempting to put what I had experienced into words, I could not but lose the quality of luminous certainty it had contained. I was ready to accept Ouspensky's rebuke, but I could not deny my own vision. During the ten years that I had studied and worked with Ouspensky, I had tried several times to speak of some deep inner experience, such as that which had come to me at Fontainebleau in 1923; but I had either been unable to speak at all or Ouspensky had rejected what I had tried to say.

At that time, I was so despondent about myself and my attempts to put into practice what I firmly believed in theory that I was ready to believe that anyone was right except myself. That year, 1932, my wife and I spent four weeks in Shoreham. The Ouspenskys were still at Sevenoaks, but preparing to move to Gadsden. I was invited to go there one Sunday with two or three of my group. My wife and Lucien Myers and one other came with me. After lunch we were invited to put questions to Madame

Ouspensky. The atmosphere was tense and we waited in silence. At last, Lucien Myers started, and she answered one or two questions without demur. Then he put another, reading from a manuscript, but she interrupted him saying: "Only one question is necessary: What is work?" He was not perturbed and, looking at her solemnly, said: "That is my question number twenty-three." Everyone laughed and the air cleared.

My own questions were roughly handled, Madame Ouspensky saying: "You do not know yourself and you have not yet realized your own mechanicalness." I accepted this rebuke as well-merited, but the next day my wife took me to task, saying that I had been far too meek, and that Madame Ouspensky did not want people to behave as doormats.

We went back to London. I was so full of my own self-accusation and searching of heart that I did not even notice how heavily it was weighing upon my wife. At last - it was on 1st September 1932 - I became aware of her suffering. A few days later two members of my group came and poured out their hearts in distress at feeling lost between disillusion with the old world and inability to realize the new. I gave what seemed to me a clear explanation of their situation, and why it had to be so. My wife remained silent. After they had gone, she said to me: "They spoke from their hearts, but you answered from your head. Could you not see how much they were suffering and why?"

I record these incidents to show how far I was from understanding other people, even my own wife, who was nearer to me than anyone and who was my sole comfort in all my distress. People came to me because they thought I knew the answers to their questions; but as I could not understand what was behind the questions in the depths of their human souls, I could not have been much use to them.

Meanwhile life had to go on. The Grecian Mining Company ceased its operations. With great difficulty we rescued the unfortunate manager and brought him back to England. A period of my life had ended. Something in me had died and nothing was yet reborn in its place. Not only had I lost all my money, but I was left with debts. I had not taken my salary as Managing Director for nearly a year, and I had paid various expenses of the Company instead of my own debts. We decided to leave our flat in Bryanston Mansions and sell what we could. I parted with my Bechstein piano and all the best books in my library of nearly two thousand volumes. My wife unhesitatingly sold her jewelry.

We went to live with my wife's mother, Constance Alice Elliot, a magnificent old lady, the great-granddaughter of Sir Elijah Impey, the first chief justice of India. Her husband, by a strange coincidence, was great-grandson of the first Lord Minto, who, as Sir Gilbert Elliot, had prosecuted in the impeachment of Impey and Warren Hastings. Mrs. Elliot had all the dignity and courage of the Anglo-Indian society to which she belonged. She was very small but perfectly proportioned and still beautiful. Her erect carriage was a reminder that she was considered, in her time, the best horsewoman in India.

My wife's father had died before the First World War, and Mrs. Elliot was living in a small house in Baron's Court. Her great interest was the London County Council, to which she was elected three times for North St. Pancras. She had taken very kindly to me, and my wife and I went to Baron's Court and occupied a room in her house.

I had to attend to the winding up of the Company and was beginning to earn small sums of money by making translations from Greek and Turkish for an agency, when an unexpected opening presented itself. One of the engineering contracting firms which had helped me to prepare our great development scheme for Vevi was H. Tollemache and Company, specialists in powdered coal plant. The managing director, Commander Humphrey Tollemache, had been very friendly, but I had seen him only two or three times and was surprised to receive an invitation to lunch. He said that he felt sympathetic over our unmerited failure, and thinking I might be in difficulties, offered me a job as engineer-estimator with his own company. The salary proposed was less than a tenth of what I had received as managing director of the Aegean Trust three years earlier and a quarter of what I had been paid by the Grecian Mining Company. But it was a job, and it could give me the opportunity of learning something entirely new; that is, of working as a minor employee with no authority or freedom of action. My wife was sure that we could live on the small pay offered. I accepted and started work the following week. It was 9th September 1932, the same week that the Ouspenskys moved from Sevenoaks to Gadsden. The work was quite new to me, and I found it interesting and exciting. After years of grappling with the shadow of a wonderful plan, it was very satisfying to work out schemes that could be realized. When my first contract was signed and work started, I understood how much I had been starved of concrete achievement. My part was not important or decisive. I was only an estimator, but I saw my own calculations being verified, the equipment I had selected being bought and erected.

There was also a painful, but salutary, element in the work. I had always known I was prone to inaccuracy, but now my errors came quickly home to roost. When I was severely criticized for my mistakes, I learned how everyday life can teach lessons that no esoteric school can convey. I wrote: 'See yourself with eyes that do not love you.' Our own eyes can never be free from the conflict of self-love and self-hate, and we must borrow other eyes if we wish to look at ourselves impartially.

In 1933, I had the opportunity to do some research on my own. Tollemache was friendly with the chairman of the United Steel Company, and had suggested to him that it might be worth de-dusting their coal before washing it, and using the dust for firing boilers. When it came to evaluating the suggestion, it was found that no one knew how much dust the coal contained. I offered to make a study and spent several weeks at the colliery. My report was a success, and, what is more, I discovered that the quantity of dust in coal can be predicted from the distribution of the larger sizes. This was the beginning of my interest in size distribution in broken materials, which during the following ten years produced results that gave me a modest standing as an industrial research worker.

From my study of the size of coal dust particles, I had the idea that suitably graded powders could be used in foundries for protecting moulds more effectively than ungraded dusts. When I tried this idea out it proved successful. At that time, Tollemache and Company had started to manufacture powdered coal at Grimethorpe Colliery in Yorkshire. We packed the powdered dust in paper bags and began to sell them to foundries. In order to develop the business, I offered to go out as a salesman.

The experience was most revealing. Canvassing for orders was strangely distasteful to me. Salesmen have told me of the pleasure they take in their work. To me it was unmitigated suffering. Even when good orders came my way, I was harrowed by the fear that I had misled the customer or promised more than we could perform. I was so extremely timid that each visit was an ordeal; yet I would not for anything have missed the months I spent travelling through industrial England selling coal dust. They showed me how narrowly limited I was in what I could do. The experience forged a closer link between my inner and my outer life than I had known before.

Throughout 1933, I was desolated by my inability to achieve positive results in my work with Ouspensky. I was constantly getting myself into trouble, and it seemed as if Ouspensky's main object in dealing with me was to teach me discretion. I could never hear of anything that was interesting or valuable to me without the impulse at all costs to tell others. Often the costs were very unpleasant. So week after week and month after month I struggled on, sometimes in hope, more often in despair.

In August 1933, when I was going for the third time to Shoreham with my group, Madame Ouspensky sent for me privately and said:

"You go now with your group. Try to be yourself. Why do you imitate Mr. Ouspensky in everything? You even copy his mistakes in speaking English. Why? You have your own way of working. You can never succeed in work by imitating others. Remember the saying in the Bhagavad Gita which I made you read this afternoon." This was the thirty-fifth verse of the third Adhyāya which reads:

"Better one's own way of life - dharma - even if it lacks merit, than that of another, even if one well performed. The way of another is fraught with danger; salvation comes only by following one's own way."

I said that I could not trust myself, and that I was afraid of saying the wrong thing. She replied: "Of course you cannot trust yourself; you cannot trust anyone else either. There is only one way to learn what you can trust in yourself, and that is by your own actions proceeding from your own intention. When you imitate others, you learn nothing about yourself, and you can never grow strong. You have in you the possibility of being of great value to the Work, but for that you must prepare yourself and gain your own experience."

I went down to Shoreham greatly heartened by this talk, for it came only a day or two after a distressing scene when I had to tell the board of directors of the Grecian Mining Company that we could not hope to pay our debts and must put the Company into liquidation. One director, who could well afford the money he had lost, had been very angry, and had accused me of holding out false hopes. Although I knew that I had never intentionally deceived my colleagues, I felt terribly guilty. It seemed to me that I could have managed the business better.

When I went home and told my wife of my talk with Madame Ouspensky, she smiled wryly and said: "That is what I have been telling you again and again. Why is it that you will listen to everyone except me? Yet you know that I love you and believe in you more than anyone else. Why don't you trust me more?"

It was true that we loved one another dearly and were only happy in one another's company. We could share nearly everything that matters in life, and we both cared very much for the work I was doing with my group of pupils. But in spite of this, I would never listen to her. I tried to understand the reason for this. I wrote in my journal that I was overbearing and insensitive towards those who really cared for me and only attentive to those who disliked me. But this is an over-simplification. The truth is that I was so much at war with myself, so bewildered and distressed by my own inadequacy, that anyone who trusted and spoke well of me seemed to me to be misguided or wilfully blind.

During our stay in Shoreham in 1933, I had to come to London on business and returned by way of Lyne to visit Ouspensky. He then had the habit of sitting up half the night drinking claret and, nearly always, of talking about his own early days in Russia. He seemed to be obsessed with the need to put himself back into the life he was living before he first met Gurdjieff in 1915.

That night the two of us were alone. The whole night passed. Towards morning, when we had drunk between us four or five bottles of claret, I was speaking and expressing my opinion about some question - I have completely forgotten what it was. But as I spoke I went quite outside myself and heard my own voice and even watched my own thoughts as if they were going on in someone else. I saw myself as completely artificial; neither my thoughts nor my words were my own. 'I' - whoever at that moment 'I' might be - was a completely indifferent spectator of the performance.

Quite suddenly the spell broke, and I was back 'inside' myself. I said to Ouspensky: "Now I know what self-observation really is. In all these years I have never seen Bennett as he really is until this moment." He replied very seriously, saying: "Was this worth sitting up all night for?" I said: "Yes, indeed, or for twenty nights if necessary." He continued: "If only you can remember what you have just seen you will be able to work. But you must understand that no one can help you in this. If you do not see for yourself, it is impossible for anyone else to show you."

Soon afterwards he went off to bed, and I took my car and drove to Shoreham as the sun was rising. The intense beauty of the summer morning filled me with a joy that I had rarely known before. And yet, even then, I knew that I would lose what I had just gained. I would forget, and I would no longer know who and what this 'Bennett' was, whose life was somehow grafted on to my own true life. I saw it all with calm resignation, and it did not touch my joy at having my eyes open to see reality - if only for an hour. I watched the swallows skimming over the morning fields and said to myself: "One vision does not make a conscious man." Nevertheless, at this seminar I got further than ever before in reaching a sense of unity with those I worked with.

15: NEAR-DEATH AGAIN

On 1st October 1933, I completed the thousand days that I had set myself to keep a journal. It had shown me that this was possible for me, and it had also been a constant reminder of my fluctuating states. I decided to continue. Through the next two or three years, the exercise of constant repetition of the Lord's Prayer held a dominant place in my inner life. Sometimes I kept count and found that I would repeat it between three or four hundred up to a thousand times a day or more. It was my sheet anchor and a great comfort.

By this time my wife and I had found a small basement flat in Bayswater and were living happily with very little money. But, early in 1934, my chest symptoms began to grow troublesome. On 6th May I wrote: 'I have been brought face to face with the problem of health. I shall have to stay in bed for at least a month.' I was then very tired, and my work at Tollemache's was a heavy burden. I had become so thin that my wife became alarmed. She insisted that I should see a doctor.

A good friend in Ouspensky's group, Dr. Francis Roles, was a noted authority on tuberculosis. He diagnosed me as having an active T.B. lesion in my left lung. He thought it might heal if I could remain perfectly still for three months, never allowing myself to get out of breath. Failing this, I would have to go to a sanatorium in Switzerland. Tollemache generously gave me three months' leave with pay, and I set myself with my usual impetuosity to be completely inactive. Complete inactivity was a new experience. All my life I had driven myself - particularly since my talk with Gurdjieff at the Prieuré in July 1923. I did not know how to be still, especially as I was warned not to read or allow myself mental activity. We had a back yard, with a small lawn and a rock garden. I lay on a mattress all day, taking care of miniature alpine plants. This gave me great happiness, and made the time pass easily.

By the end of the summer, I had so completely recovered that Roles recommended me to resume normal activity. The only unusual treatment I had received was given on Ouspensky's advice. I drank twice a day an extract of aloes, the fresh leaves being sent by a friend in South Africa. Ouspensky was very solicitous throughout my illness. I cannot tell whether it was the aloes or the rest that brought so rapid a cure. My own belief is that this illness was a phase in the process of dying and rebirth, which had started in 1929.

When I returned to work, I became increasingly interested in the waste of coal in England, due to the inefficiency with which it was burned. Before 1914, coal had been so very cheap and plentiful that few were concerned about its efficient use. The work I was doing for Tollemache largely consisted in demonstrating that money could be saved by burning coal efficiently, as a powder rather than in large lumps. I got to know the manufacturers of other types of coal-burning appliances, and conceived the idea of an association of manufacturers, which would educate industrial and domestic consumers in the better use of our dwindling coal reserves.

The coal industry was then awakening to the converse problem of making good the markets for large coal, threatened by the increasing competition of gas, electricity and oil. The Coal Utilization Council was formed and financed by coal producers and distributors. Very soon it was realized that the Council needed the cooperation of the appliance makers. I found an ally in Kenneth Gordon, the first director of the C.U.C., who encouraged me to take an active part in starting the Coal-burning Appliance Makers' Association. By 1934, this Association had become so vigorous that I was invited to leave my job and become its first director. Thus began a phase of my life that lasted for sixteen years, during which my main outward interest was research into the better utilization of coal.

Burning coal to produce heat, mechanical energy and electricity was then, and still is, the foundation of the industrial activity of the world. I was astonished to discover how little scientific study had gone into this vital process. Since long before the advent of coal, the open log fire has been a decisive factor in making the winter bearable in such a climate as ours. When used for burning on an open fire intended for logs, coal is not only very wasteful but contributes to the grime and smog of cities. Yet since the time of Count Rumford, in the eighteenth century, little has been done to improve either the efficiency or the cleanliness of coal fires. I was sure that a systematic research could work wonders in this and in other appliances for burning coal.

When I told Gordon of my ideas, he was enthusiastic and promised financial help from the Coal Utilization Council. The coal owners were at first skeptical, but when I went to visit Sir Robert Burrows, then chairman of the Lancashire Coal Owners, he told me to go ahead and promised a thousand pounds to start a research department of the Coal-burning Appliance Makers' Association. We began very modestly, in a back room of our offices in Victoria Street. A first small success with a device for reducing smoke gave us our start. Sir Evan Williams, chairman of the Mining Association of Great Britain, a man with all the capacity for enthusiasm of the Welsh, asked me to put a plan before the coal owners.

At that time Lord Rutherford, one of the greatest experimental scientists of this or any age, was chairman of the Government's Advisory Council for Scientific and Industrial Research. I went to see him, and spoke about the prodigious waste of our greatest natural resource. He at once saw the significance of working upon the apparatus for using coal, rather than upon the properties of coal itself, which most coal research had followed until that time. He agreed to speak as guest of honour at the annual lunch of the Coal-burning Appliance Makers' Association, to which we invited all the leading coal owners and many scientists. He spoke so convincingly that, within a few weeks, the coal owners decided to make a levy for research on every ton of coal mined, and the Government gave pound for pound. From a small struggling research department, we were launched as the British Coal Utilization Research Association, of which I was appointed director. We became at one bound the second largest industrial research association in the country. I was congratulated upon having made the British coal owners 'research-conscious', but the truth is that the stream was flowing by itself. Some big coal owners, such as Powell Duffryn and United Steel, were already doing a great deal of research, but saying little about it. I did no more than help to dig out the channel that allowed the stream of research to flow as a truly cooperative effort, in which coal owners, coal merchants, and the coal-burning appliance makers could work together.

Everything was new and exciting, and I was happy in the work. Lord Rutherford, who was not only chairman of the Advisory Council, but also Cavendish Professor at Cambridge, helped me with ideas and with the recruiting of staff direct from the University. I was also fortunate in finding J.S. Hales, a genius in the practical design of equipment. He undertook the task of studying the coal fire, improving its efficiency, and reducing its tendency to smoke. The outcome of the pioneer work started in the B.C.U.R.A. (short for British Coal Utilization Research Association) can now be seen all over England in the form of the new convector fires for coal and coke, of which scores of designs are now on the market. The efficiency of the coal fire has been increased by thirty to forty percent as a result of Hales' work.

In 1936, I was invited to join the Coal Research Club on the strength of my researches into the physical behaviour of coal. This was a small body of scientists including two remarkable women, Dr. Marie Stopes and Dr. Margaret Fishenden. The club had been formed in 1921 on the initiative of Drs. Lessing, Wheeler and Sinnatt - all passionately interested in the enigma of the chemical nature of coal. My election was a recognition that its physical properties are no less enigmatic. Professor Wheeler had been one of the few to discourage the formation of the B.C.U.R.A., on the ground that coal research had nothing more to give. He was a brilliant but disappointed man. I have never ceased to be interested in the Coal Research Club, in spite of a certain narrowness of outlook that unfortunately is only too common among scientists. A notable exception was Dr. Clarence Seyler, the founder of Coal Systematics, who died recently at the age of ninety-two. His interests ranged as widely as my own, and he became one of my closest friends.

Between 1936 and the outbreak of the Second World War, my relations with Ouspensky changed. Although I went regularly to his big house at Lyne, near Virginia Water, I was no longer in his confidence. With Madame Ouspensky it was different, and I received immense help from her during these years. She had persuaded Ouspensky to allow a selected group of pupils to study Gurdjieff's exercises with one of his former pupils. I was allowed to join this class and resume work that I had found so valuable at the Prieuré fourteen years earlier. The classes began in October 1937 and continued for nearly two years.

The opportunity to attend these classes meant being away from home two evenings a week, as well as going to one or two of Ouspensky's meetings in London, and as I also went off to Lyne every Sunday, my wife was in danger of being left alone. I asked Madame Ouspensky, who said she was welcome at Lyne, and she began to go there and work.

Nevertheless, at this time she began to be tormented by the fear that she was standing in my way. She offered several times to leave me, saying that I should have a younger wife and more children. I could not take this seriously, because I had no doubt whatever that we would remain together for the rest of her life. To be with her was my greatest happiness, and I was sure that she felt as I did.

I completely failed to understand what goes on in a woman's mind. My sense of almost hopeless inadequacy in front of my own inner problems was a present reality. When my wife spoke of her sense of inadequacy she seemed to be speaking nonsense. She was not inadequate, and I thought no more was needed than to tell her so and encourage her as well as I could. I was quite unable to understand that her trouble had nothing to do with the logic of the situation. She said to me once: "I have had a wonderful life with you. It is nearly twenty years since we met, and I was always sure that you would find your place and do great work. You are now well established on the way to success. You do not need me any more. More than anything, you care for your work with Ouspensky. I cannot find my place there; they do not really need me nor want me. I do not wish to be invited just because I am your wife. It would be much better if I disappeared altogether."

We had several such talks, which always ended in my supposing that I had reassured and comforted her. Like so many men, I thought that perhaps she was jealous because of some other woman and felt that she should know by my behaviour that her place was secure as the one woman with whom I could share my life, as much as I could share it with any human being. It did not for a moment occur to me that she was speaking seriously and quite sincerely felt that it was time for her to go out of my life. Only now, looking back after more than twenty years, can I see how woefully ignorant I still was of people, and especially of women. When my wife said that she cared for my well-being more than for her own life, I took this for an expression of feeling, not a statement of fact. So I was wholly unprepared for what was to happen.

We were then living in Bayswater. On 24th January, 1937, I went as usual to my office in Victoria Street. Without knowing why, I felt restless and telephoned to my home at about four in the afternoon. Getting no reply, I became anxious and went home at once. When I went in, I called: "Polly, where are you?" Getting no answer I went to our bedroom and found her breathing very heavily and sprawled over the bed. There was a note to me, and an empty bottle of her sleeping medicine. I ran out of the house, found a taxi, carried her from the bed and drove straight to St. Mary's Hospital.

The house physician on duty, Dr. Smiter, came at once, and after a single glance had her carried into a ward and told me to wait. By a wonderful chance, Smiter was doing research under a noted neurologist on the effect of barbiturates on the nervous system. This gave him the courage to take very drastic steps. He came out and said to me: "She is nearly gone. I propose to give her lumbar punctures until the cerebrospinal pressure comes down. You had better wait."

Only then could I begin to think again. I saw how completely I had failed to understand her anguish. It was entirely my fault that she had been driven to this extremity. It was incredible that we should love one another so dearly and be so close together, and yet not be able to understand. How could she imagine that I could live without her? How could I imagine that she had not been serious in saying that it was time for her to go?

At eleven p.m. I was allowed into the ward. She was in a profound coma. I sat by her bed holding her hand. Dr. Smiter said: "If she shows any sign of moving, speak to her and try to rouse her up." I sat very close and spoke to her all the time, assuring her that I needed her and calling her to come back to me. The hours passed and there was no sign. Her breathing grew weaker, and I was panic-stricken.

All the following day and night, and again the next day, I sat by her bed, speaking and calling to her. I was convinced that she knew I was there, although she gave not the smallest sign.

At last, after three nights and three days, she opened her eyes and looked at me. She said: "You", or "Yes", I could not tell which, closed her eyes and went into a normal sleep. Dr. Smiter, who had devoted himself to the case with all his skill, was called. He told me to go away and rest. I had scarcely moved from her bed for three days and did not know if I was awake or dreaming. Slowly her strength returned. The next day she woke up and said to me: "I have seen a miracle. I went out of my body and was in a place where I heard heavenly music. It was not like any music on earth. I knew that Jesus was there. I was quite sure of His presence, though I could not see Him. I wanted to remain. Then I heard you calling me. I told you not to call, but you could not hear me. You called me back into my body. I did not want to come, but your wish was too strong for me. I could not stay out of my body. When I came back, I could hear you speaking, but I could not see you. Then all went black, and when I woke up I was again out of my body, in a blue light. I was very peaceful, but it was no longer the place where Jesus is. Then I knew I must return and live my life out. But I was happy because I knew you really wanted me." She remained silent a long time and added: "You must not tell anyone about this until after I am dead. Perhaps I shall tell Mr. Ouspensky - but I must wait."

Ouspensky had been informed; though no one was told that the overdose was anything but an accident. He enquired daily for news, and asked to see my wife as soon as possible. When she was able to go to Lyne, I drove her down, and she had a private talk with Ouspensky. Afterwards she told me that he had said: "I know that something important has happened to you. Will you tell me about it?" She replied that she had decided to wait a year, and if then she still remained convinced of the reality of her experience, she would tell him. He accepted her decision. From that time on he gave her much more attention, and she began to feel welcome at Lyne.

She undertook to make quilted curtains and counterpanes for Madame Ouspensky and worked at these in all her spare time for several months. I was very happy to see that a real friendship had been formed between the two women I most admired in the world. They were of almost the same age, and perhaps just because they were both very strong they had been somewhat wary of one another until that time.

After her experience of death my wife was greatly changed. She acquired a degree of non-attachment that I had never seen in her before. I do not mean that her enthusiasm and joy of life was abated. On the contrary, we were much happier than ever before, but she was no longer torn by the feeling of her own uselessness.

In 1938, my first wife Evelyn died. I had not seen my daughter for eighteen years. When I asked permission to see Ann after her mother's death, her grandmother invited me to their house in Wimbledon. We were complete strangers to one another. I felt helpless to make any contact with her, and yet I was aware of a great tenderness and gratitude that I was able to be with her again. During all the previous years, I had never broken my decision to make no attempt to see her or interfere in her life. I now saw that this had been utterly unfeeling and artificial. Her mother was a gentle person and would not have wished to keep father and daughter apart. But there again, I had been sadly lacking in understanding of women.

Although I could not understand people, I had the power to arouse their interest and confidence in my own visions. During the years just before the Second World War, my outward life turned towards success. I was engaged in the activity best suited to my type and temperament, of building something new and infusing it with life. My days were very full, and yet I had no doubt that all I was doing in science and industry was as chaff compared with my work with Ouspensky.

My deep conviction that the unseen world is more truly real than the visible world had been reinforced by my wife's experience. As she was reluctant to speak of it, I put it out of my thoughts. Quite unexpectedly, a message came from Ouspensky reminding her that the year was up and asking to see her. She went down to Lyne and had a long talk with him. When she came home, she wept and said to me: "I am deeply sad for him. I had not understood how much he suffered. When I told him all that had happened to me, he was on the verge of tears and said that since he was a young man he had been waiting and hoping to have for himself the experience which proves the reality of the other world, but it had never come to him." She went on to tell me how she had said to him that she felt herself like his mother, and that she knew that he must give up his pride in his own strength. She added: "He is a great man and I have always respected him, but now I feel differently. I feel warm towards him for the first time. Only I am very sad for him, because I do not believe he will get what he is looking for. It only came to me because I was willing to die. He understood me, but not altogether, and that is why I am sad: because he is terribly lonely." She told me that when she was leaving he had said: "I have neglected you too much; you must come and see me more often."

I could see that she was deeply moved and supposed that it was the outcome of her talk with Ouspensky. At last she said: "There was more in my experience than I have told you. It concerns you and your own future, but I know that I must not tell you yet. The truth is I don't know how I can ever tell you, because you would not believe what I have to say." I assured her that I did believe all she had told me, but she said very sadly: "Yes, you believe what I tell you about myself, but you would not believe what I could tell you about yourself. If I can speak to you, one day I will do so, but not now."

These events made a deep imprint upon my inner life. I saw that in nearly twenty years I had learned only with my intellect; I was still lacking in inward sensitivity. It might have been expected that this discovery would have been a turning point in my life. But I was not ready. For many long years I was to continue to be dominated and ruled by my own stupid cleverness.

In the spring of 1939, Ouspensky once spoke to a few of us about his fading hope of making contact with the source of Gurdjieff's ideas. On an impulse I wrote to the Bash Çelebi, the hereditary chief of the Mevlevi Dervish Order, who had gone into exile in Aleppo in Syria. I received a warm reply, inviting me to visit him. When I told Ouspensky, he was delighted. He borrowed the letter and showed it to the people at Lyne. My wife and I began to make preparations to take a month's leave and go to Syria in the spring of 1940. The outbreak of war forestalled us.

Meanwhile, all was going well with the B.C.U.R.A. As our work in new laboratories at Fulham was about to explode into full activity, the war came. On 3rd September 1939, my wife and I were on the way to the South Coast and heard Chamberlain's declaration on the wireless in a garage where we had stopped for petrol. We had intended to take a few days' rest and to see my daughter, who was staying with her grandmother in Bognor. I returned to London, expecting big changes and the probable loss of most of my staff. Instead, we were informed by the Government that the Research Associations were regarded as necessary for the war effort, and that our staff would not be recruited for the armed forces. I quickly devised a new programme of research, aiming at enabling motor vehicles to be run on coke gas if the threatened submarine warfare should cut off supplies of imported petrol.

While we were waiting for our wartime task to become clear, I had less to do than for several years. My thoughts turned again towards the fifth dimension, and the task of expressing in mathematical terms my intuition of the character of eternity. With this was an urge to write about Gurdjieff's System and connect it with contemporary discoveries in science and pre-history. Throughout 1940 everything that I touched went well. My wife and I had moved to Tite Street in Chelsea, where we took a large studio. She made it very comfortable, and we lived in a style that I had never enjoyed before. At that time we both used to go down to Lyne on Sundays. Many of our group also went there to work. There was a more natural balance between my work with B.C.U.R.A. and my work with Ouspensky; also I was not driving myself quite so unreasonably as I had during the previous years. In spite of the war and the air raids, this was one of the happiest periods of our married life.

On 4th January 1941, Madame Ouspensky left for America. My wife was one of a very small number to see her off at the station. When she returned, she commented on the desolation of those who were left behind, saying: "They are too dependent. What is the use of having worked on themselves for ten, fifteen or twenty years if they are still as dependent as ever upon Mr. or Madame Ouspensky? You would be as bad as they are if Mr. Ouspensky had let you, but you certainly have no right to be so passive. You can and must be responsible for your own work."

A fortnight later I heard that Ouspensky was following his wife to America. He was convinced that Germany would win the war, and that this would be the prelude to revolution. He told us that Communism was bound to sweep over Europe, and that the only hope lay in America keeping aloof. When I went to say goodbye, I put three questions to him. The first was: "Is my lack of progress due to lack of effort, or wrong effort, or is it due in part to there being some method or technique we do not know and have yet to find?" His answer did not surprise me: "It has nothing to do with methods. Your trouble is that you always make false starts. All your work consists of false starts. And if you keep returning to the starting point, how can you hope to make progress?" I then asked him: "How do I stand in relation to your group here?" He would not say much about his plans. "I can only consider the work at Lyne. The rest, so far as I am concerned, is dissolved. I have given my instructions for continuing the work at Lyne as long as possible. You and your wife can, of course, remain in contact with the work there." Then I put the question that had been troubling me for months: "Have you any objection to my trying to write out the System as far as I can remember it?" 'System' was the name we gave to the teaching and methods we had learned from Gurdjieff, as transmitted by Ouspensky. His reply was disheartening: "In my opinion, writing is not useful. Mental recapitulation is better. In any case, the System cannot be written in ordinary form. If you do write, it can only be to convince yourself that it is impossible."

He added that he had, at that moment, no intention of publishing an exposition of the System, though he might change his mind later.

On 29th January 1941, Ouspensky left for the United States. I never saw him again. I felt that there was more than a physical separation. Even before he left, I had resolved that I must in future work independently. I wrote in my journal: 'It is not a sharp break, or any diminution in my respect and deep gratitude towards him. He has taught me everything, and the contact with his work has had the supreme advantage for me of teaching me my own weakness and foolishness.'

At that time, I had thirty or forty pupils who wished to continue to study with me and to work together according to the System. We were meeting regularly, in spite of the fierce air raids on London. Life at that time was very dangerous. My wife was reported killed, and had the unusual experience of seeing her obituary notice in the Daily Telegraph. Her cousin, Field Marshal Lord Birdwood, invited me to lunch with the Turkish Ambassador in London, and the possibility suddenly arose that I might go on a special mission to Turkey. I remembered my correspondence with the Bash Çelebi and wondered if I would have the chance of going to Aleppo. The plan fell through, and Sir Denison Ross went instead of me on the mission to Turkey.

At this time, the constant repetition of the Lord's Prayer, which I had been practising for seven years, had an unforeseen effect, inasmuch as it completely removed the fear of death. We were often close to death and yet, so long as I repeated the Lord's Prayer, I had the conviction of immunity from danger. It was not so much that I felt that death did not matter as that I was not destined to die in that way and at that time. Nevertheless, the air raids began to threaten our laboratories. One night a large bomb fell in the cemetery next door and hurled a gravestone through the roof. When we arrived in the morning we found it in a desolation of broken apparatus.

We were in a target zone for the German bombers, and we were advised to move our laboratories out of London. The Government offered to requisition a place, but left it to us to find it. In spite of the danger and discomfort, this was a happy time. On 10th April my wife and I went for a week's rest in the Malvern Hills. We had never been closer or happier together. I wrote: 'It has been a week of as near perfect happiness as it is possible for me to conceive, until I change entirely.' The day after we returned to London, Tite Street was directly hit by a bomb, and we were surrounded by blazing houses. We got out unscathed. My wife and I were able to share the conviction that our earlier experience had brought to us; that the destruction of the physical body need not be a disaster to the soul.

Although our own flat escaped complete destruction, it was not possible to remain there. My wife and I went to live in a small house next door to the laboratories. The air raids on London were at their worst. Our neighbours came and shared our air raid shelter. It was a real slum area, and I met for the first time petty criminals and prostitutes, living with their delightful children in unembarrassed promiscuity. We took some of the boys and girls to work in the laboratories. My wife became librarian and thoroughly enjoyed the work, especially that of training her young assistants. The need to find a new place to live and work was becoming urgent, and I spent such spare time as I had in visiting houses on the outskirts of London which we could expect to be outside the main target area for the German bombers.

16: COOMBE SPRINGS

I was drawn towards Kingston Hill. I inspected several large houses vacated because of the war, but none was suitable. On Saturday, 5 May 1941, an estate agent telephoned to say he had just been offered a large house with seven acres of land, to be let for the duration of the war. I got into a car with my wife, and we found our way to Coombe Springs. We drove through handsome, but rusty, wrought-iron gates up a short drive to reach the house, which lies out of sight of Coombe Lane, the main highway between Kingston and Wimbledon. The house was in an appalling condition, rank with the smell of cats and dogs. Seven fierce chows and twenty-two cats disputed possession of the ground floor. To keep the animals from fighting, the house was divided in two.

Mrs. Hwfa Williams was almost totally deaf. We could make no headway with her. She either could not, or would not, tell us the name of her solicitors, with whom we wished to discuss a lease. She insisted upon telling us of the past glories of Coombe Springs, of the golden days when King Edward VII and his friends used to come and spend week-ends with her. She showed us her visitors' book, in which the names of the royalty and nobility of Europe mingled with those of the set that surrounded the King. She told us that her husband had at one time owned Claridge's Hotel and was a well-known race-horse owner. Since his death, she had lost all his fortune gambling in Monte Carlo and was now living alone with her Italian maid.

We went out to see the grounds and could hardly make our way through the dense growth of brambles and thistles. A small bomb had fallen in the rose garden, and the greenhouses were derelict. The place might well have produced upon us the most desolate impression, but on the contrary, we were exhilarated beyond reason. Both my wife and I were convinced that we should come and live there, and that it would become a great centre of spiritual life.

That night I wrote in my journal: 'We saw Coombe Springs. My heart tells me that this is where we must go. Again and again, I have been drawn back to Kingston Hill to look for a place to transfer part of our work. And here I have found what looks all and more than I had hoped for. If it all comes true, I shall have to say that something guided me there, for there was a persistent, unmistakable urge to go and look in that area, and I have rejected other good alternatives without logical reasons. Polly and I were so happy that we dared not think of it too much. If we can get Coombe Springs, such wonderful opportunities will open for us that I can really hope to make some progress. At the same time, there will be great perils and great responsibilities.'

When I told my group about Coombe, several wanted to take it for our work and not for the research laboratories, but it was obvious that we could not afford such a commitment. The Council of the B.C.U.R.A. found it suitable for the temporary research laboratories, and after negotiations with Mrs. Hwfa Williams, strange to the verge of farce, we signed a lease 'for the duration' and received permission to build temporary laboratories there.

Sir Edward Appleton, later Nobel Physics laureate, the author and Sir Evan Williams, BCURA chairman, at the opening of new research laboratories at Coombe Springs, 1943, known as "The Fishbowl".

I was now the director of the largest industrial research association in England, and one, moreover, serving coal, the basic industry of the war effort. I had neither the academic qualifications, nor the training in research, of my colleagues who directed other such associations, but I did have ideas. My strong point was my ability to see more deeply and more quickly than others into the potentialities of a situation. I saw clearly that the era of cheap coal, on which Britain's industrial supremacy had rested for a century, was ended, and that we must compensate by increased efficiency for the higher wages and better living conditions that must be assured to the coal miners in the future. This conviction led me into various activities that were mutually related by the one theme of advancing the more efficient use of coal. I did much to bring about the formation of a Solid Fuel Industries Committee at the British Standards Institution and, for most of the war years, was its chairman. I was the B.C.U.R.A. nominee on the Parliamentary and Scientific Committee, a very influential body of nearly four hundred members, drawn from the two Houses of Parliament and more than a hundred scientific societies. The Committee, with Sir John Anderson as Chairman, elected me Honorary Treasurer. I was responsible for drafting its report on a National Fuel Policy and took an active part in most of its work. The Minister of Fuel and Power appointed me as a member of the Fuel Efficiency Committee under the chairmanship of Dr. E.S. Grumell, of Imperial Chemical Industries. I acted as chairman of the subcommittee on the better care of fuel in industry and also of a small committee appointed to examine and report on inventions in the field of fuel economy.

This account of my activities may give the impression of a self-confident man making his way successfully towards a moderately important position in public life. The reality was ludicrously different. All that I was doing seemed to be incongruous, unnecessary and worlds removed from my true destiny. I knew that I had renounced the prospect of outward achievement twenty years earlier when I had refused Ramsay MacDonald's offer of a political career with the Labour Party. The only satisfaction I felt was that I was not required to do anything from the beginning to the end of the war that concerned the taking of human life. I had pacifists on my staff, and, when convinced that they were sincere, I was ready to go and testify for them at the Conscientious Objectors' Tribunal. My own attitude towards the war was that a consistent pacifism is impossible. We have the right to criticize and oppose violence only if we neither allow ourselves to be violent nor profit from the violence of others. I could claim neither justification. On the other hand, I found war itself detestable. I mistrusted our own propaganda and knew that the Germans were as sincerely convinced of the rightness of their cause as we were of ours.

My dominant conviction was rather of the stupidity than of the wrongness of war. I did not have the passionate belief in the sacredness of human life that converted many into pacifists. Taking life, even indirectly, was sinful, but not horrible. I was certain that the life of a man's soul is not dependent upon the existence of his body. It seemed to me that modern man's horror of war is connected with his fear of death and this, in turn, has resulted from the decay of faith. I observed that many atheists were pacifists; many sincere believers in God, in Divine

Providence and in the immortality of the soul have not been pacifists.

I was living in a state of great strain. The war and the bombing were not the worst disturbance of my life. The irreconcilable conflicts within my own nature overflowed into everything I was doing. I could not look at the simplest situation without seeing the absurdity of human life. There is, however, one exception that I must record, and this is the influence of music and the musical friends with whom my wife and I made new contacts at this time. Through Hilda Dederich, a gifted pianist and the wife of my chairman, Herman Lindars, himself a fine musician, I came to know Denise Lassimonne and Myra Hess and other pupils of that great teacher Tobias Matthay. My wife and I often visited him at High Marley, above Haslemere. I took piano lessons from Hilda Dederich, who taught me something of the art of touch. We spent Christmas 1941 with Matthay and his nearest friends. I wrote: 'We spent a beautiful day: kindness, music, laughter, the whole atmosphere harmonious and peaceful. Nothing but goodness and beauty seems to live down here. And, moreover, it is not passive, but spreads its beneficent influence all over the world. Uncle Tobs is the source and mainspring of it all. From him there radiates a true love of the beautiful, a sincerity unshakeable which creates, in those of his pupils who can receive it, a new set of values.'

We remained close friends of Uncle Tobs Matthay until his death in 1945. It was a perpetual astonishment and delight to us that he wished to have us with him as often as possible. Our last visit was a week before he died. He professed himself to be an agnostic. He knew that I believed in a conditional immortality and often spoke to me about the soul. When he died, I was entrusted with the solemn duty of scattering his ashes on the hillside above High Marley. I have never doubted that he had attained to that degree of liberation from terrestrial influences which enables the soul to enter into a fuller existence after death. Such a soul continues to transmit good influences after its departure from the earthly scene.

In 1942, I was elected a member of the Athenaeum Club. On my first visit, I sat on the seat I had shared with MacDonald twenty years earlier. My life passed before me in review. The Second World War, which I had seen as inevitable in 1922, was now upon us. The vanity of political endeavour was as evident to me now as it had been then. All round me were earnest, elderly men engaged in discussions that all concerned, in one way or another, the conduct of the war. I felt as remote from it as if I were not living in a physical body on this earth. I was no wiser and no better than all these respectable and famous men; but I could see clearly what appeared to elude their vision: that human cleverness will never solve the fundamental problems of human life.

If war is not the greatest crime, it is perhaps the greatest folly which man can commit. I was certain that the Allies would win the war. This certainty was based on belief neither in the rightness of the Allied cause nor in the wisdom of their counsels, but in the abstract principle that every attempt at universal domination must eventually fail. But I had no great hope that an Allied victory would bring peace. I had not forgotten my experiences of peace-making twenty years earlier. I believed that the world was entering a long time of troubles. This would involve all mankind, and my belief, at that time, was that individuals or small groups of people could avoid involvement. This belief was confirmed by the observation that the group of thirty or forty people working with me in my group were very little affected by the war. None was killed or seriously wounded, either by air raids or in the armed forces. This was done without deliberate withdrawal from war activity, and it appeared to be the consequence of having set ourselves to serve an aim beyond our own welfare. In the years that have passed since that time, I have seen further evidence that there may be an invisible protection for those who are called to serve a great purpose.

These ideas were made explicit by the task that I had set myself of writing all that I could remember of Gurdjieff's System. From the time that Ouspensky left England, I had been devoting all my spare time to writing. I would draft a chapter during the week; read it to the group, and revise it in the light of their questions and comments. This work seemed to me particularly necessary, since nothing had been published of Gurdjieff's System. Ouspensky had said that he probably would not publish what he had written, and there was a danger that his manuscripts might be destroyed. At that time, I was quite unaware that Gurdjieff had spent years writing his own version in the monumental All and Everything, of which scores of copies were scattered over three continents.

Ouspensky had said that a systematic presentation of Gurdjieff's teaching was impossible, but I believed that it could be done by taking one central theme to give coherence and structure. I found this theme in the notion of the triad; that is, the theory that everything that exists or happens in the universe is the conjunction of three independent factors.

As the study of this Law of Three occupied a large place in my thoughts for more than twenty years, I must go back to the time when I first saw something of its significance. This was in 1934, when Ouspensky suggested that some of his pupils might undertake research into the law of three, and accepted my offer to study it in the sacred writings of

India. Much reading of the Vedas, the Upanishads and the Mahabharata had led me to a chapter in the Sixth Book of the great epic in which the variability inherent in all existence is ascribed to the six possible combinations of the three gunas or qualities of nature: Sattvas or purity, Rajas or dominance, and Tamas or inertness. I also found in the Sankhya Karaka, which I studied in an old Sanskrit edition, a similar discussion, with the additional statement that the three gunas are perfectly balanced and unified only in the world of primal Being.

When I reported these discoveries to Ouspensky, he said that he had come to the conclusion that there must be six or perhaps seven fundamental laws governing all existence, derived from the six possible, and one impossible, combinations of the three qualities that Gurdjieff described as the affirming, denying and neutralizing forces. He spoke of this at one of his general meetings and invited us to try to work out the form of the six laws. He encouraged me to speak of my own researches, and this was a surprise and a satisfaction to me after having been I snubbed so many times when I had ventured to put forward ideas of my own.

For about two months, all our meetings and discussions were occupied with this theme. Suddenly, as was his way at that time, Ouspensky dropped the subject and refused to discuss it further. My interest had been too deeply aroused to let me drop it, and I continued to study alone.

Before long, I found that I could make no progress and reluctantly put the study away. I suppose that Ouspensky had dropped it because he had reached the point where some quite new notion was needed in order to bring the abstract law into closer contact with concrete facts, and this notion would not reveal itself before its time.

Seven years went by, and in 1941, soon after Ouspensky left for America, the notion of the triad spontaneously engaged my attention. I connect this with our coming to Coombe Springs. It was July 1941, and my wife and I were to live in the house. I wanted to combine the use of the house for research with a voluntary effort to bring beauty back to the neglected grounds. The strange manner in which the house had been found and secured illustrated a triad that I had never been able to understand. New ideas were fermenting in me, and I felt the need to translate them into action. As a first step, I proposed to the Executive Committee of the B.C.UR.A. that I should invite friends down to work at weekends, and so improve the gardens without spending money intended for coal research.

On 3rd August, I took a party down to Coombe - just over twenty people - and we worked all day in the garden. That night my wife and I remained there alone, and we were alone the next day. I wrote in my journal: 'We remarked how strange it is that all my life I have had no attachment of any kind to a place, nor have I wanted a home. Even the thought had been foreign to me, for I have visualized my future always as an escape to the East. Then, suddenly, this place appeared, and there has never been any doubt in my mind that this is where I have to be.'

On 13th August we had a small family party in London, interrupted by an air raid, for my daughter Ann's twenty-first birthday. I had been searching for three years for the right relationship with her. I see how far I still was from any ability to enter into the feelings of others. My daughter wanted a father, not a good parent, and I did not even guess that these are not the same. And yet my own father had been a very good father and a bad parent. Not for anything would my sister and I have had him different.

A few days later I went with a small group to Snowdon, in North Wales, staying near Pen-y-Pas. It was no small achievement to travel two hundred and fifty miles in an ancient Packard car with a producer gas trailer in tow. Our journey, made with coke, an unrationed fuel, instead of petrol, then severely rationed, aroused much interest. The gas producer had been designed and built by the B.C.UR.A. staff.

We all, old and young alike, camped in tents. About a dozen managed to make the journey, and we were together for twelve days. During that time I did what seemed to me then, and since, the most important creative work of my life in the realm of philosophical speculation. This was the elucidation of the six fundamental laws of existence, and the manner in which they produce secondary laws in passing from one level to another. Since the results of this work are given in detail in Volume II of *The Dramatic Universe* I need not refer to it here. The manner in which it all came to me is, however, very strange and worth recording.

I had intended to work on psychological themes, but on the first morning of our arrival, I rose at dawn and walked into the great horse-shoe of hills that lies to the east of Snowdon. I was alone. There was no sound but of bleating sheep and an occasional bird. The sunrise was majestic, and I was overwhelmed by the contrast between unfortunate London, writhing under the German bombing, and this place of peace and splendour.

As I walked, I began to see the laws that governed all these processes. I saw involution and evolution: the descent of Power from Above, and the struggle of Existence to return to its Source. I saw how all that exists is what it is eternally and indestructibly, and yet is always changing, merging with everything else and filling the universe with endless activity. I saw the universal Order and finally, I saw how Love and Freedom redeem everything. I shouted for joy in my aloneness, thanking God that I had been shown such wonders.

When I returned to the camp, I breakfasted, and sat down to write. The others went off climbing. By the evening I had written down what I had seen, and one of the girls who had come with us, Hylda Field, typed it out. That evening I read it aloud and we all shared in the exhilaration.

The next morning I went out again, and this time I saw how every law has a pure and an impure form. Then I understood why we had failed to make headway with triads eight years before. Ouspensky had failed to recognize the true cosmic character of several of the triads. Once again I wrote and Hylda typed.

This continued day after day. Sometimes the complexity of what I saw was too much for me, and I could not transcribe it. I saw how out of the simplicity of the triad arises all the intricately interwoven patterns of our experience. I could only formulate a small part of what I saw, but it was enough to lay a foundation on which I continued to build for fifteen years.

The last phase of these experiences was a fitting climax. I had to go up to Glasgow on coal business. The gas-producer car took me to Bangor and a long slow journey began. I reached Crewe four hours before the London-Glasgow train was due. The refreshment room was ill-lit and dirty, crowded with soldiers, talking, shouting or sleeping, many drunk. In this turmoil, I sat down and went to sleep. When I awoke I found myself saying: "There are also negative triads." The meaning of the sentence was clear to me at once, and finding some sheets of paper, I wrote down a description of the six negative triads.

The task was complete. The negative triads were in some ways the most extraordinary discovery of all. The names I have since given them are: Imagination, or Negative Involution; Self-worship, or Negative Evolution; Fear, or Negative Identity; Waste, or Negative Interaction; Subjectivism, or Negative Order; and Identification, or Negative Freedom. These are the central defects of the Will, and as I saw their significance I felt that a veil had been drawn aside, revealing the secrets of human sin and suffering.

When I returned from Glasgow the next day, our visit was nearly ended. I read what I had written about the negative laws. I believe that those who took part in that visit will never forget those twelve days. We had shared in an experience. These visions were different from any that had come to me before. This time, I was being shown truths that were not for me alone.

When I returned to London, I put aside what I had written at Snowdon. I did not feel ready to work upon it further. The strain upon me must have been very great, for I fell ill with impetigo. My whole body was covered with sores, and I was very miserable for about a week. I returned to work on 17th September. I believe that there is a close connection between the condition of our bodies and that of our psyche. If I was brought for a time into a state when I could be aware of great truths, my coarse body, which reflected my psychic impurity, had to suffer the consequences. Looking back, I saw that I had suffered unaccountable physical ailments each time that I was passing through some psychic experience of a higher reality.

During the autumn of 1941, as my journal shows, I was in an irritable condition. I was trying to write a chapter about the Higher Centres in man and found that I was torn between the conviction that several times in my life I had known the working of higher powers within myself, and the fear of being led away by imagination. I took refuge in the descriptions in the mystical literature of the East and the West, but the more I read, the more did the conviction grow upon me that there was some secret connection with the sexual function and mystical experience. Ouspensky had always been reticent about questions of sex, and yet, in his own book A New Model if the Universe, he had spoken of the transmutation of the sex function as a necessary element in the fulfilment of an individual destiny.

When I wrote a section of the chapter on the sex function, I read it to my wife who said, after listening carefully: "You may have missed the most important element in this. There may be very much more in the sexual powers of man that we do not suspect. I long ago became convinced that one of the tragedies of modern man is his inability to grasp the true significance of sex. People think of sex as something exclusive and separate, whereas it may really be the power by which mankind should be united. You had better not read this chapter to the group, as they may understand it wrongly. You have a negative attitude towards sex which is not genuine; until you are free from this you will never understand women." I followed her advice.

When we had this talk, we were already living at Coombe Springs. On 1st November 1941, my wife and I were invited to Lyne to hear a message from Ouspensky. He wrote to say that a magnificent estate in New Jersey, called Franklin Farms, with several hundred acres of farmland, had been offered to him and Madame Ouspensky by his American group. He was having great difficulty in getting started, owing to the lack of experienced helpers, but he had decided to remain in the hope of establishing a permanent group in the United States. He wanted the work at Lyne Place to be maintained on the highest possible level, so that each group would help the other. He added his belief that the chief danger to world security was still Bolshevism, and was not at all sanguine about the future of Europe even if the Allies should win the war.

A wave of emotional sympathy passed through everyone present at the prospect of close connectedness with the work in the United States. I was personally disheartened by Ouspensky's political attitude. It was evident that in the future I should be thrust back more and more upon my own resources. The demand that Lyne Place should be maintained on the 'highest possible level', while at the same time being forbidden to take any initiative, seemed to me to be impossible of fulfilment. For me the Work was something dynamic that was alive only when it was expanding. The history of religion and of spiritual movements shows that, when the impulse to search and move forward gives place to the impulse to hold on and preserve, the death knell has been sounded. The uplifted, excited feelings of the day before at Lyne were no more than the effect of a momentary stimulus after a long period during which nothing had happened. It was soon, as subsequent events showed, to give place to a slow but steady decline, the inevitability of which could have been predicted from the start.

Within a few months, my relations with Ouspensky began to go from bad to worse. In his groups a habit had developed, based on the principle 'There must be no secrets from the Teacher', of making reports on the real or fancied misdeeds of other members. This caused no serious trouble so long as we were all in personal contact with Ouspensky and misunderstandings could be corrected. When he went to America, great harm was done by mischievous reports. I was only one of several victims. Ouspenky's natural and justified mistrust of my impulsiveness was aggravated by reports that I was giving lectures and writing a book on the System. The first intimation that in our last talk he had intended not merely to discourage but to disallow my writing came in May 1942, when I received a message drawing my attention to the rule that no one was allowed to write anything without his permission. I tried the experiment of putting aside my writing for a few weeks and of reading nothing at my meetings. This convinced me that my writing was both necessary and useful. I wrote to Ouspensky, reminding him that I had talked the matter over with him before he left England, and went back to my writing. I began also to give lectures, at that time only to people privately introduced by my own pupils. Once a fortnight the group used to come to Coombe Springs and work together. I also began to teach the rhythmic exercises I had learned at the Prieuré and at Lyne, and which now had, for some reason, been renamed 'Gurdjieff's Movements'.

The opportunities of meeting Ouspensky's close pupils were restricted by the war. I myself was very busy with the new laboratories at Coombe Springs, where I had been given a free hand to plan the Research Station. In spite of war-time building restrictions I was able to introduce several ideas that I had learned at Fulham, and the laboratories were designed to enable us readily to carry our work from the small-scale bench experiments to pilot plants that could be used to design commercial installations. The laboratories were completed in 1942 and opened by Sir Edward Appleton, who was then Secretary for Scientific and Industrial Research under the Lord President. Our own president was Sir Evan Williams, Bt., the wise and experienced head of the Coal Owners' Association of Great Britain.

I was very proud of the staff that I had collected round me under the difficult conditions of war-time research. I was greatly drawn towards the work and yet I could not avoid the feeling that it was at best a passing interest and value, whereas the work of my groups could make a contribution, however modest and imperfect, to the eternal welfare of those who were seeking for spiritual values. I could never look upon coal research as an end in itself.

Nevertheless, the B.C.U.R.A. continued to make visible progress. It was agreed that a concentrated effort should be made to produce more efficient appliances for using coal in the home. We were also at that time cooperating with the research department of Imperial Chemical Industries on the use of alkali to make coke more reactive, and so more effective, in gas producers for road transport. I was empowered to increase the staff and build new equipment.

I continued during these months to fret over my defects, and especially my wastefulness in thought and action. In retrospect my fretfulness looks foolish. The truth is that I was attempting far more than I could accomplish, and driving myself too hard.

Despite the appearance of harmony, the seeds were sown of the misunderstanding that was to arise between myself and the Coal Owners' Association, the all-powerful body to whose good will the future of the B.C.U.R.A. was tied. My personal hopes and aspirations were all directed towards the ending of my activities in coal, in order to devote myself to teaching and writing about the System. But my advocacy of a rapid expansion of research in industry appeared to others as empire-building - an ambitious plan to force the hands of the coal owners to provide the B.C.U.R.A. with more and yet more money for my personal advancement.

Once I gave an address to the Northwest Branch of the Institute of Fuel, in which I said that we must face the fact that the age of cheap coal had gone forever; and that, in future, industry could only avoid a heavy burden of fuel costs by a great increase in efficiency. I added that this would inevitably lead to a reduced consumption of coal. This address, which was reported and favourably commented upon in the financial columns of The Times, drew upon my head a stinging rebuke from the Mining Association. I was told that coal industry price policy was none of my business.

I should have seen the writing on the wall, but my conscience was clear. I knew that I was not trying to make a great place for myself after the war and, with my usual inability to enter into the feelings of others, did not suspect the jealousy and distrust that my actions aroused.

The winter of 1941-2 passed. The worst bombing of London was over. The war situation was serious, and yet we were already preparing for reconstruction, everyone sharing in the conviction that an Allied victory was already assured. My work at the B.C.U.R.A. prospered. In 1942, I was elected Chairman of the Conference of Research Associations, under the Department of Scientific and Industrial Research. This was a surprising honour, as I was the only director, of twenty-five research associations representing the chief industries of the country, who had neither academic qualifications nor long experience of research. I was elected because I was able to see the future of industrial research in Great Britain on a much larger scale than my colleagues, who were directing associations which had been struggling along on small incomes for ten or twenty years. It was clear to me that the fearful destruction of the war would leave England so weakened financially that our only hope of survival would lie in the scientific and technical genius of our people. Research, from being the Cinderella of industry, would become its favoured child. I had not forgotten the lesson I learned from John de Kay, that it is easier to win acceptance for large projects than for small ones. I insisted upon the need to think of industrial research in terms of millions of pounds, where others were still thinking in tens of thousands. As Honorary Treasurer of the Parliamentary and Scientific Committee, I had many opportunities of preaching the need for a bolder approach to scientific and industrial research.

At the end of the year, I was invited by the chairman of the most powerful British coal company to spend a few days in his house in Wales. He encouraged me to speak of my own ideas of a research policy for the British coal industry. I came back feeling that I was in danger of being drawn altogether into a public life that would drown my inner aspirations. In the train, I wrote this prayer: 'O Lord Creator, and all you Conscious Powers through whom the Divine Will is manifested, let me be liberated from sleep, mechanicalness and slavery and find refuge in Conscious Action from which no evil can come. Let me turn from the part to the Whole; from the temporal to the Eternal; from myself to Thee.'

This prayer was answered, but only at the price of very bitter experiences. My whole world had to crumble before I could return to the path which, in the depths of my conscience, I knew to be right.

17: INSIGHTS INTO COSMIC LAWS

After we had been living at Coombe Springs for about a year, a rhythm was established which to some extent harmonized my various interests and activities. This made me aware of the degree to which my life had, until then, been divided into compartments. My work with the coal industry had nothing in common with my work with Ouspensky and his groups. My interest in the geometry of higher dimensions, and my conviction that Eternity was as real as Time, seemed to have no place in either. I had maintained a desultory correspondence with friends in the Near East and had never quite abandoned my dream of a long, secret journey in Asia; but it was still no more than a dream. I kept up my languages, but seldom used them. In my more intimate, personal life I was no less divided. My wife represented one and my daughter another set of impulses, and besides these I had others that did not fit into any pattern. In short, I was not one man, but several men; sharing one body and yet living separate lives.

I did not fully see the extent of the inner conflicts which these separate lives engendered, until they began to coalesce. In an obvious sense this came because I was living at Coombe, where during the week days I was engaged in coal research and at weekends I worked with my group of pupils. My wife had become librarian of the B.C.U.R.A., and we worked together in a way that we had not known before. Still more remarkable was the fact that I found on the staff of the B.C.U.R.A. mathematicians and physicists who were not only interested in my five-dimensional theory, but were able to bring to bear on it a far greater analytical skill than my own.

Two of the Cambridge scientists recommended to me by Lord Rutherford, M.W. Thring and R.L. Brown undertook in their precious spare time to study the geometry by which eternity can be represented as a fifth dimension. Thanks to their skill we obtained remarkable results, which were embodied in a paper that we hoped jointly to publish. We were, however, very diffident of launching a theory that departed so radically from those which had their origin, and derived much of their prestige, from Albert Einstein. Through my very dear friend Professor Marcello Pirani, I had come to know and greatly admire Professor Max Born, who agreed to read our paper. We sent it off in great trepidation on 14th August 1943. At that moment I felt great hope for our work. I wrote: 'This paper may change the course of history.' But I added: 'But only if on its own scientific merits it wins acceptance by men of science. That is why this moment is so pregnant and so strange.'

In the summer I took a party of twenty-five up to the English Lakes. We found a hospitable place in Langdale, where an old gunpowder factory had left behind dozens of solidly built stone huts and one large building, turned into a hotel. Many streams flowed through the grounds. We were almost alone. Every day we wandered in the hills and returned to practice Gurdjieff's exercises in the squash court. After dinner was the meeting. At that time, I was greatly interested in the relationship of different Orders of Beings.

Darwin's *Origin of Species* had diverted the attention of philosophers from the Scale of Being developed by biologists from Aristotle to Cuvier, yet I felt that in this natural hierarchy, the reality of which is obvious to all, we should find one of the keys to understanding human destiny. At that time, I was writing an essay that later became Chapter 35 of *The Dramatic Universe*.

While at Langdale, we received a letter from Professor Max Born saying: 'I found the paper very interesting, but I need a good deal of time to make definite comments.' He agreed to come and stay with me at Coombe Springs and did so. He said that he found no fault in the mathematics, but did not believe that we were right in the fundamental assumption that time and space were merely conditions of existence. He thought they were inherent in the nature of matter; or more exactly, that matter was only the name we give to our perceptions in space and time. We were encouraged by his interest, but saw that we had to be more cautious in the way we presented our basic assumptions. We little guessed that five more years of work were ahead of us before the paper could be published in the Proceedings of the Royal Society.

When I returned to London after the seminar at Langdale, I found that the powers that ruled the destinies of the Mining Association of Great Britain had found it wise to curtail my freedom of action and speech. My first impulse was to resist and manoeuvre to retain my position. I recognized that my true interest lay in letting myself be restrained; I was overworked and needed to reduce my activities. Instead of doing so, I took on more and more. In addition to our weekend meetings at Coombe, I committed myself to give a series of lectures in London at the Church House, Westminster, with the title Man and his World. The lectures went well, and our group was growing stronger from month to month. But I had mismanaged my relationships with the Mining Association. My chairman, Herman Lindars, was sincerely distressed. He was convinced that I was overworked, and that the strain of the war conditions was affecting my judgment. I lacked both gratitude and

wisdom in my attitude towards him. Our close friendship and collabo-
ration over seven years was overshadowed by my impatience of any kind
of restraint.

I could see how unwisely I was behaving. I wanted to be free from
commitments, and yet I fought hard to keep everything in my own hands.
I remember quoting to my wife from The Egoist: "It is hard to relinquish
that of which one would fain be rid." She could not understand how I
could see my own foolishness and yet not act differently.

At this time, I began to be deeply concerned with the problem of
self-will. I saw that I was self-willed. I did not wish to be self-willed, and
yet there was nothing I could do about it. The unceasing repetition of
the Lord's Prayer, which I had practised for nine years, was a constant
reminder. *Fiat Voluntas Tua* I said hundreds of times a day, but when I
stopped to ask myself whether I could mean and intend that God's Will
should be done in all things, I saw that there were always reservations.
"Yes," I said to myself, "I wish God's Will to be done, only I wish, in this,
that or the other situation, His Will to agree with mine."

I could go a long way towards saying "Thy Will be done," but never
unconditionally. This seemed to be quite useless. "With God, one cannot
bargain," I said to myself, but the bargaining was unabated.

So strongly did this impress itself upon me that I could not keep it
to myself. At one of my public meetings, a man stood up and asked me
the question: "What part does prayer play in your teaching?" I answered:
"Prayer is a very great thing, but you must understand where it begins.
The first prayer, on which all other prayer is built, is expressed in the
words 'Thy Will be done'. If I cannot say these words with the whole of
my being, what right have I to pray in any other way? So long as I am at
war with myself, and one part of me says 'Thy Will be done', and another
part says 'Let my own will be done', what can be the sense of my prayer?
It is better to put prayer aside until you know yourself and your own
contradictions. At present, the only prayer appropriate to our condition
is that we may be made able to see ourselves as we really are."

This answer gives a picture of the intolerant and uncompromising
attitude I had towards human problems. I drove myself and was never
satisfied. On 7th September 1943, I had written: 'Madame Ouspensky
always used to say to me: "You are too kind to yourself." I know that
this is true. But what is worse, is that I am too indifferent to the welfare
of others.' With such an outlook, it was inevitable that I should have no
weapon but my own self-will with which to say *Fiat Voluntas Tua*. The
absurdity of this did not occur to me, and even when my wife spoke
to me about the obvious inconsistency of my attitudes, I still did not

understand. I not only loved her, but greatly admired her penetrating insight into people. I recognized that it was far more sensitive than my own, and yet I did not trust her insights when they concerned myself. Inside and outside, my life was riddled with conflicts.

Not only were my relations with the coal owners deteriorating, but my relations with Ouspensky reached breaking point. I sent him a copy of the paper I had re-written with Thring and Brown after receiving Born's criticisms. Just before Christmas, I had a reply written by him personally, the last I was to receive. Reading it again after seventeen years, I can see a far deeper significance in this letter than I did at the time. He summarily dismissed the paper on five-dimensional physics with: 'If successful it will only amount to a new theory of Thermodynamics, and nothing more.' He then went on to say that nothing new can be found by intellectual processes alone, and that there is only one hope: that we should find the way to work with the higher emotional centre. To this he added the sad comment: 'And we do not know how this is to be done.' He ended by saying that he forbade categorically the use of any ideas of the System, whether contained in his lectures or not. If I wished to quote him I could refer only to his published book, A New Model of the Universe.

Ouspensky was concerned about the possible distortion or misrepresentation of the System. This was clear from a letter he sent to one of his most trusted pupils and friends, in which he said that 'all in London should make sure to avoid the smallest departure from the letter of the System as contained in the writings I have left.'

These messages brought into a new perspective all my problems of self-will and its surrender. It was irrelevant whether Ouspensky was right or wrong in demanding the surrender of all personal initiative on the part of his pupils. The whole point was that I never had surrendered and never could surrender my own independence as others had done. I wrote: 'I do not know in myself what complete surrender or complete obedience really mean. I have, of course, surrendered in my outward actions for many years. For a long time - from 1933-1938 perhaps - I did nothing rebellious in the smallest degree, and I followed the lines of the Work without asking why or whither. But all this outward conformity only covered an even more stubborn inward self-determination.'

I had no doubt that it was my duty to write. When I first met him, Ouspensky had preached the gospel of grow or die. Why then did he deny our right to grow? "Can we," I asked myself, "eternally struggle only to stand still?"

The winter of 1943 passed. My wife fell ill. She was then sixty-nine years old, and this illness was the warning that her active days were numbered. She herself copied from a book of Tibetan maxims the saying: 'It is supremely necessary to understand that time is meted out to us like the last few moments of a man who has received a mortal wound.' She had this mounted in a blood-red frame and kept it constantly before her.

I was getting more and more weary, and in consequence making mistakes in my work. Herman Lindars, in the most friendly way, urged me to go away and take a month's rest, saying: "If you do, I beseech you not to take any work to do. Have a rest." It was no good. I went with my wife to stay at the Old Bell Inn at Hurley, but I took my writing with me and worked all day long. I had never learned how to rest or be peaceful, yet the stay at Hurley was a very happy time for us both. My wife recovered her health and I felt myself at peace again. But still I would not or could not rest.

We had long talks about our future plans. It was clear to me that I should draw out of coal research as soon as the war ended. I was confident that we could buy Coombe Springs when the B.C.U.R.A. moved out. I had no doubt that my future lay in the search for spiritual values and not in the pursuit of material success. During this time we went to Lyne Place, and had long and serious discussions with Ouspensky's closest pupils still remaining in England. The conflict between 'conservation' and 'development', between what appeared to me as the static and kinetic attitudes towards any ideas or values, was unmistakable. It was clear that our ways were parting. I felt an intense sadness. I foresaw that very soon Ouspensky would repudiate all connection with me, and that I would again be left to struggle on alone.

Immediately after Easter, I returned to Coombe Springs and discovered that, during my absence, decisions had been taken that further curtailed my authority. My feelings were deeply wounded by what seemed to be a stab in the back. I was appalled to see that I could be so disturbed by outward events. For several days, I was plunged in hatred of myself and all about me.

Early in the morning of Thursday, 14th April 1944, I awoke and as usual went down to the Springs for my accustomed dip. Day was dawning, but the sun had not yet risen. I had slept badly and was in a rebellious state, seething with resentment against Ouspensky and his pupils; against Lindars and the Council of the B.C.U.R.A.; even against my own group because they could not understand my difficulties. As I walked down the woodland path, I said to myself: "Now is the moment to sacrifice all this self-love and self-pity." I said aloud the words *Fiat Voluntas Tua*, and for the first time in my life I was conscious of speaking them with no reservation of any kind. With the incredible speed of conscious vision that leaves thought limping lamely far behind, I saw the future: not one future, but all possible futures. I saw myself losing my job. I saw myself triumphantly successful. I saw Ouspensky repudiating me, and all his pupils shunning me in the streets. I saw myself followed by people who loved and trusted me. All this and much more was presented to me in the merest moment of time. And I accepted it all. Whichever the future God might send, I was ready to follow it without question.

In the same moment that I made the decision, I was flooded through and through with love. I said aloud: "Jesus!" Jesus was everywhere. Each new-born spring leaf on the willow trees was full of Jesus, and so were the great oak trees, still bare of green. The spiders' webs glistened under the morning dew. The eastern sky glowed with the coming sun. Jesus was everywhere, filling all with love. I knew that Jesus is God's love.

I saw also that each separate part could contain so little of God's love just because it was so small. I said to myself: "Unless concentration can occur, He is as if not there." As I spoke the words they were full of meaning, but now I have forgotten what they meant, except for one thing: that in order to live in the Love of God - that is, in union with Jesus - we must pray without ceasing. This practice, which for many years I had followed so conscientiously, had been as nothing, because without love, prayer is empty.

I returned to the house and made tea. I took it to my wife and woke her and told her what I had seen. She rejoiced with me. She said that she had known that Jesus was the same as God's Love when she had been as dead, and had never quite lost her vision.

I remained for three days in the state of ecstasy produced by this experience. It was unlike anything I had known before, because it came not by deploying my own strength in a supreme effort, but from the simple act of surrendering my own self-will. While the state was on me, I could not act against the manifest Will of God. For example, the day following I received in my morning post a letter that was both unjust and dangerous. I could have dealt with it sharply, demonstrating that my correspondent had wilfully distorted the facts. I was about to write a personal letter to someone who would have put the matter right. As I took up my pen to write, a voice within me said: "That pen contains Jesus. How can you misuse it?" Peace came over me and I saw that I should not try to defend myself.

If I had not written down my experiences during those days, I should not now trust my memory. For a short time, I was able to see and even to enter that realm in which Divine Love is a reality. But when

I could no longer see, I returned to myself, and many years were to pass before I again became directly aware of that reality.

Even now, I can scarcely believe what I wrote in my journal concerning the real Presence. I find the words: 'We can see the literal truth of "Take, eat; this is My Body ..."' I was penetrated with the eternal quality of the great religious truths. I wrote that morning: "We must see literally, as I have seen, how Jesus is the uttermost reality of personal existence, and yet is not a person in any sense that has meaning for human conception." I had made the step which leads from understanding of symbols to participation by way of gesture. This experience led me to make the distinction (in my book, *The Dramatic Universe*, Vol. I, pp. 71-3) between Symbolism as Being-language and Gesture as Will-language.

Those April days of 1944 were crowded for me with intense happenings. I had been awarded the J. Arthur Reavell Lectureship of the Institution of Chemical engineers. This award had aroused considerable jealousy and criticism from a section of the Institution that wished the award to go to a Fellow of the Royal Society. I had worked hard to prepare the lecture, the theme of which was *Coal and the Chemical Industry*. It was to be delivered on 18th April, four days after my day of surrender. I knew that I should have a critical and even hostile audience, but I was quite unconcerned.

The President, who had to introduce me, was well known for his mordant humour, and he did not fail to make his dislike of my appointment clear. Yet I found that I could give the lecture without using my notes, and gradually a feeling of warmth came over the hall. The lecture was a success. My thesis was that the British coal industry could not survive solely as a purveyor of cheap energy. It was necessary to turn to account the endless potentialities of coal as a raw material of chemistry, of which I gave an imaginative, perhaps over-bold picture. At the time, little notice was taken of the paper except in the technical press, one of which described it as a 'blue-print for the New Age of Coal'. Seventeen years were to pass before the government appointed a commission to study the potentialities of coal as I outlined them in this lecture.

Almost immediately after the Reavell Lecture, I began a series of public lectures on Gurdjieff's system. I did not mention him by name, and some of the audience assumed that the ideas I was expounding were my own, and referred to me as a 'New Teacher'. I hastened to repudiate any such role, or any suggestion that what I was telling them was original. Nevertheless, the lectures aroused much interest, and many wrote to ask if they could continue to study with me. I was faced with the question of what I would do when the war ended. I discussed this with my oldest pupils and friends, and we agreed that we might have to start some kind of Institute or Society, for researches in the realm where life meets with spirit.

Preparations for the end of the war were in the air all about me. It was recognized that, owing to planning restrictions, the B.C.U.R.A. could not remain at Coombe Springs, and after much searching, a large plot of land was bought at Leatherhead and new, imposing laboratories were being designed. I was offered a private Director's laboratory, where I could supervise researches in which I was especially interested. When the plans were finally approved and building was ready to start, I went to Leatherhead with a small party to witness the cutting of the first sod by my dear friend Dr. Clarence Seyler, the doyen of coal research in England. As he spoke of the hopes he placed in my leadership of the new laboratories, I had, as so many times before, the experience of separating from my body and surveying the scene from another dimension. I saw clearly that I myself would never go to Leatherhead, and that no Director's Laboratory would ever be built.

This was hardly prophetic, for my situation at the B.C.U.R.A. was deteriorating fast. It was being said openly that I had done well in launching the project, but that I was too unreliable and self-willed to be a good administrator. I had made enemies, mostly by my own fault. There was also a sincere conflict of convictions as to the aims of Coal Utilization research. On the short view, the aim was to preserve markets for coal against the threat of conversion to oil-firing. For this, appliances had to be made easier to use, more efficient and less productive of smoke and fumes. Our work in this field was going ahead well, but it could not create new markets for coal. On the contrary, by making two tons of coal do the work of three, it was bound to reduce consumption. Post war experience has fully confirmed this forecast. I believed then and still believe, that there are unexplored possibilities of using coal as a chemical raw material. This belief appeared to most of the coal owners a scientist's dream that would never be realized, and they resented money being spent on it.

The issue was brought to a head by a line of research that I had initiated early in the war, the aim of which was to find a way to make use of the fact that coal is a natural plastic, like resin. Early in the war, there was a threatened shortage of raw materials for the plastics industry. I had suggested to the Ministry of Supply that an unlimited quantity of plastic material was available in our coking coals, and that a way of using it directly for making electrical and other parts might be developed.

It is not difficult to describe the effect I was looking for. Thermoplastic materials soften when heated and harden again when cooled. They are made into useful shapes by pressing them in moulds while they are hot, but if they are overheated they decompose and will not set again. Now, although coal softens, it decomposes at the same time. This is what produces coke, the pores of which are made by the gases that come out while the coal is soft. It occurred to me that, by making coal into a very fine powder and pressing it just below its natural softening temperature, it would set hard and strong into any desired shape.

I was invited to make some experiments. As so often happens in research, these were very promising, and the B.CUR.A. was offered a contract to develop the method. For the reasons I have given, the Council of the B.CUR.A. was not enthusiastic about this proposal, which in their view went outside the broad programme of research into the use of coal as a fuel. I asked and was given permission to seek for independent support of the project. Four great industrial firms headed by Imperial Chemical Industries agreed to back the research, which we called 'Coal Disaggregation' because the idea behind it was first of all to break coal up very finely and then put it together again. I put the research under the direction of Professor Marcello Pirani, whom I have already mentioned as my colleague in my first scientific paper. Pirani had discovered, before the First World War when he was chief of research of the German Osram Werke, how to make very strong carbon filaments for lamps, and he had original notions about doing the same with larger shapes.

By June 1944, these researches had made good progress. A number of patents had been applied for but, owing to war restrictions, could not be completed. The work was recognized as my baby, and the Council of the Association displayed a marked lack of interest in its progress. I saw in it a possible way of making myself independent of the B.CUR.A.

Everything in my life was in flux. The move of the B.C.U.R.A. to Leatherhead was decided, and Coombe Springs would fall vacant. Mrs. Hwfa William's solicitors offered me the opportunity of buying her out at a very favourable price. My public lectures on the System were going well, and many people came to Coombe Springs each Sunday to work with the old group who came to help in the garden.

I was still trying to do too much and, by the end of May 1944, felt very ill. My wife and I again went to Hurley - this time with the intention of staying a month. I was torn by the struggle that was raging within me between one 'self' that could not bear to admit defeat and wanted authority and an important position, and another 'self' that remembered the experience in the garden and knew that my true destiny lay in surrendering outward success and giving up the desire for power.

Slowly, the second self was winning the struggle. Each time I felt myself free from desire and ready to say 'Thy Will be done', my inward peace returned, but the demon of self-will was far from exorcised. I could accept my destiny, but I could not stop myself from struggling to change it. This struggle made me ill.

At this time I was holding my meetings during the week at Park Studio, the home of Mrs. Primrose Codrington, who generously threw her house and unique garden open for us to work in. We also regularly practised Gurdjieff's exercises in one of her studios.

On 8th June, my forty-seventh birthday, I became aware that the corner had been turned. I was able to relinquish the desire for power and was able to try at least to be patient. This sounds simple enough, but patience and non-action were so foreign to my nature that I felt myself torn to shreds. Early in June, I was told that if I were to resign as Director of the B. C. U.R.A., I would receive generous compensation, and also that I could, if I wished, take away with me the research in the field of coal plastics. My wife and I made ready to leave Coombe Springs, where we had been living for less than two years, but which we already felt as our home. We went up to Langdale alone, having arranged that the group would follow in a week. Although in her seventieth year, my wife was amazingly active, going for long walks with me over the dales. I was then writing the last chapter of my book on the System. The subject was Salvation, which I understood to mean the liberation of man from the powers that bind him to his lower nature.

As the days went by and we enjoyed the rare happiness of being alone together, the strain of the preceding year lifted off me. I had been saved from being drawn into a path in which I would have found neither peace nor spiritual welfare.

The seminar at Langdale that year was a joy to all of us. It was a release from London; not only from air raids and restrictions, but even more from the tense atmosphere, the quarrelling and the misunder-standings. The link with my awareness of the Presence of God's Love, so weakened over the past months, was renewed. I saw the beginning of hope that I might become less self-centered and self-willed. How little did I foresee the next ten years and what they would bring.

At that time the world situation seemed very dark. Storms of wickedness were sweeping over the earth, and the search for spiritual values seemed to have lost its hold on men's lives. I looked upon my task as the building of an Ark in which one could take refuge from the destruction that seemed inevitable.

We returned to Coombe Springs on 20th August. My plans were

settled: to retire as soon as possible from the B.C.U.R.A.; to found the Institute for Psychokinetic Research and prepare the way for our return to Coombe Springs in1946. A surprise awaited me. I was asked to meet the directors of a great industrial company and was offered the post of Scientific Adviser to the Board of Directors, at a higher salary than I had ever earned before. The job would mean leaving London, and it was stipulated that I should devote my whole time and energy to their work. Also I would be required to sign a service agreement for a minimum period of five years. It was hinted that if I proved a success I might hope to succeed the managing director. The prospect of being a 'captain of industry' was a sop to my wounded pride. The announcement of the appointment would vindicate my conduct of the affairs of the B.C.U.R.A.

I returned and talked it all over with my wife. When she had listened to the whole story, she said: "Why do you hesitate? What interest have you in money and position? These are the only reason for going. You would not achieve anything that you wanted for yourself." I need not have asked, for my own decision had been taken. It was not my way. I remember that I tried to find my real motives. It was not true that I had no interest in money and position, or rather in these as evidences of success. I liked the people who had made me the offer and knew that I could work with them. I was only forty-seven years old, and I could hope within ten years to be free to do what I wanted.

The truth is that there was no weighing of reasons for and against. I simply knew that this was not for me. As soon as I had declined the offer, another came. This time, to work on the coal disaggregation project, with the backing of two strong industrial groups. This could be done in London, and I was able to stipulate that my job should be part time. I was offered generous terms and accepted.

In October I came to an agreement with Mrs. Hwfa Williams' lawyers, and our return to Coombe Springs after the war was assured. With the help of members of my group, I put down the agreed part of the purchase price. My wife and I went to live at Park Studio and remained there for eighteen months. A chapter was closed. The experiences of the preceding twelve months had been very unpleasant. I had made bad mistakes, and I had paid for them. I wrote on the fifth of October: 'I have, for a year, passed through a period of purgation in which I have come to realize fully my own weakness and my inability to control myself or my life.'

The tide of the war was beginning to turn. I decided to regard the next year and a half as a time of preparation, and hoped that I would succeed in avoiding commitments beyond my power to fulfil.

18: SIGNS AND PORTENTS

On New Year's Day 1945, I set myself to make an honest assessment of my life and its fruits. A quarter of a century had passed since my first wife, Evelyn, had returned home from Turkey to give birth to our daughter. From that time, my life moved in a new direction. I made the contacts that led me in turn to Sabaheddin, Ouspensky and Gurdjieff and to my second marriage. The idea of work on myself in order to achieve a higher level of being had been the common thread running through all the diverse events of the intervening years. I had never doubted that such achievement was possible and that Gurdjieff's System, as taught by Ouspensky, was a key to its attainment. It was no longer a theory that fascinated my mind, but a conviction based upon my own experience. And yet, when I asked myself whether I had made any effectual progress towards the goal of Higher Being, I could find no positive assurance. I had certainly changed in many ways, but was there anything that could not be ascribed to the natural maturing of a man who had lived an eventful life? I wrote down my thoughts, and reading them today, I see that I had no confidence at all in my own progress, and yet was sure that my wife had really changed. But in her case, this might be due to her nearly fatal illness seven years earlier, and the revelation it had brought her of the secrets of life and death.

Ouspensky had convinced us all that the crucial test of a man's being is his ability to remember himself. A man who is asleep is a machine; the helpless slave of his environment. Only the man whose inner consciousness remains free from his outward activity can rightly call himself a responsible being. By this test, I was nowhere. I could not remember myself as much as I could when I first made the effort in the early days of Ouspensky's lectures in London. I was no more free from my environment than those whom I professed to teach.

There was something radically wrong. When I spoke about this to my wife she said: "You have changed more than you know, but you still make the mistake of driving yourself too hard. You do not trust yourself, and that is not good. Perhaps it is better than being eaten up with vanity, but it is a weakness all the same. Why don't you follow your own line more and stop trying to imitate Mr. Ouspensky? You are not like him and you never will be, but you are worthwhile for what you are, and you should not be so concerned about remembering yourself. You are doing good and useful work, and that should satisfy you."

As usual, I would not listen to what she said but went off on a new

line of my own. I said to myself: "My efforts to arrive at self-remembering by force have failed; let me try by gentleness." I set myself to spend
half an hour every morning, after waking up, in the practice of quiet
self-collection. I hoped by this to acquire patience.

Very soon after I had started this practice, I heard, from one of
Ouspensky's old pupils, that Gurdjieff was alive and had been in Paris
throughout the war. Gurdjieff, as a man, had so far receded from my
thoughts that this news came as a shock. It was very strange that I should
have almost forgotten the man who had determined the whole direction
of my life, and I resolved to go to Paris as soon as the war was over and
find him for myself. Such a thought would have been quite alien to me
a year or two earlier, when my attitude was dominated by Ouspensky's
insistence that we should have nothing to do with Gurdjieff. But since the
previous summer, my wife and I had been drifting further and further
away from Ouspensky and his people. That year we held a New Year
party for all our group at Park Studio. This was a distressful landmark,
for in previous years we had always gone to Lyne Place for the New Year
celebrations. This was the first time for twelve years that we had not been
invited.

My depression soon passed, as all our states, good and bad,
disappear and are forgotten. My work was interesting, and I had more to
do than I had time and strength to accomplish. Yet I did not wish wholly
to abandon the book that was beginning to take shape. In February, I
went with my wife for the first of several visits to Crowborough in Sussex.
It was an interlude of wonderful harmony and we had seldom been so
happy together. In intervals of my writing, we walked in Ashdown Forest
under the brilliant February sun. My pessimistic mood was forgotten
and I wrote in my diary: 'I wonder if I can ever repay one tenth of the
happiness I have been given! I often feel how great is my debt to the
world. So many good things have happened to me and I have done so
little with them. I pray that I may be more worthy.'

The first six months of 1945 were a time of steady progress in coal
research. We discovered that we could produce a new form of carbon with
many valuable properties. I joined with the other inventors in taking out
many patents. At one time I was the joint holder of more than fifty British
and foreign patents. The new material was given the name Delanium, to
indicate that it behaved in some ways like a metal. At that time it was
difficult for industrial firms without a reputation for research-minded-
ness to attract first-class scientists. By using unorthodox methods, I was
able to get some young men of exceptional originality and was building
up a team from which I hoped for great results.

I was no less successful in attracting people to the study of the System. During the spring, I gave a new series of public lectures of Gurdjieff's System, with large and more interesting audiences than ever before. Several Americans joined our group at this time. Some of these returned to the United States, where I gave them letters of introduction to Ouspensky. They must have given him very garbled accounts of what I was doing in London. Only much later did I learn that they had supposed that the lectures I was giving were copied from Ouspensky's lectures given before the war.

Whatever may have been the immediate cause, the cup of Ouspensky's growing suspicion and disapproval finally overflowed. My first intimation was a letter from Ouspensky's solicitor in London, asking for the 'return of all Mr. Ouspensky's material, including his lectures'. Next, I heard that a letter had gone to Lyne instructing Ouspensky's pupils to break off all relations with me, and never again to communicate with me on any subject.

At that time, we were still living in Park Studio, and next door were George Cornelius and his wife Mary. He was an American from the Middle West, working in the Naval Attaché's office. He had brought several naval officers to my meetings, and he and his wife had become close friends of ours. One day, seething with indignation, he brought me a letter from an American naval commander, who had recently returned to the U.S.A., warning him that he was the victim of charlatanism. He informed Cornelius that I had stolen Ouspensky's lectures and was passing them off as my own. He advised him, without delay, to break away completely from me, failing which he could never hope to be accepted as one of Ouspensky's pupils.

It was a bitter day for me. I had left Gurdjieff and the Prieuré in order to follow Ouspensky and had tried for so many years to conform to his discipline. I knew well enough that I was self-willed, and that I had not obeyed him when ordered to stop writing. But the whole point of my writing was that I should express my own, and not borrowed, ideas. I had been accustomed to regard Ouspensky as a man of higher wisdom and could not imagine that he would credit foolish tittle-tattle. I searched for some higher motive for his action and could find none.

I was determined not to justify myself or to explain what I had done. If Ouspensky were acting from some mysterious motive of testing and proving me, justification was pointless; if he were merely suspicious and angry, it would be a waste of time to try to put matters right by letter. I can now see, only too well, how in this reasoning, there was an element of self-martyrdom, as if I were saying: "Let all my friends turn against me, let me be misunderstood and misrepresented; I will suffer in silence."

Yet the suffering itself was genuine enough. I did not at all like to meet friends of many years' standing and see them turn ostentatiously or sheepishly away from me. I did not enjoy reading out to my group the letter in which I was described as a charlatan and a thief. I said each one must make up his or her own mind. They could stay with me, recognizing that I was all alone, bereft of guidance and teaching, or they could go and join the group of Ouspensky's pupils and never see me again. Their reaction was consoling to my wounded feelings, for nearly all declared their confidence in me.

I tried to make it clear that their decision should not be based either upon faith in me or on lack of faith in Ouspensky, but solely on their own understanding of the principles of the Work. I did not wish to influence them by giving my own reasons for disobeying Ouspensky. These were clear enough to me: I had to choose between a static and a dynamic attitude towards the spiritual life, between conformity and creativity. However much I might distrust myself and my motives, I was sure that it was better to risk all than to do nothing.

I expected a great turmoil and much searching of heart. There was very little reaction. They could not understand how serious and how painful for me was the ending of an association of pupil and teacher that had lasted for twenty-three years. Few of them had ever seen Ouspensky, and still fewer had been regular members of his groups. It was a shock to be brought face to face with the realization that all these people would henceforward depend upon me. I was taking upon myself to influence the spiritual destinies of more than a hundred men and women, and I was agonizingly uncertain of my own.

In spite of my varied and extraordinary experiences, I felt myself to be a child in spiritual matters. I remembered how Ouspensky had said to me at Lyne on the night of my self-discovery: "You are like Madame. Both of you have young souls. You have not the experience of living many times on this earth." He was referring to his theory of Eternal Recurrence, which most of his pupils took to be literally true. I was much less confident about it, though I believed that it contained an important element of truth. My wife accepted it as the best way of accounting for her conviction that, in some previous existence, she had taken her own life. As Ouspensky had the same belief about himself, it seemed that there must be some substance in the 'I have been here before' experience that so many have described.

A great merit of Ouspensky's theory of Eternal Recurrence is the avoidance of many of the absurdities of the naive reincarnation doctrine as popularly understood. So far as I could judge, the 'I have been here before' experience cannot refer to some other life in a different place and time. Moreover, reincarnation beliefs tend to disregard the influence of heredity on the destiny of the individual. It was clear to me that parents and children are connected by a link that is organic and therefore subject to natural laws. It cannot be explained in terms of 'previous lives'.

My own belief, at that time, was that there is a deepening and ripening of that stands apart from time; that is, from 'before-and-after'. A few years later, my researches in geometry and physics led me to extend my notion of higher dimensions to include a third kind of time that I called Hyparxis. This dimension is connected with the depth and quality of existence that I defined as 'ableness-to-be'.

The quality of ripeness is almost impossible to express in practical terms. We are aware of it in Greek tragedy and in the greatest poets. Shakespeare puts it into the mouth of Edgar in King Lear:

Men must endure their going hence, even as their coming hither.
Ripeness is all, come on.
Gloster. And that's true too.

I was now before the reality; no theory could sustain me in the responsibility I had taken upon myself. I was aware of the difference between experience and ripeness. Edgar, surrounded by wickedness, blindness and madness, though young in years, is the one ripe soul in the tragedy, and he remains to say the last word. Gurdjieff's words to me at the Prieuré in 1923: "You already know too much, but your knowledge is useless without Being" returned to me. I was forty-eight years old, and according to the vision that came to me in Scutari Cemetery, I would not meet my true destiny until I was sixty years old, and even then it would only be the beginning.

True destiny or not, there was no going back, and during the summer of 1945, the work at Park Studio reached its greatest intensity. At that time we worked regularly in Primrose Codrington's garden. Alongside were the derelict gardens of houses bombed in Onslow Square. We bought hens and grew vegetables. Frequent meetings and hard work together, against the background of the peace that came over London with the end of the German war, produced in us all a sense of regeneration, of a new and hopeful life in which the work was to spread and prosper. But though outwardly all was going well, I was still secretly anxious and insecure, wondering where I was being led.

At the end of July, with a party of thirty-five, I went for our third and last visit to Langdale. Though the war with Germany was over, the Japanese seemed determined to fight it out to the bitter end. One member of the group had been in attendance at the Potsdam Conference in July 1945. He came to the seminar with gloomy prophecies about Russia that seemed to confirm all that Ouspensky had foretold. We had burned our boats with Stalin, and any hope of friendly cooperation after the war had vanished.

On the fourth day of our stay in Langdale came news of the dropping of an atom bomb on Hiroshima. I was completely overwhelmed. I had known something of the search for an atom bomb. I had refused to believe that it could be realized in practice. I had been so rash as to say, in a public lecture on the future of coal, that atomic fission was as elusive as a needle in a million haystacks. It may be that my refusal to believe it possible came from a far deeper refusal to accept the picture of the future that it implied.

Now it had come. The prodigious consequences were obvious to me as I listened to the account on the morning radio. It was the death-knell of the Epoch in which mankind had lived for two thousand five hundred years - the epoch of reason and of confidence in human wisdom. From now on, madness was to be the master of human destiny. There it was; I saw it, and yet it was inconceivable that there should be no remedy, no way out.

Pondering on these things as I walked through the heather and bracken, I began to see the significance of our work in a new light. It must be the precursor of an action in the world that would counteract the terrible consequences of the atom bomb. I spoke of this to the assembled group, leading them step by step through the events of the century. I said that I believed that within ten or twelve years - anyhow in the nineteen-fifties - there would be an external manifestation of the Work of which we had seen only a small fragment. The task before us was to prepare. Hitherto, our Teaching had remained hidden and known only to a few. The time would come when it would be made public and be followed by many. When that time came, the chief need would be for people who could teach others. Our immediate aim should be to gain experience in the conduct of group work, and I said that I hoped that as many as possible would undertake this when we returned to London.

Our visit to Langdale was not the gloomy affair that this description might suggest. It was the first post-war outing. Rationing was still general. Meat was almost unobtainable in the towns, but in remote farms rationing was already a dead letter. George Cornelius, whose reputation in the Naval Attaché's office rested mainly on his unrivalled ability to procure anything and everything that was wanted, managed to buy a whole lamb. We had a riotous barbecue in the hills on one of those rare fine days by which Lakeland contrives to tempt us into her mists. It was the end of the war, the end of the old regime, and all of us looked forward with confidence to the acquisition of Coombe Springs and the start of a new era.

Although our immediate plans were centered upon Coombe Springs, I felt myself once again powerfully drawn towards the East. Not knowing quite why, I went to the School of Oriental Studies to enquire about Tibetan lessons. I met a Chinese scholar, Mr. Wu, who had lived many years in Tibet. He was interested in Osmanli Turkish. We came to a peculiar arrangement. I was to take one lesson a week in Tibetan at the School and to exchange another lesson with him privately. An Englishman teaching a Chinese Turkish, and learning Tibetan from him, made an unusual combination.

My wife decided to join me, and we started work on 9th October. I still do not understand why I wanted to learn Tibetan. It is an easy language to speak, but the literary forms are fabulously complicated. Fifteen years have passed, and I have only twice had an opportunity of using my slight knowledge of Tibetan.

We entered the New Year full of hopes, and ready for anything. On the whole, our expectations were fulfilled. I was then earning a very good salary as managing director of the Coal Plastics Company. The B.C.U.R.A. had gone to Leatherhead. The contract for Coombe Springs was signed, and the money raised. We worked on the constitution of our new Institute. Many names were suggested. In the end, I proposed that we should choose one that would mean little and convey less, and that would be so awkward to pronounce that it would soon fall into disuse. I wanted to remind them that the Institute was merely the outward form, and that the inner content would come from our own Study groups. The title we selected, The Institute for the Comparative Study of History, Philosophy and the Sciences, Limited, fulfilled our unusual require-ments well enough.

We fixed our return to Coombe Springs for 6th June. I wanted to be there for my forty-ninth birthday. We had to choose the first residents. Many of the group wished to come, but my wife wanted as far as possible to have married couples. Four, in addition to ourselves, were chosen or, more truly, chose themselves. One husband changed his mind, but at the last moment his wife decided that she would come alone. The first group of residents numbered twelve. Several of us were living at or near Park Studio, so that the exodus on 6th June became an event. Miss Kate Woodward, later to become one of the pillars of Coombe, brought her car with a trailer, on to which we loaded a henhouse and the dozen hens, under the care of Elizabeth Mayall and George Cornelius. The hens insisted on laying eggs during the journey, and the trailer arrived gay with yellow splashes. George was amazed and delighted to learn that Cockney jargon is really spoken when one of the removal men asked him if a sofa was to go 'up the apples'. It was an electrifying day for us all; for the first time we had a place of our own, to be devoted wholly to the creation of a centre for spiritual studies.

With memories of the Prieuré, I was consumed with zeal to encourage effort and more effort - mental, physical and emotional. On the very first evening, when we were all tired with the move, I started to wash the walls, and everyone joined in until midnight. It was a Thursday, and I announced that we would have a birthday party on Saturday the eighth. We invited all the old group, and about forty came with their children. Mary Cornelius, who had undertaken the catering, pretended to be in despair. We had no paid staff, and everyone shared in the work. All were enjoying the excitement of the new life. We agreed that there should be no speaking at meals. The day began with a pilgrimage to the Spring House for a plunge in the icy spring water.

My mother was living nearby with my only sister, Mrs. Winifred Udale. She had been active all her life, but was now bedridden, having suffered a stroke the previous year. Soon after we came to Coombe I was able to give her a home, and apart from short visits to a nursing home for treatment, and to my sister's house, she remained with me to the end of her life. Olga de Nottbeck, one of the first members of our community, helped to nurse her through her last illness.

In August, we held our first seminar at Coombe Springs. The theme I chose for our study was *Being and Consciousness*. About forty people came, and we worked from morning till night in the torrid heat of that very hot summer of 1946. We demolished a laboratory built on the site of the hard tennis court. Hours every day were spent in a choking haze of dust. This was for many their first experience of extreme physical effort. Every night we had long meetings to discuss various aspects of the theme of *Being and Consciousness*. Some of those who took part had, though in a minor degree, the experience of breaking through to a different state of consciousness by means of extreme physical exhaustion. Some were frightened and were unwilling to go through with the effort. This was enhanced by having two days of complete fasting without any relaxation of the physical work or mental exercises.

There was nothing original in all this, for I was merely copying what I had seen at the Prieuré, in 1923, under another torrid summer sky. For the pupils who came, the experiences were as new and astonishing as they had been for me twenty-three years earlier. If I had not passed through them myself, I would not have dared to set them before others.

The seminar did good in an unexpected way by forging a link between those who had come to live at Coombe Springs and those who came only for weekly group meetings. There was a danger that the little community might become isolated from the world. The life was so strenuous that there was no time for any outside interests. From June to September 1946, not one of the women living at Coombe went outside the gates, except the woman designated to buy household necessities. The day began at six o'clock, with goats to be milked, hens to be fed and breakfast to be got ready. We often remained up till midnight, finishing the day, as at the Prieuré, with Gurdjieff's rhythmic exercises. The hard physical work was only one element in creating an atmosphere of strenuous endeavour. Both my wife and I were intent upon creating conditions for self-remembering and self-study. These often took the form of the exposure of weaknesses in terms that would, in any other circumstances, have led to open revolt. The most outrageous attacks were accepted as necessary means for self-study, and no one complained. Indeed, as I learned later, the members of the community, now increased to about twenty, felt themselves to be so inadequate that their one fear was of being sent away.

I myself felt that physical effort and emotional stress were not sufficient. I looked for a way to maintain a state of mental alertness also. With this in mind, I set myself, in September 1946, the task of proposing every day a theme for meditation. These themes were called the 'Daily Topics'. I undertook to formulate a different topic every day for a thousand days. I gave out the topic early in the morning, and members of the group telephoned to learn the topic of the day. The task was to keep the theme in one's attention in order to avoid wandering thoughts and idle daydreams. I kept this task going through the shattering experiences that were awaiting us in the unseen future, until the end of the thousand days on 16th May 1949. I cannot tell if the effort was worth making. For me it was a severe self-discipline and for the others a means of sustaining their own sense of direction and purpose. There is another side of such practices that needs to be understood. They easily degenerate into what Gurdjieff used to call 'working to avoid work', that is, making efforts that are easy in order to hide from oneself that one is shirking the sacrifice that is really called for. In the religious life and in the search for spiritual values, this is a great pitfall. At its worst it leads to the pharisaism that says: "Thank God that I am not as other men are." But even at its best it is a perilous self-deception. I have seen many fine spiritual movements drift and finally stagnate through the adoption of regular practices of prayer, meditation, fasting, self-criticism, as well as through works of piety and charity. All these can very easily become smoke-screens that hide the true target, which is the deep-seated egoism and self-love that no effort can conquer.

Therefore, I am doubtful whether I did any good to myself or to others by devising various spiritual exercises. Though their purpose is to provide a fulcrum through which our desire for perfection can exert its pressure, they can easily become ends in themselves.

The spiritual life is far harder than the material, for in the latter self-love can be a most powerful ally. I could see this well enough in my coal research work, where my desire for success was stimulated by the need to think well of myself. I was still concerned in many scientific activities. I had retained my interest in the Parliamentary and Scientific Committee, of which I was still Honorary Treasurer. In December 1946, we brought out a report on Universities and the Increase of Scientific Manpower. Re-reading this report after fourteen years, I see the value of the cooperation between scientists and parliamentarians which the committee fostered. Our proposed expenditure of an additional £10,000,000 pounds per annum on higher scientific education was regarded by many as wild extravagance. Today the present figure of £43,480,000 is criticized as being inadequate. We live in an age where it is seldom wrong to have a bold approach to the problems of the future.

I felt that my usefulness to the Parliamentary and Scientific Committee was coming to an end, and I wished to devote myself more to the work of our own Institute. In 1948 I ceased to be a member.

Our life at Coombe Springs was varied and full of colour. I wrote a play based on the burning of Chartres cathedral in 1187, and its rebuilding by a prodigious effort of the entire countryside. This was rehearsed during the autumn and produced at our New Year party at Coombe Springs. In it I tried to represent the power that enters a human community when all are joined by a common aim beyond all personal gain. There came to me, when I was writing this play, the conviction that the Virgin Mary began to influence human destiny with the beginning of the second millennium of the Christian Era. I tried to convey some feeling of the love that grew between mankind and the Blessed Virgin in the rebuilding of Chartres.

My mother had watched the play from her wheeled chair and had enjoyed her first evening out for many months. The following week, she had another stroke and this time remained completely paralysed. She could scarcely speak but made it clear that she hated her helplessness and wished to die. My wife probably understood her inner state better than anyone and visited her room often to console her. They were more like sisters than mother and daughter-in-law. Mother would say to her: "Polly; will it be long?" and she would answer: "Not much longer."

As her life drew towards its close, my mother began for the first time to take an interest in my spiritual quest. I had not been able to understand why she cared so much that I should have worldly success, and so little for my inner life. She had never liked Ouspensky, whom she had met once or twice in the 1920s and persisted in speaking of him as 'your Koupensky'. Her chief interest, apart from her children, had always been reading history and biography, and she had the New England intellectualism of the 1890s that seemed strangely out of place in the 1940s. She was a woman of unquenchable courage and devotion; upright, and a hater of any kind of sham or hypocrisy. Although she sacrificed everything for the welfare of her three children and loved us all dearly, she would avoid any outward show of affection like the plague. It was very hard for me to get behind the barrier of her intellectual pose.

When she began to ask me to explain what I understood by eternity and to tell her what I believed about death and the soul, I was both astonished and greatly moved. I did my best to explain in simple terms, and to make her see for herself that the relationship between her and my father and us children could never be broken. When her mind wandered she mistook me for my father, whom she had never ceased to love though he had been dead thirty years.

She died in the lodge at Coombe Springs. I had been with her half an hour before and had gone out for a walk. When I returned she had ceased to breathe. I sat beside her for a long time and for the first time in my life became aware of a kind of mystic participation in the condition of a dead person. I could sense her bewilderment, and a heart-rending sadness took hold of me that had nothing to do with myself or with past or future. It was the sadness of her own dawning realization that she had put her trust in the wrong things and would have to learn all over again to live according to her true destiny.

This experience suddenly lifted, and I felt that I had lost touch with her. The sadness vanished and a peaceful quiet took its place. It was not until two years later that I was able to make a step towards understanding what the experience signified.

Looking back over the intervening years, I connect my mother's death with the beginning of a change in myself that was to lead, a few months later, to experiences so overwhelming as to give a new direction to my whole life.

From the beginning of 1947, I introduced the practice of early morning meditations, which any resident or visitor at Coombe was free to attend. I also initiated some of the members of my groups into the practice of repetition as I had learned it from Ouspensky. We also worked regularly at Gurdjieff's rhythmic movements and ritual dances. The life at Coombe grew ever richer and more varied, but some of the original members of the community were beginning to feel the strain. Interest in our groups was growing, and the meetings I held weekly in London in the spring of 1947 were attended by men and women who were beginning to take the ideas and methods of Gurdjieff's System very seriously indeed.

In the meantime, I had signed a contract with my publishers for The Foundations of Natural Philosophy, which later became the first volume of *The Dramatic Universe*. I thought it was ready for publication, but each attempt at a final revision showed me so many serious defects that I had to rewrite it over and over again. I showed them the transcripts of my lectures on *The Crisis in Human Affairs*, and they agreed that these should be published first. Miss Rina Hands, who had made the transcripts, undertook also to edit them. When later the book was praised for its clarity, I ascribed the credit to Rina Hands far more than to myself. It was a bold venture to agree to publication, for it was the first book to appear with an account of some of the main features of Gurdjieff's System. It was also the first publication of my conception of Eternity as the domain of potentiality, both material and spiritual. It would be more accurate to say that, through understanding Eternity, we can recognize that spirit and matter differ only in their form of consciousness.

My own state during the summer of 1947 was peculiar. Everything was going well. Delanium, the new carbon material we were developing in our research laboratories, was full of promise. The board of directors of our parent company decided to make an early start on commercial production, and a fine factory was bought in Hayes for the purpose. Coombe Springs was flourishing. More people than ever were coming to my lectures. I was very happy with my wife, who had found at Coombe scope for her power to awaken and inspire people. She had taken under her wing a young French-Canadian doctor, Bernard Courtenay-Mayers, who had played an heroic part in the French Resistance movement, but had escaped with his nerves shattered by concentration camp horrors and other heartrending experiences. He had won the M.C. serving as an officer in the R.A.M.C. under an assumed name. Bernard came to live at Coombe, and he and the other young people, especially Elizabeth Mayall, formed a circle round my wife. The little community at Coombe Springs was, on the whole, well balanced. Our ages ranged from under twenty to over seventy. Several races were represented, and we had many visitors who came to stay for short periods to learn about our work. To all appearances, the undertaking was flourishing; membership was growing, and there was an intense activity in research and psychological study.

With all these outwardly promising conditions, I felt inwardly a sense of foreboding. I was alone, and I knew that my ability to help and guide people was limited by my understanding and hampered by my own defects. I began to think of finding Gurdjieff again. When Cornelius went to Paris on a mission, I asked him to make enquiries. He came back with the assurance that no such man was living in Paris; he had asked the French police through the United States Embassy, and since Gurdjieff was an emigré Russian they would certainly have known his whereabouts. Enquiries made through Bernard Courtenay-Mayers were no more rewarding.

August 1947 approached, and with it our second seminar at Coombe Springs. Several who had been aghast at the rigours of the previous year kept away. Others, who had not come before, were attracted by the hope that they could learn something about 'super-efforts'. I myself came to it with foreboding, having rarely felt so acutely my own inadequacy.

The theme I had chosen was *The Ideal Community*. We were already contemplating the need to leave England, where war and destruction seemed inevitable. South Africa seemed the most promising place to which to go, and we were to discuss the form which a spiritual community might take.

As things turned out, the seminar developed on quite unexpected lines. We undertook to paint the house and to clear some of the garden of weeds and brambles. We had days of fasting, as in the year before. But the direction of our discussions was taken out of my hands, as if some unseen power were guiding and directing it. The theme emerged more and more clearly from day to day, and yet we could never put it into a formula. It concerned the whole life process on the earth, the Biosphere. We saw that man should occupy a special position, but cannot fill it without help from beyond the earth itself.

Our meetings that year were held under the great oak tree that stands in the centre of the grounds and dominates them. This oak was probably planted, with several others still living, when Cardinal Wolsey had the Spring Houses built in 1513. Its branches, which cast a shade over a thousand square yards, make it one of the finest oaks in England. Visitors to Coombe Springs seldom fail to recognize the majesty of its presence.

On the last day of the 1947 seminar, we sat together, each making a hesitating, confused contribution to the expression of what we had all experienced. That day was strange, for though the fifty people present afterwards agreed that it was supremely important, not one could remember just what was said. My recollection is that we saw all life on the earth as a female Being who passes through great cycles of fertility and sterility in her spiritual receptiveness. When her moment of fertility comes, the cosmic male Power descends upon earth and all life is inseminated with a new spiritual power. From this is born a new Epoch. Not only man, but everything that lives, takes part in this cosmic ritual.

Told in this way, the account must give the impression of a flight of imagination. For those of us who shared the experience it was, for one brief summer afternoon, a present reality. After the day had passed, none of us could speak of it, and even now, after thirteen years, I cannot bring myself to write the whole of it. Another strange feature of this seminar is that one of the members present, Gerald Day, undertook to write an account of our discussion and did so. But his manuscript of nearly two hundred pages was irretrievably lost before it could be copied.

As the seminar came to an end, it was as if we all were coming out of a world of mystery and wonder. Coombe Springs had been for a fortnight a secret place, and we were as if sworn to secrecy not to reveal what we had been shown. To remind myself of the day when a veil had momentarily been lifted, I planted a bank of ferns and promised myself that, as long as I lived at Coombe, I would never let it die. Often, as I walk past the bank, I remember and wonder if it was all a dream. But the strange events of the year were not at an end.

On 15th September, I was due to give the first of a series of talks at Denison House, just by Victoria Station. Those who had come to my lectures in the spring had been invited to write and explain why they wished to continue the study. I had received eighty replies and was astonished that my own doubts and hesitations had not communicated themselves to my audience. I tried to prepare my first talk, but whatever I wrote stared back from the page with empty eyes.

On the morning of the lecture I was no nearer to finding my way. Bernard was causing my wife anxiety. He was suffering from a sense of guilt over some failure in the war that I took for a figment of a morbid imagination. I spoke to him, but saw that no advice would help. I myself was restless, almost feverish, and after lunch decided to go for a walk on Wimbledon Common. This is crowded with memories for me, because I was born close to it, and had been to King's College School, which stands at its southwest corner; had walked there as a youth with my first wife, and more recently had made it a refuge from the turmoil of our life at Coombe Springs.

I usually walked in the woods, but this time I found myself crossing the open heath and entering the gates at King's. I had not returned to my old school since 1917 - just thirty years. I wondered why. I walked through the grounds past the laboratories, over the playing field where for two years I had been captain of rugby football. Little was changed. I walked, half in a dream, up to a monument. Idly, I noticed its resemblance to the choragic monument of Lysicrates on the slopes of the Acropolis, when I became aware that it was the memorial of the First World War. I started reading the names. One after another I saw the names of boys with whom I had played rugby or cricket. Hardly one seemed to have escaped. I knew then why I had never returned; I had never reconciled myself to the loss of so many of my best friends.

I was all alone in the great playing field; but, as I stood, I was no longer alone. All these boys were still there, still living, with their powers undiminished. A Great Presence enveloped us all. An immense joy flooded through me. Past all understanding, it was yet true that premature death is not necessarily a disaster. Potentialities are not destroyed by death. I was, quite irrationally, convinced that an angel had been sent to make me aware of this truth.

I walked back across the Common quite certain that the angel was still with me. I understood that I must speak that evening of death, of what it can and what it cannot destroy.

When I came to the door of Coombe Springs, Elizabeth was waiting for me: "Mrs. B. wants you at once." My wife was at the head of the stairs: "Bernard needs you at once." I went into his room. He was writhing on the bed, his face distorted, uttering pitiful moans and sudden screams. I stood at the head of the bed for a few moments and then said: "Bernard, you need not suffer - they are all right." He lay still, gave a deep sigh and went to sleep. I knew that I had told him what was necessary and that he had believed.

That day, Coombe Springs was visited by some Great Presence. It might have been some angel or an even greater Being. When I spoke that evening at Denison House, it was neither I nor my own voice that spoke. I was, during the whole of that day, completely certain that in some utterly incomprehensible way the boys who had been with me at school, and had died on the battlefield, were as much alive as I was. This experience was quite different from that of my own state when I nearly died. It was not a personal experience nor remotely resembled any kind of direct communication with them, for I had no notion, no picture, of how and where they were living. Only I was aware that their potentialities had been preserved intact and undiminished.

I cannot remember what I said that evening, nor was any record made of it, but afterwards several who had lost sons in the war came up to me and said that all grief had been lifted from them.

The next day all of us at Coombe Springs were subdued, and many were awe-struck. I discovered, as the days went by, that several others had been aware of a Great Presence and of a blessing that had come to us.

A few weeks later, I was down at the Springs early in the morning for my dip in the waters when my nephew came and told me that Ouspensky had died. I knew he had returned to England and that he was ill. I had written and asked to see him but had no reply. Now he was dead.

An hour later, I was summoned to the telephone to take a call from New York. George Cornelius was calling to tell me of Ouspensky's death and to say that he had a message that I should see Janet Collin-Smith, the wife of the author Rodney Collin, one of Ouspensky's closest associates. I did not know her well or where she lived. I found her address quickly and went straight to London. She met me at the door of her house, as much surprised as I was that I should have received such a message, for she, like others, had been forbidden to speak to me. She accepted the message and told me about Ouspensky's last hours. Throughout the day I felt a great love towards him, such as I had never known while he was alive. Nevertheless, I was strongly aware of the difference between death after a long life on the earth and a premature departure. Ouspensky's potentialities had been brought into time, and they had undergone an irreversible transformation. There was something that I could not understand and should not try to understand. A great cycle of my own life, which had lasted nearly twenty-seven years, had closed. I felt love and gratitude towards Ouspensky, but I felt no nearer to him than I had before.

19: SOUTH AFRICA, SMUTS AND THE AFRICANS

I was in my fiftieth year. There were now more than two hundred regular students following my courses at the Institute. I was receiving invitations to lecture on the Psychokinetic Philosophy not only in England, but also in France. My wife was happier than I had ever known her. She loved Coombe Springs, and felt that she had found at last real work that she could do. She had reached an age, seventy-two, when she felt that she need no longer care what people thought of her, and said and did just what she pleased. Sometimes the results were magnificent, sometimes disastrous; they were never dull.

I did not find it difficult to combine my activity each week-end, including lectures, meetings and work in the grounds at Coombe, with a hard week's work at the Research Laboratories in Battersea. We were preparing to produce Delanium on a commercial scale, and I hoped to repay, by a financial success, the trust and personal kindness I had received from the Chairman and other directors of the Company.

With all these favourable omens, I was deeply dissatisfied and uncertain within myself. It seemed to me that a third world war was inevitable. Never in history had the accumulation of arms prevented war, nor had human nature proved able to withstand the temptations of fear, jealousy and personal ambition. All the factors that make war inevitable were present. Why should we remain in the danger zone? Ouspensky was dead, Gurdjieff had disappeared. There was nothing to hold us in Europe.

Our thoughts and discussions were dominated by the symbol of Noah's Ark. We had learned much, and had proved that we could hold together as a community. Would it not be right to go away to some remote place and make ourselves independent, so that we might weather the coming storm and afterwards return and help in the rebuilding of a new civilization?

Various influences combined to turn our attention towards South Africa. Two friends, Cecil Lewis and his wife Olga, had decided to emigrate, and offered to explore the possibilities of Rhodesia and South Africa and send us their report. Cecil was an airman and an author. He decided to buy a small plane, fly it to Africa and sell it when he arrived. The week after Ouspensky's death, his little plane circled over Coombe Springs; we watched them turn south as if they were to discover a new world.

Soon afterwards I had an opportunity of going there myself. Powell Duffryn were inclined to invest some of their capital in coal-mining enterprises overseas, and when I offered to go out and make a report they gave me every encouragement. Another friend, Keith Thorburn, was also interested in South Africa on behalf of a great financial group of which he was a director. He offered to charter a plane and fly me down with him. We arranged to leave at the beginning of January 1948.

Meanwhile, I had arranged through Bernard Courtenay-Mayers to give lectures in Paris. He had a wide circle of friends, mostly connected with the French Resistance movement of General Leclerc. I took the word 'psychokinetic' to define the theme. One lecture was on *Psychocinétisme et Psychanalyse*. I arranged to fly to Paris on the morning of the lecture, but dense fog all day kept me grounded. I had to dictate the lecture by phone to Dr. Godel, who had agreed to be my chairman, and he read it to the disappointed audience. In spite of this setback, the second lecture on *La Prâtique du Psychocinétisme* was well attended. Both were given at the École des Sciences Politiques, through the kindness of one of the professors.

While in Paris, I personally made enquiries about Gurdjieff, but no one I met knew of him. This is hard to account for, as he was very well known in the city where he had lived for twenty-five years.

The lectures aroused intense discussions, and several score people asked me if I would open a French branch of the Institute. I could do nothing then, as I was due to leave for Africa in a few weeks. We flew in a converted Lancaster bomber; very fast for those days, but very uncomfortable. As Keith had business in the Sudan, we stopped a few days in Khartoum. This gave me the chance to visit o and see the junction of the White and Blue Niles. The city of Omdurman made a deep impact on me. It was then more than twenty-five years since I had been to the midnight prayers in San Sophia in Constantinople. I had almost forgotten the impression the Islamic religion had made on me, but here in Omdurman, it was greater than ever. There must have been some white people in this city of a million souls,but I saw not one. The midday prayer was a dramatic experience. The entire life of the city came to a standstill. Most of the men went into the mosques; but thousands took out their mats and made the seven-fold prostration on the banks of the Nile, in streets, anywhere and everywhere. It was the same in the evening. I had never before seen a great city whose daily life was wholly regulated by religious observance.

As I stood upon the bridge that crosses the Nile where the waters from Ethiopia and Uganda flow together, I was transported into the past:

an age even more remote than ancient Greece. The Badarian colonists, who had descended into Egypt from the mountains eight thousand years ago, must have gone past this spot. At that time, long before any recorded history, similar migrations must have been stirring all over the world as mankind entered the promised land of material power. "What in eight thousand years," I asked myself, "have we achieved that is worth more than the sincere worship of these illiterate Sudanese? They have neither motor cars nor radio and they know little of what the modern world has achieved, yet they are nearer to God than we are."

I returned to Khartoum, to the small artificial world created round the Government and business offices by the British rulers of the Sudan. Here were good people, with a sense of duty and fairness. Most of them loved the Sudanese, and I think that they were loved in return. But neither could understand the values by which the other lived. I had long wanted to visit Africa, because the few contacts I had made with Africans had convinced me that something had been preserved on the African continent that the rest of the world has lost. I remembered a strange man, Tracy Philipps, whom I had known in Istanbul, and his stories of the powers of extra-sensory perception he had seen and personally verified in Central Africa. I had at that time a suspicion that the northern hemisphere of our planet was doomed, and that a new civilization would arise in the south. This would be the first civilization of the New Epoch, and in it the balance of races would be quite different from the present time. I must say that, as time has passed, I have become less and less inclined to attach any importance to this notion.

We went on to Nairobi, where once again Thorburn had a few days' business to occupy him, and my time was my own. In Nairobi I was acutely uncomfortable. Wherever I went I was surrounded by people who had run away. Some had run away from the war, others from social difficulties or matrimonial scandals. I do not remember any place that I have visited that so filled me with sadness for the petty, mean way of life into which people fall who care only for their own safety and comfort.

As soon as possible, I also escaped. I took a car and drove out to a farm to visit an old friend. The scene is magnificent as one comes to the Great Rift, descends two thousand feet and crosses the valley where little grows but cactus and prickly pear. I was heartened by my visit, because I saw that the decadence of Nairobi was not the whole Kenya story. There were also Englishmen who were working hard to make the land live and bear fruit.

Next I went to visit the National Park and the game reserves. The sight of wild giraffe, great herds of zebras, hippopotamus in the swamps and vultures in the treetops was a new and thrilling experience. But nothing could match the moment when we came upon half a dozen lions basking on rocks beside the road. The driver said that they never attacked cars and that I was perfectly safe looking at them through the open window; so close that, if I had stretched out my hand, I could almost have touched them. I watched the great animals peacefully resting after the night of hunting zebra, sometimes opening an eye to look, indifferently, straight into mine. I said to myself: "If I had faith I could walk among those animals and they would not fear me nor I them." But I knew that I did not have such faith and, what is worse, that my motives in wishing for it were not pure.

During my visit to the game reserves in Kenya and other parts of Africa, I became convinced of the truth of something I had written about, but without much feeling (cf. *The Dramatic Universe*, Vol. II, pp. 3I0-II): namely, that every animal genus contributes a specific mode of feeling to the whole experience of life on the earth. If lions disappear from the earth, something will be lost that the Biosphere needs, and if we men are responsible for that disappearance, we shall have to pay the price of our blood guilt. Much good, unselfish work is being done to preserve animal and vegetable genera from extinction, but even those who do this work are seldom aware how vital it may be for the survival of mankind. "He that lives by the sword shall perish by the sword" is a warning that refers to more than human life.

When I returned to Nairobi, through the coffee plantations and fruit orchards, I felt more strongly than ever the unhealthy atmosphere of the city. This was January 1948, long before the Mau Mau troubles had started, and I heard no complaints of the Kikuyus. It was not racial discrimination or exploitation that distressed me, but the awareness that I was among people who were not facing life as men and women should.

I retired to my room in the hotel and remained alone for nearly twenty-four hours. I was in agony of mind. Was I not also running away? In what way was I better than any of these people who considered themselves so clever to have 'got out' before trouble came in England?

I could not sleep that night, but prayed that I might see what was right. At about two in the morning the noise of music and dancing below me ceased. Slowly the night grew quiet. I was aware again of the same Presence that had spoken to me of death in the school field at King's, a few months before. This time it was a personal message or instruction: 'You are not meant to stay in Africa. Your place is in London. Trouble will come; not as you imagine, but differently, and you have to be in the midst of it. There is no need for Noah's Ark, for this time there will be no flood. The task before you is quite different from what you suppose.'

I have expressed what came to me in words, but it was an unspoken message, the meaning of which was clearer than words could make it.

I slept almost at once, and awoke feeling calm and assured. I did not know whether I should speak of what I had received. It seemed to me that the message was for me personally, and that if others wished to go and found a colony in Africa, I should help rather than oppose them.

We left the next day for Rhodesia, where nothing of interest happened, and then went on to Johannesburg. Thanks to introductions from Thorburn and others in England, I was given permission to visit many coal mines and to study chemical analyses, costs and market figures - in fact all that I could need for my report. As the programme would take a week or two to arrange, I decided to go for a quick run in Natal and Eastern Transvaal, to form some idea of the prospects of founding a colony in some isolated valley.

We were five in all; two Lewises, two Thorburns and myself. Mrs. Thorburn had been immobilized by a fall that had seriously damaged her back. She did not come on our first expedition, which was southward to the foothills of the great Basutoland plateau. We saw a well-cultivated farm for sale, but the land was expensive, and it was too near the main route to qualify as a secluded valley.

We returned and met together in Durban. I felt that the atmosphere was not at all propitious. There were cross-currents of feeling, and I had not helped matters by my own change of plans. We were due to leave for the Eastern Transvaal to visit the area favoured by the Lewises. Having one spare day in Durban, I suggested that we should forget everything and go for a picnic. We had been told of the beauty of the Umzimkulu valley in the foothills of the Drakensberg Mountains and we agreed to go there for the day.

We took two cars and set out for the hills. As I write the words Umzimkulu Gorge, it is hard to resist sitting back and reveling in the memory of that splendid day. The road up into the Drakensberg Mountains from Durban must be one of the most spectacular car drives in the world. We went through the Valley of a Thousand Hills that leads from Durban to Pietermaritzburg, sunk deep in the scorching heat of a South African summer, and then up the foothills three or four thousand feet, through mile after mile of mimosa in flower - smelling so strongly that the scent penetrated everything. Then round other cliffs into the Umzimkulu Gorge, where nature has thrown everything together in a wild formation of rocks and varieties of vegetation.

We stopped to picnic, and I suggested that we should spend one or two hours in meditation upon the Beatitudes as they are set down in St. Matthew's Gospel. I have always been convinced that a very high inspiration guided the compilers of the passage known as the Sermon on the Mount, and the Beatitudes have been for me the highest objective test of my own condition. We went apart for ten or fifteen minutes at a time to meditate upon each of the Beatitudes, and when we returned we gave our own impressions. I think that none of the six who shared in the experience of that afternoon has forgotten how our state gradually changed and how the irritations and frictions evaporated. For several weeks afterwards our party worked together in harmony, and we were able to agree upon the steps to be taken about the valley.

We went by way of Johannesburg through Belfast, the highest town in South Africa, just seven thousand feet above sea level, to Machadodorp, only a thousand feet lower. There we heard of the Crocodile Valley, and the possibility of buying several thousand acres of land rather cheaply. By now the others were reconciled to the thought that I would not come out to stay, though at that time I expected to make regular visits if a community were established.

The Lewises had already almost decided upon their own homestead. Thorburn was willing to buy a large tract on his own account and make a part of it available to settlers. With this in mind, we drove out to see the valley. I was carried away by the beauty of the Crocodile Valley, lying two or three thousand feet below the high veldt of Machadodorp and Belfast, and linked to it by the Crocodile Falls, hidden deep in the dense tropical forest that surrounds the low veldt. It seemed to me an ideal place, by its beauty, its isolation, its rich soil and abundant water supply, to be the home of a community of several hundred families. I advised that the land should be bought, if Thorburn were satisfied that the upper farms on the high veldt would guarantee his investment.

I could not remain long, because I had before me a big job for Powell Duffryn, and I wanted to do it well. I was extremely lucky, and in ten days collected enough information, and saw enough of the coalmines and chemical industry of the Transvaal and the Orange Free State, to have a clear idea of what might be done.

Before leaving England I had written to the Prime Minister of the Union, Field Marshal Jan Smuts, whom I had met almost exactly thirty years before when I was convalescing as the Master's guest at Christ's, Cambridge, his old college. He had invited me to visit him, and I did not want to miss the chance. I therefore flew down to Cape Town as soon as I felt that I had something to tell him about the prospects of the coal industry. I called on his secretary, and was given an appointment for the next morning. I left a proof copy of my book The Crisis in Human Affairs, which my publishers had sent me for the purpose.

Having heard that Smuts had little opinion of people who had not climbed the Table Mountain on foot, I set out to do so, supposing that it would not be any harder than the Pen-y-Groes track to the top of Snowdon. I chose a track on the sunny side of the mountain overlooking the Bay. It was a burning hot summer day, and I had had no idea how hot and dry the climb would be. In five hours I struggled to the top; looked southward towards the Antarctic, and climbed down again exhausted; but the climb was worth making.

Smuts gave me back my book, saying that he had read it during the night. He said: "I agree with you that we are now passing through a great crisis in human affairs, and with reservations I agree with your theory of Epochs. But I do not agree with your pessimistic attitude towards human nature; the process of integration continues in spite of all appearances to the contrary. Now tell me why you have come to South Africa."

I said that my job was coal research, and that Powell Duffryn had sent me to report on the scope for investment. I said that my enquiries had convinced me that South African industrialists greatly underestimated the potentiality of the Transvaal coalfield: "Gold mining is so dominant, that they do not realize that they have the cheapest source of power in the world. South Africa should be able for at least fifty years to produce coal more cheaply than any other country, owing to the shallow, massive disposition of the coal measures, and their suitability for mechanization. Everything that Canada can do at the Niagara Falls, South Africa could do more cheaply. If the Kariba Dam is built, the capital charges will be so high that Zambezi power will not be able to compete with the Transvaal. South Africa should have the greatest electro-chemical industry in the world."

Smuts interrupted me, saying: "What you are telling me is interesting and valuable, and some of it is new to me. I want you to go and tell it all to Hofmayr. He is my Finance Minister. I shall soon retire, but I hope that he will remain to carry out all these schemes. I can only give them my blessing."

I took this as a hint to speak of my personal reasons for coming, and referring to my book said: "I believe that there is a great danger that European civilization will collapse. With a group of about two hundred, I have been wondering whether we ought not to emigrate and found a colony in some remote valley in Africa, where we could preserve what we have found and bring it back after the storm."

Smuts asked me a few questions, and then sat back and spoke to me very seriously: "It is my duty to encourage emigration, especially from England, and I do encourage it. But you and your friends are not ordinary emigrants. In my opinion, you have a wrong appreciation of the world situation. You think that if European civilization is destroyed, something can still be preserved. I do not believe this. Europe is still, and for at least a century will continue to be, the bearer of the hopes of the human race. An ancient and a very stable culture has been established in Europe, with which for this purpose I include the British Isles. There is nothing like it in the rest of the world.

"Recently I was in San Francisco for the signing of the Charter of the United Nations. It has made a fine start, and in many ways it is more hopeful than the League of Nations; but it will not save the world from disaster. Only Europe can save the world. What is the use of coming to South Africa? This is a new-born country. We have not even begun to grow up. All our troubles are still ahead of us. There will be no culture in South Africa for a hundred years. I will go further, and say the same for the United States. The most profound and disturbing impression I received from my visit to America was of the immaturity of the country. They have become the most powerful country in the world, and are being forced into world leadership. They are still unfitted for this task, and this is a grave danger. The crisis in human affairs, as I see it, consists in the premature acquisition by mankind of powers which it cannot use wisely. But this crisis cannot be solved by running away from it. If you have understood the situation a little better than others, then your place is at home. Go back and preach the supreme importance of your European heritage."

In its practical consequences, his advice agreed with what I had been shown in Nairobi, though the reasons there had seemed altogether inward and private, whereas his were political and general. I told him how I had attended two of the peace conferences and had heard Briand speak much as he had done. That was twenty-eight years ago, and Briand had been destroyed by his own vision. Smuts said rather sadly: "And so shall I too be destroyed by my vision. But there are now people in Europe, and people with influence, who see as I do that we must bend all our efforts towards the salvation of European culture. This is possible only if we can preserve the political independence of Europe."

At this point his secretary entered to say he was half an hour late for an appointment. Smuts turned to me with a kindly smile and said: "That is a measure of how much you have interested me. Go and see Hofmayr and tell him all about coal. There, at least, is something we can do."

Hofmayr received me at once and made me give my report on coal much more fully. He asked me some questions about quantities and prices which astonished me. I am very quick at making mental calculations, and I had studied the subject thoroughly. But Hofmayr was far quicker. I would rate him among the three or four finest brains I have met in my life. He was also obviously a very good and sincere man.

I said that the seams were almost ideal for mechanization and that I was sure, from having watched the Bantu miners at work, that they would easily learn to handle the machinery. I was surprised that there had been so little mechanization. He said: "You do not understand our industrialists. The wealth of the Transvaal has been built upon cheap and abundant labour, and they cannot think in any other terms. The future of this country demands an immense improvement in the standards of living of the Africans. Everyone would benefit by it. But very few can see it. Maybe they will not see until it is too late. Nevertheless all that you say interests me very much. I want you to go and talk to Sir Ernest Oppenheimer; he and his son are the wisest of our rich men and they will listen to you." He told his secretary to write to Oppenheimer.

After I had left him, I felt sorry that I had not spoken about the spiritual side of my mission. I felt sure that he would not only have given me practical advice, but have been interested in our deeper search.

In the outcome, I returned to Johannesburg, and met Oppenheimer and other leading industrialists of South Africa. They were attentive to what I said, but evidently thought that they were already doing well enough with the cheap power available, and were not ready for further expansion. These very rich men in South Africa made a good impression on me. They had a sincere warmth of feeling towards the Africans, and were whole-heartedly behind Smuts and Hofmayr in their policy of bringing the Africans forward. Several told me regretfully that there was little hope that this policy would continue when Smuts went. They admired Hofmayr's ability, but said that he did not know how to win popular backing in the country.

Having finished my task, I went for a second visit to Machadodorp. The Lewises were already installed. The Thorburns had bought some two thousand acres of land. Thorburn himself had been so encouraged by his reception in Johannesburg that he had advised his group to invest boldly in South Africa. This advice was taken, and, I believe, never regretted.

This time, I remained in the Crocodile Valley. I wanted to get the feel of it all alone. There were no European or Asian inhabitants, only a tribe of about two thousand Basutos who, under their Chief, an awe-inspiring old lady now over a hundred years old, had left Natal sixty years earlier in order to get away from the European settlers. They were living the traditional tribal life in five or six kraals.

I set off very early one morning to walk alone to the Crocodile Falls. I only had a very doubtful map to guide me. My friends had warned me to beware of snakes and told me of the terrors of the black mamba that strikes unprovoked. These stories spoiled some of the pleasure I might have had in striding in a vest and shorts through the rich grass of the valley. All I saw was a couple of unbelievable butterflies with wings as large as my hands, and all I heard was the chatter of invisible baboons.

Following a lightly trodden path, I came upon a Basuto village. All the inhabitants were out hoeing mealies. Their ages must have ranged from seven to seventy, and they were singing and hoeing to the rhythm of their own music. As they saw me they all stopped and stood straight up in surprise. Then with one accord they began to laugh. I have never heard such laughter. It was pure joy and friendship, without malice and without thought. I joined in, and we all laughed together for several minutes. I waved my hand and walked on, and they resumed their gravity and their hoeing.

This was one of the unforgettable moments of my life. A lifetime's experience had convinced me that happiness is greatest where material prosperity is least. I had seldom seen a happy rich man, but I had seen many happy people among the poorest villagers of Asia Minor or Greece. I had seen happiness in Omdurman, but this happiness that I saw before my eyes was beyond all the others. Here was a village totally lacking even the smallest of the benefits of civilization. They had not even a plough or a cart. And yet they were the happiest people I had ever seen. They were without fear and without pride.

I could not help comparing them with the detribalized Africans of the suburbs of Johannesburg, or even with the far happier coal miners of the Transvaal. And yet, even as I made the comparison, I knew that there was no going back. No power on earth could save this happy Basuto tribe from civilization. It was only a matter of years before a kind government would start schools and shops and provide them with tools and tractors.

With a terrible pang I asked myself the question: "Have I seen the last happy people on the earth? Is all mankind to come under the yoke of material success? What does Smuts know? Europe is happy compared with America. Europe is mature and has a tradition. But what of these Africans? Are they not perhaps more mature and more firmly rooted in tradition than all the rest of us? What have the Americans done to the Red Indians - the bearers of a tradition perhaps twenty thousand years old? What are we all doing? Selling happiness for progress, selling our human birthright for a mess of machinery!"

The beauty of the valley restored my peace. I plunged into the forest, making my way up the banks of the Crocodile River, still only a stripling near to its source. The waterfall swept away the last vestiges of pain. It is not one of the world's greatest or loftiest falls, but it must surely be one of the most beautiful, and it was then still quite unspoiled. In the thunder of its voice, I prayed that I might never forget that if man has created cities, nature is still God's handiwork.

I understood why I had been so powerfully attracted to this valley, but I knew that I would never live there. I was melancholy because I had never seen in the world a place so beautiful, so secluded and so happy.

Soon after I returned to England, I wrote my report, but I have never gone back to South Africa. A community was started. I helped to raise funds for it. But those who went out were lacking in experience, and after two or three years it was sold up. I believe it was bought for the trout fishing for which the Crocodile River is famous. Rich South Africans probably go there for weekends to escape from Johannesburg.

I returned to London alone, and found that great preparations had been made to welcome me. My wife had prepared a feast and a demonstration of Gurdjieff's exercises and ritual dances, on which twenty-four selected pupils had been working under her direction. Costumes had been made as they had been at the Prieuré. I was taken by surprise, and behaved with a complete lack of understanding. Even before we came back to Coombe, I had been afraid of being put upon a pedestal and treated as a superior being. I was afraid of it for myself, and I thought it most harmful that others should look to me rather than to themselves for strength. This was the one point on which my wife and I were most liable to disagree. She thought it was good for the others to show respect towards me, and also considered that my constant self-deprecation was a weakness that I should overcome.

In most cases, I managed to keep a balance between our two conflicting interpretations of my role, but this time I was wholly unreasonable. Instead of praising the really great effort that had been made, I scarcely spoke, and went off to my room as soon as the performance was finished. My wife did her best to console those who had worked so hard, and indeed they took it as a test that I had deliberately inflicted upon them, to see whether they had done the work for its own sake or for reward or praise. Since then, several of those who were then at Coombe have reminded me of those early years, and of the attitude that regarded all I did as conscious and directed to some high but obscure purpose.

I can say sincerely that I did nothing to encourage so foolish an attitude. On the contrary, I tried to avoid hiding my own mistakes and faults, which were many. I have made a few references in this book to my relationships with women. I was always far too ready to fancy that I could help some woman in her difficulties, or in her solitary life, by showing affection or more than affection. All I can say for myself is that I never in my life tried to come between a woman and her husband or responded to any overtures in that direction. But I was always liable to make attachments with unattached women. Two of these lasted many years and were important factors in my life. My wife did not like them, but told me that she regarded them as inevitable, having regard both to my own nature and our difference in age. But they were really quite unforgivable where a relationship of teacher and pupil also existed, and I constantly struggled with myself to get free from them.

I only mention this side of my life because it seemed to me that my actions, which I tried neither to hide nor to parade, should have destroyed any illusion that I was a superior being worthy of special respect. Another obvious fault was my particularly irritating habit of telling lies, either from the desire to please people or from the impulse to avoid awkward situations. Everyone was aware of this habit, and yet they continued to treat my actions as if they were directed by some higher intelligence.

Those who had to deal with me were above all exasperated by my habit of agreeing with almost anyone who might urge upon me some course of action and then, upon further reflection, feeling it to be mistaken and doing something quite different without either warning or explanation. I could see all these and other defects, and was under few illusions about myself.

When I had been back in England a few weeks, I realized that my wife was not only tired, but that something was seriously wrong with her health. She had borne the whole burden of keeping Coombe Springs going for two years without a holiday, and I proposed a car trip in France.

I had just heard of the discovery of the palaeolithic cave paintings at Lascaux, and as pre-history never failed to interest me, I wanted to see them for myself. We were fortunate in seeing the caves just as they had been discovered, crawling under the overhanging rock and seeing them by the light of torches. The effect was prodigious. Here, before our eyes, was proof that men of the highest culture and considerable technical skill had been living on the earth at least twenty thousand years ago. The paintings have so often been described that I need add little, except that I was convinced that there must have been two widely different levels of culture. One was that of the esoteric society that knew the purpose of these underground sanctuaries, and wielded technical resources that were far in advance of the age in which they lived. The other level was illustrated in the cave dwellings around Les Eyzies, where everything had the primitive character popularly attributed to the men of the Old Stone Age. I was convinced, by a week's stay in the Dordogne and visits to the Musée de l'Homme in Paris, that esoteric societies did exist in ancient times, but were quite different from the fanciful descriptions given in the theosophical and occult literature that Prince Sabaheddin had so dearly loved. I could picture the great herds of deer and bison; the tribes of hunters following the retreating glaciers and, in the background, the wise men who were preparing for the future that we have inherited.

My wife returned home much happier, but still suffering from some unexplained pain. I took her to various doctors, but no clear diagnosis was forthcoming. In May, I learned that Powell Duffryn required information about research in the United States, aiming at the production of oil from coal. I offered to go and make a report. When this was approved, I wrote to Madame Ouspensky, without very much hope of encouragement, asking if I could see her. To my delight, I received a most cordial reply inviting me to go and stay at Mendham.

I arrived on 7th June, the day before my fifty-first birthday. Madame Ouspensky's grandson Leonide had the same birthday, and I was invited to share in the feast. I was surprised to find two old pupils of Ouspensky, of whom I had heard that they had withdrawn from all active participation in the groups. Madame Ouspensky was by that time already confined to her room, and was seeing very few people.

I was invited to her room, and after enquiring about my wife's health she abruptly asked me the question: "Now Mr. Ouspensky has gone, what will you do?" I learned afterwards that she had put the same question to several others. I replied that I had hoped to find Mr. Gurdjieff, but could not trace him. I supposed that he had either died, or, as someone had told me, had gone mad. She said: "He is not mad. He has never been mad. He is living in Paris now. Why do you not go to him?"

Nothing can convey the shattering effect her words had upon me. In a flash I saw how foolish I had been not to search more systematically. I remembered my last talk with him, since when nearly twenty-five years had passed. I felt mortally afraid. I was no longer a young man. Would I be able to stand up to Gurdjieff's methods? What might he not demand of me now? And with all this flood of questions, came an immense sigh of relief. I was no longer alone. The one man of all those I had known whom I could trust, as having an insight incomparably deeper than my own, was there to give help once again.

I said to Madame Ouspensky: "I have a job to finish in America.

When it is over, if you will tell me what to do I will go."

She said: "It is not so simple. You are not the only one involved. You do not know Mr. Gurdjieff's situation." She told her companion, Miss Darlington, to read me a letter she had sent to Lyne, asking the group there the same question she had put to me, and inviting them to consider a return to Gurdjieff. This letter had provoked a storm. Some considered themselves bound by their promise to Ouspensky never again to have anything to do with Gurdjieff. Others wanted more information. Only two - those who had come to America - had already decided that they would make the attempt to work with Gurdjieff again. It transpired further that Madame Ouspensky, in inviting me, had aroused the indignation of the fanatical section, who held that every word spoken by Ouspensky was an immutable law, which no one could break without betraying a sacred trust. He had said: "No one is to speak or communicate with Bennett," and this held good whether he was alive or dead, and whether or not he had been misinformed when he said it.

There was nothing in all this that surprised me, because history shows that whenever a spiritual leader, small or great, leaves the earthly scene, his followers invariably divide into factions. Each claims to preserve and transmit what the teacher has brought to it, but one faction understands this duty literally; preserving every word, every memory, every injunction as if they were crystallized and fixed forever. Another faction secretly or overtly rejoices to be set free from the constraint of the teacher's presence, and goes off to do whatever their own impulses dictate. Yet another seeks to keep alive the spirit of what has been given, and is prepared to see the outward forms changed and even distorted if only something new can grow.

Thus described, I suppose anyone would approve the third way of acting. It is in accordance with the parable of the talents, which condemned the servant who wrapped his lord's money in a napkin and hid it in the ground. But the reality is never so simple. Many believe they are following the Way of Life when they are led only by their own self-will or willfulness. Those of the first path would indignantly repudiate any suggestion that they were burying the talent confided to them.

Turning again to the lessons of the past, we can see how all the followers of a great man are convinced that they are doing justice to his memory. It is only in the perspective of history that we can clearly see the factions separating. In the long run, the passive preservers die away, as did the Jewish Christian Community in Jerusalem or the Ehl-I Beit, the 'People of the House', in Mecca. It is the near-heretics like St. Paul or Mu'awiya, the fifth Caliph, who see beyond the outer form to the inner grandeur of the message, and make it live and give fruit in the lives of men. The Buddhist scriptures paint the contrasting picture of Ananda the close disciple, who committed to memory every word the master had spoken, and Sariputta, the searcher, the propounder of dangerous views. Ananda and his like disappeared into oblivion after the death of Buddha. The active searchers, the near-heretics, kept the Dharma alive.

If then Madame Ouspensky appeared to many of her husband's followers to be a near-heretic, this was because she looked at the living content and not at the form of his teaching. She knew that no teaching that begins and ends in a man can be a living power. She looked beyond Ouspensky to Gurdjieff, and beyond Gurdjieff to the Great Source from which comes every good gift and every perfect gift.

I did not have a moment's hesitation. As soon as I knew that Gurdjieff was alive and in full possession of his powers, I wanted to go to him. But I had my own work to do first. I set out on a tour of the coal research laboratories of the United States. Although my mother was American to the fourth generation on both sides, I had never been in the U.S.A., and I found everything exciting. Two incidents illustrate the contrasts of this great country.

I had to go to Golden, Colorado, to visit the Bureau of Mines Research Station, then working on the carbonization of brown coal. Golden is a mining town that goes back to the prospecting days, when Colorado was a remote state. It stands nearly 8000 feet above sea level on the foothills of the Rocky Mountains, behind Denver. I had been told that a certain steak house was famous throughout the Rockies for its beef. The owner was the grandson of the founder, who had opened it when cattle were first ranched in the State. I found it without difficulty; sat down and ordered beef. I was told it would take three-quarters of an hour to prepare. I wandered round the town, and returned twenty minutes too early. Looking through the menu I saw Rocky Mountain trout, and ordered it, to pass the time. An immense fish that must have weighed a pound and a half was soon placed before me, and I realized that I had a complete meal. The fish was delicious, and I finished it. By now I saw that the habitués of the steak house were watching me curiously. The beef was brought in on a great oval plate. It was an entire rib, weighing two and a half pounds: five weeks' meat ration in England. I had never eaten such tender beef, and I did my best to do it justice, but my thoughts could not help turning to the millions of men and women starving in the labour camps of Europe and Asia.

The next day, Doctor Perry, the director of the Research Station, drove me over the Rockies to Rifle, two hundred miles to the west. It was the end of June, and Denver had been like an oven. As we rose the air grew cooler, but I was unprepared for the sight that met us: an immense panorama of snow-covered mountains and a great glacier, at the foot of which grazed a herd of wild bison. They looked so exactly like the bison in the caves at Lascaux that my heart missed a beat. At that moment, I became convinced that the American Indians were a link with remote antiquity - perhaps the Ice Ages - and that we had perpetrated a hideous crime in destroying their culture instead of learning from it.

Rifle is a mining town in a desolate part of Colorado, with the high mesa stretching for a hundred miles. My purpose was to visit one of the greatest oil shale deposits in the world, and see how it was mined. This was but one of many visits, and I saw many parts of the country.

If I were writing for scientists, I should devote a chapter to this journey. I made many friends, and saw something both of the strength and of the weakness of American research and technology. The tendency to rely too much on apparatus robs them of flexibility and stifles initiative. On the other hand, they were far better aware than most industrial research organizations in England of the serious problems that arise when the scale of an operation is multiplied ten- or a hundred-fold. We in England often come to grief because we are in too much haste to pass from the research stage to large-scale production.

We were making the same mistake at Powell Duffryn, and I was largely to blame. Delanium was a really good invention, and it could have been made a commercial success with small risk of the capital involved. But we went too fast, and Powell Duffryn Carbon Products had painful teething troubles. I should have foreseen this, but I did not wish to damp the enthusiasm of the directors. As usually happens when there is enough money behind an enterprise, it came out right in the end; but I had to pay the price of my lack of caution.

All this happened later, and I refer to it only because it is important to understand the difference between the British and the American approach to technical problems. For us, the right idea is all-important. For the Americans, what matters is to have the right machine. When they have to deal with material problems, the machine often counts for more than the idea behind it. The Russians have an advantage over both of us in that they pay more attention to the balance between thought and mechanics.

On my way back to England, I revisited Mendham and found that my two friends had already left to go to Gurdjieff. I wrote every day to my wife. In my last letter before sailing, I said: 'This seems to me to be our last throw. I cannot and will not go on at Coombe alone. Madame

Ouspensky says she never has and never will allow herself to be looked upon as a teacher. She has warned me that Gurdjieff may make extreme demands upon us. She set the entire group here at Mendham the task of answering the question: "What would you do if a Higher Teacher came?" The answer must surely be that one puts oneself unreservedly in his hands. Suppose that what he wrote in the Herald of Coming Good is true, and that he really has a hidden school in Persia to which he sends people? And suppose he tells me to leave England and Coombe and you also, and go there? What am I to do?"

I travelled back on the Mauretania, using the six days at sea to write my report for Powell Duffryn. On the fourth day out I received a cablegram from my wife: 'You must do whatever he says even if it means going away forever.' This was an heroic reply, because I knew well enough that she would not survive my going.

When I reached home at the end of July, I found that her condition had grown alarmingly worse. She was in constant pain. Bernard was in great distress. He took her to one specialist after another. One said it was her kidneys, another an injury to her spine, a third hinted darkly at cancer. The nights were agonizing. She could not sleep until four or five in the morning, when she had to be lifted into a very hot bath. This gave her relief, and she slept for a few hours. In spite of the pain and her growing weakness, she insisted on going with me to Paris.

We went over on 6th August, 1948. Bernard feared that she would not survive the journey. He telephoned to a doctor friend to meet us at the Gare du Nord with an ambulance. Her courage was prodigious. She would not hear of being carried, but walked to a taxi. I took her to a hotel on the Left Bank, as we were to go the next day to the Rue du Bac near the Boulevard St. Germain to meet Madame de Salzmann, whom I had not seen since she had made a short visit to Gadsden seventeen years before. We discovered that she lived up five flights of stairs, and that there was no lift. I wanted my wife to wait below, but nothing would daunt her. Slowly and painfully she climbed up the stairs. We met Madame de Salzmann; small, very erect and with snow white hair; much changed from the young woman I remembered as one of the best pupils of Gurdjieff's exercises at the Prieuré in 1923. As soon as we arrived, she asked if we would like to lunch with Mr. Gurdjieff. Astonished that it should be so easy, we agreed at once. We had been expecting to be kept waiting for days, and to meet all kinds of demands before we were allowed to see him.

20: THE RETURN TO GURDJIEFF

SLOWLY and painfully, my wife climbed down the narrow, steep and winding staircase into the ancient courtyard of 44 Rue du Bac. Slowly she climbed into a taxi and we drove off, crossing the Seine at the Pont de l'Alma, driving round the Etoile and down through the flowering catalpas that line the Avenue Carnot. The hot summer day could not remove the chill in my heart. My wife's fortitude seemed unnatural, rather as if she were possessed by that mysterious strength that sometimes enters those who are about to die.

Mr. Gurdjieff's apartment at 6 Rue des Colonels Renard is on the first floor left. As we entered, the odours of Asia, saffron and tarragon and others less definable, produced the impression of being transported into another world. The flat was a strange contrast to the Prieuré. Here all was small and dark and dingy, giving an impression of poverty of a kind that was neither European nor Asiatic. Recalling the magnificent salons and gardens of the Prieuré, the great Study House with its ornate decoration and the brilliant sunshine of 1923, it seemed that Gurdjieff had turned his back not only on splendour but on sunshine itself. It was early afternoon and yet all the shutters were closed and electric lights were burning.

Madame de Salzmann made my wife enter a small sitting-room to the right and went down a passage to the left, returning in a few moments with Gurdjieff. I turned to see him standing on the threadbare carpet, changed even more than his surroundings. The dark, sweeping moustaches had turned white and the brilliant, mocking face had lost its firm outline. He was old and sad; but his skin was smooth and he held himself as erect as ever. I felt a sudden warmth towards him, very different from the youthful awe and the timidity with which I had approached him at the Prieuré. He wore a red fez, in the style of the Ottoman Turks rather than the Egyptians or Moroccans. His open shirt and untidy trousers were more in keeping with his whole appearance than the smart French suits he wore in 1923. He moved, as always, with a grace and an economy of gesture that were in themselves enough to induce in those near him a sense of relaxation and well-being.

Madame de Salzmann introduced me, saying that he would remember me from the Prieuré. He said: "No, I not remember." He looked at me for a few moments in silence and added: "You are Number Eighteen. Not big Number Eighteen but small Number Eighteen." I had no idea what he meant, but his manner made me feel happy and at home.

He might not remember me, but I was satisfied that he accepted me. It was twenty-five years to a month since I had left the Prieuré; but seeing him, time disappeared and it was as if I had never left him.

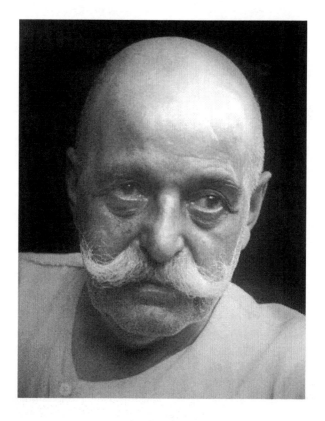

Gurdjieff in Paris 1949

There were only a few people at the flat. Lunch had not started, though it was past two o'clock. We went into the little parlour, barely eleven feet square. The walls were covered with hideous oleographs and daubs of oil paintings. There were two glass cases filled with worthless bibelots: dolls in costumes and trinkets of uncertain origin. The smells from the kitchen pervaded everything.

An American was reading aloud in English from a typescript. Every word was clearly pronounced but I could make little of it. After a short time a young woman put her head in through the door and said: "Chain." Gurdjieff repeated: "Chain!" Without explanation, most of those in the room went and took their places a yard or so apart in a line from the kitchen to the dining-room. Madame de Salzmann took my wife and sat with her at the table, asking her questions in a low voice. I joined the others, not knowing what to expect.

Gurdjieff went into the kitchen, where I could see him filling plates from several large pans. The plates were neatly arranged in tiers with stew below, soup above, each covered with a plate. They were passed from hand to hand and laid out on the table. I saw the advantage of this method of serving a few weeks later, when forty people were crowded into a dining-room large enough for six and were so wedged in that no one could have moved in and out to change the dishes.

I was placed on Gurdjieff's right and my wife sat opposite him, to the left of Madame de Salzmann. The lunch was eaten with the elaborate ritual of toasts and the sharing of morsels that has often been described in books about Gurdjieff. After a time he stopped eating and spoke to my wife in English: "You are in pain?" "Yes." "Bad pain?" "Yes." He left the table, and returned with a small flask from which he took two pills, saying: "Eat. If pain goes, I will know what to do for you. If not, you tell me." He resumed the meal, taking no further notice of her.

All our attention was taken by the series of toasts. I remembered Gurdjieff's toasts to various kinds of Idiot at the Saturday feasts at the Prieuré, but the ritual had now become much more elaborate and apparently had acquired a set form. Gurdjieff sat and listened. The toasts were proposed by the same American who had been reading. He sat on Gurdjieff's left and was referred to as 'Director'. Gurdjieff explained that this was an ancient custom, well-known in Central Asia and it could be recognized in the Gospel story of the Marriage at Cana of Galilee, where the Ruler of the Feast, or Chamodar, fulfilled the same functions as the Director at Gurdjieff's meals.

While giving these explanations, he broke off and turning to my wife, said: "Where is your pain now?" She answered: "It is gone." He insisted: "I ask where is it now?" Her eyes filled with tears and she said: "You have taken it." He replied: "I am glad. Now I can help you. After coffee, Madame Salzmann will show you an exercise."

The meal did not end until nearly five o'clock. When we rose from the table, he invited me to a still smaller room to take coffee. This was his office and pantry, hung from floor to ceiling with dried herbs, dried fish and sausages, and with shelves all around the wall loaded with tins and jars of food. Food was still severely rationed in England, and this display of provisions was a very unusual sight. However, Gurdjieff at once captured my attention by saying, "You know what is the first Commandment of God to man?" While I was fumbling for an answer, he gave it himself: "Hand wash hand!" He paused to let this sink in, and said: "You need help and I need help. If I help you, you have to help me." I said that I was ready to do whatever he wanted. He spoke about his difficulties in Paris; how he did not have enough money to go on a trip to Cannes which was very important for him. As I had come prepared to give him as much money as I had available, this did not surprise me. Then he said: "What do you wish from me?" I replied: "Will you show me how to work for my Being?" He approved with: "It is right. Now you have much Knowledge, but in Being you are a nullity. If you wish, I will show you how to work, but you must do as I say."

There was something unearthly about this conversation. It was the exactly fitting continuation of what he had said to me at the Prieuré, and that, in its turn, followed directly from our very first talk at Kuru Cheshme with Prince Sabaheddin, twenty-seven years before. I said to him: "I know that if I remain as I am, my situation is hopeless. That is why I have come back to you." He said: "If you will do as I say, I will show you how to change. Only you must stop thinking. You think too much. You must begin to sense. Do you understand the distinction between sensing and feeling?" I said one is physical and the other emotional. He answered: "More or less. But you only know this with your mind. You do not understand with your whole being. This you must learn. Go and tell Madame Salzmann to show the exercise of sensing and feeling to you and Mrs. Bennett."

As I was leaving the room, he called me back and asked: "Have you read Beelzebub?" I understood that he referred to the book that was being read aloud before lunch, and I said that I had never seen it. He said: "Must read it many times. Take now chapters about Ashiata Shiemash and read them three times before you come to dinner tonight."

I found my wife sitting with Madame de Salzmann and telling her about Coombe Springs. When I said that we were to learn the exercise of sensing and feeling, Madame de Salzmann asked if I was sure I had understood rightly, as this exercise required preparation. However, it proved to be what he wanted, and she explained very simply and clearly what the exercise was, and how often and how long we should do it. She also gave me the typescript of the three chapters he had prescribed. I went back to the flat in Avenue d'Eylau, and read them over and over again. The description of the mythical prophet Ashiata Shiemash, and his 'Organization for Man's Existence', made a deep impression on me.

I saw in it a prophecy of events to come. Gurdjieff later confirmed this interpretation.

My wife was electrified by her experience. I myself had seen that she was, at least temporarily, relieved of her trouble, for she had risen from the table with her customary vigour, and not slowly and painfully as she had done for several months. She had a private talk with Gurdjieff the next day, about which she would never tell me anything except that it concerned me more than herself, and had satisfied her that he really could help me.

Bernard had brought us to the flat of two close friends, a young married couple, both heroic fighters of the French Resistance. He had come with little or no expectation of meeting Gurdjieff. Elizabeth Mayall had also travelled with us, but she had gone southward to the Dordogne, wishing to see for herself the Lascaux cave paintings that had so impressed us.

When we returned to Avenue d'Eylau, Bernard was delighted with my wife's condition. She did not recover at once, but within a few days she slept without pain, and the mysterious illness had gone. To the end of her life that particular pain never returned, and she was convinced that Gurdjieff had cured her.

We were invited to dinner that same evening, and Gurdjieff announced that he was leaving for Cannes the next day. I had given him a fairly large sum of money, and hoped that this had helped to make the trip possible. He invited me to go too, but I had not brought my car. He said: "Send for your car and follow." I telephoned to my wife's nephew, Pierre Elliot, who said he would come over the next day.

Gurdjieff went off, in a borrowed car, with the American who had been reading on the first evening, George, his Russian chauffeur, and a young girl called Lise Tracol. My wife and I expected to follow the next day. Having seen Gurdjieff leave, my wife, Bernard and I spent the day quietly together. He was very close to us, and we wished that he could share our experience at first hand. This seemed unlikely for a long time, as I had understood from Madame Ouspensky that, whereas my wife and I could meet Gurdjieff, I was not to ask permission to bring any of my pupils.

The next morning, as arranged, I telephoned to say that my car was coming, and to ask if there were other passengers to go with me. I was told that there had been a serious accident in the night, and that Madame de Salzmann had gone off to find Mr. Gurdjieff and bring him home. I brought back the news. We were all stunned. What if he should die at the very moment we had found him again?

The sun had set by the time my car arrived, driven at top speed from Dieppe by Pierre Elliot. I drove to the Rue des Colonels Renard to offer my services. At the same moment, two large cars drove slowly to the door; they had only just returned. My first impulse was to go away, so as not to be a burden. Then I realized that they must be deadly tired, and that I could help with the luggage.

I pulled up my car and stepped out into the road. It was already dusk, but somehow it seemed unnaturally dark. There were no passers-by. I stood and watched and waited. The door of one car opened, and Gurdjieff came slowly out. His clothes were covered with blood. His face was black with bruises. But there was something more, that made me realize that I was looking at a dying man. Even this is not enough to express it. It was a dead man, a corpse, that came out of the car; and yet it walked.

I was shivering like someone who sees a ghost. I could not believe that he would remain upright. But he reached the door and then the lift, and went to his apartment on the first floor left. I followed like one hypnotized.

He walked into his room and sat down. He said: "Now all organs are destroyed. Must make new." He saw me and smiled, saying: "Tonight you come dinner. I must make body work." A great spasm of pain passed through him and I saw blood flowing from his ear. I thought: 'He has a cerebral haemorrhage. He will kill himself if he continues to force his body to move.' He asked Madame de Salzmann: "How is X?" I could not catch the name. She replied that he was in the American Hospital. He said: "Go and see him. How he is?" Then he added: "I wish water-melon. Buy water-melon when you come back."

I said to myself: "He has to do all this. If he allows his body to stop moving, he will die. He has power over his body." Aloud, I offered to drive Madame de Salzmann. At that moment, I saw something of her heroic courage. She was grey with exhaustion and could not bear to leave him at such a moment, but she obeyed without argument.

She said: "Drive carefully. I cannot bear much." At best my driving was no pleasure to my passengers, and that evening I was in no fit state to drive. Somehow we managed it, even stopping on the way home at the market in the Place Saint Ferdinand to buy water-melons: but every shop was shut.

Pierre appeared from nowhere, waiting anxiously at the door for news. Gurdjieff asked who it was, saying: "Tell him fetch water-melon. If he brings, he has right always to come to my house." Pierre, always at his best in a crisis, was off to the Halles, and returned with an armful of melons. I went to fetch my wife, and to tell Bernard that Gurdjieff wanted an injection of morphia to still the pain.

The dinner that night was agonizing beyond description. The doctor had come, and said that Gurdjieff must lie absolutely still, and that he was likely to die of pneumonia if not of the injury. Gurdjieff disregarded all advice and came in to dinner. He ate a few mouthfuls and listened to four toasts. Then at last he went off to bed. Bernard arrived with the morphia, having gone to one after another of his doctor friends before finding one at home. Gurdjieff said it was no longer necessary, as he had found 'how to live with pain'.

The next day he was very ill. He had fractured a bone in the skull. This alone would not have been serious, but he had also broken several ribs and his lungs were full of blood. He had been driving through the town of Montargis, when a small lorry with a drunken driver had shot out of a side road and caught him amidships. The driver of the lorry and his passenger were killed instantly. Gurdjieff's car had buckled up, pinning him between the wheel and the seat. It had taken an hour to extricate him. He had remained perfectly conscious, and directed each move so as to avoid fatal loss of blood. The three passengers in Gurdjieff's car had escaped with minor injuries.

At that time, nearly all Gurdjieff's French pupils were away on holiday. Those who could only spare a few days had taken advantage of his journey to Cannes to visit friends in the country. On the second day, Elizabeth, who had returned by now to Paris, and Bernard were invited, to their great surprise and gratitude. They never missed an opportunity of being with him until the end of his life. There were very few at the flat besides the five of us: my wife and Elizabeth, Bernard, Pierre and myself. We were told to come for meals. On the Wednesday after the accident, Gurdjieff came in and said to us solemnly: "Never allow doctor to give you penicillin. It is poison for the psyche of man." He had been given an injection for his pneumonia when he was very ill, but after the first day he had refused to see a doctor. A French professional nurse came in to take care of him. At first she was in despair, and said: "*Veut-il donc mourir? Il se tue.*" He insisted on joining us for every meal.

My wife and I both observed an extraordinary change. Before the accident, he had been the enigmatic Gurdjieff that we had known, of whom so many stories are told. For four or five days after the accident, it seemed that he either could not or did not feel the need to play a role, to hide himself behind a mask. We then felt his extraordinary goodness and love for humanity. In spite of his disfigured face and arms - he was literally black and blue from head to foot - and his terrifying weakness of body, he was so beautiful that we felt that we were looking at a being from another and better world. Bernard and Elizabeth, who had not seen him before, found it impossible to reconcile their impressions with all that they had heard and read about him.

I believe that, for a few days, we caught a glimpse of the real Gurdjieff, and that all his strange and often repellant behaviour was a screen to hide him from people who would otherwise have idolized his person instead of working for themselves. The next week he was already able to get about, and on the second Wednesday, as he himself had foretold, he resumed his daily routine; going to his cafe in the morning, shopping for the household, seeing innumerable visitors, and above all receiving more and more people for meals twice a day. He became once again more like the Gurdjieff we had known before, and as enigmatic as ever. On the third or fourth day after his accident, he said to me: "You have how many people in England?" I said there were about two hundred, and that eighty were at that moment collected at Coombe Springs for a seminar. I had left them with a programme of work for three or four days, expecting to return almost at once. When he heard that many would be free to come to Paris, he said: "Let all come. Now my French group are away on holiday. Necessary not to lose time. Go home and bring whoever wishes to come."

I took my wife back to England by car and collected all who were at Coombe for the seminar, and a few others hastily summoned by telephone. I said to them: "Some of you know that Mrs. Bennett and I have been to Paris to see Mr. Gurdjieff. We were able to see him, and intended to go with him to Cannes. A fearful accident that nearly killed him has upset all our plans; but it has opened the possibility for those of you who wish to do so to go over and see him for yourselves. As you know, I have always looked upon Mr. Gurdjieff as the Great Teacher from whom our System originated. If we can place ourselves directly under his guidance, we may hope to make progress that now seems impossible. But I must warn you that there will be many difficulties."

I then gave them a description of our arrival and of the accident, and of Gurdjieff's promise to show us how to work on Being. I went on to say: "In the ten days since I left England I can say that a miracle has happened. I now have hope: not blind hope, but what I would call Objective Hope that I can achieve the transformation of Being that has been my aim for nearly thirty years. I believe that the same objective hope exists for all of you. I must warn you that Gurdjieff is far more of an enigma than you can imagine. I am certain that he is deeply good, and that he is working for the good of mankind. But his methods are often incomprehensible. For example, he uses disgusting language, especially to ladies who are likely to be squeamish about such things. He has the reputation of behaving shamelessly over money matters, and with women also. At his table, we have to drink spirits, often to the point of drunkenness. People have said that he is a magician, and that he uses his powers for his own ends. I cannot pretend to know what is true and what is false in all these rumours. What I do know is that he can show us the way to work effectively so as to get results from our work. He has shown me an exercise that has completely transformed my understanding of self-remembering. Whereas I went to Paris convinced that self-remembering is both indispensable for man and impossible of attainment, I am now sure that it can be attained, and moreover by the very simple means of invoking the powers latent in our own bodies.

"From my point of view, whatever may be the risk and however great may be the payment, the game is worth the candle. But I do not want any of you to follow me blindly. Remember the advice that was written over the door of the Study House at the Prieuré: 'If you have not a well-developed critical faculty it is no use your coming here.' If you go, you must do so with your eyes open. I do not believe that the scandalous tales told of Gurdjieff are true, but you must take into account that they may be true and act accordingly."

Several spoke and said that they were impressed, not so much by what I had said as by the obvious change in myself. Before the evening was out, the great majority of those present asked me to take them over to Paris.

During August 1948, I did bring about sixty of them to Gurdjieff's flat. Scores more clamoured to go, but the flat at the Rue des Colonels Renard, even when crowded to suffocation, would not hold more than sixty people, and at that time Gurdjieff's pupils new and old from all over the world were beginning to flock back to him. We were extremely lucky to strike a quiet period, and the amazing experience of his last nearly fatal accident.

When the French group returned from their holidays we began to come to Paris as often as possible for long weekends. Some of my pupils volunteered to help with the work in Paris, and especially with the production of copies of Beelzebub, then still in typescript, and greatly in demand. We of the English group were deeply grateful to the French, who did all they could to make our approach to Gurdjieff easy by withdrawing into the background. For seven years they had had Gurdjieff almost to themselves, and he had given them more consistent and continuous teaching than any of his pupils had previously received. They had a deep respect for Madame de Salzmann, who had sustained them through the trials and bewilderment that everyone who sought to learn from Gurdjieff was bound to meet.

Soon after the influx from Coombe Springs began, Kenneth Walker came to see Gurdjieff with the two men I had met at Mendham. He arrived a sad and bewildered old man. Gurdjieff received him with true compassion, restoring his faith and hope far more through his feelings than through his mind. It was a great joy to watch the transformation taking place under our eyes. Within a few days, Walker was rejuvenated and filled with a new hope. He returned to England and spoke to as many of Ouspensky's former pupils as were prepared to listen. As a result, many came to Paris. Soon there were three streams, by no means harmoniously blended, flowing between London and Paris. The third was led by Jane Heap, a remarkable woman, joint founder of the Little Review and well known in avant-garde circles in America forty years ago. She had for nearly twenty years upheld the flag of Gurdjieff and only Gurdjieff in London, refusing to have any contact with Ouspensky and others whom, in her uncompromising way, she regarded as renegades. Each group had reached Gurdjieff's table from a different direction and brought with it different ideas of what the word "Gurdjieff" meant.

At Gurdjieff's table all these differences were forgotten. We were learning something new and altogether extraordinary: that is, the deep significance of the physical body of man and its latent powers. Gurdjieff showed us exercises so new and so unexpected in their effects that we all felt that a new world was opening for us. He also conveyed, but only to those who came with a sincere desire to be shown the way, a feeling of the importance and urgency of working upon oneself, in order to liberate the self from its state of illusion and dependence. At every meal, the director was called upon to propose the toast of All Hopeless Idiots, and to clarify the distinction between those who are subjectively hopeless, inasmuch as they are fully aware of their own nothingness and therefore are destined for an honourable death; and those who are objectively hopeless, inasmuch as they are unable to repent of their sins, and are therefore doomed to perish like dogs.

No description can convey the terrifying reality of this distinction as it was conveyed by Gurdjieff, with the burning eyes and the vibrant tones of a Jeremiah. I saw old men break down and sob who perhaps had not been so moved since their childhood. Sometimes the effect was too powerful. Several men and women left Paris after a weekend with Gurdjieff, so shattered that they required treatment in mental hospitals. He himself never relaxed his efforts: every day from morning till night he was seeing individuals, listening to readings, presiding over midday and evening meals, taking classes in his rhythmic exercises and often ending the day improvising unearthly melodies upon a hand organ.

The evening meals, coffee drinking and music lasted late into the night. Frequently it was two or three in the morning before we left the flat. By that time, we were so fully aroused by what Gurdjieff had been saying that we could not contemplate sleep. Small parties of three, four and sometimes even a dozen, would go to a nearby cafe and sit for an hour or more, reconstructing what Gurdjieff had been saying. This led to a strange observation that was verified many times by all of us. One person would have a clear and exact recollection of what Gurdjieff had said on some topic. Another would flatly contradict the account, saying that something quite different had been said. Sometimes several people would insist that Gurdjieff had spoken exclusively and privately to them, giving them a deeply important message. Other people who had been sitting a yard away would not have heard a word.

After some time we concluded that Gurdjieff had a peculiar kind of Māya that enabled him to appear differently to different people at the same time. He was, indeed, as Madame Ouspensky had put it, X - the unknown quantity. To convey some impression of his infinite variety, forty people, men and women, who saw most of him at the various periods of his life would have to write forty different books. Unfortunately most of those who could have written of him have died, leaving little or no record of their experience.

I am reluctant to describe any of Gurdjieff's spiritual exercises, as I am sure that they should never be undertaken without supervision by some experienced guide. Herein indeed lies the chief obstacle to the spread of Gurdjieff's method. His pupils are generally agreed that at least seven years of intensive training are needed to form a group leader. The majority of those who attempt this training fall by the way, or become so acutely aware of their own defects that they refuse to take responsibility for others. In consequence, those who have at different times accepted the task of guiding others have been overworked and overstrained. Dependence upon highly trained and rarely equipped teachers is a serious defect for which it is difficult to see a remedy.

One exercise which opened for me a new field of understanding I feel able to describe, as it could not rashly be imitated by a curious minded reader. One day Gurdjieff called me into his room and asked me about my mother; when she had died and how I felt about her. He then said: "She is in need of help because she cannot find her way by herself. My own mother is already free, and I can help her. Through her, your mother can be helped, but you have to bring them into contact." He gave me a photograph of his mother, who had died at the Prieuré twenty-four years earlier, and said: "Every day for half an hour you practise what I say. First look well at this picture until you can see my mother with your eyes shut. Then place two chairs side by side, and on the right chair picture my mother and on the left your own mother. Stand in front of them and keep your attention fixed upon the wish that they may meet and that your mother may receive help. This is a very hard exercise, and you must have a great wish to help your mother. You cannot help her yourself, but through my mother I can help her."

I took this exercise even more seriously than others he had set me. When my mother had died I had been acutely aware that she needed help after she was dead, and I had no idea how it was to be given. The task proved to be unexpectedly painful. After a few weeks the effort of standing for half an hour before two empty chairs became almost intolerable. To my surprise I found myself bathed in sweat from head to foot, as if I had been doing heavy manual work. One day, I burst into tears and sobbed for the entire half-hour. Yet nothing at all seemed to be happening. I was invaded with doubts, and a feeling that the whole affair was a cruel joke that Gurdjieff had played upon me. Then a change began. After I had done the exercise for a month, I began to be aware that there were presences in the room. These presences, which at first were fleeting and nebulous, took the shape of my mother and Madame Gurdjieff. I felt distinctly that my mother was resisting, and would not turn her head to the left. Then, one day, the contact was unmistakable. A wave of relief and gratitude flowed through me. It seemed at that moment that Gurdjieff himself was with me in my bedroom at Coombe Springs.

A few days later I was in Paris, and told him what had happened. He said: "I am very pleased. Now you are part of my family, and we will not be separated."

I felt towards him as a son, and took his hand to kiss it. He drew it away sharply saying: "Not you must kiss my hand, but I must kiss yours." I have no idea what he meant by this, and he changed the conversation abruptly by speaking of some practical question that I have now forgotten. From that day, I was unable to repeat the exercise, although I often became aware of some delicate and almost imperceptible contact with my mother.

21: GURDJIEFF'S LAST DAYS

Meanwhile, Gurdjieff himself was making plans to go to the United States. The chief obstacle was his passport. He had never been popular with the authorities of any country. Nothing less than the intervention of very influential friends in Washington had saved him from deportation from America before the war. The French police regarded him as a dangerous suspect. He had been arrested after the war on the charge of illicit possession of foreign currency, and his dossiers with the Sûreté Publique and the Prefecture of Paris were bulging with reports of unlawful activities of all kinds. Gurdjieff himself was quite indifferent to the impression he created, and even seemed to take pains to let himself appear in a bad light.

The French Group told the story of his arrest. A French friend connected with the police had warned him to avoid keeping any foreign currency in his flat. Foreign pupils, especially Americans, coming over to see him after the war would bring him gifts of money - sometimes a thousand dollars or more. By law, these should have been exchanged at once for francs. But Gurdjieff liked to keep the foreign banknotes.

One day he was warned that the police intended to raid his flat, and he was implored to make sure that he had nothing suspicious. He had said: "They can never find anything in my apartment." The same day the police came, looked under his mattress, and found a variety of foreign currency notes. He was taken to the police station and locked up with petty criminals. Afterwards, telling the story against himself, he said that one of them came up to him and said: "Old boy, how many times have you been inside?" When he said that it was the first time, he saw that he had lost face. So next time he was asked, he replied: "Eighteen times!" and he had been the admiration of all. To appreciate the story it would be necessary to hear the magnificent tone in which Gurdjieff proclaimed: "Dix-huit!" This number had a hidden significance, for in Gurdjieff's series of idiots it represented the highest level to which any individual being in the universe can attain by his own efforts.

When brought before the magistrate, Gurdjieff had played to perfection the part of a poor old man who understood nothing about foreign money, and could scarcely speak French. He had been discharged, and went back to the flat to tell the story with many embellishments to his pupils and friends. When he was asked why he had ignored the warning, he replied: "I had never before been in prison. One must have every kind of experience." He liked telling this story, with many others against himself, and we heard it many times. Whenever he came to the place where he hid the money under the mattress, he would pause, look round the room with a beatific smile of child like innocence and say: "Good place? Hein?"

Such exploits, though amusing and instructive to his pupils, could not have ingratiated him with the police. He had never been able to get French citizenship, and travelled on the Nansen passport issued to White Russian émigrés. The holders could not enter any country without evidence that, at the end of their stay, another country was prepared to receive them. When Gurdjieff applied to the French police, they were adamant in refusing him a re-entry permit. Without this, there was little hope of an American visa unless some other country would accept him. But he insisted that he must be assured of a return to France.

No one could see a way out. I was asked to help. It happened that two of my pupils were on very friendly terms with a powerful minister in the then French Government, who, on being asked, assured them that it would be the easiest thing in the world to arrange the permit. In point of fact, a former prime minister of France had to give his personal guarantee before the French police very reluctantly agreed to give the re-entry permit. The visa for the United States was arranged by myself and another Englishman, once again through having just the right connections.

Gurdjieff sailed for the United States with Madame de Salzmann from Le Havre on 30th October, 1948. I was asked to go with them on the boat train in case of trouble at the last moment. There was a large party at lunch that day. I was Director, and took upon myself to break the ritual of the toasts by proposing his own health. He said: "No. I will propose myself health of English. Thanks to the English I sail to New York free from all debts. Pure *comme bébé.*" Indeed, very large sums of money had been collected for him by the English groups. There was a great crowd of the French pupils at Gare St. Lazare. As he leaned out of his carriage window he distributed, as usual, sweets and nuts, and gave his last parting message: "Before I return I hope with all my being that everyone here will have learned the difference between sensation and feeling."

On the way to Le Havre, Madame de Salzmann was unusually nervous and ill at ease. It was not easy for me to grasp the dread of the police that obsessed those who had lived in Paris through the German occupation. When, at last, without incident, we were safely on board the American liner, Gurdjieff began to let off steam. He made a great scene over his cabin, which was on the inside. He had insisted on a single cabin, and the purser pointed out that all single cabins were on the inside. Then he said he would not go to America, but would leave the ship at Southampton, and that I was to arrange to meet him there the next morning. Finally he marched up to the deserted grill-room, told me to fetch bottles of Armagnac, jars of caviare and zakuskas of various kinds that he had brought in a basket from Paris. The stewards were furious, but he mollified them with a generous tip. He told me to be Director - that is, to propose the toasts. We sat drinking until the last minute for me to leave the ship.

It was midnight before I got off. I had missed the train back, and it was raining heavily. I wandered through the quays; no hotels were open, so I settled down to sleep under a railway arch. A prostitute came by, and thinking that I was down and out, offered to share her bed with me. I refused as gently as I could. She was immensely fat and kindly. As she walked away I said to myself: "I am sadly ignorant of life. Is she good or am I good?"

Daylight came, and I returned to London to pick up the threads of my complicated life. It was indeed very complicated, because my preoccupation with Gurdjieff's affairs was beginning to interfere with my duty to my employers. Also my own pupils at Coombe Springs had been thrown into turmoil. For some the thought of meeting Gurdjieff and learning from him had been the crowning satisfaction. They had no problem, except that of contriving to see more of him than was easy so long as he lived in Paris. Others were affronted by his behaviour. They could not reconcile themselves to the drinking at his table and his obscene language. Several were terribly distressed by what they heard in Paris about his private life, and especially his relations with women. They took literally his boasting about his many sons and daughters and his irresistible appeal for women.

I had somehow or other to hold things together. So far as I was concerned, Gurdjieff's private life was his affair, and all that mattered was that he most certainly could and did help me, and all who came to him. I reminded those who were volubly distressed of the warning I had given them all. I myself was not in the least disturbed by all that I saw and heard. It may be that I was too uncritical. The new hope that Gurdjieff had so firmly implanted in me made any doubts seem trivial. Moreover, I had seen him after his accident. I was quite sure that the loving, God-fearing and gentle being that we had become aware of during those terrible days was far nearer to the real Gurdjieff than the one who delighted to scandalize, and even to terrify, those who came to him with no clear idea of what they wanted. To me, it was obvious that he was not only a most extraordinary being - far more so than he had appeared at the Prieuré in 1923 - but that he was also a good man, who had undertaken a prodigious task and was carrying it through regardless of the cost to himself.

Soon after the normal life around Gurdjieff had been re-established, he began to speak of the need for a large place that would enable him to resume the work he had started at the Prieuré. He was offered the Château de Voisins at Rambouillet, a magnificent castle, probably the finest built in the present century. The owner, an immensely wealthy sugar baron, wished, for taxation reasons, to lease it cheaply for a number of years, and I was deputed to undertake the negotiations. Gurdjieff himself visited it several times, and declared it to be very suitable for his work. As Madame de Salzmann and the other French pupils took the proposal very seriously, I did the same, and worked out a financial plan by which it could have been acquired, and the heavy running costs covered, by the stream of visitors from the United States and England, who were expected to come in search of help and guidance in their work. When Gurdjieff left for America he took with him concrete proposals, and he appeared to be confident of getting the support he needed to lease the Château. I must confess that I was never able to tell when Gurdjieff was serious and when he was play-acting.

The opportunity of a short business trip to America presented itself. I arrived in New York a few weeks after Gurdjieff. It was the New Year of 1949. He was installed in the Wellington Hotel, where I found a room also. I had to visit Washington to attend a hearing at the U.S. Patent Office of our claims for the invention of Delanium, but I was able to spend several days in New York, including 13th January, which Gurdjieff claimed to be his eightieth birthday. He was, in fact, a good deal younger, and it is doubtful whether 'Midnight on the first of January, Old Style' was more than a symbolic birthday. Nevertheless, it was celebrated by all Gurdjieff's followers, and they were coming from different parts of America for a feast arranged in Gurdjieff's apartment at the Wellington.

He had just taken the final decision to publish the first volume of All and Everything – Beelzebub's Tales to His Grandson, and had been asked by Madame Ouspensky to decide whether or not Ouspensky's own book, Fragments of an Unknown Teaching, should also be published. He remained undecided about the latter for some time, pointing out when he heard it read aloud that certain of his ideas were far more clearly and strongly expressed in Beelzebub. He finally agreed, on condition that it should not be published in advance of his own book.

I cannot tell what was Gurdjieff's private opinion of Ouspensky, but he nearly always spoke of him in scathing terms as one who had exploited his ideas, brought many of his pupils to grief, and in the case of Ferapontoff and Ivanoff, even caused their death, and who, if he had not left Gurdjieff to set up on his own, need not have 'perished like a dog'. This last utterance, made in front of fifty or sixty friends and pupils in New York, provoked an uproar, which was probably Gurdjieff's intention. One brave young man stood up to him and said: "If it had not been for Mr. Ouspensky we should not have been here now!" To which Gurdjieff retorted: "What is use of your being here? You also are candidate for perishing like a dog." Gurdjieff frequently complained that Ouspensky had ruined his pupils by his excessively intellectual approach, and that he did better with people who came to him with no preparation at all. On the other hand, he praised Ouspensky for the accuracy of his reporting. Once I read aloud in front of him an early chapter of In Search of the Miraculous. He listened with evident relish, and when I finished he said: "Before I hate Ouspensky; now I love him. This very exact, he tell what I say."

Once when he complained to me of Ouspensky's pupils when we were alone together, I asked him if mine were spoiled also. He said: "No; your people are not spoiled, but lunatic. With lunatic I can do something; not with spoiled." Nevertheless, his method, from the start, was to do all he could to turn my pupils against me and break up the work I was doing at Coombe. When I heard that he told people close to me that I was immature, ignorant and useless to them as a teacher, or that there was nothing he could do to help me and they had better find someone else to work with, I was not in the least dismayed. On the one hand, I was convinced that what he said of me was true and, on the other, I could see perfectly well that he set himself to break down all personal attachments, first of all towards himself and then towards others.

No words will reproduce the atmosphere of wonder, of tension, suspicion, exasperation, hopefulness, delight, sheer enjoyment and of abject misery that Gurdjieff succeeded in creating about him. I returned to New York from Washington to plunge into just such a situation. Gurdjieff had announced the day before his birthday that he intended to send a circular letter to all his pupils, past and present, telling them of his decision to publish Beelzebub, and of his wish that unlimited supplies should be available without cost, so that everyone could read it for himself. He also desired it to be published in at least four languages and distributed all over the world, including Russia. There was an animated discussion at dinner as to how this letter should be worded, but he brushed all suggestions aside. Gurdjieff treated me with exaggerated deference as the 'esteemed representative for England'. I knew that this boded no good, but could not tell what was behind it. While in New York, Gurdjieff paraded photographs of the Château de Voisins, saying sometimes that he had bought it, at others that he needed money to buy it. He offered permanent suites in the Château to anyone who would contribute $5000 to the cost. At the last dinner before his birthday, he linked Beelzebub and the Chateau, saying that thousands would come to visit him when it was published, and he needed a very big place. He even spoke of resuscitating his Institute for the Harmonious Development of Man, and making the Château de Voisins its world headquarters.

The next morning, I went to the Child's Cafe on Fifth Avenue at 56th Street, knowing that this used to be his 'New York Office'. I cannot recall if he told me to go or whether I went on impulse. I found him sitting alone. He offered me tea, which we drank in silence. Then he said to me: "You now write letter." I asked for a sheet of paper, and wrote without knowing how or what I should write. In two or three minutes the letter was written. The manner of writing was completely foreign to me. I had used the word 'adept' instead of pupil. This both surprised and annoyed me, as the word 'adept' grated harshly on my ear as savouring too much of occultism. He said: "Read!" I read the letter aloud:

6, RUE DES COLONELS RENARD,
PARIS, 17

13th January, 1949

This circular letter is addressed to all my present and former adepts and to all those who have been directly or indirectly influenced by my ideas and have sensed and understood that they contain something which is necessary for the good of humanity. After fifty years of preparation and having overcome the greatest difficulties and obstacles, I have now reached the moment when I have decided to publish the first series of my writings in three books under the title of An Objectively Impartial Criticism of the Life of Man, or Beelzebub's Tales to his Grandson. By this publication I shall begin to actualize the plans I have prepared for the transmission of my ideas to the whole of contemporary and future humanity.

In order to accomplish this task, I shall need the help of all those who have understood something of the value of my ideas and especially those who have gained personal benefit and help from their study. I intend that the first series of my writings shall be made freely available without payment to all who are in need of their help.

The first edition of the first series is now in course of preparation in one volume of nearly 1000 pages and will be printed in four languages. The distribution of such a great work will cost a very large sum of money and in order to make it possible, I ask you and all my other pupils to buy one copy of the first printing for a sum of £100. If you can buy more than one copy you will correspondingly help more people to enjoy the benefit of free copies. Those who cannot buy a copy alone may join with one or two others. By means of this action, it will be possible for all those who have gained personal help from contact with my ideas to do something to repay and to help to reap the harvest which I have sown.

G. GURDJIEFF

He reached out and took the paper without a word.

That day at lunch, he took the letter out of his pocket. I was sitting next to him, and he gave it to me to read aloud as if I had never seen it. All those present were loud in approval, saying that it was exactly right; only Mr. Gurdjieff could have written it, and so on. I remained silent, knowing that I had been made the subject or the victim of one of those tricks of thought transference, or suggestion, that Gurdjieff loved to play.

He then said: "I need three representatives for France, England and America." He named me for England, Lord Pentland for America and M. René Zuber for France. The letter was to be dispatched independently from each country, and everyone was asked to give £100, or the equivalent in dollars or francs.

That afternoon there was a children's party. Gurdjieff was always at his best with children. He regarded them as unspoiled material, and taught them with the utmost delicacy. Someone asked him how best to introduce children to his ideas. He said: "Never try to teach directly. Always with children begin from afar. Children must find for themselves; otherwise they will grow up as slaves." He did not mean that children should be left free to do as they liked. On the contrary, he believed in very strict discipline, and impressed upon children that they must always be ready to conform to the society in which they happened to be present - but never put on artificial manners with him. A valuable book could be written describing the innumerable ways in which Gurdjieff showed parents the right way to handle their children. When children were brought to him he used to say: "Love your parents. They must be for you like God. Who does not love his parents can never love God."

When the children's party broke up, the elders either left the apartment or went to prepare dinner. I was left alone with him. He was seated on a low divan at the end of the long drawing-room. I knelt beside him and thanked him. He said: "What I have done up to now for you is nothing. Soon I return to Europe. You come to me, and I will show you how to work. If you do what I tell, I will show you how to become unmortal. Now you having nothing, but if you will work you can soon have soul." This was for me a very solemn moment, because I knew that, for the second time since 1923, he was speaking to me seriously, and was making me a promise which, from his side, he would certainly keep.

I will not describe the extraordinary events at his birthday party that night, the last before he died ten months later. Within two days I left for England, and plunged again into my work at the laboratories. I was determined to make up for the neglect of my business during the previous summer. The Powell Duffryn Research Laboratories were at that period doing their best work, and I enjoyed it for its own sake. We had the full, even enthusiastic, support of our directors, and the satisfaction of seeing the fruits of many years' work in the laboratories ripen into articles of commerce. When I visited the great factory in which the large-scale production of Delanium was getting under way, I was in wonderment that my timid brain-child of seven years before should have been so transformed.

I had been ready to abandon everything and go wherever Gurdjieff might direct. When I asked him what he wished me to do he replied: "What you already do. Change nothing. You can be most useful to my work by what you do now in England." It was with the conviction that I could best serve Gurdjieff by making a success of my business life that I prepared a plan of action that would enable me to devote nearly all my energies to the Powell Duffryn Research Laboratories. However, I met Gurdjieff at Cherbourg on his return, and he was scarcely off the ship before he called me to sit with him in the restaurant car. He gave me two pills which I was to take, adding that after half an hour I was to do an exercise he showed me. It was strange to sit with him wholly isolated from the turmoil and the shouting that accompanies the berthing of a great liner.

So began a period of eight months which was the hardest and most painful of my life. It is quite impossible to write about the most significant events, because they were of such an intimate nature that to describe them would be a kind of public confession.

On the one hand, Gurdjieff showed me a sequence of exercises for the control and transformation of the psychic energies in man. On the other, he set to work to destroy my closest and most precious relationships. Whereas the previous year he had treated me and my wife as one, he now came between us to create a most difficult situation. He told my wife that I must learn to do without her, and me that I must free myself from attachment to any woman - even to herself. This demand was made almost impossible to fulfill by the circumstance that since we had been together during the terrible week of 9th August of the previous year, a deep attachment had formed between myself and Elizabeth Mayall. She for her part placed all her hopes in Gurdjieff. The year before, she had passed through a prolonged state of despair over her own inner life. I advised her to leave Coombe and go to live in Paris, suggesting that she should ask Gurdjieff to accept her as his pupil. It seemed to me that only a complete transformation of all our natures could resolve the impossible situation in which we found ourselves. She took my advice, and in the outcome saw far more of Gurdjieff during the last eight months of his life than I did. During her stay in Paris, Elizabeth accompanied Gurdjieff on several of his trips to Vichy and other French cities. He had brought back with him from America the daughters of several of his pupils, to undergo special training in the rhythmic movements and become instructors. One of them, Iovanna, daughter of the great architect Frank Lloyd Wright, became particularly expert, and later taught Gurdjieff's movements to young architects at Taliesin. The girls were known as the 'calves' and Elizabeth, though older, was usually treated as one of them. Gurdjieff gave her special responsibilities, and indeed I believe that only Lise Tracol saw more of him than she did, as she was at his apartment for many hours each day. He gave her his confidence to an unusual degree, and entrusted her with many delicate missions.

I had not reckoned that Gurdjieff would use my close personal relationships to create an almost intolerable tension between me and everyone near me. In addition to this, he made constant demands for services that risked my reputation, and obliged me to jeopardize the good standing that I had acquired through fifteen years of work in coal research. I also had, during the spring and early summer of 1949, to make the transition from the conditions of work so laboriously established over the years since I had parted from Ouspensky, and which depended upon my leadership, to the new condition where I was a pupil like the others, and where everything had to be learned again from the beginning. I made many mistakes during this time, and Gurdjieff did not fail to use them to sharpen his knife.

One of the few consolations of this agonizing year was the great improvement in my wife's health. She went over to see Gurdjieff a number of times, and he must have told her something about the reasons for his treatment of me, because having vehemently rebelled against it at first, she afterwards told me that it was necessary, and that her one hope was that I would succeed in doing what he required of me. If I had known clearly what this was, it would have perhaps been easier, but I had to read between the lines and guess his intentions.

Nearly every weekend I took a plane for Paris or, going by car, brought three or four pupils to visit him. Each time, when I arrived, some new task or proposal was awaiting me. He was then receiving requests for help from all over Europe, and frequently turned to me to go and start a new group or meet some important personage. I learned to refuse what was wholly beyond my powers, but even so I undertook far too much. And yet I know that if I had done less, I should have missed opportunities that would never return.

One Saturday in May, I arrived in time for lunch. Gurdjieff asked me if had a group in Holland. I said I had no contacts in Holland. He said: 'Why not? I have need of a group in Holland; you can arrange.' Elizabeth, who was sitting in her usual comer by the piano, told him that she had a Dutch school-friend now living in The Hague. He said: 'She can help. You write to her.' As we already had undertaken a big task in organizing classes for the rhythmic exercises or 'Movements' in London, I decided that the Holland Group project need not be taken seriously.

Gurdjieff would often insist that some scheme was vitally important and then never refer to it again. For example, the proposal to lease the Chateau de Voisins had not been mentioned again, and Gurdjieff was now negotiating for a much smaller place. The following weekend I went to Paris again, and was somewhat taken aback when Gurdjieff asked me as soon as we went in to lunch whether I had done anything about Holland. When I said that I had not had time, he shouted at me, saying: "I too have no time. You think I will live forever? I have need of contact with Dutch because of India. Not your English India which not have interest for me; but with their India. I need Dutch group, for contact with Dutch India." I could not understand what he was driving at, but it was evident that he was serious. Elizabeth wrote at once to her friend, who happened at that time to be Secretary of the International Grass Association, and to have many useful contacts. In the outcome, I was invited to give a public lecture on Gurdjieff's System in The Hague, and a Dutch group came into existence. It was not until nine years later, with the coming of Subud, that I could find an explanation for Gurdjieff's insistence upon the need to have contact with the Dutch Indies.

I was in Paris for my birthday on 8th June. Gurdjieff said that he would play a special piece of music for me on his organ. As I listened, I became aware that I was holding something back, that I had to find a new relationship with him, and that he was opening a door that I could not enter because my perceptions were not fine enough. At that time, Gurdjieff had set me to work upon a spiritual exercise that completely baffled me, for it required the attainment of a state of motionless equilibrium of all the psychic functions, and yet the absence of any constraint or effort of attention. When he first explained it to me, it seemed simple compared with the complicated and very difficult exercises, connected with control of the energies of sensation, feeling and thought, that I had been working on before. Its very simplicity made it supremely difficult to accomplish. It seemed to me that I was failing, and that I must contrive to spend more time in Paris, and place myself entirely under his guidance. I cancelled the plans for a seminar at Coombe Springs - the only time in fifteen years that there has been no combined work there in August - and arranged to take four weeks' holiday. On 21st July, 1949, I began again to keep a journal, and continued for two years. My aim was not so much to record events, as my own inner experiences. As I re-read the pages after eleven years, I see how I was driving myself day and night to very little purpose. Every page is evidence of my lack of understanding of what was required of me. I was convinced that I needed to dominate all my bodily and psychic functions, and that I could only acquire the power to do this by long and painful exercises. I was especially bewildered and even outraged by all that Gurdjieff said in public, and advised me in private, about the subject of sex. He spoke of women in terms that would have better suited a fanatical Muslim polygamist than a Christian, boasting that he had many children by different women, and that women were for him only means to an end. The general impression that Gurdjieff produced shocked those accustomed to regard the sex relation as sacred - even if their private behaviour might be anything but sacred. Gurdjieff always showed the worst outwards and kept the best hidden.

Sometimes young women would come to Paris to visit him. He would then flirt outrageously with them, and invite them to come back to the flat late at night when everyone had gone. Often thinking that this was some kind of mysterious test, or just frankly curious, they would go. In all cases that I heard of, Gurdjieff would open the door, look astonished and say: "Why you come now?" give them a handful of sweets and send them away. It was, however, inevitable that the worst interpretation should be placed on his actions. Troubled parents would ask me if it was expected that their daughters should sleep with him. I always answered: "Certainly not; he only does this to see if you have enough common sense and strength of character to stick to what is right." Nevertheless, I am bound to say that the advice that he gave older men and women resulted in many irregular relationships being formed. The whole atmosphere among those who surrounded Gurdjieff was impregnated with a feverish excitement that made it hard to tell what was right and what was wrong.

I believe that Gurdjieff's own actions were guided throughout by a deep and direct awareness of the unity of all life and of our dependence upon the Mercy of God. Once, a newcomer told a malicious story against someone present. Gurdjieff, who had been telling his harmless and apparently meaningless jokes, broke off to say in a very serious voice: "Every breathing creature has self-love, and this we must not offend." There could be no doubt that his dearest wish was that his work should help to deliver mankind from slavery and dependence upon the good opinions of others. But this required that they should not depend upon him either, and this made him a severe taskmaster. In spite of my trust in Gurdjieff and the complete faith I had in his goodness, I felt nervous about going to stay in Paris, not being at all sure of my own ability to find my way. However, the decision was taken. Before I describe those dramatic weeks, I should refer to three incidents that added spice to my life during the summer of 1949.

The first was the publication by the Royal Society of the paper on Unified Field Theory on which Thring, Brown and I had been working for so many years. We had submitted it nearly a year earlier, just before I went to America, and it had been severely handled by the referees. In its final form it owed much to the help of a fine mathematician, now a Fellow of the Royal Society, who wished to remain anonymous. It attracted very little attention, and I saw that Ouspensky had not been far out in saying it would be 'just another physical theory'. Nevertheless, it was a considerable honour for three scientists standing outside the academic world to have so abstract a paper accepted by the most exacting scientific society in the world.

The second was an invitation from Dr. Maria Montessori to give an address at a great educational congress, to be held in her honour at San Remo. Among our activities at Coombe Springs was an experimental Montessori school, which we kept going for several years. The friendship that had grown between myself and the *dottoressa* had little to do with her schools, and sprang rather from the strong feeling we both had for the unity of mankind.

The third event was an invitation from the Government of Ceylon to become Adviser on Industrial Development. I learned that they had asked the Royal Society for a recommendation, and Sir Alfred Egerton, then Physical Secretary, knowing my interest in the East, had put forward my name. The Government stipulated that I should sign a five-year contract. The work was very attractive and I had long wanted to go to Ceylon, but I could not leave Gurdjieff for so long unless he thought it really useful. I consulted the directors of Powell Duffryn. They, apparently interpreting my action as a hint that I was not satisfied with my position, offered me a five years' service agreement as head of their Research Laboratories and director of three subsidiary companies. As I was sure in my heart that I would have to give up business before long, I refused. When I consulted Gurdjieff, he said: "If for one year, good, but not five. I will need you in Europe and America after one year."

When I look back to that time, it is hard to believe he really could have needed me. My idea of working on myself was merely to make life as unpleasant and exhausting for myself as I could. After so many years, my lack of understanding was pitiable. I will give an example of the uncomprehending efforts I was making at this time to reach by main force a different state of consciousness. As we were having no regular seminar, I invited some forty pupils to spend the August Bank Holiday at Coombe, and undertook to read Beelzebub from start to finish. The book in typescript had 2100 pages - more than half a million words. I read it all aloud: four hours' reading and two hours for eating and rest, all through the day and night. Before the end my tongue was so swollen that I had to drink iced water to prevent my teeth from cutting it. It was no less of a struggle for the others to listen to sixty hours of difficult reading. We finished on Monday night, with a feast of Persian pilaf and grilled steak. The pilaf was made from Persian rice that Gurdjieff had given me. It was cooked in two and a half pounds of butter and three pints of milk. Fifty-four eggs were whipped up and added. The whole was stirred until it was just setting. This was at a time when food was still rationed in England. Each member of the party had brought one or two eggs for the purpose.

I ask myself today whether such efforts had, or could have, any value. And yet at the time I was convinced that they were necessary. Behind these efforts was the regular daily practice of the exercise that Gurdjieff had set me to master. It appears to me today that I would have done better to force myself and others less, and to have relied upon the spiritual exercise, the true significance of which I only began to understand many years later.

On 5th August I went to Paris. My wife came with me. We began the ritual of readings and meals twice a day. For some reason Gurdjieff made me read, three or four times over, a chapter from the Third Series of All and Everything called 'Life is Real only then when I AM'. We called this the 'I AM Chapter', and it contains an account of the task that Gurdjieff set himself as a young man of denying himself the use of his immense psychic powers, except to cure diseases and to help others. The chapter draws a vivid picture of the extraordinary demands Gurdjieff made upon himself throughout his life. Did he mean to show me that I must make more demands upon myself? I probably misunderstood him, and what he really intended to show me is that there is little or no value in torturing oneself, either physically or emotionally, and that what is needed is a 'reminding factor' that will prevent us from sleeping. This need not be painful, like a hair shirt that one ceases to notice when the skin becomes accustomed to the irritation.

At last, I began to understand something. Gurdjieff was making greater and greater demands upon me. Some were absurd and even impossible. It dawned upon me finally that I could and must learn to say "No." It was like a blinding light. The inability to say "No" was my greatest weakness. He had stretched this weakness to breaking point, without explaining why, or what he was doing. Of course he could not explain, or the task itself would have vanished. When I told all this to my wife, she looked at me pityingly, saying: "Has it taken you all this time to see this? I have seen it for years, but as usual you would not listen to me." I would not listen to anyone, but I did have the utmost confidence in Gurdjieff. My wife had to return to England. When we parted, she said to me: "You must do the task he has given you, whatever it costs. It is as hard for me as for you - but I accept it. Only I cannot help you any more until it is done."

Until then, Gurdjieff had evaded every attempt to speak about my problems. Finally he saw me, and when I told him all I was doing, he said: "Physical efforts are unnecessary." I told him about the paper to the Royal Society. His comment was: "Mathematik is useless. You cannot learn laws of World Creation and World Existence by Mathematik. You must only look for Being. When you have Being, you will know all these things, without the need of Mathematik." I was about to explain my purpose, but fortunately held my tongue, for he went on to give me explanations about the inner life of man that were beyond price.

Two or three days later, I had the experience of leaving my body without the special conditions of previous occasions. I was reading aloud before the evening meal. Suddenly, without any warning, I found myself several feet away from my body. My voice was still speaking, but it was not 'my' voice any more, but a stranger's. I said to myself: "How can he read? He can't possibly give the right intonation!" I could see the other people from quite a different perspective, and wondered if anyone else knew that an empty shell was reading. I wondered if Gurdjieff knew, and at the same moment the body's eyes looked up from the reading and saw him, and, without knowing how, I was back in my body again and the reading continued. The sense of separation from the body persisted for several hours, although I remained inside it.

This was only the beginning of an avalanche of amazing experiences that continued for four weeks. I became conscious of internal organs such as my liver and how they worked. The condition of complete command over my emotional states that had come to me at the Prieuré returned unexpectedly one morning. This time I found that I could be aware of events happening in another place. I rang up my wife in London, and verified that I had been aware that she was at a meeting with the women of the house, and what she was saying. There were many extraordinary talks with Gurdjieff at meals. Once he spoke of the Last Supper and the role off Judas. He spoke in rather a low voice to me. He said that Judas was the best and closest friend of Jesus. Judas alone understood why Jesus was on earth. Judas had saved the work of Jesus from being destroyed, and by his action had made the life of humanity more or less tolerable for two thousand years. He then looked at me very intently, and said: "You know what I say of Judas and how differently the Church teaches. Which do you believe is true?" What was I to answer? I saw that I had accepted without self-searching the account that Gurdjieff gives in Chapter 38, on Religion, of All and Everything. Now I was called upon to pronounce my own judgment.

The crowded dining-room disappeared, and it seemed as if Gurdjieff were leading me back through the centuries to the Jerusalem of A.D. 33. It seemed that I had been there before, but this was not at all important. I was strongly aware of the prodigious forces at work - good forces and evil forces at war. Judas was unmistakably on the side of the good forces. That was all that I needed to know. In a moment we were back in the fiat and I was speaking to Gurdjieff. "You are right. Judas was the friend of Jesus, and he was on the side of good." Gurdjieff said in a low voice: "I am pleased what you understand." He was almost inaudible, and someone asked from the end of the table if he would repeat it. He said: "I speak only for him. One day Mr. Bennett will give a conference on the Last Supper, and many people will be thankful to him." This was but one of many enigmatic prophecies about my future.

On several occasions he said that my relationship with him was the same as that between Judas and Jesus. Once he pointed to me and to an old friend of mine sitting next to me, saying: "Mr. Bennett is like Judas; he is responsible that my work is not destroyed. You are like Paul; you must spread my ideas." In the sequel the second part at least of this prophecy was fulfilled, for the friend in question took the lead in securing the publication of *All and Everything*. My own role has been obscure. Once Gurdjieff said: "Judas is universal type: he can enter into all situations - but he has no type of his own." This, at least, seemed to agree with my own estimate of myself.

Taken together, Gurdjieff's references to me during the summer of 1949 all conveyed the impression that, at some time in the future, I would have a special role to play. At this time also, Gurdjieff began to make dark references to his own departure. He never spoke of death, but of going far away. I did not guess at the time how seriously he was speaking and warning us that he was soon to die. Once when a visitor from America said to him: "Mr. Gurdjieff, what shall we all do when you die?" he replied in a furious tone: "I am Gurdjieff! I not will die."

The stream of visitors from all over the world grew in volume, and in the insistence of their demands for private interviews with Gurdjieff. He refused no one. The atmosphere of unbearable tension was not confined to the fiat, but spread out to the hotels where visitors were staying; the Belfast, the Rena and the San Remo, and the cafés where we met and talked in the middle of the night, and to the studios of the Salle Pleyel, where movements classes were held several times a week, and which he rarely missed.

Throughout August, I was absent from Paris only for two days, when I went to San Remo to give my talk to the Montessori Conference. I spoke of the need for teachers of children to learn to work upon themselves. I gave the talk in Italian, to the delight of the dottoressa, who herself took the chair. The address was mentioned on the Italian radio with a reference to Gurdjieff and his ideas on the role of teachers. When I returned to Paris he was delighted, and said: "Perhaps Pope Rome heard. One day Beelzebub will be read in Pope's Palace. Perhaps I will be there."

During the summer, before I came, Gurdjieff had made several long trips by car, accompanied by his 'calves', to Geneva, to Dieppe, to Cannes, to Vichy. I had heard often of these extraordinary journeys, and hoped to go at least once. Gurdjieff was beginning to get very tired, and looked much older and moved with greater difficulty than when I had come to Paris a year before. Nevertheless, he was determined to make one more trip. He wanted to see the prehistoric cave paintings at Lascaux, of which

I had spoken with more enthusiasm than judgment.

The last trip made by Gurdjieff before he died was to Vichy and Lascaux. We set out in three car-loads, and others went by train to join us at Vichy. One of Gurdjieff's unexpectednesses consisted in starting before the agreed time. Unless you knew this trick, you were liable to arrive punctually and find the party had left half an hour earlier. Consequently, before any trip, those invited would collect an hour or more in advance. Lise Tracol, Gurdjieff's sister-in-law and his niece Luba, and others close to him would come from time to time to the window of the flat and look down at the cars. The loading would begin. He always travelled with hampers of food; several water-melons if they were in season would fill the back of the car. The voluminous luggage of the calves would be loaded on to the roofs of the cars, while they wandered aimlessly up and down the street as if bored with the whole proceeding - which indeed most of them were. Finally, Gurdjieff himself would appear, smoking a cigarette in a big black holder, with his red fez at a jaunty angle on the back of his head and a pocket book bulging with thousand-franc notes.

On this occasion, we lost touch with Gurdjieff in the outskirts of Paris, but by some strange freak caught up with him in the middle of the night as he was approaching Nevers, where we stopped for the night. Although it was nearly midnight, the hotel staff turned out and served a cold dinner, to which was added the caviare, salad and other delicacies brought from Paris. Wherever he went, even if he stopped at a hotel for lunch, the ritual of the toasts was never broken. It was evident that he was well-known and popular wherever he went.

While at Vichy we had several talks, both during and between meals, which opened new and wonderful vistas so far as we could understand them. Once he spoke of the 'Inner God' who can be the directive power in all our actions. He said: "If you learn to obey Inner God, this is a thousand times better than the Ten Commandments, which only tell us how to live, but cannot help a man to work." The same evening he spoke about immortality, saying: "Unmortal is very big thing, but is not all. If a man works he can become of use even to God." He pointed to me and added: "There are two kinds of unmortal. He now has already Kesdjan Body. This is unmortal, but not real unmortal. Real unmortal only comes with higher body. He have body for soul but must also have body for 'I.'"

He then went on to speak of the difference between Paradise and what he called the Sun Absolute. "You can go to Paradise with Kesdjan body. But Paradise is only good for two or three days. Imagine what it would be if next year, year after, hundred years. Must not be satisfied with Paradise - must find way to Soleil Absolu."

This conversation may mean little to those unfamiliar with Gurdjieff's language and methods. To me, it meant that a great step had been taken towards the fulfilment of the promise he had made to me in New York, eight months before. I could not sleep that night for wonderment.

He went on to the caves at Lascaux. The long drive tired him very much, and his legs were beginning to swell ominously. But he insisted on going down into the caves. As he stood looking at the paintings, he seemed completely to belong there. He explained various symbols, and especially the strange composite animal, which he said was, like the Sphinx, the 'emblem' of an esoteric society. I said: "Symbol?" He rejected the correction. 'No. Emblem. At that time there were societies with special knowledge, and each society had an emblem by which the members recognized each other. Same way as we have Enneagram." He said that the deer were the totems of individual people. By the number of points on the antlers you could know the degree of attainment of the man they represented. He bought pictures for everyone. A special album was given to Iovanna Lloyd Wright with injunctions to give it to her father and "tell him that such place exist."

We turned back to Paris; starting as a convoy of three cars. One car was despatched straight to Paris. He took four in his own car, and I followed, expecting to remain with him, according to my promise made to Madame de Salzmann before leaving Paris. However, he made it plain that he did not want me. Finally, at Tulle, without any ceremony, he said: "I go right, you go left." I tried to keep an opening by saying: "Then we must say goodbye to you?" He said shortly: "Yes, goodbye!" and after drinking a glass of iced Vitelloise drove off very fast towards Clermont Ferrand. We turned north through Uzerche, and on our way back to Paris stopped at Fontainebleau and visited the Prieuré, which two of those with me had not seen. We also went to visit the station hotel at La Grande Paroisse on the Seine, which Gurdjieff was negotiating to buy. He had long abandoned the project of leasing a big chateau. He had been telling us wonderful stories of his plans to build on the steeply sloping ground behind the hotel, and to make this place in the future the centre of his work. He said that without a place where people could live and work together, his method could never give the best results. His description was a good example of the deep significance he could convey by means of an improvised symbolism. He said: "There will be a house at the top of the hill where I will rest from my labours, and to this only my nearest will come. Below will be a hall like Study House for movements, classes and lectures, and under that will be rooms where visitors will live. On each side of the hotel coming up from the outside street will be a path. This double path will be paved with mosaic. I will bring special architect to make this path, which will have many thousand stones of different colours." As he was saying this at lunch one day, a young English architect with a pointed beard, whom he had nicknamed Mefistofel, interrupted and said: "I can find you good mosaic artists here in Paris." Gurdjieff turned to him with majestic scorn saying: "Idiot! Such mosaic as I need no artist can make!" It was evident to all who were accustomed to his idiom that the mosaic represented his pupils from all countries and races and that the three houses stood for the three bodies of man.

The morning that Gurdjieff returned to Paris, I had a kind of vision of the horror of reincarnation. The condition of being out of my body and separated from my own mind came over me again; but this time I saw that if I died without fulfilling my destiny I might be required to leave 'all this' and live again in another person's body, think with his mind, feel with his emotions. And I saw the terror of such a situation, and that it might happen to me if I could not acquire that higher body of which Gurdjieff had spoken in Vichy. It seemed to me that perhaps this had not happened to me before, and that I could escape such a fate. But all dissolved into vague images and I could retain nothing definite or convincingly certain from the experience.

At our first meeting after his return, Gurdjieff treated me as if I were an outcast. Complaining at lunch that he had not been able to eat on the journey for lack of company, I said to him: "But you sent me away." He shouted at me: "But you tell you have to go fetch wife - but she here all the time. You not honest. Your manifestations are disgusting." He took every opportunity to tell me that I was a disappointment to him. I fell into despair and wished that I could die. My wife, who had in fact arrived after me in Paris, was also deeply distressed. It seemed to us both that all my time had been wasted, and yet I had done my best to follow his guidance and instructions. I had failed in understanding what was required, and in Gurdjieff's method this is the worst sin. Anyone can do what they understand, but not to understand is like the sin against the Holy Ghost which cannot be forgiven in this world or the next.

On Sunday, 4th September, my month in Paris ended. The previous night I had passed in agony of mind. In the morning I went round to Gurdjieff's cafe in the Rue des Acacias, having seen him go past my hotel on his way there. When I arrived, he would not let me sit at his table, saying in an angry voice: "People come, sit here and waste my time, and then I lose my clients. They not come, because they think I occupied."

I sat some distance away and for nearly half-an-hour he interposed a barrier of hostility between us. Then I asked him some questions about money arrangements he had asked me to make, and he answered shortly. Then slightly relaxing, he spoke of having cured someone, and "putting him on feet", and the obligation of his mother to pay heavily for this. I recognized the case he referred to, and knew that he had achieved a near miracle that was not sufficiently appreciated by the young man's family.

I had come to see him mainly to ask him if he would see my wife before we returned to England that night. He had told her that she would need special help for her health, and wished her to come over from England before I left. Although the moment was scarcely propitious I asked him, and his voice changed to an unusual gentleness as he said: "Tell her come at a quarter past one." I said that I was very grateful for what he was doing for her, and added: "I cannot thank you for what you have done for me. That I can never repay." He said nothing, but continued to drink his tea as if he had not heard me.

A long time passed, during which various people came and spoke to him. When we were alone again, he turned to me and said slowly: "What you say about never repay - this is stupidity. Only you can repay. Only you can repay for all my labours. What you think is money? I can buy all your England. Only you" - with great emphasis – "can repay me by work. But what you do? Before trip I give you task. Do you fulfil? No; you do just opposite. Never once I see you struggle with yourself. All the time you are occupied with your cheap animal."

He spoke very simply and quietly, and was going to say more when one of his patients came in. I got up to go, and he said: "Go for walk and then come back." I went round to the hotel to let my wife know that he was expecting her at a quarter past one, and returned to the cafe.

He told me that the man who had come had been a paralytic, and that he had cured him and "put him on feet." He had just brought 50,000 francs. "How he get, I don't know. Very difficult for a Russe. But he get." Then he added, with a very kind smile: "I think this have some connection with our conversation. I two nights not sleep because of you. Now you must repay - by your work."

I wanted to ask him where I had gone wrong, but he was again unapproachable. Soon he got up and drove off in his car, saying: "Let wife come at a quarter past one."

At lunch, after he had seen my wife, he spoke of Conscience, saying: "Conscience all have. But it is out of reach. It can only be brought into consciousness by the intensity of inner struggle. When conscience and consciousness are together, then you will not make such mistakes."

After lunch I drove Madame de Salzmann home, and told her of my sense of failure. She said: "The work changes. Up to one point, one gets fairly clear guidance. Then comes a time when it is made so confusing that you can easily do exactly the wrong thing in the conviction that it is right." I have not written much about the part Madame de Salzmann played, because she dislikes her good works to be seen of men. But she was to me, and to many others, a wise counsellor and friend in our fumbling efforts to discover what Gurdjieff wanted of us.

I returned to London saying to myself: "It is better to go with Remorse of Conscience for my failures than with Pride of Achievement." There was a difficult task for me to do in England. I had made the mistake of showing to those of my own pupils who could not go to Paris some of the simpler exercises that we had learned. When I told Gurdjieff this, he said: "That is very bad. You now make it difficult for me to work with them." So when I returned I had to disentangle the skein I had ravelled.

I continued to wrestle with the sense of failure. It seemed that I could make any effort and any sacrifice except the one needed. Then to my surprise George Cornelius came back from Paris and said that Gurdjieff was going to America and had said at lunch: "Bennett is my best pupil; I need him in America. But everyone takes his energy!" When my wife returned, she said that in her last talk with him he had said that he could help me with what I now needed, but that it would take time. Meanwhile I must rest. About herself, she said that he had promised her some special medicine, but nothing had materialized. Nevertheless she felt better, and did not think that the dangerous illness of which he had warned her could be imminent. She also said that he was very tired, and that it cut her to the heart to see everyone stealing his energy. He gave to everyone that asked, regardless of his own growing physical weakness.

I had, as quickly as might be, to resume my normal life. It was not easy. The difficulties I had foreseen in connection with my work for Powell Duffryn were beginning to emerge. One day the Chairman, the kindest of men and a firm supporter of the Research Laboratories, which some of the directors regarded as an extravagance, spoke to me about the "great harm that is being done to us all by the talk that is going round that pressure is being put upon people at the factory to join your Institute." The implication of partiality was, I knew, not justified. I had been particularly careful to show no favour to those who came to Coombe for study. I saw that it was inevitable that jealousy and suspicion would be aroused. I gave instructions to those of the staff who were also members of the Institute to be doubly careful to keep the two interests separate and to avoid giving offence. Yet I knew that sooner or later I would have to make the choice. To combine the work I was doing at Coombe with any responsible position in industry was scarcely possible: either I would 'love the one and hate the other, or cleave to the one and despise the other.' I wanted to retire, but did not feel that the time had come. I had enough money to live on, but I felt myself under the obligation to see the research work through to the point where Delanium was a commercial success, and the confidence which had been placed in me was justified.

I was well aware that I had no stable attitude. I had often compared myself to a chameleon that takes the colour of every background. I was one man in Paris, another at Coombe, a third at the Laboratories; one man with the directors, another with the staff. I would say "yes" to them all, and the result was chaos. It was astonishing that I achieved anything. I went back to Paris for a weekend at the end of September. I saw Gurdjieff at his cafe, and said that I was struggling to understand what he meant by 'Real unchangeable I'; all I could find was a succession of different 'I's. He waved his hand towards the street. We were sitting by the open window, looking on to the Avenue des Ternes, and a bright hot sun was shining on us. He said: "Those people all look for taxi. Everyone can get on your taxi. But you are beginning to have own motor-car. You must not let people get on your taxi. This is real unchangeable 'I' - to keep one's own motor-car. Now, you have only taste, but one day you will have such 'I', and when you know it has come, you will have such happiness as you cannot imagine."

I have not given any examples of Gurdjieff's extraordinary gentleness and goodness to those in real distress. The following incident occurred four weeks before his death. I brought a Russian lady to see him. She had suffered terribly in the Revolution, having been raped by soldiers at the age of thirteen. She had never forgotten the horror of the experience and looked upon life itself as utterly vile. Finding in Gurdjieff's teaching no trace of the sentimental optimism she abhorred, she had taken to it with all the fanatical zeal of which Russians are capable. When at last I was able to arrange for her to go to Paris, Gurdjieff was already a very sick man. Yet he accepted her, treating her as a daughter, and taking infinite pains to gain her confidence. He then set about convincing her that her life had a great meaning, providing only that she would allow that meaning to take shape. Her bitter feeling of the injustice of life prevented her from believing in the love of God. Gurdjieff was at pains to show that we as individual essences are not God's handiwork, but the results of heredity and the conditions of our conception. I had never before heard him speak of the importance of the moment of conception. He described the state of the father and mother: how they lie together in bed and experience the sounds and scents coming from the garden, and are happy; and so a human seed is sown that is destined for happiness. But if they are full of passion, angry with one another or with anyone else, or if the father is only thinking of his cheque-book and how much the baby will cost - then all these influences enter the seed, and the essence is formed with tendencies to hatred and avarice. God is not responsible for this. He made man to be clean: if he is now dirty it is his own fault.

I was in wonderment to see how this apparently harsh account of our human weaknesses brought peace and comfort to her. From the time of her visit, she was completely changed, as if the horrors of the past had been wiped clean away. I can remember many such instances of Gurdjieff's completely disinterested goodness towards those who came to him with real sufferings. But if anyone came with some false motive, trying to get some personal benefit, Gurdjieff would be merciless. I saw tough businessmen so shattered that for a whole day they could not speak for weeping. Those who came from curiosity were treated usually to filthy or blasphemous language, especially directed against their own country and race, or anything else that might touch them on the raw.

So it went on into October, 1949. I undertook to give a series of lectures in London called Gurdjieff: the Making of a New World. After the first, Madame de Salzmann came on a flying visit to London. One hundred and eighty-three people met her in a studio in West London, and she gave a remarkable lesson in Gurdjieff's Rhythmic Exercises, in which all those present, young and old, strong and weak, were able to take part. I read the 'I AM' chapter from the Third Series of Gurdjieff's writings. This also made a deep impression on the many who had never heard it.

I returned to Paris on Friday, 21st October, with Madame de Salzmann, convinced that we should establish a strong centre in England for Gurdjieff's work. News reached us that Gurdjieff was much worse and was now too ill to go out, but as I was going up the rue des Acacias I saw him with Bernard, buying enormous quantities of bananas "pour les Anglais." He had for a year kept up the joke that the poor English were starving, and could get no bananas. He looked so frail that I was alarmed, and telephoned to London to urge my wife to come over. She had been advised not to do so because of her own health. Only ten days before, Gurdjieff's doctor had assured me that there was not much the matter, and that his journey to America by sea would set him up. The tickets had been bought. Elizabeth Mayall was one of those who were to go with him. It was impossible at this time for me to get away from London. Then, catastrophically, his physical condition collapsed. On Saturday the

22nd, he walked out of his flat for the last time. I found him alone at the cafe. He had not been there for two or three weeks, and men and women from the Quartier des Ternes crowded in to salute him. None seemed to notice how ill he was. He spoke of the future, saying: "The next five years will decide. It is the beginning of a new world. Either the old world will make me 'Tchik' (i.e., squash me like a louse), or I will make the old world 'Tchik'. Then the new world can begin." He did not say much, and when he got up to go I saw that he could scarcely walk. I had to lift his legs into the car, and was nearly in tears to see how his condition had degenerated. In spite of his weakness, he insisted on driving himself, although his legs were so swollen that he had not the strength to put on the brake. It was the most terrifying car drive of my life. Crossing the Avenue Carnot, a large lorry bore down on us. Gurdjieff could not even slow down. By a miracle we crossed the street, but he could not turn the car. He let it run down and just succeeded in pulling up. I had almost to carry him to the lift. He did not leave home again until he was carried out dying on a stretcher four days later.

It was agonizing to witness the difference between his present illness and the time of his accident fifteen months earlier. Then, he never lost his vitality and interest in the future. Now he was indifferent. It even seemed that he wished to go as soon as possible. The previous night he had seen the proofs of the American edition of Beelzebub. Perhaps he felt that this was the sign that his work on earth was ended. I am sure also that he had been waiting for the assurance that all would be well in England. He certainly wished to keep his promise to return to America - but this was beyond his power.

There was great confusion between his own doctors and various specialists that one or another friend or pupil insisted on sending to see him. Half a dozen conflicting reports came out to us, anxiously waiting all day on Sunday. He sent for me on Sunday night. I was only with him for twenty minutes. He was in bed. He spoke of his plans for the future: his wish for a large place outside Paris, and how he would not go to America if he could get the support he wanted in England. He said that when Beelzebub was published he wanted all his pupils to make a task of getting it spread through the world. I could not think what to say. Spontaneously the words came: "In future times, next year will be called year One, because it will start a new age." He looked at me strangely and said: "Very perhaps!" meaning that it was quite possible. He was terribly weak: I had to help him to get to the stool. He said: "This never happen in my life before." But his whole demeanour and everything he said entirely deceived me. I was sure that he would again summon the amazing power he had over his body, and recover his strength. I wrote in my journal that day: 'Altogether I was greatly reassured.' My wife and I returned to London in time for me to give the fourth lecture of the series Gurdjieff: The Making of a New World. More than three hundred and fifty were counted at the hall, and judging by the questions, interest in Gurdjieff and his work had been deeply aroused.

Each morning I telephoned to Paris. Gurdjieff had refused to have a nurse. His American doctor had arrived, but said that he could not administer the serum he had brought, as Gurdjieff's blood pressure was too high. No one had any authority to act. Hitherto he had taken all decisions, and Madame de Salzmann had obeyed his orders without question. She would not now disregard his wish to be left alone.

The doctor took the situation in hand, and moved him to the American Hospital. He tapped his dropsy. Gurdjieff watched, smoking a cigarette, cracking jokes and saying "Bravo America." He lay down, and never rose again. He passed into peaceful sleep, and his breathing gradually died away. At eleven a.m. on Saturday morning, 29th October, he was dead. The autopsy showed that most of his internal organs were so degenerated that no doctor could understand how he had lived so long.

At ten a.m. Elizabeth telephoned to tell me that the doctor had said: "By all ordinary standards, he has only a few hours to live." My wife and I took the first plane. Elizabeth met us at the airport and one look at her face told me that he was dead. We went straight to the American Hospital. Madame de Salzmann was there with Thomas and Madame de Hartmann, waiting for the body to be embalmed.

When I went in to see him, I broke down and wept bitterly against the stone wall of the chapel. He looked inexpressibly beautiful, with a happy smile. I returned later with my wife, and we sat with his body for a long time. All sadness left me, and I felt first calm, and then so blissful that I wanted to shout for joy.

I was certain that though he himself had left us for ever, his power remained, and that his work would continue. I noticed one phenomenon that I have since observed at least three times. I was convinced that he was breathing. When I shut my eyes and held my breath I could distinctly hear a regular breathing-although no one else was in the chapel.

Later still, I returned to see his death mask taken. This broke the last link with his body. I could not feel the slightest value to myself or to him in seeing or thinking of it again. The best death is that which is the most complete separation of the mortal and the immortal parts of man: everything told me that Gurdjieff had gone away completely and finally, never to return.

22: PAINFUL EXPERIENCES

For a week, Gurdjieff's body lay in state in the chapel of the American Hospital. By day and by night, his pupils kept ceaseless vigil by his side. Every corner of the chapel was filled with flowers, and there was a deep serenity. I went from time to time to spend an hour there, usually after midnight when there was little coming and going, but I felt that what we were doing was rather a testimony of respect than a communion with the soul that had left us. Within a few hours of his death, Gurdjieff had ceased to be located in time and space. I was convinced that he had demonstrated in his dying what he had asserted during his lifetime, that death is a successive separation – Rascuarno - of the different constituents of the living man, each of which goes to the sphere to which its nature corresponds. Over the years, the conviction had grown on me that dying is a process far more complex and diversified than people suppose. It is hard to express just what had been added to this conviction by the manner of Gurdjieff's passing. His was a clean, decisive dying to which he gave his willing consent and for which he was fully prepared. There were no loose ends; no sense that any part of him remained attached to some unfinished experience. Each element had gone to its own appropriate place. If I were asked what I meant by this, I could not have replied, but much later I began to understand it better.

My personal situation was painful. I had lost my best friend and teacher, and I had lost him just when I most needed his help in order to make the next step. During the idle week spent in Paris before the funeral, I should have had time to survey my situation and make plans. I could do neither. Going for drives out of Paris with my wife and Elizabeth, I was at one moment gay and confident, at another irritable and unjust. All of us had shared in that moment of illumination, when we became aware that our essential relationship with Gurdjieff would never be broken, but now that this had passed, we were beginning to feel our own helplessness. Matters were not made easier by quarrels that flared up in the French groups. I was invited by rebels against the authority of Madame de Salzmann to take sides against her, or to support some proposal for future action. The contrast between the serenity of Gurdjieff's chapel and the turmoil of the groups was reflected in my own inner state.

At last, the day of the funeral arrived. I had dreaded it a little, fearing that there might be a display of personal emotion. Indeed, the scene in the Russian Cathedral in the Rue Daru was charged with emotional force; but there was very little personal feeling, except among those who knew him only as a kind old man who gave sweets to children. The requiem mass of the Orthodox Church is most impressive in its beauty and the depth of its symbolism. The church was crowded. Pupils had flown to Paris from America and England. There were also scores of humble people of the Quartier des Ternes to bear witness to his kindness. We had thought our capacity for feeling had been exhausted by his death, but this day was different, as if it were a foretaste of the benefits that multitudes would receive from his life of devotion to the welfare of mankind.

That evening Madame de Salzmann spoke with some forty or fifty of her French pupils. One or two English people were there. She said: "When a Teacher like Mr. Gurdjieff goes, he cannot be replaced. Those who remain cannot create the same conditions. We have only one hope: to make something together. What no one of us could do, perhaps a group can. We no longer have a Teacher, but we have the possibility of a group. Let us make this our chief aim in the future." Having seen the friction between those who had been closest to Gurdjieff, I could not but marvel at her optimism, yet I was bound to agree that in unity lay our only hope.

The situation in England was not easy. People had gone to Gurdjieff from various groups that had been closed, and even hostile, towards one another. There were still sharply conflicting loyalties and differences of understanding. Gurdjieff had done nothing to harmonize these differences. On the contrary, his very method of work often required that people should needlessly be set in conflict. Again and again, he would give two or more people, without telling the others, authority to act for him in a particular matter. They would all set to work, and find the others in the field. Each was sure that he alone was the one Gurdjieff had intended to do the job. This led to endless friction and misunderstanding, which we accepted as the stimulus that would make us search within ourselves for a deeper understanding. Too easy outward conditions could lead to the illusion that we understood and accepted one another. One of the Aphorisms in the Study House at Fontainebleau read: 'The worse the conditions the more productive the work: providing you work consciously.' Gurdjieff would never be satisfied with the illusion of harmony if the substance were lacking.

Although he had named me in his circular letter as his representative for England, I knew that I was unacceptable to many. My own inner world was in confusion. I had been left in mid-air, well aware that I had not received from Gurdjieff the final teaching which he had promised. I could continue the exercises he had shown me, and I could learn more from Madame de Salzmann: but I was convinced that something more than spiritual exercises was needed. I was even clear just what that something should be: it was an action so profound that it would enable me to die to the old man and to be born again. Gurdjieff had once said: "In order to be born one must first die, but in order to be born awake, one must die awake!" All that I had done up to that time might enable me to die awake, but it could not give me the secret of death and resurrection. It seemed to me that unless one knew that secret one could never be, in the truest sense, a Teacher, and this alone was sufficient to make me draw back from any suggestion that I might become the leader of Gurdjieff's followers in England. I remember that I said to myself: "If it is God's Will, you will receive this also; but it will be in God's own time. Until it comes you can do nothing but prepare yourself, and for that you have the means at hand."

Early in the New Year of 1950, I had to go for Powell Duffryn to Washington. Madame de Salzmann was in New York. I was then inclined to take literally the behest to seek salvation in the group. Everywhere I went, I found discord: groups were such only in name. In America there were two factions: one consisted of the group started by A. R. Orage twenty years earlier, and the other was the one more recently formed by P. D. Ouspensky. The first owed allegiance exclusively to Gurdjieff, whereas the latter looked primarily to Madame Ouspensky for guidance. I was impatient to see all barriers broken down and all the fragments united. When I spoke of this to Madame Ouspensky she laughed at me, saying: "Always Mr. Bennett wishes to serve humanity. He wants unity, and does not see that it cannot come without understanding." After speaking with some of the leading members of the two factions, I saw that I could be of little use, and returned to England with the renewed awareness that my true work lay in Coombe Springs. There, I could make my own contribution without going beyond my own limitations.

Soon afterwards, Madame de Salzmann came to London and allowed herself to be persuaded to take responsibility for the work there. I was very thankful, as it was evident that she commanded the respect and confidence of nearly all the factions, and that in her leadership lay the best hope of unity. I encouraged members of my own group to enter the new groups she was forming in London, and all the pupils at Coombe Springs who were able to do so, to take part in the classes at which Gurdjieff's movements exercises were taught by members of his French class.

Jeanne de Salzmann, 1949

During 1950, I often visited Paris to seek advice and help from Madame de Salzmann. During one of these journeys, I passed through an experience that was the shortest in duration and the deepest in significance of my whole life up to that moment. I cannot fix the exact date, for I kept no record. It has been present with me ever since, and though the memory of it remains unchanged, I have seen more and more wealth of meaning in it as the years have passed.

I was travelling alone to Paris by the Golden Arrow. I had just finished lunch an hour or so beyond Calais, and was drinking coffee. As I put my cup down my attention was drawn to my breathing, and in the brief instant when the flow of breath changed from inspiration to expiration, I became aware of Eternity. This was the first time in my life that I lived through a timeless event, though it is common enough between sleeping and waking to have long and vivid dreams that occupy seconds and seem to last for hours. This was not at all like a dream - there were no visions, no images, nothing happened, not even a thought. It was a state of pure cognition, a luminous certainty. The central truth was the imperishability of the will. Body perishes, all the functions that depend upon the body turn into dreams and eventually fade away. Even my very self, my own existence and the feeling of 'I' that accompanies it, could endure only for a time. But my will was out of time and space, and nothing could destroy it. So long as the will was the prisoner of my functions, that is of my sensations, my thoughts, feelings and desires, it must be involved in their fate. If they perished, it must perish with them. But if my will were free from all these, especially from 'being' anything at all, then it would be truly imperishable, immortal and able to create for itself whatever vehicle it might need in order to exist and work. This freedom is the will to do God's Will, and I understood once and forever that this is the secret of everlasting life. All the mysteries of the Christian creed, and not those of Christianity alone, but of all that has been revealed to men through the ages, became one clear consistent truth. All this and infinitely more was revealed to me, age upon age and world upon world, and yet the entire experience did not occupy the time of a single heart-beat.

From that moment, I have been convinced that the consciousness of eternity is possible for man, and that it gives a contact with the reality behind appearances that is incomparably more direct and complete than our ordinary consciousness of events in time and space. The very incommunicability of such an experience is the most convincing evidence that Facts are not everything. No doubt Wittgenstein and his school are right in asserting that all that is Fact can be described clearly and without ambiguity, and that whatever can be said at all can be said clearly. The factual content of the experience, within the limits of my fleeting memory, could be described in as much detail as you please, but there are literally no words to convey the certainty that in one moment I had left time and space and entered the state of eternal consciousness. It is of the very nature of time that events succeed one another; this is equally true of time as we find it in our everyday sense experience, and of the refined notions of time developed in mathematical physics. All our language is so linked to time that we cannot express a timeless situation, except in temporal terms. But Eternity has no succession, neither before nor after.

There is, I believe, only one form of expression well-known to man that can express eternity; and that is the painter's art. The artist does more than seize the moment and fix it on the canvas; he displays a depth of significance that goes beyond the mere fact. There are, for example, dozens of self-portraits of Rembrandt in the world's art collections. It would be ridiculous to place them in a temporal sequence, and speak of Rembrandt's 'development'. All the pictures, and every one of them, represent the soul of Rembrandt contemplating its own outward form. Time means little, perhaps nothing at all, in this contemplative awareness. When the artist allows us to see the stages of his creative work, as Picasso has done in such a series as the drawings of David and Bathsheba, it is obvious that time is being eliminated to leave the eternal moment free from any hint of successiveness.

It therefore seems to me that awareness of eternity is by no means a rare experience for man. My own awakening in the Golden Arrow was extraordinary for me, chiefly by the immensity of the vision; the vanishingly short duration did no more than underline its timeless character. Since then similar experiences have come to me several times, and have served only to strengthen the impression that Eternity is always here and now.

During 1950, I was torn by conflicting forces. I threw myself wholeheartedly into the task of submerging my personality in a group, but the seven men and women who were joined in the undertaking were too diverse in their understanding of what was required to make its fulfilment possible. We were getting nowhere, but none of us dared to admit it. Once again, I could not but admire the courageous optimism of Madame de Salzmann, who saw progress where we could find none, and encouraged us to continue by the force of her example.

During this year, the activity of the Powell Duffryn Research Laboratories reached its zenith. We investigated coals from all over the world, for all possible purposes. It was necessary to expand both our facilities and our staff. This was a time when experienced research workers were in demand everywhere. The big companies earmarked promising young men at the universities, before they had even proved their value by the quality of their degree. I had to build up a staff without the prestige that attaches to a famous research organization. On the whole I was fortunate, but I had to choose men with a capacity for original work, but reputedly difficult to get on with, rather than those who were blameless in character, but pedestrian in their work. The real treasures could go where they liked and earn what they asked. I had no hesitation in risking trouble by taking on men with original ideas, whether they were reputed to be good team workers or not. My chairman supported me in this policy.

I was greatly interested in the psychology of scientific discovery. It is well known that in some fields, such as mathematics, the greatest discoveries have been made by men like Newton and Einstein when in their early twenties. Chemists are at their best up to thirty, and each branch of science seems to have its most fruitful age. It is difficult to give young men enough scope without unfairness to the older ones. I tried to find a solution for this problem, which confronts every industrial research laboratory. The universities, enjoying a constant flow of research graduates, do not have quite the same difficulty.

The usual solution is to form a number of small teams, each under a good leader, and give them a very free hand in following a definite objective. This method works, but it is wasteful, since the younger and often more original workers have to wait a long time before they become leaders of a team, and then their most creative period may have passed. The method I followed was to leave the individual workers as free as possible, and let them choose their own helpers. This usually meant that the outstandingly original men would work alone, while others would form small or large teams.

This method leads to a large output of ideas. It is then necessary to choose which will be followed up and which put aside. This is called 'killing babies', and it is often nearly as painful as infanticide. The judgment of the research director must be exercised here very firmly, or energy will be dispersed with little result.

All through the summer of 1950, I worked hard and regarded our research activity as being, on the whole, remarkably productive and successful. There were one or two brilliant young men on the staff, one of whom, as ill-chance would have it, was an avowed Communist. I was so sure that neither I nor any of the senior staff had any political interests or connections, that I only laughed when I was warned that "So-and-so will get you into trouble." By the autumn the Research Laboratories at Battersea were beginning to find their feet. I was thoroughly enjoying the work. The relative quiet at Coombe Springs and the cessation of my visits to Paris allowed me to give nearly all my time and energy to the laboratories. The commercial production of Delanium was not yet going well. We had made several mistakes, particularly in assessing the markets in which it would prove most valuable. Nevertheless, I was sure that with patience and courage it would come right, and justify all the money that had been spent.

I did not reckon with the changes that were taking place in the higher direction of the company. Nor did I realize quite how much harm had been done to my own standing with the directors by the rumours spread about that I was connected with a very queer secret society. It certainly never occurred to me for a moment that I should be suspected of dealings with Communism, but as it appeared later, Gurdjieff's name had been mentioned as a Russian spy, and it was assumed that he was a Communist. Thus, without knowing it, I was treading on very thin ice;

the more so as some of the work we were doing in the research laboratories had a bearing on the production of atomic energy, then associated in everyone's minds with atom bombs.

The ice broke unexpectedly, and with unnecessary drama. One night I worked late to finish a report. The next morning I arrived to be told that the laboratories had been sealed and no one was to enter. The newspapers got wind of it and the afternoon papers appeared with front-page headlines: Research Laboratory working for Atomic Energy a Communist Spy Centre. I was besieged by reporters who had heard that there was another side to the story. It was obviously necessary to say nothing whatever, and my own name did not even appear in the papers.

I at once offered my resignation, with the sole request that it should be clearly acknowledged that no suspicion of Communism or spying was suggested. It turned out that rumour had bred suspicion, and suspicion more rumour, until it was seriously believed that incriminating documents were concealed in the laboratories.

Of course, all my friends and business associates knew of the drama. As always happens, most people believed that there could not be smoke without fire, and that something must have been seriously wrong. I had learned enough wisdom to make no attempt to defend myself, but to wait quietly until passions had calmed down.

The story thus told may seem harmless enough, but to me it was very painful. I was fifty-three years old. I was a member of several government and scientific committees. I still had something to contribute in the field I had worked in for just twenty years. I had expected to retire and keep an advisory position, which would enable me to preserve the balance between spiritual and worldly interests that I believe to be right for men in our modern world. All these expectations vanished overnight. Nor could the disaster have fallen at a worse time for me personally. Less than three weeks before the blow fell, my wife nearly died from a coronary thrombosis. Struggling to keep Coombe Springs going at a time when all interest was ebbing away, she had driven herself too hard. One morning, she found that the week's washing had been neglected by the woman assigned to the task, herself overworked. She had gone to the wash-house and had done the work herself, allowing no one to help her. When I arrived home in the evening, she was exhausted but triumphant. In the night she had a heart attack and was taken to the Westminster Hospital. Her condition remained critical for days, and she was half paralysed. It was agony to see her face distorted - but many people have experienced that grief. I was allowed to visit her twice each day. When the blow fell at Powell Duffryn, I felt that strange aloofness, of being other than myself, that came over me at most critical moments of my life. One part of me suffered acutely; another part looked on with unassumed indifference.

It was exceedingly unpleasant to have to go to the office with my secretary, and collect my personal belongings under the suspicious eye of a former clerk. It was painful to learn that my closest friends in the laboratories had all been given notice. Promising researches were nipped in the bud, and I was denied the satisfaction of proving that my method of administering a research laboratory could achieve a high proportion of original work. At no time did I feel inclined to blame anyone but myself, but that also is not very pleasant. The directors of the company, probably feeling a little foolish at having acted with such precipitation, treated me kindly, and I was offered and accepted a fair compensation on my retirement. I found myself in the situation that I knew to be right for me, and could devote all my time to Coombe Springs and my own studies; but I had achieved it in the most painful way possible.

There was one immediate consolation: I was free to spend all the day with my wife. Her condition was giving the doctors great anxiety. She was soon able to speak, but the paralysis of her left side remained and she was growing weaker. She begged me to take her away from the hospital, saying that she could not bear the nights alone. The doctors said that it was out of the question to move her and that she needed nursing that only a hospital could give.

In the end she decided the issue by getting out of bed and saying she would walk home. The surgeon, a famous heart-specialist who took a close interest in her case, told me that her heart was tired out and that further treatment was useless. She was over seventy-five years old, and at her age one could not hope for a miracle. I could take her home if I wished, but he must warn me that I was taking her home to die. He doubted if she would survive the journey.

Meanwhile I had heard from Madame de Salzmann of a Russian doctor, Professor Salmanov, who had done wonders for members of Gurdjieff's French group, and said that he could treat my wife through Bernard Courtenay-Mayers, provided she were at home and had good nurses.

The next day an ambulance moved her cautiously to Coombe. Salmanov directed her treatment by telephone from Paris several times a day. It was terrifying in its apparent brutality as applied to a woman so near to death. Enemas, injections and above all, leeches had to be applied. Our search for leeches in London was a tragi-comedy, but they were found, applied and brought her immediate relief. Her mind was wandering, but as they drew blood she exclaimed: "Ah. The biter bit!"

The name, 'the biter-bits', became current among us. It is hard to say what saved her: whether her own courage, or Salmanov's treatment, or the loving care she received from all around her. It would probably be truest of all to say that the hour of her death had not yet come. Within a few weeks, she had made a spectacular recovery.

In the spring, we went for a motor trip in France. It was one of the happiest times of my life. She and I were alone together. We drove to Chamonix, and then followed the route of the High Alps, the most spectacular road in Europe. We went south to Cannes, and spent a week with Dorothy Caruso and Margaret Anderson in a magnificent hired villa, and returned by way of Provence. Her illness had liberated her from some of the agonizing sense of urgency that used constantly to drive her to more and more effort, and made it very difficult for her friends to keep pace with her. We were both convinced that her illness had been foreseen by Gurdjieff, and that he had intended to show her the way to protect herself. Perhaps he had, and she had not understood. She herself told me that at their last talk he had said to her: "You must not work any more. Let others work. Now you must prepare for dying, maybe in many years - still you must prepare." She had been unwilling to take him literally. Who was I to blame her? I had done no better.

I was then working hard upon my book *The Dramatic Universe*. I had set myself, as usual, an impossible task. I wanted to bring all that I had experienced and discovered about the inner spiritual life of man into harmony with all that was known to science and history about the world of the senses and the mind. As the task progressed, it grew. I spent hours reading, digesting, writing, re-writing. What I wrote seemed good enough at the time. When I looked at it again three months later, it appeared to be incomprehensible rubbish.

At the end of 1951, my wife had another attack. This time, although we had Salmanov's treatment ready, she very nearly died. One night I sat beside her. She developed the deadly Cheyne-Stokes respiration, an alternation of heavy panting and almost complete cessation of breathing. Again and again, I thought she had died. I relived the agony of St. Mary's Hospital fourteen years earlier. This time I was sure that however deep might be her coma, she would know I was there and what I said to her.

She remained for twenty-four hours between life and death, and then returned. This time she was very much changed. Her brain had been affected by what the doctors took to be a cerebral haemorrhage; for many weeks she was in a state of dementia. But, once more, she made a marvellous recovery, and by the spring was again in full possession of her faculties, though much weaker. She could not recall her experience while in the state of coma, beyond the memory that she had been very happy and strong in the assurance that all was well.

In 1952, the life at Coombe Springs resumed some of its former vigour. I gave public lectures, and many new students came to the Institute. We kept close and friendly relations with the groups under Madame de Salzmann's direction, and shared with them in the study of Gurdjieff's rhythmic exercises and temple Dances. A public demonstration was given at the Fortune Theatre on 17th May. I myself learned very much from the preparations for this demonstration. I had worked at the exercises regularly since I first went to Paris in 1948, and was fairly competent, though my size was against me. I had been chosen to take part in at least one of the ritual dances, known as The Great Prayer. This has always deeply moved me since I first saw it in Constantinople forty years ago. It is one of Gurdjieff's finest creations, and contains a progressively deep symbolic significance, of which one becomes more aware by working on it month after month. Special costumes are worn; the accompanying music is deeply religious, and the whole effect extraordinary, both for those who witness and those who perform it. During the last rehearsals I began to feel very ill and to make mistakes, and so was quite rightly asked to stand down from the actual performance. I took part in the final rehearsal, aware that I should never take part in this experience again as long as I lived. This realization penetrated into my deepest consciousness. I lived every moment as if it were my last.

When it was over, several friends came up to commiserate with me at being left out of the public performance. I replied: "I am the luckiest man alive, because I have done this for the last time in full consciousness that it was the last time." I knew that I had penetrated one of the secrets of life. I had often heard it said, and had told others and even myself, that one should do everything as if it were the first and last time, but I had never lived through the experience with such a clarity of consciousness. The memory of that day has often helped me since. However, I was beginning to be rather seriously ill. I became strangely weak and my breathing grew more and more troublesome. I was X-rayed and it seemed that my tuberculosis had become active again. My wife insisted that I should go to Paris and see Salmanov. He diagnosed my trouble quite differently, but said that my life was in danger unless I took a complete rest. He would not even let me return to England, but made me go to Fontainebleau and lie on my back in the forest for a month. My daughter Ann came over and took care of me.

My strength gradually returned, but when I came back to England I disregarded Salmanov's warning and started working again too soon.

I was pruning an apple tree in the garden, fell off a ladder and cut my hand badly. The shock started some action that resulted in my entire body being covered with sores. I was burning and could scarcely lie on a sheet covered with flour which Salmanov recommended. No one could do anything for me, as the sores kept breaking out in new places. Remembering what Gurdjieff had said, I refused to have penicillin or other antibiotics. In any case, I was sure it was not an infection, and that the illness was not ordinary. It had come on me so suddenly and the pain was so unbearable that I was sure that I was intended to die. This condition lasted for three days.

I lay as still as I could, there being no other way to reduce the pain. Without any warning, I found myself leaving my body. I no longer felt pain, or any other sensation. I went out of my body very gently and can clearly remember a kind of wordless recognition that could be expressed in the words: "This is death and I had no idea it was so peaceful." I was aware that my body was on the bed and supposed it had ceased to breathe. I looked for my own breathing and it was there - but not a physical respiration. I could not think, but only be aware of my experience. This is hard to describe; it was rather as if my experience was being presented to me: I ceased to see, hear, think or breathe voluntarily. I knew that I was in some kind of body, but it was certainly not the body I had just left.

I do not know how long this state lasted, but I heard my wife call my name. I felt a sharp stab of pain and I was once again in my body. Nothing had changed, but within a few hours the sores began to dry, and in a week I was well again. I have never understood what happened to me so far as the illness is concerned, but I surmise that the 'out of the body' experience belonged to what Gurdjieff calls the second or Kesdjan body of man. This taught me something of what he meant by the need to build a different body for the 'Real Unchangeable I'. While I was out of the body I had no 'I', only an awareness that was blissful and peaceful - but in which there was no power of action.

Later that year, I went to America to lecture on Gurdjieff's System at the invitation of Madame Ouspensky and Madame de Salzmann. I gave four lectures at the Carnegie Hall in New York. I was glad to be of service, but I did not feel that I belonged. I wanted to be wholeheartedly united with those who were carrying on Gurdjieff's work and spreading his ideas. I was as convinced as ever that Gurdjieff had brought to the world the most powerful instrument of self-perfecting that has ever been known. He was in the best sense a Master.

After he had left us, nothing was the same. However, it would be wrong to say that Gurdjieff had ceased to exist for us. We felt his presence. Every year at the anniversary of his death, requiem services in his memory have been held in Russian churches in many countries. The bond that unites those who learned from him is renewed on these solemn occasions.

All this was true for me, and yet I could not forget what Gurdjieff had said at a very serious moment near the end of his life: "After I go another will come. You will not be left alone." I remembered also Ouspensky's insistence that something more was to come from the Source from which Gurdjieff had received his inspiration. Gurdjieff had defined his own role in that prodigious 'I AM' chapter that he had so often made me read aloud before him. He had seen in 1924 that his ideas could not be made to serve mankind in practice during his lifetime, and he had therefore set himself to ensure that they would enter human life in theory after his death. Since he had also said that theory has no value unless it opens the door to practice, it must follow that his work was a preparation for a further stage in the Manifestation of that Providence that guides mankind from Epoch to Epoch.

If our task was to prepare and not to fulfil, then even our disunity made sense. We should keep alive what we had received, and be alert for whatever might come.

Not everyone saw the situation in the same way, and even those who did so were divided as to the best means of fulfilling the task. As after the death of Ouspensky, so now, the typical factions began to appear. Some favoured the meticulous preservation, unchanged, of everything that Gurdjieff had said or done. Others were sure that he had given them a private directive that entitled them to work independently of the rest. Others were prepared to sacrifice everything for unity. Many, of course, were content to leave the problem to others and were happy if they could receive personal help and guidance from those more experienced than themselves. I believed that unity was all-important, and was ready to form part of whatever whole might take shape, but I was also quite sure that unity does not mean uniformity. It seemed that I could play my part best by strengthening the life at Coombe Springs. I remembered how Gurdjieff had said that a place was necessary where people could live and work together, gaining thereby experience which would serve later when they had to go out and work with others.

I set myself the difficult task of subordinating myself to the whole and yet preserving the integrity of my own part. I asked myself whether I could find, either in myself or in the group with which I was then working, the resources to give real help to the three hundred pupils who were then attending groups. I could take them a certain distance. For two or three years, the majority gained very much from the teaching, the exercises and especially from the practical work we did together at Coombe Springs. But I saw that those who had been working in this way for many years were beginning to move at an even pace. I put it in this way, because I had no sense of a decline. We had been endowed by Gurdjieff with such a vast wealth of ideas and methods that it was possible constantly to devise new exercises, and create new conditions, that kept everything alive. Nor was it in my nature scrupulously to adhere to the letter of the teaching. I was ready to experiment with new ideas and new methods, providing they conformed to the fundamental principles of Gurdjieff's work.

I understood these principles to be that the human organism and all the psychic functions of sensation, feeling, thought and desire are no more than a very complicated machine, incapable of independent action. The true man, the 'permanent unchanging I' should be the master and ruler of the machine. But in nearly all people this inner ruler is asleep or absent. Thus, although outwardly they appear to be human beings, in sober fact they are automata, acting only in response to the stimulations that come to them through their senses. The illusion, for it is surely such, of having an 'I' comes from the nature of consciousness, which gives the taste of reality to whatever it touches. What people believe to be 'I', or 'myself' is no more than the ever-flowing stream of consciousness. In this Gurdjieff was in full agreement with the sceptical philosophers, and especially with David Hume. It was, however, possible for man to acquire his own 'permanent unchanging I', if he was prepared to pay the price. No man can pay this for another. Each has to work for himself, but very few, if any, can do this alone. Therefore groups and teachers of groups are a practical necessity for the creation of right conditions: not for giving the help that each must find within himself.

The creation of right conditions depends upon the strength and wisdom of the one who undertakes it. I was increasingly aware of the limits of my strength, and even more of my wisdom. I could never dare to take the risk with the inner world of others that Gurdjieff was prepared to take. I remembered how once he had behaved in a particularly outrageous manner towards a dignified lady at his table, and had turned to me and said: "You not astonished that I have such impudence?" I said: "No, I am not, because you know what you are doing." He said: "Yes. That is science. I have science of man and human psyche. That is why I can do what others cannot. If others do what I do, they could kill. Even I sometimes make mistakes: but then I can repair."

The seminar in 1953 was hazardous. Without my intention, the conditions were much more intense than I had foreseen. Several people went through days of violent emotional crisis. At one moment, it was alarming; but, as if by a miracle, everything fell into place, and many of those who came, went away with the conviction that more strenuous conditions of work were necessary. Others were frightened, and did not wish to repeat the experiment.

During the fortnight that we were together a very clear indication came to me during a period of meditation. I was aware of a voice in my breast that said several times over: "Go to the East." I told my wife and closest friends of this experience, and they agreed that I ought to follow the indication I had received.

23: SOUTH-WEST ASIA

The East is vast. It stretches from the Mediterranean to the Pacific and contains twice as many people as the rest of the world put together. Where was I to go? I reflected that it was little use going to a country where I could not speak the native tongue. The only eastern language I knew really well was Turkish. I knew not only Ottoman and modem Turkish, but also several of the central Asian dialects. The Turkish language in its widest sense is a *lingua franca* with which it used to be possible to travel from the Balkans to Chinese Turkestan, from the Volga to the Nile, and always find someone who could understand.

Although there had been great changes since the war, those whom I needed to see were of the older generation. If I travelled in Turkish-speaking countries I would be at home. I decided to spend three or four months in Turkey, Syria, Iraq and Jordan and then decide what I should do next. I had no compunction in leaving England. Although my wife was now more or less confined to her room, she was surrounded by loving friends and was convinced that the journey should be made. Also I wanted to avoid drifting into the position of an indispensable leader. From such a danger I would escape at all costs, even if it should mean leaving everything and everyone.

I had one clue to follow. When I was in Constantinople thirty-three years before, I had met the Sherif Ali Haidar, the last Sherif, or Warden of the Holy City of Mecca, and a direct descendant of the Prophet Muhammad. He had five sons of about my own age, one of whom was my very good friend, Prince Abdul Medjid. The piety and simple goodness of these men of ancient race had impressed me, and I had greatly regretted the - to my mind - baleful influence of Lawrence of Arabia, who had given all his support to the younger branch of the family, and prevented the return of the legitimate Sherif after the First World War. The history of our relations with the Arab peoples might have taken a much more favourable course if we had supported the Sherif Ali Haidar, who knew how to deal with the Wahabis. However, all that was now ancient history; Ali Haidar was dead and his son had given his allegiance to his cousin, the Hashemite king of the Jordan. He had been Jordanian minister in London, but in 1953 had transferred to Paris.

I went over to see him, and told him of my urge to go to South-west Asia and the reason for it. Being a pious Moslem he said: "No doubt it is the Will of God, for it was shown to you without your searching. As you know I am a Sufi and a dervish at heart. During the war, when my fortunes were at their lowest, I found a remarkable sheikh in Damascus. He is a man of great piety and wisdom. I advise you to go and see him. He will certainly do everything he can for a friend of mine. His name is Emin Chikhou." The Prince went on to tell me about the Naqshibendi order of dervishes; the most flourishing of all at this time, with its sheikhs and groups of *murids* throughout the Muslim world from Morocco to Indonesia. He knew that I was a follower of Gurdjieff's ideas, and had come at my invitation to the demonstration at the Fortune Theatre the year before. He said that I should be interested in the Naqshibendi Order because they do not retire into *tekke*s, nor make use of outward exercises like the Rufai and Mevlevi, but fulfil all their worldly duties without losing the worship of God in their hearts.

The Prince's kindness touched me deeply, but I did not imagine that I could so easily meet with an authentic source of the esoteric traditions of Islam. I decided to start in Turkey and gratify an old wish to visit Konya, the home of the greatest of all Islamic mystical writers, Jellaluddin Rumi, founder of the Mevlevi Order, among which, in the early twenties, I had made many friends.

I had no planned itinerary, but I did set myself three tasks. I took a cine camera so that I could share with those left behind some of the impressions of the journey. I also set myself to keep a very full journal. I decided, thirdly, to make a study of the buildings old and new which had been used for various rituals and spiritual exercises by Christians, Muslims and the lesser sects of South-west Asia. My aim was to discover, if possible, the way in which enclosed spaces can concentrate psychic energies. My own theoretical studies had led me to the belief that the shape and size of buildings and the disposition of the masses have an effect upon the psychic state of those who enter them to share in an experience.

I set out on 15th September, 1953, travelling by way of Rome, where I stopped for two days. In Istanbul I met Prince Muhiddin Haidari, whom I had known as a boy in his father's palace. His wife is probably the best living singer of old Turkish music. Listening to her, I became aware of the strength of the bond that unites me with the Asiatic peoples. I felt at home and yet very shy; like a boy who returns home and finds that he does not know what to say to his own family.

Every day I wandered on foot through old Istanbul. Beside the wall of the old market under the shadow of Sultan Bayazid Mosque, I found the lokanta of Kebabji Kiamil, where I used to eat kebab in April 1919, when I was working in the Turkish War Office. Old Kiamil and his son had died, but his two grandsons made me welcome. I went out of the old city through the Adrianople Gate, and found the monastery of the Mevlevi dervishes which I used to visit in 1920. Though it had been deserted since the dervishes were exiled thirty-five years ago, nothing had changed. I found a guardian to open the Sema Hane and the old memories flooded back. I wondered at my own former blindness. As I stood on the dust-laden floor and looked at the crumbling woodwork, I saw what the dervish attitude towards life had meant to the Turks for more than seven centuries. They had been the leaven of practical mysticism that had saved the religious life of Turkey from degenerating into formalism. I began to ask myself if thirty years of secular government under Kemal Ataturk could have destroyed the deep religious feelings of the Turks.

Before leaving the *tekke*, I measured the Sema Hane and made sketches. Later, I did the same at the Mevlevi Hane in Pera, now a police station, and found that the basic dimensions were identical. I went at dusk to the great Suleimaniye Mosque, the youthful masterpiece of Sinan Mimar of Kayseri, one of the world's greatest architects and mathematicians, whose very name is hardly known in the West. My vision had grown more sensitive with the years, and I stood upon the outer wall enraptured with the subtle marvels of its domes and interlocking turrets, cascading down and down in a harmony that seemed to unite earth and heaven. How lifeless beside this prodigious building is our great St. Paul's on Ludgate Hill or the massive, meaningless church of St. Peter in Rome. In this supreme work of art, Sinan Mimar fulfilled his promise to Suleiman the Magnificent that he would outdo the Byzantine architects of Santa Sophia. I went inside, and heard the voice of the muezzin chanting verses of the Koran. Once again the purity of the acoustics brought tears to my eyes, but now I was aware of a sound within the sound, and realized that the architect had built a spiritual temple within an earthly temple.

On 22nd September I left by train for Konya. I had made up my mind to travel and live like a Turk, with little money to spend. It was not easy to find a hotel; but the Belediye, the town council office, helped me. The hotel I found was emphatically not intended for foreigners. In the old days when there were no hotels, the inns at caravanserais were called konaks or 'alighting places'. The Turks, being by nature nomadic, still like sleeping together in large rooms as if they were in tents. There is no demand for single bedrooms. I, rather fastidiously, insisted on a room to myself, and paid the equivalent of six shillings for a room with three beds, but no other furniture. The Turks, like all good Muslims, are scrupulously clean, and the floor was washed daily. Cleanliness is, however, not incompatible with a lively fauna, mainly fleas and bed bugs inhabiting mattresses and rugs. The Turks regard us as dirty people because we do not wash our privy parts several times a day. They are fastidious in ways that do not occur to us at all. But we for our part find them dirty because their sanitary arrangements adhere to principles different from ours.

By the time I had settled in the hotel, the midday call to worship echoed from all the minarets of Konya, and I went to the Selimiye Mosque to follow the prayer. The city has never lost the deep religious feeling that goes back to the Seljuk Sultans. Nearly every shop closes at midday so that the owner can go to the mosque to pray. I was moved by the sincerity of the worshippers and wrote this note: 'As I listened to the reiterated cry of God is Almighty, I realized how true is this creed of surrender to the Will of God. The need constantly to make this inward act of submission and to put aside our own self-will entered me and I realized that this at least is something I can learn here.' Every day that I spent in Konya I went to the great Mevlevi *Tekke*, the home of the poet Jellaluddin Rumi - founder of the Order of Mevlevi Dervishes. The Sema Hane was built in the thirteenth century under the direction of his son, Sultan Veled, by the Seljuk kings of Konya. It is the prototype of three hundred and sixty-five similar buildings, distributed throughout South-west Asia. As I studied it, I became convinced that the size and proportions of the building were derived from some lost art of creating a concentration of psychic energies, that could influence the inner state of those who met in it to worship God.

As I sat and made notes, the guardian of the tomb of the Mevlana came close and, having caught my attention, indicated an elderly Turk who wished to speak to me. I had noticed him the previous day, and felt that he was watching me. Since the days of Abdul Hamid, plainclothes policemen have shadowed the life of Turkey; the suppression of spying is a reform no revolution has accomplished. I had assumed that I was being watched, as a foreigner behaving in a strange manner would inevitably be. I was glad to find I was mistaken. He was a dervish and a pious Muslim. We went to a chai hane and drank tea. After some cautious probing, he said: "A country without dervishes cannot exist. One true dervish can redeem the sins of a thousand people." I asked the difference between a dervish and a true believer who is not a dervish. He replied: "The latter lives in one world, but the dervish in two. There is a visible prayer which you see in the mosque; but there is also the invisible prayer of the heart. The dervish has both." I said that we read of the prayer of the heart, but to practise it one must have a murshid; that is, one who shows the way. This was the opening he had evidently been waiting for, because, looking at me keenly, he said: "Of course nothing can be done without a murshid; but there are teachers everywhere." After some talk of their presence in Turkey, he said, in a doubtful tone of voice: "In Adana, there is a Great One, but I do not know him." As he said no more, I told him that I was going to Adana, and that one of the reasons for my journey was to ascertain if the ancient ways of Sufism were still followed in Turkey and Syria. He said that he knew a pupil of the Great Teacher, and would try to arrange for me to meet him.

Later in the day he told me that the man he had in mind was out of Konya, but would return in a few days. I did not see him again, though I went to the hammam and to the chai hane to enquire.

A long chapter would be needed to describe all that I experienced in Konya. It was like shedding one skin and putting on another. When I left Konya, I felt more like a Turk and a Muslim than an Englishman and a Christian. One day, while I was resting in the Turku Hammam, the vision came to me of a Sema Hane at Coombe 'built by our own hands'. I wrote that 'it may take two or three years, but the very making of it will be our great work. I must fear nothing, but go forward with a fine design, and little by little we shall see how to continue.'

From Konya I went by a slow train to Adana. Passing through the wild Taurus Mountains, I saw a golden eagle. The Cilician Gap, great twin rocks only a few hundred feet apart, leads suddenly from the icy steppes to the coastal plain where cotton flourishes and bananas ripen.

Adana in September was baking in the sun. I was disappointed to come, after Konya, to a flourishing city of 130,000 inhabitants, the centre of the Turkish cotton industry. Keeping to my plan, I went to the Baghdad Hotel that is not even mentioned in the guidebooks, but was several classes higher than my konak in Konya. At midday, I went to the nearest mosque. Standing at the back, behind the worshippers, I watched a latecomer hastily perform his ablutions and join the prayer. I was attracted by his evident piety. As the worshippers were dispersing, this young man came after me and invited me to tea. When we were seated, he said: "I saw that you were a stranger and did not even know if you could speak Turkish, but I felt that I must speak with you, because of the sincere way you followed our prayer. I must tell you that I vowed my prayer to you and asked God to open your heart to the Muslim faith."

Without the preliminary skirmishes usual in such conversations, we began to speak about faith. He said: "I am a simple man and cannot explain our path to you, but if you will come with me, I may introduce you to someone who can." At that moment, he looked up and, seeing a tall elderly Turk with a beard and rough country clothes passing by, hailed him and asked him to join us. He introduced him as Hassan Effendi. The old man was above medium height, dressed in a nondescript garment aged and almost ragged. He had fine gnarled hands and erect bearing, and magnificent eyes looking steadily from beneath heavy brows. His grey beard was long, but carefully trimmed. He made a strong impression by his complete freedom from all embarrassment and the deep peace that suffused every gesture and every word he spoke. It turned out that Hassan Effendi was a pupil of the Great Teacher of whom I had heard in Konya. He invited me to spend the next day with him in an orchard not far from the city. We were together for three days, and during this time I learned from him so much that a volume would be needed to write it all. He was a true saint, though a very simple man, who lived by trading in the market place in second-hand clothes.

After three days, I went on to Damascus, where I stayed for several weeks. I chose a hotel occupied only by Turks and Syrians. It had been the first hotel in Damascus fifty years earlier, but now was lost in an unfashionable and derelict quarter of the city. Damascus, as I saw it, delighted me beyond measure. Nearly every morning, I rose very early and went to watch craftsmen at work; weavers, metal workers, carpenters, basket makers, leather workers. Their way of living seemed to me as nearly perfect as possible. Fathers teaching sons; whole families working, singing, laughing and living together. But the educated Syrians were ashamed of the old quarter. Students would prevent me from making films, or even from wandering in the back streets. Damascus was, and probably still is, divided into the sophisticated modern quarter, slavishly imitating what they profess to despise - the French and British way of life - and the simple old quarter, true to itself and imitating no one. No one with half an eye could walk through the streets and fail to observe the contrast between the sullen, suspicious and unhappy modern Damascene and the gay yet serious, natural and open dwellers in the old city. As the days went by, I loved Damascus more and more.

As soon as I arrived, I set out in search of the dervish Emin Chikhou. I had no address, except that he lived in the quarter called Muhajireen - that is, the area allotted to Muslim emigrants from countries lost by Turkey in the Caucasus and the Balkans. Thousands of refugees had been settled there by the Ottoman Government in the nineteenth and early twentieth century, with little concern for their welfare. Muhajireen extends for two or three miles up the hills to the north of the city. After three days' searching and many adventures, I found Emin Chikhou, and from that time on, spent several hours in his company and that of his pupils every day of my stay in Damascus. Emin Chikhou is the sheikh or leader of an unorthodox branch of the great Naqshibendi order of dervishes. Being by race not an Arab but a Kurd, and having been an officer in the Turkish Army, he had known Turkish perfectly, but like myself had not spoken it for many years. Nevertheless, we had no difficulty in understanding one another. He had at that time about two hundred men pupils, mostly young, in Damascus alone, and others scattered throughout South-west Asia. He told me in great detail the story of his most unusual life, insisting upon the evidence that he had been guided and directed throughout by the Divine Wisdom. I learned from him the nature and method of the spiritual exercises used by the Naqshibendi Dervishes. I could not doubt that these exercises, if faithfully practiced, would both purify the nature and awaken the inner consciousness of the pupil. I agreed to practise one exercise which he recommended for half-an-hour each day; but it did not give the quick results he evidently expected.

The central theme of Emin Chikhou's teaching, and of all his talks with me, was the New Dispensation that he identified with the Second Coming of Christ. He spent hours in showing me the prophecies preserved in the sayings of Muhammad and the Muslim saints, all of which indicated that the end of the age was to come when mankind had conquered the energies of nature. I told him that I too was convinced that we were entering a New Epoch in human history, but that I did not take literally the prophecy of the Second Coming, of Armageddon and the Millennium of Righteousness. Though I could not accept his literal eschatology, I was deeply impressed by the man himself. I could speak with him as I had not been able to do with anyone - not even with Gurdjieff. He asked me to tell him of my life, and I recounted many of the incidents described in this book, and others that are too intimately personal to be written down. I found his explanations enlightening and often quite unexpected. He many times drew attention to the strange parallels in our two lives and more than once called in his pupils and translated for them into Arabic what we had been saying.

Commenting on some of the events of my life, he said: "Be quite sure that such things do not happen to everyone. There are certain people in whom God discerns a capacity for response, and He teaches them in a special way. Other people live as they wish - they do not see the results of their actions until it is too late. But you have been chosen by God to serve a great purpose, and therefore He has directly undertaken your training." He affirmed that he had seen the Prophet Muhammad in a vision, and had been told that the end of the age would come during his lifetime. He assured me that I would witness the coming of the Power of the Lord, and that I had a special part to play in preparing the Western peoples to receive this Power. I could not bring myself to take these prophecies seriously, and yet I found Emin Chikhou himself deeply impressive. I was permitted to attend several meetings with his pupils. The veneration in which they held him did not surprise me, as it is usual among the Sufis for pupils to regard the sheikh or murshid as the vicar of God. I was more impressed by the complete harmony that prevailed, and the devotion of all the pupils to the ideal of service to their fellow men. I saw how they took care of the sick and bereaved, and how those few who were rich shared their wealth with those who needed help. When later I met some of Emin Bey's pupils in far-away Mosul on the Tigris, I saw how the sense of brotherhood overcame separation in space and time.

Judging by the fruits of his work, I would say that Emin Chikhou is an outstanding spiritual guide. He is also a man of penetrating intelligence. I could not disregard his glowing faith in the coming of a New Dispensation, and hence I had to take seriously his affirmation that I would have a special part to play.

Once I was visiting the cemetery where a saint is buried, who gave his right arm to save a pupil's life. As I walked between the tombs, I found myself transported back thirty-three years to the evening in the Mezarlik of Scutari, when I had so clear a vision that the great moment of my life would not come until I was sixty years old. Now I was in my fifty-seventh year, and Emin Chikhou was assuring me that within four years a great event was to occur, and that I was to play an important part in it. He was, however, convinced that the event would occur in Damascus, and quoted with approval the tradition - many centuries old - that Jesus would appear in Damascus and that the Mahdi, the Announcer, would make him known from the minaret of the great Umayyad Mosque.

In all that he told me, there was a bewildering blend of inspiration and good sense; of a broad, even modern, outlook and a generous tolerance towards all shades of opinion; of archaic notions, ancient traditions, quoted as if they had the validity of Divine Revelation; of shrewdness with naiveté, of simple piety with a rather extravagant assessment of his own mission. I could neither accept nor reject what he told me, but after three weeks I became convinced that he lacked the profound insight that distinguished Gurdjieff from all other teachers I had met. It seemed probable, if I had time and were patient enough, that I could learn much from Emin Chikhou, but that I would not, through him alone, find the ancient Sufi tradition which has undoubtedly been preserved in South-west and Central Asia. I hope that, in quoting his references to myself, I have not given the impression that I had any sense of being a 'chosen vessel'. On the contrary, I felt embarrassed, for I was too acutely aware, not only of my moral defects, but of my spiritual insensitiveness, to take them seriously.

During my stay in Damascus I visited the Jebel Druze, and was fortunate in meeting one of their elders who could speak Turkish, and who told me of their belief that there are millions of Druzes in China who will, at the appointed hour, cross the steppes of Central Asia and descend upon the West and liberate their co-religionaries in Syria and Egypt. The peoples of South-west Asia have widespread and varied eschatological beliefs. I met Maronite Christians of the Lebanon who are waiting for the Parousia in their own lifetime. Strangely enough, only the Jews seem to have lost interest in the Messiah.

Before leaving Syria, I went for a few days to Jerusalem, where my chief impression was of the contrast between the human, superhuman and sub-human forces working in the Holy City. It was a heart-breaking experience, for I was perpetually torn between feelings of awe and reverence, and of disgust, horror and amazement that so holy a place could be so desecrated by those who profess to worship there. It was agonizing because I could recognize in myself the same conflicting forces, and knew very well that I had no right to pass judgment.

From Jerusalem I returned to Damascus, and a few days later left for Baghdad by one of the great coaches of the Nairn Transport. To leave behind us the sun setting over Lebanon, to travel all through the night and meet the sun again rising red over the Euphrates is an experience to be recommended to anyone. When later I had to make the same journey by air, I was really sad to witness the extent to which we are cutting ourselves off from life-giving experiences by the lust for speed and comfort in travel.

I visited Babylon and Ur, Mosul and Nineveh. In each place I learned something new - especially when I went without companions, and steeped myself in the life of the local inhabitants. I will describe only two out of a score of incidents. While in Mosul, I was taken by Ross-Thomas of the British Council to visit Sheikh Adi, the principal sanctuary of the Yezidis. This sect has always interested me because they are commonly called 'devil-worshippers', and yet are known to be a sect of high morality and steadfast faith. For fifteen hundred years, they have been persecuted and often massacred in thousands, and yet they have held firmly to their beliefs and practices. When I met Kemal, the permanent Sheikh or guardian of the Sanctuary, I had no doubt that I was in the presence of a spiritually awakened man. He is one of the very few Yezidi Sheikhs who, on account of the peculiar sanctity of the shrine they guard, are vowed to perpetual chastity and poverty. With much difficulty and the help of a Kurdish interpreter, I was able to ask and receive answers to the questions that interested me.

It became clear to me that the Yezidi religion is a survival of true Mithraism, which has thus remained alive for fifteen hundred years after the downfall of the Sassanian Empire. The Yezidis are wrongly called devil-worshippers because they believe that the earthly life of man has been placed by God under the dominion of Ahriman the Adversary - the Great Angel, as they call him. They have two emblems: the Black Serpent and the Silver Peacock. I saw the serpent carved in the rock beside the third portal of the sanctuary. The Sacred Peacock is never seen except by the Sheikhs, and then only after a special ritual of purification. I understood from Sheikh Kemal that a strict moral life is regarded as the only protection against the Serpent, whereas ritual purification and worship lead to the Peacock, the symbol of heaven. As I spoke with Sheikh Kemal, I remembered Gurdjieff's tales of the Yezidis, and saw how they are a living link with an age long dead. I also saw that travelers who go to find their secrets can never penetrate very deeply, for it is not their doctrines nor even their practices that are important, but the inner experience that enables them to face persecution and even martyrdom without turning back.

The second incident was my first visit to the ruins of Babylon. Everyone I met, both English and Iraqis, warned me that I should be disappointed. "There is nothing to see in Babylon except an obscene statue of a lion copulating with a woman." "See the Ishtar gate and go away - the rest is rubble." These were the typical comments of my friends.

I hired a car, and the driver offered me a round trip to Babylon, Kerbela and the Hindya Barrage on the Euphrates. We started before daybreak to avoid the heat of the day - which was then 120 dgrees F. in the shade. I was fulfilling the wish of a lifetime, but I was prepared to be disappointed. Instead I was overwhelmed. All day long I wandered through the remains of the German excavations, made shortly before I was born. The city came to life, and I became aware of its people and their extraordinary achievements in art and science, of their religious beliefs and their spiritual search. I saw how very great Babylon had been, and that its greatness still remained though its people had departed and its buildings were in ruins. I could understand why Gurdjieff, in his early days, had spent so much time in the ruins of Babylon, and why he had situated of his most dramatic writings in Babylon at the time of its greatness. Since that day, I have visited Babylon several times, and I have always received the same impression of a living force that still pervades the ruins of the city.

Throughout the journey, I adhered as well as I could to my decision to live in the cheapest way possible and to avoid contact with Europeans. Sometimes I found myself in difficulties, but as the weeks went by, I felt as if another skin had been shed and that I had been renewed. I wrote nearly every day a long letter to my wife and sent her my journal, which she had read to those living at Coombe with her. In a hundred days, I wrote more than a thousand pages of manuscript. Reading them through after five years, my adventures seem even more significant and extraordinary than they did at the time. The whole experience was a preparation for the new life that was to begin for me three years later.

The climax of self-revelation came on 3rd November, when I left Mosul by train for Aleppo by the route of the old Baghdad railway. Far away to the east, I could see the smoke rising from the oilfields at Kirkuk. I remembered my talk with Walter Teagle at the Ritz Hotel in Paris in 1924, when I was offered two and a half per cent interest in the Mosul Oilfields - now producing half a million pounds worth of oil a day. The black wisp of smoke reminded me of the black serpent symbol that guards the third gate into the Yezidi sanctuary at Sheikh Adi. To the north the snows were visible on the great mountains of the Kurdish Highlands. To the south was the desert, stretching for a thousand miles to Mecca and the Red Sea. In places, the railway runs in the midst of the dry, dusty desolation of the Syrian desert. As the train rumbled slowly over the lonely single-line track, I sat and pondered upon all that I had seen and heard. I made plans for what I would do in Aleppo and in Anatolia.

We reached Tel Kotchek, the Syrian frontier post, after four hours. Although it was November, the midday sun was scorching and there was no shade. The Syrian officer in charge refused me a transit visa, although he gave it to three Turkish travelers on the train. The conductor told me that it was usual to offer a gift of twenty Syrian pounds. I suddenly became obstinate, and refused. I could see myself behaving as I had done scores of times on similar occasions. Twenty Syrian pounds - four times the cost of the visa - was not an exorbitant bribe to ask. After all, he had a miserable assignment and was certainly underpaid. I said all this to myself, and yet remained as stubborn as a mule who has been asked to do something of which it does not approve.

The result was that the train went on without me, and I had to choose between waiting two days for the next passenger train east or returning at once on a goods train, in a cattle truck full of live poultry and half a dozen Iraqi soldiers. I chose the latter, and had a most interesting journey. We had to wait for several hours at Tel-el-Hugnah, and I climbed a small eminence to watch the sun setting. In a few moments the clear blue sky was filled with clouds on fire in the rays of the sun. The distant mountains of Kurdistan were a pale, pale blue, as if they were made of the clearest water.

I was all alone in complete stillness. I experienced an intense happiness as I became aware of my own inner consciousness, still and unmoved even by the manifestation of my own stupidity. The cold night descended on the desert, and the engine driver whistled for me to return.

A few hours later I was in Mosul, just in time to catch the night train to Baghdad and to make my way back to Damascus across the desert by the Nairn transport, as I had done a few weeks before. We ran into a desert sandstorm, and were delayed for five hours. We stopped near a semi-oasis, where a hundred Bedawi tribesmen were camped with their sheep and camels near a well. One stunted tree - the first for two hundred miles - marked the place.

At noon on 5th November I entered Damascus for the fifth time in four weeks.

My involuntary diversion through Damascus enabled me to pay a short visit to Amman, the capital of Jordan, where I had the opportunity of doing some business for a friend in England, and so of earning something towards the cost of my journey. I had my last meeting with Emin Bey. I had disputed his thesis of the infallibility of the Prophets and the sacred books. He insisted in regarding me as being in full agreement with him. In front of his assembled pupils he said: "There are few Muslims as near to God as Mr. Bennett. That is because he surrenders to the Will of God. He has no need for the outward practices of our religion." I was not very happy about this, because I could not accept his central thesis; that he was himself the precursor of the Second Coming. I could not doubt his faith, sincerity and love of God; and these made it hard for me to argue with him, even when I disagreed. His broad attitude towards the profession of religion was in curious contrast to his insistence upon literal interpretations. He told me of a Christian priest he had converted to belief in Islam. When the priest proposed to make a public declaration of his conversion, he had said this would be folly. "Islam has degenerated," he had told him, "no less than Christianity. No one will be brought back to religion by your sacrifice, which will be regarded as mock heroics. No, I advise you to remain where you are. Live by the precepts of the Koran, which are identical with those of the Gospel. Do your prayers in secret, but do good to men openly. Those who see your good works may come to you for advice, and then you can try to show them how to think rightly. You will do much more good in this way than by any public confession."

His last words to me were: "Never forget that the epitome of all religion is contained in the one word MAN. Our task on earth is to become MEN - that is, beings whose inner consciousness is awakened to know and to do the Will of God. To become a man is all that matters - outward forms mean nothing."

I left the next morning for Aleppo, where I met the grandson of the last of the hereditary chiefs of the Mevlevi Order, and also a venerable dervish, Farhad Dede, a Dedeghian, one of the few Muslim orders that take vows of poverty and chastity and devote themselves to the contemplative life. I have never met a man who more completely exemplified, in every moment of his life, faith and submission to the Will of God. He was infinitely patient in telling me in the minutest detail about the methods of spiritual training that have for centuries been practised by the Mevlevi dervishes. At that time the sheikh of the little community was a real scoundrel, a tool of the Syrian Government, who, to enrich himself, connived at the expropriation of all the lands owned by the monastery and kept his little flock of dervishes, now reduced to three old men, on the brink of starvation. Farhad Dede never complained and endured the outrageous treatment meted to him in my presence by the sheikh without so much as the flicker of an eyelid. Once, when we were alone together, he said to me: "I have been a dervish for nearly sixty years. My first sheikh was a great teacher - he had been formed when discipline at our parent *tekke* in Konya had lost none of its traditional rigour. Since then I have known many. I have been in *tekke*s in Istanbul, Cairo, Cyprus, Jerusalem, Afyun Kara Hissar, Aleppo and, of course, Konya. The sheikhs do not take, as we of the Dedeghian do, the vows of poverty and chastity. They have to be worldly men, and everything depends upon their training. One thing is certain; no one is fit to teach who has not worked under a teacher. Only a true spiritual guide, a murshid, can form a true murshid. True sheikhs have always been rare, and now none are left, and soon our order will die out. All is finished.

"For myself, I am content, for my soul is delivered to God, and whatever He wills is pleasing to me. If I could come to England and you would accept me, I would take you for my sheikh, for I see that your will is surrendered to God. For me it is enough that I have my ragged cloak and food to eat; I want nothing else in this life." He made me a cup of tea with the slow exquisite care that the Mevlevi dervishes bring to every act, large or small. I left him, refreshed and greatly enriched in my knowledge of the Sufi traditions.

From Aleppo, I went by way of Iskenderun to Adana. As we left Syria we passed under a Roman triumphal arch. This drive northward can be recommended to anyone who loves the beauty of nature. The narrow coastal plain is flanked by hills. Every ten or twenty miles are the proud ruins of crusader castles. The Taurus Mountains rise majestically far away to the north. It was the season of autumn colours; plane trees and oaks, yellow, red and gold. The pass of Mount Belan looks down from 4,000 feet upon the blue waters of Zakie Asnuk.

In Adana, I found a letter waiting for me from the United Nations Organization in New York, saying that they had recommended me to the Turkish Government to advise upon the development of the Turkish coal industry. The salary offered made me gasp, and I felt bound to consider the proposal seriously.

The next day I went eastward again, to a little town not far from the place where the Euphrates comes down from the steppes of Anatolia, to water the Mesopotamian plain. Here I lived for a few days with a small community of dervishes, under conditions unlike any I have known before or since. I stayed in the house of a dying man, the father-in-law of the young dervish who had accosted me in Adana six short weeks before. We slept in a hut on the dry earth. His breathing was very painful and during his sleep he constantly moaned and writhed on the ground. Each morning, an hour before dawn, he got up to pray.

With an effort painful to watch, he dragged himself to the nearby mosque for the first prayer of the day. His inward prayer, or zikr, never ceased.

I decided that I would enter as completely as possible into their life. Since leaving London, I had let my beard grow, and now had a straggling grey beard and a venerable appearance, which earned me the title of Baba, father, when I wandered in the bazaars or sat in the *chai hanes* or tea-houses. I went five times every day to the mosque for the ritual prayers, and spent the rest of my time in visiting the dervishes at their various avocations, in learning by heart chapters of the Koran or in repeating the zikr that Emin Bey had shown me. In the evening, we met in the hut where we slept. A little group of dervishes would come to pray and talk together. I confess that, throughout my stay, the nights distressed me, chiefly because I could not get used to cockroaches crawling under my blankets.

On the third evening, we were joined by a bearded man of about thirty, called Hadji Hassan of Kayseri. I learned that he was famous in the remote Turkish provinces for his impassioned preaching and for his beautiful voice, which moved the congregation to tears when he chanted the Koran or recited the call to prayer. Hassan Effendi, my old friend from Adana, told me that the young Hadji was only a preacher for the sake of outward appearances. In reality, he was one of the chosen initiates of the Great Teacher.

We ate together, sitting cross-legged on the floor and taking food with our fingers, or in the pieces of thin unleavened bread usual in the villages. After the meal, Hadji Hassan went out and performed his ablutions. When he returned, he sat on the far side of the room, instead of beside me as before. I wondered why, until he began to sing in Turkish, improvising, in excellent verse and music, a long chant of welcome to me. His voice was of a delicate purity, unusual for Turks, and he had none of the customary nasal intonation. He must have sung for ten minutes, changing the metre and rhymes and the mode or key of the music two or three times. He sang about their joy in my coming, about what I would take back with me to England; he invoked blessings on my pupils, but above all he prayed that the desires of my heart should be fulfilled to find a murshid-i-kiamil - a perfect Teacher - and that I would myself advance far in the way of perfection. He expressed the joy that all the dervishes felt in having me as a brother, and their hope that I would either stay long or return often.

It was all beautifully done, with no personal sentiment, and yet with deep feeling. After the song was finished, he soon rose and sat beside me again. No one present either then or later referred to the song.

They asked me to tell them all that I had witnessed in different countries about the state of the religious life. We sat together for hours, while they listened with rapt attention to the story of my adventures.

I told them of the proposal made to me to become adviser on coal to the Turkish Government. They regarded this as a sign from Heaven that I was intended to leave England and devote myself wholly to the life of a dervish. They told me of a great spiritual teacher, who lived unknown to the world in a remote part of Kurdistan. They said he was the Mutessarij-uz-Zeman - that is, the Regent of God on earth - and assured me that if I were patient I could meet him and enter the circle of his close initiates, of whom I would be the first European member.

So strong was the influence created by the unquestioning faith and deep piety of these men, coupled with the incessant practices of prayer and meditation, that England, my wife and friends and my responsibilities at Coombe Springs had grown remote and shadowy. I felt a peace and well-being that I had seldom known in my life before, and it seemed to me that this must be due to the environment, for I myself was not changed. While I was meditating on what had been said, Hadji Hassan took my left hand in his right and sat quietly for some time, his body swaying gently in the manner of one who is repeating an inward prayer. I could feel that he was very sensitive to my inner state and fixed my own attention on the question: "Should I accept the Turkish offer?" When he returned to himself, he said: "I advise you, before sleeping tonight, to wash your body from head to foot, make thirteen prostrations and prayers and commit your question to God. He will answer it in the night."

I awoke spontaneously at four-thirty a.m. It was perfectly dark in the hut. The other occupants were sleeping. I was wide awake instantly and, sitting on my heels, began silently to repeat the name of God. I saw before me a dim light, which became a well. A thirsty man was leaning over the well, but there was no bucket. In my hand was a bucket and a voice said to me in Turkish: "*Evvela vasifa yap sonar kendine bak*", the translation of which is: "First do your duty and then see to yourself." This vision passed, and I felt myself back at Coombe Springs. It was early dawn and I was alone in the garden, waiting for the morning's work to start. This again passed, and once again I was listening to the stertorous breathing of the dying man.

When I recounted my experience the following evening, all agreed that it was an indication that I should return to England for a time. But they were equally convinced that it also indicated that there would be a new dawn at Coombe Springs, and that I should prepare myself for great changes there.

The days I spent with the dervishes were by far the hardest trial of the whole journey. I was living in conditions to which I was wholly unaccustomed. I, a Christian, was being treated as a practising Muslim.

After a few days, I found it embarrassing to go to the mosque, for young and old would press round me to put their hands on my clothes. I discovered that the dervishes had put about the story that I was an English convert to Islam, a man of exceptional piety, and that various marvellous signs had been shown to me. The ancient notion that virtue is gained by touching a holy man is, of course, still widely held in the villages and towns all over Asia. The experience distressed me, because I had never been more acutely aware of my unholiness. My faults seemed to be thrown with grotesque vividness on to the screen created by the artificial situation in which I found myself. As my stay drew to an end, I began to count the hours till my liberation, and yet I would not for anything have missed the opportunity. If every hour became like a day and every day like a month from the intensity of the experience, I could not complain. I had come to the East to get new impressions, and I was getting them, pressed down and running over!

After my visit to the dervishes, I went to Ankara, and then set out eastwards to visit Kars, where Gurdjieff had spent his early years. Unseasonable snows and bitter cold held me up in Kayseri, the ancient Caesarea, home of St. Basil the Great and the centre of Cappadocian Christianity. When I went out to walk up the slopes of Mount Erciyes, the great volcanic mountain that dominates the Cappadocian Steppe, my beard froze solid. When at last I reached Erzurum, it was forty degrees below freezing. Only a few weeks before, I had been scorched in the sun of Babylon. So thick were the snow-drifts, that I had to turn back at Sari Kamish, "where," according to Gurdjieff, "the tallest pine trees grow."

24: NORTH PERSIA

I returned to England as if to another world. My wife soon persuaded me to part with my beard. The problems of Coombe Springs again began to press upon me. I was faced with a decisive choice. Either our work must expand and attract more people, or it would collapse for lack of support. I had held back as long as I dared, in the hope of achieving unity of purpose and of action with the other groups following Gurdjieff's ideas. It was apparent that the time for unity had not yet come. Subordination does not produce unity unless it is spontaneous and unforced. I could force myself to accept trends that could only lead to the sterilization of all that Gurdjieff stood for, but I could not inwardly agree with them.

The year 1954 was one of great suffering for me. My wife, now in her eightieth year, suffered a cerebral haemorrhage which nearly killed her. Once again she hung for days between life and death, and when she returned, her mind was deranged. It was hard to recognize her as the woman who had lavished her love and care on Coombe Springs; now she seemed to hate the place. I tried taking her for motor drives, but she would incessantly try to throw herself from the car, or turn upon me and tear at my hair in a way that made driving impossible. For hours on end, she would scream like a terrified animal, and no sedatives could calm her. Thanks only to the love and devotion of her friends at Coombe, it was possible to keep her with us, though she could never be left alone, day or night.

Only those can know the agony we all suffered who have had to witness the same apparent disintegration of a noble soul from causes that seem to lie wholly in the bodily organism.

Throughout the year, I continued my group meetings and scores of pupils came regularly every Sunday. My wife's behaviour was quite unpredictable, and we neither could restrain her nor attempted to do so. It was a searching test for us all, but I believe that it was hardest for me. For more than thirty years we had been man and wife; we had endured suffering and disaster and we had enjoyed almost perfect felicity together, and now I could do nothing for her.

After a few months, she became quieter, but outwardly she was no longer the woman I had known. Strange hidden fears and resentments that I had never suspected came to the surface. The feeling that she was not wanted alternated with demands for incessant attention. Before this year, I had thought that I knew what suffering meant, but now it was worse than anything I had known. I felt deeply that I was to blame, that I should have understood her better.

It would be beyond my power to describe the experience of living in the presence of dementia, nor do I believe it would be right to do so if I could. Throughout all the terrible months, I never lost faith that she would recover. I was convinced that her true self remained unchanged, and that what seemed to be a disintegration of the self was, in reality, only a failure of the machinery of communication.

Her closest friend, Edith Wichmann, who had been living with us at Coombe Springs since 1947, carried the heaviest burden, but the care she needed was made possible not by two or three, but by scores of her friends. I was advised again and again to send her to a hospital. Doctors told me that there is no recovery from senile dementia. Friends outside Coombe expostulated with me for subjecting the household to such bitter grief. But no one flinched, and no one near her doubted for a moment that it was right to keep her with us.

During this time of troubles, I turned towards my writing. For years I had been struggling with *The Dramatic Universe*. I had already written and re-written it four or five times. I was little nearer to a satisfactory version than I had been ten years earlier. It was this year that Dr. Maurice Vernet advised me to divide it into two parts - separating the material from the spiritual; the attempt to systematize all Fact from the attempt to relate all Value to a new principle. Dr. Vernet is one of the few close friends I have made in my life. I met him when he was lecturing at the French Institute in London in 1952, and, though we have seen little of one another through the years, I have always been sure that we could understand and love one another. I owe him a special debt in that he advised a treatment for my wife that English doctors had not tried. She responded well, and within a year of her cerebral haemorrhage she was relatively free from the terrible periods of acute dementia, when she could do nothing but scream and curse at everything that she loved and held sacred.

During the fine summer, we arranged places for her to lie out of doors in the lovely sun-lit garden. Unfortunately, people would go up to her and make mechanical conversation, such as: "Aren't the roses lovely?" Any insincerity jarred on her, and she would scream: "I hate roses, never speak to me of roses again!" Those close to her slowly came to realize that she had been set free from all the restrictive mechanisms that produce 'well-bred' and 'civilized' behaviour. She expressed exactly what she felt at the moment.

This was sometimes intensely painful, but we came to value beyond anything those 'moments of truth' when she would say with the most brutal frankness exactly what she felt about the person in front of her. Once an old friend came to visit her after a long absence. She had always been secretly afraid of my wife and had avoided her outspokenness, which, even when her health was normal, was not always easy to bear. As she was leaving the house, she saw my wife sitting, dozing in the drive in her wheel-chair, went up and, leaning over her, close to her face, said: "Goodbye, Polly darling; I do love you!" My wife opened her eyes, pushed her away, and said in a ringing voice: "Liar!" closed her eyes and went to sleep. The lady in question never visited our house again. Those who were present and detected the note of insincerity were not surprised at the response. But often visitors could not understand at all, and went away angry or disgusted.

For me, the whole experience was a re-education. My own faults and weaknesses were exposed to me by the very voice that for so many years had hidden them from me and from others. I learned that what appears to be dementia to the psychiatrist, may be the unveiling of a hidden wisdom that the ordinary self of man fears and does not wish to recognize. In this I was not alone. Several others knew that to be with my wife was to experience the sufferings of purgatory, and since they wished to be purified, they were profoundly thankful for all that she said and did.

My troubles were not confined to my wife's illness. Disharmony surrounded me on all sides. During the summer of 1954, it became increasingly clear that we were not going to achieve unity with the groups directed by Madame de Salzmann. My wife's illness had a profound bearing upon all our relationships. I was certain that what was happening to her was both a purification for herself and a deep teaching for those round her. Those who saw her simply as an old woman whose brain had been damaged by a haemorrhage and who would be better in a mental home, branded themselves in our eyes as insensitive to the deeper realities. A heart-rending experience need not be either a tragedy or a disaster. It can increase faith, though it can also shake or even destroy it.

There was a deep cleavage between those who regarded my wife's illness as a terrifying but immensely valuable lesson, and those who regarded it as a disaster or even as a sad misfortune from which we should pray to be quickly delivered.

In life, unequivocal distinctions never occur, and it would be quite wrong to suggest that all who had known my wife were divided into two camps. Yet, there was a separation. Only those who had the courage and the love to keep close to her could see how much more she was giving to us in her demented state than when she had kept a rein upon her inner feelings. Those who kept aloof could not be expected to see what we saw.

We were further divided from Madame de Salzmann by our attitude towards Coombe Springs. We believed in its value. Visitors were coming from many countries, and it was coming to be known as a focus of spiritual activity. So long as I had been earning a good salary, I could help to keep it going, but now I could no longer contribute financially. To maintain Coombe Springs without undue strain, we needed the support of three or four hundred members and students. To get these I had to give public lectures, but there were considerable divergences of opinion as to the desirability of lectures or indeed of any action that might arouse a wider interest in Gurdjieff's teaching. I could not understand this attitude, for he himself had repeatedly insisted that when All and Everything was published, it should be made known all over the world by any and every kind of publicity. He wanted all his pupils to carry copies of the book wherever they went, and even to stand up and begin reading it aloud in public places.

I felt that he had been betrayed by the decision to distribute the book through ordinary commercial channels. His circular letter of 13th January, 1949, which I had written for him at Child's, had brought in large sums of money, and it would have been possible to print thousands of copies of the book and distribute them freely. My common sense told me that this would have been disastrous: no one reads a book that is given away free. Yet I remained with the feeling that more should have been done to make it available. It seemed to me that, on the contrary, Beelzebub was being treated as a disreputable elderly relative, best kept in the background. This alienated me from those who did not share my feelings.

The causes of separation were, of course, not wholly on one side. I was, and have always been, very hard to work with. My exasperating habit of agreeing upon a course of action and then doing something quite different, is tolerable only for those who can value a little gold even when mixed with much dross. I could make real sacrifices for the sake of unity and then destroy all the good-will I had gained by following a course of action I had agreed to forswear. When I was at school, my Sixth Form Master would shake his head at me and quote: "To obey is better than to sacrifice, and to hearken than the fat of rams." After more than forty years, I had not yet learned the lesson.

Here Elizabeth Mayall, now Elizabeth Howard, with her two sons George and William, re-enters the story. After Gurdjieff's death she had remained in France, and it was only three years later that she decided to come with her children to live at Coombe Springs. The intervening years had not touched the mutual understanding that had grown up between us in Paris. From the time that she had first come to my lectures at the end of the war, I had been convinced that our destinies were interwoven. I had never met anyone else towards whom I could feel that complete trust that comes from an identical sense of what is really important in life.

Elizabeth had, at that time, an aloof air that disconcerted people who could not recognize her timidity. Her acute sense of humour, not untinged with malice, made people who did not see her deep humility feel uncomfortable and even resentful. From their first meeting, my wife had enjoyed her company, and we had made many expeditions together. I felt no contradiction in the deep love for my wife and the bond that existed between Elizabeth and myself. Being a man, I could not understand either of them, and I could not tell if I were causing suffering of which I was unaware.

During the acute stages of my wife's illness, when no communication, in the ordinary sense, was possible between us, Elizabeth had been unfailing in her support and consolation. We watched the gradual emergence of a deeper consciousness, set free by the disruption of the ordinary consciousness. She evaluated the change, as I did, in terms of the true and false selves of man. What we saw was a marvel, but not a miracle. It is very probable that many people, certified as insane and subjected to various destructive treatments, are for a time channels to the deep subconscious wisdom of the human soul. Whenever I am told that a mentally sick person is 'uncooperative', I remember my wife. Once a psychiatric social worker visited her to sign an order for a wheelchair from the Ministry of Health. She had a rough reception and beat a hasty retreat, saying: "I have rarely seen anyone so uncooperative.

Are you sure that it is wise to keep her at home?" Lest I appear critical of the admirable British Health Service, I would add that we could not possibly have kept my wife at home without the help of excellent trained nurses, and the support of all the forty or fifty people living at Coombe. I dare not think of what might have happened had we been living in a small house or among unsympathetic people. It is unfortunately still true that what is possible for one may be impossible for many.

I must return to March 1955, when I received an invitation from Paul Beidler, an American architect and former pupil of Gurdjieff, to visit him and his wife Margaret in Baghdad where he was stationed. By then, my wife had recovered sufficiently to make it safe to leave her for a short trip to the East. I decided to go for a fortnight with Elizabeth

Howard, profiting by cheap excursion tickets available via Cyprus. We left by night on 11th May, expecting to arrive in Cyprus in the early morning, but were diverted to Benghazi where, for a few hours, we tasted the sights and sounds and smells of Africa. We did not reach Cyprus till evening, and had barely time to transfer to a plane for Beirut. We were met by friends, Ronimund von Bissing and his wife. They told me that a Turkish dervish had been waiting all day to give me a message. I spoke to the young man, who asked me to visit his *murshid*, Sheikh Abdullah Daghestani, who lived in the Kurdish quarter of Damascus. I said that it would not be possible, as we were to leave early in the morning for Baghdad. He did not insist, but said that the sheikh would expect to see me.

Hiring a taxi at the airport in Beirut, we went straight to Damascus, by the route I had several times travelled when I was last in Syria. On arrival in Damascus, we found that the Nairn coach was not leaving until the next day. I therefore decided to visit Sheikh Abdullah.

Elizabeth came with me as far as the tomb of Muhiddin Ibn Arabi. As Emin Chikhou had firmly refused to speak with women, I expected the same from Abdullah, and therefore sent Elizabeth back to the hotel. I had not been told where the sheikh lived, but I was to find him by enquiring at the shop of a barber called Turkish Ali, opposite the Ibn Arabi Mosque. Turkish Ali had been taken ill and was in hospital, no one knew where. It looked as if I had drawn a blank but, as I left the tomb of the Saint, I came face to face with the same old Hadji who, eighteen months before, had guided me to the sanctuary called Arbaein. He was evidently expecting me, and when I asked if he knew the house of Sheikh Abdullah, he simply said: "It is near the path we went by last time." On the way, he told me that the sheikh was known as a very holy man. He was born in Daghestan, near the Caspian Sea, and is known therefore as Abdullah Daghestani. He had lived for many years in Turkey, and could speak the language perfectly. He had travelled widely, and received visitors from many countries. We should probably find him in a small mosque which had been built by his pupils for his private use.

The sheikh was waiting for me on the roof of his house. It was high up above the city, commanding a superb panorama. Abdullah Daghestani was of middle height, with a white beard, but looked far younger than the seventy-five years attributed to him by the Hadji. I felt at ease from the start, and very soon I experienced a great happiness that seemed to fill the place. I knew that I was in the presence of a really good man.

After the usual salutations, and compliments on the excellence of my Turkish, he astonished me by saying: "Why did you not bring the

lady sister who is with you? I have a message for her as well as you."
It seemed unlikely that anyone could have told him about Elizabeth.
We had walked straight to his house, and the Hadji, my guide, had left
me at the door without speaking to anyone. I replied that as he was a
Muslim, I did not think he would wish to speak with a woman. He said
very simply: "Why not? Rules and customs are for the protection of the
foolish; they do not concern me. Next time you pass through Damascus,
will you bring her to see me?"

I promised to do so if the opportunity came. We sat for a long time
in silence, watching the ancient city. When he began to speak, I found
it hard to come out of the deep reverie into which I had fallen. He was
saying: "I was expecting someone today, but I did not know it would be
you. A few nights ago an angel came to my room and told me that you
would come to visit me, and that I was to give you three messages. You
have asked God for guidance about your wife. She is in God's keeping.
You have tried to help her, but this is wrong. You disturb the work that
God is doing in her soul. There is no cause for anxiety about her, but it is
useless for you to try to understand. The second message concerns your
house. You have asked God for guidance as to whether you should go
your way or follow others. You must trust yourself. You will be persecuted
by the Armenians, but you must not be afraid. You have to attract many
people to you and you must not hesitate even if other people are angry."

He fell silent again. I was astonished at the two messages, for it was
perfectly true that I had prayed for guidance on just those two questions.
If he was right, then the way before me was clear. I was already beginning
to plan a series of public lectures that I would give in the autumn, when
he broke into my thoughts again.

"The most important message is the last. You must know that there
is great wickedness in the world. People have given themselves over
to the worship of material things, and they have lost the will and the
power to worship God. God has always sent Messengers to show the way
out of such situations, and he has again done so in our present age. A
Messenger is already on earth, and his identity known to many. Before
long he will come to the West. Men have been chosen to prepare the way
for him." He had led up to this point in a quiet, matter-of-fact tone of
voice. Then his manner changed, and he spoke more slowly to hold my
attention, saying: "It was shown to me that you are one of those chosen
to prepare the way. You have a duty in the West. People will listen to you,
and you will recognize the time to speak. The Messenger will come to
your country and even to your house. You have now to return to your
country and prepare your house to receive him. You must not speak to

anyone of what I have told you, for you will not be believed until the time comes. The followers of the Armenian will persecute you if they know what you are doing. Therefore you must keep everything to yourself."

I could not understand what he was referring to, and said so. He replied that it was not necessary to understand, but only to be prepared. He said: "You should never cease to worship God, only you must not show it. Outwardly you must behave as others do. God has appointed two angels to take care of you. One will guide and direct you so that you will no longer make mistakes as before. The other will perform the religious duties that you cannot do for yourself."

He said that he had finished telling me the messages, but wished to add as personal advice that he recommended to me to practise incessantly the act of submission to the Will of God. He said that no harm can come to anyone when he is actively and consciously surrendering himself to the Will of God. He said: "I advise you frequently to repeat in your heart the words *la ilahe il Allah* - which means surrender to God alone." When I said that this was the Muslim profession of faith, he replied that it is as much Christian as Muslim, for the foundation of all religion is that man should not follow his own will, but the Will of God. He repeated what he had said before: "You have nothing to fear, for you are henceforward under protection. Nothing will go wrong with you."

We sat together for some time longer. I asked him about the great Murshid of the dervishes I had heard of in Anatolia. He said: "I know him. He is my friend, and came here to visit me recently. He looks outwardly an insignificant little man, but he is a true Wali" - that is, a saint. He added that there were others in the Muslim world who knew what was to come, and were preparing themselves and others. He went on to speak in eschatological terms - but in some respects what he said was significantly different from what I had heard from Emin Chikhou. When I mentioned Emin's name, I fancied a trace of hesitation before he replied: "He is a good man, and he does much good."

When I had to leave, I asked his permission to come again in ten days' time. I returned to the hotel by tram, and as it rattled down the hill, I asked myself whether these strange prophecies should be taken seriously. His two 'messages' about my wife and my home were indeed remarkably apt. He could scarcely have known enough from any human source to realize that these two questions were so important for me at that moment. The reference to Armenians haunted me. Gurdjieff's mother had been an Armenian, and his family was more Armenian than Greek. The warning could be interpreted as meaning that Gurdjieff's people would turn against me.

Did he have clairvoyant powers? Had he indeed been warned by an angel? I remembered the angel that had 'spoken' to me about death in September 1947. I believed in angels, though I had no idea of their true nature. If Abdullah Daghestani could have authentic knowledge about me, not attributable to sense perception or thought, then he might also have authentic knowledge about the presence on earth of a Messenger from God. I recoiled from such an inference. The world has tired of announcements of its imminent end, and mankind has grown weary of new prophets. And yet I myself had written seven years earlier of the New Epoch, and of my conviction that there would be a fresh manifestation of the Divine Mercy. There was nothing so very wrong with what the sheikh had said, except its inherent improbability. I could not reach any conclusion, and resolved to take his own advice to make no attempt to understand what he had told me.

I rejoined Elizabeth, who was disappointed to hear that she might have met the sheikh. That afternoon, we left for Baghdad by the desert route as I had done before. The Beidlers were waiting for us and, in spite of the heat and our fatigue, we decided upon a visit to Babylon the same day. The impressions I had gained on my previous visit, that Babylon was not a dead city, but had preserved memories of its former experiences, were strengthened and shared by the others. We did not wish to stay longer in Iraq, and set out early next morning by car for the Iranian frontier town of Khanikin. We did not reach the frontier until noon, by which time the customs and immigration offices were already closed for the siesta. I went into the darkly shuttered customs office, and found an elderly Turk dozing alone at a desk. He woke up and greeted me, and we fell into conversation, from which it transpired that he had formerly been a Turkish Government official and had been employed at the Sublime Porte. He remembered some of the officials I had known, and this made a bond between us. Being of Iraqi origin he had left Istanbul with the fall of the Sultanate, and was now working for the Iraqi Government. He gave me the impression of a man who had found, in the spiritual or religious life, a serenity that made him indifferent to his fallen fortunes.

He put himself to considerable trouble to pass us through the frontier without hours of waiting. As we were saying goodbye, he said to me quietly: "Most people driving to Tehran stop for the night at Kirmanshah. I venture to suggest that you might do well to stop at Kerind. There is a good guest house, and you may find other interests there." His manner suggested that there was more in his advice than the recommendation of good lodgings, and we decided to take it. We were rewarded by meetings that were of great interest for all of us.

One was with a solitary dervish, and the other took us to a community of dervishes living in a *tekke* on the outskirts of the little town. We stayed in Kerind on our way out and also on our way back. A more beautiful site could not be imagined. North Iran is traversed by ranges of mountains. From the Kabir Kuh in the south-west to the Elburz in the north-east, the successive chains rise from ten thousand to nineteen thousand feet. Travelling eastward, we went over three or four passes. Kerind itself lies in a narrow valley leading up to the high mountains from the plain of Kirmanshah. Rivulets run everywhere, and the sound of waterfalls is the background to the clatter of horses and mules. Dark Kurdish shepherds with their stern, rugged faces mingle with the handsome Persians, who in that region are often as fair as Circassians. Both the men and the women of Kerind are uncommonly handsome.

The little town has for ages been a centre of metal-working crafts. It has assimilated without losing its ancient character the educational reforms of the late Shah, and has now a good secondary school. But there was no radio, no electricity, no newspapers, scarcely a motor-car. Paul Beidler, who has made a deep study of the problem of rehousing Asiatic peoples in connection with irrigation and other development projects, was delighted with what we saw, for it was evidence that the tranquil life of Asia could be preserved without depriving children of the opportunities of education, or their elders of the benefits of sanitation. We said to one another that if we could ever retire, we would rather come to live in Kerind than any place we knew. Beauty was everywhere, and the laughing hospitable Persians, so different from the suspicious, sensitive Syrians, thronged round to have their photographs taken, or to show us their children.

The dervish Ahmad Tabrizi lived then a mile above the town, in a hut beside the tomb of a forgotten saint. Paul Beidler walked up the ravine and found him sitting alone. I had stayed behind to write down - this being the first opportunity since leaving Damascus - my impressions of Sheikh Abdullah Daghestani and all that he had told me. Finishing my work, I followed the others from the indications of the villagers, and found them drinking tea on a roof with the family of a gendarme. Paul told me of finding the dervish and, as it was already near sunset, suggested that we should visit him in the morning before leaving. Without thinking, I said: "Let's go at once." I felt a need to meet this old man without delay. We all walked up the narrow gorge under the shade of large plane trees, until we came out to a broad valley two or three thousand feet above the plain. Far away to the south-west, the snow-capped peaks of the Pusht-i-Kuh caught the rays of the setting sun. The scene was both majestic and peaceful, as we came into the little enclosure where Ahmad Tebrizi sat before his hut. He was no longer alone; several young men - whom we afterwards ascertained were dervishes - were seated on the ground at his feet. He could not speak Arabic, so Paul took one of the young men aside and began to ask him questions. The dervish and I spoke in Turkish. He spoke the dialect of northern Persia, which is close enough to Osmanli Turkish to make it easy for me to understand him. To start the conversation, I spoke about Sheikh Hassan Sebisteri of Tebriz. He had heard of him, but evidently was not interested. I asked him if he had been to Bokhara. He said that he had wandered far and wide throughout Turkestan and Afghanistan, and had made pilgrimages to Mecca and Kerbela. He had lived for some time in Kerbela, but had not attached himself to any order. "All my life," he said, "I have walked alone. Where I could learn something useful about religion, I stopped. When I had learned all I could, I went on. Now I am satisfied that I have found all that I need on earth and, if it is God's Will, I shall remain in this place until the end of my life." I said: "You have followed religion all your life. Will you tell me what, according to your understanding, makes the true dervish?" In reply, he made the distinction between the Tarikat and Marifat; that is, between the Ways and Illumination. He had a great respect for the Ways, and knew that for some men a murshid or guide is indispensable. But there were many dangers in the relationship of pupil and teacher, and he had preferred to wait for God to enlighten him. God had been merciful, and had guided him through many perils. He added that he was convinced that the beginning and end of religion was surrender to the Will of God. It was this alone that made the true dervish. Whenever man relies upon his own understanding and his own will, he is in danger of mortal sin.

When I said that the trouble, so far as I was concerned, was that I did not know the Will of God, he said: "Then you must wait patiently. Your patience is your submission, and it is the proof of your faith."

At this point Paul Beidler, who had been speaking animatedly in Arabic to two of the dervishes, came up to us and said that he had been told that there was in the village a dervish *tekke* of the Djellalis; that is, the Order of the Perfectionists. I asked Ahmad Tebrizi's opinion, and he said: "These brotherhoods are good. They call constantly upon the name of God. In my opinion such practices are unnecessary, for God's angels constantly watch over us, and they know the secrets of our heart. Nevertheless I advise you to go and visit them. You will see for yourself who and what they are."

I was reluctant to leave the old man. He had not taught me anything new, nor had he explained anything old, and yet in his presence I felt a surge of faith and love towards God. By contrast I was coarse clay. Even Farhad Dede had not attained the same degree of awareness of the Presence of God. I felt my own unfitness; I was still the slave of my own self-will. I might be able to say with sincerity: "Thy Will be done", but I could not say with the same conviction: "Let my own will be annihilated in the Will of God." I was well aware of the gulf that lies between acceptance of God's Will and the surrender of one's own.

We took leave of Ahmad Tebrizi, and returned to Kerind with two or three of the young dervishes. They told us that the *tekke* had just been visited by a great sheikh from Turkestan, in whose honour the ritual dances and chants of the Djellali Order had been performed on the previous night. They were confident that their sheikh would repeat the performance, as we were so keenly interested. I gathered that Paul

Beidler had questioned them about the form of their private ritual, as he was curious to find a connection with Gurdjieff's ritual movements.

The *tekke* stands within fifty yards of the main route from Baghdad to Teheran and Kabul. We had passed it by on our way east and had no suspicion of its presence. No doubt hundreds of travelers pass the great walls every year and assume that they hide orchards and vineyards, like scores of other such walls that one sees alongside the roads. When we had first come to Kerind we had asked about dervishes, and had met with polite assurances that dervishes were unknown in those parts. No doubt the whole town knew of the Djellalis, but no one gave a sign of their presence. This was confirmed to me later, when I gave two or three different parties visiting Iran exact details of the *tekke* and letters of introduction to the sheikh. No one found anything. When they had enquired in the village they were assured that the dervishes had left the area.

The sheikh of the Djellalis was a tall, handsome Persian, who could speak little Turkish. The *tekke* itself consisted of several acres of land surrounded by high walls and containing numerous buildings. These dervishes were married, and when we were invited to their Selamlik or reception hall, the sheikh's wife joined us, and sat with Elizabeth and Margaret Beidler. A Turkish-speaking elder was sent for and he, with about a dozen others, came and sat with us at a long low table. Both Elizabeth and I were immediately struck by the similarity between these arrangements and those at Gurdjieff's table. I will not describe the conversation, but refer only to the fact that we could understand one another with little need of words. They all practised the spiritual exercise of repetition or zikr, as we could tell from the almost imperceptible swaying of their bodies from side to side, or of their heads forwards and backwards. When Paul asked if we could witness their ritual, the sheikh invited us to stay for a week, as it was practised only on the night before the Friday worship. Unfortunately, I had promised to give a lecture in Cyprus, and this fixed the date of our return.

When we reached Damascus, I took Elizabeth to see Sheikh Abdullah Daghestani. He said to her: "This man has been chosen by God for a great task. You have been chosen to help and to serve him. He will need you beside him, and you must never leave him. What angels will do for him in the invisible world, you must do in the visible world." Elizabeth explained that we were not married, but he brushed this aside, saying: "It is God's Will that you should be his companion and that your soul should be united with his soul." He went on to speak in some detail of the work she was required to do and then, turning to me again, he said: "Very soon you will receive an indication."

Few sights in the world are more beautiful than the view of Damascus from the hills at sunset. As we sat in silence looking over the ancient city, the sheikh beside us with his spotless white burnous and turban and his equally white beard, we experienced an intense happiness. He had dared to put into words what we secretly felt in our hearts. We had both been subjected to the prodigious impact of Gurdjieff. We had shared in the even more searching trial of my wife's illness. I had never for one moment seen Elizabeth consider herself or look for any personal advantage. Neither of us had dared to imagine that our lives would ever be as closely linked as the sheikh suggested.

When we left him it was already night. We made our way down to the noisy city without speaking. Three years were to pass before we could speak again of the message he had given us.

When we reached Cyprus, we unexpectedly met Rodney Collin Smith and his wife. They had made a quick journey in the Near East, impelled it seems by much the same need as mine, to find evidence that the ancient traditional wisdom had not been lost.

Within fifteen days of leaving London, we were back again at Coombe Springs. Two decisions had been taken. I would propose to the Council of the Institute that we should go forward with the building of a great hall at Coombe Springs, and I would give a series of public lectures in London in the autumn. I was aware that these decisions must inevitably lead to the parting of the ways with Madame de Salzmann and her groups, but I hoped that the separation would be temporary and that we should come together again in a freer association, which would be open enough and flexible enough to take in the new influences that I now expected within a very few years. The group of architects, under the leadership of Robert Whiffen, was delighted with the decision to build. The money was made available by loans made by our pupils in amounts from one pound to two thousand. A new life seemed to inspire Coombe Springs. With great joy, I found that my wife had recovered enough to understand what we had decided. Her strength was failing and she was still very far from normal in her outward behaviour, but the contact with the deeper consciousness of her true self could be made more often and for longer periods.

Coombe Springs

In July, I went to Italy, where Madame de Salzmann was resting near Como. I undertook some negotiations on her behalf with members of Gurdjieff's family, who were making difficulties over the copyright of his works. These went badly, and I felt that I had missed an opportunity of bridging the gap that separated us. I had forgotten Sheikh Abdullah's warning that I would be persecuted by the Armenians until at a certain moment, when I saw how great an embarrassment I was going to encounter, it returned to me, and I became aware that henceforward I would have to stand alone. In any case, it was clear that Madame de Salzmann could not and should not share in the responsibility for what I was doing at Coombe Springs.

In October 1955, she came to London, and arranged for the complete separation of our activities. From that time forth, no member of her groups was permitted to take any part in the work at Coombe Springs, and no member of my groups was allowed to attend the classes held under her direction. When she announced these arrangements, I told her that I hoped that the separation would not be for longer than a year. I had a premonition that by the autumn of 1956, something decisive would happen, and that if we had not reunited by that time, we would drift further and further apart.

Frank Lloyd Wright visiting the Djamichunatra, 1957

The winter of 1955 came and went. To our great delight, my wife was able to come downstairs and join a dinner party in honour of her eighty-first birthday, on 23rd March, 1956. Soon afterwards her condition again deteriorated, and during the summer months we had many heart-rending days. We marked her birthday by starting work on the great hall. Snow was on the ground as we worked. As the weeks passed, we were surrounded by crocuses, daffodils and bluebells. The team formed itself. In addition to English residents at Coombe, we had Americans, Canadians, Australians, South Africans and a Norwegian. Whenever a specialist was needed, he appeared from somewhere.

The work of the architects' group was out of the ordinary. Twelve to fifteen men, with sharply differing tastes and views on architecture, worked together without either pay or personal credit. No single feature was incorporated in the building that all did not accept. This sometimes meant waiting for weeks or months before some part of the building could go forward. I took some part in all this, but we were all convinced that no one person could do anything. The building seemed to have a plan and a purpose of its own, and all we could do was to wait until one part after another of the plan was revealed.

The first volume of *The Dramatic Universe*, with the sub-title The Foundations of Natural Philosophy, had been published in May. Apart from a surprisingly good notice in The Times Literary Supplement, it was either ignored or derided. A reviewer in Nature described it as a horrible warning to scientists to keep away from fantastic speculations. At no time did any reviewer, or any of the few readers who wrote to me about the book, make any reference to the six-dimensional geometry until, two years after publication, the American astronomer Gustav Stromberg wrote several highly appreciative articles. I was only too well aware of the shortcomings of the book, and especially of the unnecessary difficulties for the reader created by the introduction of dozens of awkward neologisms. The word hyparxis, by which I designated the sixth dimension which permits free choice, was the cause of mystification and annoyance to many. And yet I could not have written it differently. The book contains so much that is both new and contrary to trends of thought that are now fashionable that I could not expect it to be well-received by scientists or philosophers. The mode of presentation made it virtually inaccessible to the majority of readers.

I can say truthfully that my chief concern was that my publishers should not lose money by it. Working on the book for fourteen years had been a necessary part of my own education. If what I had seen in 1920 was right, then the reality of the fifth and sixth dimensions inevitably followed. Many of the experiences described in this book had confirmed and extended my first vision. If it were right, then sooner or later scientific research would lead to the same discovery. It did not matter if this should happen during my lifetime or after my death.

I was convinced - and subsequent events have only strengthened my conviction - that there is a Great Wisdom to which we occasionally have access. Even when we are unaware of it, this Great Wisdom continues to influence human affairs. If this Great Wisdom had revealed to me some deep secrets of which modern thought was unaware, it would surely in due season reveal them to others. If, on the other hand, as the reviewer in Nature had suggested, the whole book was no more than the aberration of a pseudo-scientific fantasy, then it was just as well that it should fall into oblivion.

Nevertheless, I was faced with the question of publishing the second volume, which was to be called The Foundations of Moral Philosophy. However low I might rate my own work, I had a task before me. I had set myself to write a book that would embrace all human experience, and endeavour to show that there is a great harmony underlying all the diversity and chaos of our sense experience. The second volume had been rewritten several times, but it was quite unsatisfying. I had relied too much on Gurdjieff's ideas, and had not reached a synthesis that I could really call my own. I made up my mind that I must rewrite the whole of the second volume, in terms of my own personal conviction that the diversity of values and obligations derives from the distinction between systems of one, two, three, four, five, etc., independent terms. This idea was implicit in Gurdjieff's system, but occupied only a small place in it. He had concentrated particularly on the properties of three and seven-term systems. This seemed to me artificial, and due probably to the influence of traditional beliefs that the numbers three and seven are sacred. I struggled with the task of revision, but made little progress. I was inwardly very restless, as if something necessary were missing from my life.

The work of the groups at Coombe Springs confirmed this feeling. The new groups were going well, but those that had started before 1950 were passing through a kind of crisis. The building of the hall gave a direction to our efforts, but the older people could not work at it, and were thrown back upon their own inadequacy. I could see that the entire situation turned upon my own condition. I had accepted the position of teacher or leader. I could only give what I had, and this was very limited. All that the solitary dervish Ahmad Tabrizi had said about the deficiencies of the pupil-teacher relationship came home to me. It gives admirable results up to a point, but there is always a frontier across which no man can transport another.

While I was wrestling with these problems, a cloud no bigger than a man's hand appeared on the spiritual horizon. Sometime in the early summer, I received a letter from Japan telling me about a spiritual movement that had originated in Java, and that seemed to have many points in common with the ideas and methods of Gurdjieff. I heard that a representative of this movement was in Cyprus and might come to England. I was not particularly interested in the description given by my correspondent, and yet I felt an obligation to learn more about it.

One reason why I did not follow up a suggestion that I should go to Cyprus and find out for myself was that I had formed the strange project of climbing Mont Blanc. I had grown unaccustomed to athletic undertakings. However, I had gained a little experience of rock climbing during our visits to Snowdon and the Lakes. I was not good on rock, nor was I without fear. I considered it foolish to place oneself in danger for amusement; yet now I was driven to make the attempt. I asked Elizabeth to go with me. She did not hesitate, and even seemed ready for the suggestion, although she had an instinctive fear of heights and had been unaccustomed, owing to a long early illness, to any kind of physical effort. A young Frenchman, Gilles Josserand, who, as a boy, had spent a year with us at Coombe in 1951, had since become an Alpine guide. I wrote to him, and he said he would take us to the summit, providing we did some serious training. This we did during the spring and summer.

Owing to the seminars at Coombe, we had to make the ascent very early in the season, before the snow was hard. Moreover, we only had two possible days, as Gilles was then teaching at the school of guides in Chamonix, and was free only at weekends. The weather was very uncertain. However, all worked out as if the heavens had conspired to take us to the summit. Gilles recommended a few days at an altitude of 12,000 feet to get us used to the height. We went to the Refuge du Tête Rousse below the Aiguille du Rocher. All day we practised walking with crampons and piolet. It was so early in the season that only two climbers went by; our only companions were mountain ravens, who stole the food we put out on the snow.

Not until after we were returning, did the reason for this escapade, for such it must be called, make itself apparent. We were three times in serious danger. We had to make a traverse on loose snow on the Aiguille du Rocher, and within a few minutes of passing, an avalanche came thundering down, obliterating our tracks. Soon afterwards climbers ahead of us dislodged some rocks, and we narrowly escaped being hit. On the way down, we were caught in a thunderstorm, in which two Italian climbers were killed. We did not understand the warning given by the electric shocks from our ice-picks, and did not realize how narrowly we escaped being struck by the lightning.

The quarter of an hour spent on the summit in brilliant sunshine was itself a sufficient reward, but the meaning of the whole experience only came home to me after we returned to Chamonix and I found myself blinded from the snow, my dark glasses having broken on the way up. I lay on my bed in considerable pain and asked myself whether the adventure had been anything but senseless bravado. The answer came to me that it had been necessary to place ourselves at the mercy of the forces of nature, and to have, for a time, the immediate realization of the puniness of man in the face of an indifferent and frowning universe.

We returned to London to take part in the seminars at Coombe Springs. A good start had been made upon the new hall, but a great effort was needed if it was to be completed by the following June, as we hoped. Nearly three hundred people came and spent a week or more at Coombe Springs. It was a wonderful example of unforced effort.

Several of us felt and declared that the building had come to life, and was directing its own construction. It was communicating its own form and construction to the minds of the architects, and attracting the specialists it needed. It was clear that my own role in relation to it was, for the time being, at an end. It would complete itself in its own way, and in its own time.

25: THE SUBUD EXPERIENCE

Since 1955 I had been hearing rumours of Subud, but it did not occur to me to connect them with the prophecies made to me on my journeys. The man behind the rumours, Muhammad Subuh, remained a hazy figure until the summer of 1956. My personal interest in Subud was aroused by my host in Cyprus the year before. While on a visit to England, he told me that he had met the emissary of Muhammad Subuh, by name Husein Rofé, a Jew converted to Islam. He added that Subud could not be understood unless one had practised the spiritual exercise called the *latihan*. He had quite recently been initiated, and the early results had so impressed him that he believed that Subud might be the key to solving all our spiritual problems. Knowing that Roni was not one to chase after strange gods, and that his twenty years of work with Ouspensky had given him a solid grounding in the psychology of man's spiritual development, I felt bound to take Subud more seriously than I had been inclined to do.

At that time I was wrestling unsuccessfully with the task of revising *The Dramatic Universe*, and did not want to be distracted by something new. However, I agreed to go and visit Rofé where he was staying in lodgings in Dartmouth Road, Willesden. He struck me as a man of unusual intelligence and very widely read, but his outlook was strangely materialistic. He presented Subud in terms of oriental 'success stories'. I did not find it edifying to be told of instantaneous cures of dying men, of men four score years and more restored to youthful virility, and re-marrying, of business men securing unexplained contracts or concessions, or of politicians winning adherents among their bitterest opponents. His stories of marvels, such as flights on the astral plane, of premonitions fulfilled and psychic phenomena, familiar to lovers of the occult, were anathema to me. Rofé did not seem to realize that his stories were putting me against Subud as a movement and against himself as a person. Moreover, the belief that material benefits are assured by the worship of God was a typically Muslim attitude that I had found unacceptable in Emin Chikhou. The grim realities of life are incompatible with the belief that nothing but good comes to the just man. This belief, if carried to its logical conclusion, can only lead to absurd propositions, as for example, the denial a priori that Jesus the Just Man could have died upon the Cross.

In September, I found that two or three other old friends of mine were investigating Subud. Two of them were the same men who had gone to Madame Ouspensky in 1948, and who had subsequently rejoined Gurdjieff and worked for a time in Madame de Salzmann's groups in London. Their approach to Subud was very different from mine. They had already reached the conclusion that without Gurdjieff in the flesh, his System lacked an essential element. They were awaiting something not only new but radically different from what we had before. Being convinced that work in groups, as it was being attempted in London and elsewhere by the followers of Gurdjieff and Ouspensky, was condemned to stagnation and sterility, they had withdrawn from all active participation in them. They were thus quite free from commitments both outwardly and inwardly.

My own case was not at all like theirs. I had by no means lost my belief in the practical utility of Gurdjieff's ideas and methods - even without the presence of Gurdjieff himself. I was very deeply committed, with more than four hundred pupils who looked to me for guidance, and for whose sake I had to keep Coombe Springs going. Moreover I had publicly affirmed my belief in Gurdjieff. In the Preface to Volume I of *The Dramatic Universe*, I had referred to him as 'a genius that I do not hesitate to describe as superhuman'. Even when writing these words, I had questioned their wisdom, and when I saw them in print, I had asked myself if they would be misunderstood. Now, after two years, I felt no wish to go back on what I had written. If man can in this life attain to superhuman status, as I firmly believe, then Gurdjieff was such a man. Moreover, his contribution to the re-orientation of human understanding in the coming Epoch will, I am sure, be recognized more and more widely as time goes on. If Subud could not be reconciled with all that I had come to regard as well-established conclusions of Gurdjieff's cosmo-psychology, Subud was not for me.

Madame Ouspensky had sent me a message to say that I would be welcome to go to Franklin Farms for a long stay in order to write. There was little peace for me at Coombe Springs. My wife's mental condition had again deteriorated and whenever I was in the house, she would wander from room to room, followed by her companion, looking for me and calling my name. Her doctor advised me to go away for a time, as he expected her restless phase to pass. Her general health was good, but she was losing her sight owing to cataract combined with the hemianopsia contracted at her last attack.

She was not my sole anxiety. At that time, I was carrying a heavy burden, with a constant stream of people wishing to consult me about their personal problems, and from ten to twenty group meetings every week. Under such conditions, writing was impossible. Moreover, I saw that I was taking too much on myself. If I could not find others to share the burden, the purpose of Coombe Springs as a spiritual centre would be stultified.

I had promised myself that I would continue to live and work at Coombe as long as my wife was with me. At her death, I would remain only if I were satisfied that the place was not dependent upon me personally. I was deeply convinced that no spiritual movement in our modem age could give results of any value if it was dependent upon the leadership of one man. Leadership is the easy way of achieving results, but it can destroy both the leader and the led. I was well aware that the human race is still too immature to dispense with leadership altogether, but I wanted in my own small circle to see if it could be reduced to a minimum. This would be possible only if people could understand and trust one another, and I believed that those of us who had been searching and working together for so many years were beginning to reach a measure of mutual trust. Unfortunately, my own nature was a great obstacle. I was too forceful and too hasty in action to make a good member of a team. So I veered between leadership of the most obnoxious kind - that is, dictatorship - and an equally unsatisfactory repudiation of responsibility that left everyone guessing. Such contradictions are probably inevitable in the gradual transformation of our nature, but they produced a state of chaos which was hard to bear, not only for others but for myself also.

With such thoughts in my mind, I set out for the United States, travelling on the Queen Mary. I spent about six weeks in Mendham as the guest of Madame Ouspensky. I was allowed to remain in complete seclusion in order to write. I was astonished at my own output. In five weeks, I wrote twelve very difficult chapters of *The Dramatic Universe*.

During my stay, the seventh anniversary of Gurdjieff's death, on 29th October, 1956, was marked by the usual memorial service in the Russian Cathedral. It happened that on that day Madame Ouspensky spoke to me about Subud, having received enthusiastic accounts from Roni Bissing. She asked my opinion, and I said that I could not make up my mind. I told her what Gurdjieff had said about Dutch India, and how I had wondered if he might be referring to Muhammad Subuh as the man who was to come after him. She said: "Since Mr. Gurdjieff went, I have been waiting for someone to come. I still wait, but he has not come, perhaps he will not come in my lifetime." She asked me some more questions and then said: "If a new teacher comes, how do you think you will recognize him?" I replied that he would bring something entirely new and that we should recognize it because we had been so well prepared by Gurdjieff. She did not wholly approve of what I said, but would not disclose her own thoughts.

During my stay in America, I saw little of the groups in New York. At Franklin Farms, I was treated with the unvarying kindness that Madame Ouspensky had always shown me. In New York it was otherwise. The Gurdjieff groups were cold and suspicious. One of their members told me that they were disappointed in me, because they felt that I had betrayed Madame de Salzmann. I was only too well aware of the terrible burden she was carrying in sustaining the faith and courage of hundreds of followers of Gurdjieff's ideas, and had no wish to add to her difficulties, but I could not feel that she was wise to allow complete authority to be thrust upon her. Nevertheless, I would have been grievously lacking in gratitude had I forgotten what she had done for Gurdjieff and for all of us. She alone had the strength and courage to take up the task he had left behind him. Moreover, I was sure that there had been a misunderstanding, and that the treatment accorded to me was not due to her. Later I learned that this was the case, and that, as soon as she heard how her people were behaving, she took steps to put matters right, but by that time I had returned to England.

Through all this, Madame Ouspensky never changed in her attitude. Neither approving nor disapproving, taking sides with no one, her sole aim at all times was to promote unity without sacrificing the basic principles of the Work. Of all the many remarkable people I have met in my life, Madame Ouspensky stands out uniquely for her singleness of purpose and her unwavering pursuit of her aim. Her self-discipline has been an inspiration to all who have known her. She would never undertake anything beyond her own understanding and powers. When she spoke to me of the coming of another teacher, she said of herself: "Madame is not a teacher. She always looks upon herself as a nursery governess who prepares children for school." She never said 'I', but always referred to herself in the third person as 'Madame' or even 'she'.

When I returned home in mid-November, I found my wife considerably improved. We were fortunate to have a night-nurse whom she loved and trusted. She named her 'Little Nan', and nearly always slept peacefully when she knew that her Little Nan was in the room. The care of her during the day was a harder problem, for trained nurses could not understand why we did not wish to keep her under sedative drugs. The chief burden fell upon Edith Wichmann, but many of the residents and visitors at Coombe took turns in staying with her at different hours of the day, for she could never be left alone. I could not spend much time with her, but could usually give her breakfast. Our early mornings together were always happy, and sometimes the cloud that overshadowed her mind would lift, and she would speak to me with penetrating insight about the past and the future, or about life and death. Our conversations were not always serious, for in lucid moments, she loved to speak of our adventures together and make plans, largely fanciful, about the future. Even in her fantasies, we could recognize a most significant symbolism, as if she were expressing a reality that only her unconscious self could perceive.

There was so much work to do in London that I had once again to abandon my writing. This was painful, because I had come to certain deep conclusions about God, man and the Universe which I needed to express. My own most intimate experiences and my attempts at a universal synthesis agreed, in assuring me that God is the Supreme Will, manifested as the Reconciling Power that harmonizes affirmation and denial everywhere and in everything. I am convinced that to picture God as a Being is an anthropomorphic fallacy no longer necessary at the present stage of human development. On the other hand, the notion of Spirit had acquired a deep and wonderful meaning. It seemed to me that Hegel, with his notion of Geist as the progressive principle that unifies Reality, was feeling his way towards the doctrine of the Realization of the Essence, which requires a five-term system. I had visions of an endless unfolding of systems, each more complex than those that went before. In my attempts to express what had been revealed to me, I was fettered by the limitations of language. I had to describe the most truly concrete Reality in meagre, wretchedly abstract terms. But at least I could express something when I did write. Yet at Coombe Springs I was unable for weeks to write a line.

It is scarcely surprising that I should say to myself: "I can at least stay away from Rofé and do nothing more about Subud until the book is finished." Then, to my surprise, the very same inner voice that I had learned to trust interrupted me and said: "On the contrary, you must go now."

I went and asked Rofé to perform the formal opening, or initiation, that gives contact with the Life Force that operates in the Subud *latihan*. It was on 25th November, 1956. Rofé explained the contact as being analogous to an electric current that can be switched on and off at will. He said that I would feel its presence as a thrill or vibration. He was entirely matter of fact, and seemed almost perfunctory in asking me to make a declaration of faith in God and of submission to God's Will. I was not aware of any change that could be described as a vibration, but I did observe that the restless movement of my thoughts ceased, and that I entered a state of consciousness that I had supposed to be attainable only by a long well-directed effort. Soon I ceased to think at all, but was aware of an almost unbroken consciousness, free from all mental activity and yet intensely alive and blissful. I have no idea of how long this state endured, for I lost all sense of time. I heard Rofé say: "That is enough. You can stop now", and instantly I was back in my usual state, fully aware of my surroundings. The numinous quality of my experience gave it more the character of what mystical writers call the prayer of diffuse contemplation than of Gurdjieff's self-remembering.

I was deeply impressed. Rofé was delighted, telling me that he had been convinced from the first time he met me that I would quickly recognize the unique character of Subud. He invited me to go twice a week to practise the *latihan* with others whom he had initiated during my absence in America.

It seemed right to accept, but I did not wish anyone at Coombe to know about it. Many people would be disturbed: some would wish to try for themselves, and others would conclude that I had lost my faith in Gurdjieff's methods. I needed a far longer period of experimenting before I could take the responsibility of telling others.

The *latihan* was an altogether new experience for me. In all Gurdjieff's exercises, there was a result to be achieved, a predetermined state to be reached by an intentional act of will. Here all was spontaneous. No two *latihan*s were the same; there was always something new to be learned, but there was also a striking recapitulation of all that I had learned before. All that I had learned and taught of Gurdjieff's psychology over so many years came to life in the *latihan*.

I soon realized that it was exceedingly difficult to be completely receptive and to abstain from any kind of voluntary action, but as I began to see what was required, new depths of meaning opened before my inner consciousness.

In February, after one of our exercises, Rofé spoke to the five of us about the possibility that Pak Subuh might come to England. He said: "His followers in Java told me, when I was there in 1950, that Pak Subuh had predicted as far back as 1934 that he would travel round the world, bringing Subud to many countries, and that the first would be England. He himself told me that in England there were men whose spiritual qualities would enable them to understand Subud, and that I should meet them when I came. I believe that you are the men referred to, and I would like to know whether you feel that you wish to invite Pak Subuh to come here, and make yourselves responsible for the expenses of the journey."

We met the next day for lunch, without Rofé, and took stock. I was greatly struck by the discovery that each of us had independently concluded that the action of the *latihan* is to awaken Conscience, and also that we were all convinced that it was producing results more rapidly and effectively than the exercises we had learned from Gurdjieff. We were all anxious that the opportunity of trying Subud should be given to the former pupils of Gurdjieff and Ouspensky.

At that time, Madame de Salzmann was in New York, and I undertook to make a short trip to see her and Madame Ouspensky, and tell them what we had found. I flew on 27th February, taking advantage of the cheap fourteen-day excursion tickets then available. I was again invited to Franklin Farms, and saw Madame Ouspensky nearly every day. Her strength was failing, and it was very hard for her to speak.

Madame de Salzmann, who was then very busy in New York, came out several times. The two ladies wished to hear, in all possible detail, what I and the others had found in Subud. They agreed that it was right to invite Pak Subuh to England. Madame de Salzmann said that she would be glad to meet him, as only in this way could she form any opinion as to whether or not he might be the expected Teacher.

I returned to England on 12th March. The invitation was sent and accepted. I decided to use the intervening time to complete my work on *The Dramatic Universe*. As I could not hope to write in London, I accepted the offer made by Christopher Baynes to lend me his cottage, Cae Crin, which is the westernmost habitation at the extreme tip of the Llyn peninsula in North Wales. There I went, and shutting out all other duties worked at the manuscript. It was finished a few days before Pak Subuh was due to reach England on May 21st, 1957.

During this visit, a significant event occurred that consisted in my being cured of two long-standing bodily weaknesses. The first was the residual trouble due to the dysentery I had picked up in Smyrna, and the second was the chest weakness due to my T.B. infection. These experiences, and similar ones reported by others, both men and women, who had been practising the *latihan* for some months, obliged me to take the 'healing' aspect of Subud a little more seriously.

Of far greater importance for me was a kind of moral regeneration that occurred in April, about five months from the time I was opened. This experience was truly purgatorial. A vivid inner light began pitilessly to shine upon my own past. My life stood before me in every detail. It was not like memory, which is capricious and selective. I recalled everything, pleasant and unpleasant - especially those episodes which I had wished to forget. For example, I relived, in every detail, my dealings with the ex-Khedive Abbas Hilmi Pasha, and burned with shame to see how I had justified to myself what was, in reality, a very mean action. I recalled all my affairs with women, and saw how what had seemed at the time to be compassion for their loneliness, or the desire to help them, had been the cloak for coarse animal impulses or the need to hide from myself my deep fear of women. My unreliability and untruthfulness in my dealings with men, my running away from embarrassing situations and, above all, my insensibility to the feelings of others and my consuming self-will, all were displayed and made sharply, mercilessly visible in hundreds of episodes that haunted me like malignant imps. I could not for a moment forget them. At night I could not sleep for remorse and self-loathing. It seemed to me that I must either go mad or die.

The strange thing is that my outward life was scarcely affected, and I believe that no one noticed the agony into which I was plunged. If my memory does not deceive me, I endured this purgatorial state for fourteen days.

As a relief from writing, I had spent odd hours in studying Indonesian, and by the time Pak Subuh arrived I could with difficulty read his book *Susila Budhi Dharma*, of which Rofé had lent me a copy printed in Indonesia in three languages.

When I returned to London, I found that Pak Subuh intended to bring not only his wife but also two helpers, Mr. and Mrs. Icksan Ahmad, who were paying their own fares. Where were they to stay? Rofé suggested Coombe Springs as obviously most convenient. This aroused some jealousy, and the evident fear that I might try to appropriate Subud to myself. I proposed that a furnished house in London should be hired. I had my own reason for being reluctant to invite the Subud party to Coombe. Subud was still for me only an important adjunct to what we had received from Gurdjieff; it did not take its place. Until I knew a great deal more about it, I did not consider it wise to identify myself so completely with Subud as would be implied in an invitation to the party to make Coombe Springs their headquarters.

As the time grew shorter, I grew more and more aghast at the responsibility that I was facing. My own experience of purgation had shown me that the action of Subud was real enough, but also that it was devastatingly powerful. What might happen to people less toughened than I had been by long years of trial and suffering? How was I to choose whom to bring to Subud? The others thought my predicament really desperate. They themselves were free. They could tell others about Subud, but they need take no direct responsibility. If I told my own pupils that I had been practising it for six months, most of them would certainly wish to make the experiment for themselves.

It seemed that the best way out was that Pak Subuh should stay in London and that I should bring to him only a chosen few, while explaining to the others how I understood Subud. If my plan was to work, it was necessary to say as little as possible, and not to let Pak Subuh be seen at Coombe Springs. An unexpected event impinged upon the situation. The film actress Eva Bartok had been for some years a student and member of my groups. She had impressed me by her sincerity, though the exigencies of her profession made her attendance very erratic. Without warning, she telephoned one day from Hollywood, where she was making a film, to say that she was very ill, and that her American doctors said that a serious operation was unavoidable. She wanted to come to England to get my advice. As she was speaking, it came to me that she was destined to be cured through Subud, and that through this Subud would become known far and wide. I saw that my whole life was to be disrupted, and that Subud would swallow me up. Until that moment, I had thought of Subud as something personal that had profoundly changed my inner world, but that would not greatly affect my outward life.

I invited Eva to come, saying that if she arrived about 22nd May, I might be able to offer her a special chance of receiving help. As I spoke, I knew that the die was cast and that I had committed myself to a far greater adventure than I had bargained for.

Pak Subuh arrived with his party. Our little group went to meet them at the airport. I recognized Pak Subuh sitting quietly on a chair, alone and indifferent to the excited throng of passengers, one of whom was having trouble with an immigration official. Involuntarily I contrasted this meeting with Gurdjieff's arrival from America. Both men had the same power to create round them their own environment, into which no alien influence could penetrate. Both had that extreme economy of gesture and movement, that complete stillness that is, in my belief, one of the marks of an emancipated soul. There the resemblance ended. Gurdjieff was, in any company, a striking and impressive figure. With his magnificent clean-shaven head, his fierce moustaches and his flaming eyes, he always drew attention to himself. Pak Subuh was by comparison insignificant, and seemed to deflect attention away from himself as if it were his will to remain unnoticed. When he stood up, I saw that he was far taller than other Indonesians I had met. I could not place his features; they were more like those of an Arab than an Indian, and though his skin was brown, he did not give the impression of being a native of the tropics.

That evening, those who had invited him met Pak Subuh and his party in Rofé's house, where they were temporarily accommodated.

During the evening, I asked him if those who were admitted to Subud should cease work according to Gurdjieff's method. He replied: "No. Change nothing. Bapak is not a teacher. Gurdjieff is your teacher, and once you have a real teacher you are never separated from him whether he is alive or dead. But Bapak tells you that if you sincerely practise the *latihan* you will understand Gurdjieff's teaching quite differently." He paused for the translation of what he had said, then he added: "Bapak says that later on you will learn from your teacher Gurdjieff many things that you never heard him say before."

The significance of this statement totally escaped me at the time. It then seemed to me to be the confirmation of my own belief that Subud and Gurdjieff's System were complementary and formed one whole. I was delighted, and wrote at once to Madame Ouspensky to tell her what had been said. It was not until much later that I came to understand that Pak Subuh usually told people what they wanted to hear, adding some small clue to his real meaning which they very often missed altogether. Only after two years did I begin to understand that what Pak Subuh said was applicable only to the immediate situation, and that at another time he might say, on the same subject, something quite different and even contradictory. I should have realized this much sooner, for I had quite independently reached the conclusion that logical consistency and freedom from contradictions, so far from being tests of ultimate truth, are evidences of the most limited type of thought. They are not to be looked for in the inspired utterances of a prophet or in the hesitant stammerings of a saint.

It would be hard to picture a state of greater confusion than was created at Coombe in June 1957. Instead of twenty carefully chosen and experienced pupils, I had to bring all who wished to come. Bapak Subuh insisted that there should be no selection, and said that no preparation was necessary beyond the introductory talks that I gave upstairs in my study, while groups were being opened downstairs in the big dining-room. In one month more than four hundred men and women, nearly all my own pupils, received the contact and began to come for the *latihan*. As the room would only hold twenty at a time, we often had to have as many as seven or eight exercises in one evening, starting at seven p.m. and going on until after midnight. We could not persuade Bapak and Ibu to begin earlier, as they said that the *latihan* was best made in the evening.

Asikin; Shafruddin: Pak Subuh; the author; Icksan Ahmed

Subud acted with explosive violence. Many of those who came were either terrified or disgusted by the pitiless exposure of the human self, as it was stripped naked in the *latihan*. Many of these went off and joined other groups, telling horrifying stories of what they had seen and heard. Others were lifted into such an ecstasy that they could scarcely be persuaded to restrict themselves to the two or three *latihan*s a week that Pak Subuh prescribed. We witnessed remarkable recoveries of health, heard mystical experiences recounted, were told of the fulfillment of predictions made by Pak Subuh and, with it all, were constantly aware of an immense surge of energy by which everyone was carried along, little caring where it would lead them. In all this, Eva Bartok's illness remained a preoccupation to those of us who had brought her to Coombe Springs. After a period of apparent deterioration, a visible change occurred. It was on 20th June, after three critical weeks, that her condition suddenly began to improve. Two weeks later it became apparent that she was pregnant and Pak Subuh predicted, what afterwards occurred, that she would have a normal and safe delivery. The real miracle was the transformation that we all could recognize in Eva's inner state. We were witnesses of a death and rebirth in her soul.

Pak Subuh said afterwards: "Mr. Bennett is very strong. God has prepared him to bear heavy burdens, and he will have still more to bear in the future." Such statements bewildered me. Not only did I not feel strong, but my whole life belied the assurance. I took on burdens, not because I was strong, but because I was reckless. My time with Gurdjieff had taught me to be objective in observing myself, and though as sensitive to flattery as every other man, I was not easily deceived by it. It seemed to me that Pak Subuh called me strong to encourage me to go forward at a moment when others were tempted to hold back. Pak Subuh came to visit my wife, and Ibu Subuh opened her, even though she could not understand what was being said. At that time, it seemed as though the end of her life was very near and that she would never recover her lucidity of mind.

The effect of her opening and of the *latihan* practised with her, principally by Miss Wichmann, was really wonderful. At this time, Pak Subuh changed Edith's name to Margaret, and with this change of name came a most striking change of character. Her attitude towards 'Mrs. B.', as she was called by everyone, changed in a subtle way. From being emotionally involved, she acquired a true compassion and deep understanding. My wife began to communicate with us again, and some of her conversations were deeply enlightening. The greatest mercy of all was the cessation of the agony and horror of her demented states. Once again the woman who loved her fellow-men came into consciousness, but now changed; no longer possessive and dominating, but gentle. My gratitude to Subud for what my wife received stands apart from all the rest.

So the weeks went by. In August we had our seminars, unlike any that had gone before. Visitors from America, South Africa, Canada, France, Germany, Holland and Norway came to Coombe and were opened. Subud was beginning to be known.

Then came an unexpected invitation to California. I offered to go and prepare the way. To my surprise, Pak Subuh said that Elizabeth should go with me and take her two boys. He said: "After California, you come to Java." I said that this was quite impossible: for one thing we could not afford the fares.

However, we were swept along by the stream of surprising events. After two months in California, as we were preparing to return to England, Bapak was invited to Australia. Once again, I offered to go and prepare the way, and suggested that Elizabeth and her boys should go straight back to England. Two months of incessant travelling between San Francisco, Sacramento, Los Angeles and Carmel, lectures, talks, meetings, openings, *latihan*s with great crowds or with sick and dying men and women had exhausted us both. But Pak Subuh said: "No, Elizabeth is needed, and she cannot be without her children; they give her strength."

We flew to Australia, via Honolulu and Fiji, seeing just enough of the Pacific Islands to make me understand that there was a whole world of tradition, wisdom and humanity of which I was completely ignorant. We reached Sydney tired out, and hoped for one or two days' rest.

Before we reached the customs, the reporters were on us. I had no means of knowing what had been told them, or why I was bombarded with questions about Pak Subuh, Eva Bartok, myself, flying saucers and goodness knows what! When we met Dr. Philip Groves, our host, we discovered that a hand-out to the press had aroused such interest that I was to have a press conference with about twenty reporters, an interview on television, two radio talks. Even Elizabeth's boys were interviewed, and their photographs appeared in the papers.

At last, ready to drop, we left the airport at five p.m., to learn that I was expected to open about forty men and Elizabeth fifty women that very evening. To cap it all, I had to give an introductory lecture. We were staying at Manly Beach, fifty minutes by car from the airport, so had barely time to wash and change and return to the city. The meetings were to be in the Adhyar Hall, lent for the occasion by the Theosophical Society.

This was the very place where, thirty years earlier, Annie Besant and C. W. Leadbeater had announced the forthcoming manifestation of the Messiah in the person of Krishnamurti. As we drove into Sydney, we saw the Sydney Heads through which the Messiah's ship was to sail. I was obsessed with the sense of incongruity. The reporters had asked me if Pak Subuh was the promised Messiah, and I replied that it was the first I had heard of it. But I was uneasy, even miserable. Pak Subuh was seven thousand miles away, and we were alone. My faith in Subud and all confidence in myself had been drained away by the absurdity of our reception. To enter the Adhyar Hall was to be warned of the folly of a too facile belief in signs, portents and wonders. I wanted to run away, to refuse even to see the assembled people.

Seething with inward revolt, I walked in and found about three hundred men and women filling the hall and waiting for me to speak. I have no idea what I said nor what impression I made. I spoke for twenty minutes, and probably told them that it was not the explanation, but the experience that mattered. With great trouble and in growing confusion, the hall was cleared. Reporters were firmly told that they could not be present at the opening. All the men left the room, and Elizabeth was left alone to face sixty or seventy women.

I could not get a moment to sit quietly and bring my disturbed and revolted feelings into some semblance of calm. After forty minutes, I went into the hall with the men. There were not far short of fifty.

As I faced them, I said to myself: "They cannot possibly be opened. It is all wrong. I have no right to be here in this state."

I pronounced the formula usual at the opening, asked them to keep their eyes closed whatever might happen, and commended myself to God. At that very moment, the hall was filled with a sense of Presence; an immense peace descended on me and I ceased to be aware of the others who were before me.

After ten or fifteen minutes, I opened my eyes and an extraordinary sight met them. Nearly all the men in the room were already responding to the *latihan*. More had happened in a quarter of an hour than I had seen in England in a month. In that moment, I became convinced beyond all doubt that the Power that works in Subud has nothing to do with me or with any other person. I could not understand why or how I should be a channel for its transmission, but I could no longer question its real - that is, its objective - presence. None of the men in the room had ever seen a *latihan*, nor heard any description of the reactions they might expect. And yet I saw them responding in just the same way as I had seen men in England and Holland, in Germany and America.

When, at last, we returned to Manly late that night, Elizabeth and I compared notes. Her experience had been identical with mine. She also had been aware of the numinous Presence that overshadowed her, and had known that this Presence made the opening.

We left for Singapore and Ceylon. The Subud centre in Colombo had been started by a strange sequence of events, and I was closely linked with its leading members. They begged me to stay for a longer time. It was then a period of strict curfew, and the communal riots had barely calmed down. It was scarcely a coincidence that of fifty Buddhists, Tamils, Muslims and Christians who had been opened, not one was harmed in the rioting. I wanted to stay and see all I could. Elizabeth received a cable from her sister, advising her to return, and she left immediately with the boys. She arrived too late, for her mother died on the morning before she reached home. I stayed a week, learning much, seeing much and gaining much. I hated to go but I felt, more and more, that I must get back to my wife.

At last I got back to England. My wife was waiting for me. She had indeed weakened greatly, but she was glowing with inner life, and assured me that all was well with her. Margaret Wichmann told me that during my absence from home she had, for the first time, been almost entirely free from the acute distress that she had shown before when I was away. I told Margaret that it had often happened to me that I would look at my watch and see that it was eight a.m. in London, and would then feel that I was in my wife's bedroom, giving her breakfast. Margaret told me that there must have been some real communication, for my wife had frequently spoken of me and to me, as if I were present with her, and always at such times had been calm and happy.

It seemed as if she had been waiting to see me. From the day I arrived, her strength ebbed more and more rapidly away. I was able to be with her at frequent intervals day and night. We were very happy together. Although to strangers she appeared strange, to those of us who were close to her she was wholly and most truly herself. Sometimes we spoke of the past, and the accuracy of her memory astonished me. She could fill in details of an event that I had almost forgotten. She was content to live from moment to moment. The sense of time left her entirely. When I returned after five months' absence, she greeted me as if I had just left the room. If I left her for five minutes she would say: "I thought you were never coming back." Day by day, she grew more detached and yet more loving, as if our relationship was passing out of time into eternity. As indeed it was, but not yet wholly.

On the 24th of July, an unexpected visitor arrived at Coombe; it was Sabiha Esen, at whose school in Istanbul my wife had taught English. Thirty-nine years had passed, and though they had kept up a desultory correspondence for some time, we had not heard of Sabiha for a quarter of a century. She told me that she had come to England several times and wanted to find us, but had never been able to track us down. This time, she said, the urge had been imperative, and yet she had felt helpless until, by an apparent chance, she had spoken of us to a friend who not only knew us, but had come to Coombe Springs. That was yesterday, and she had lost no time in coming.

I told her briefly of the situation and said that I doubted if Mrs. B. would recognize her. However, we went straight to the bedroom. My wife was dozing, and Sabiha began to speak quietly to her of Istanbul, the Bezm-i-Alem school and of their old friendship. Recognition came suddenly. My wife drew her down to the bed, weeping tears of joy. She was perfectly lucid, and said to Sabiha: "I am so happy that you came in time. I am going soon, and I longed to see you again."

They remained together for an hour, renewing the past. 1920 had been a turning point for all three of us, and no event could have more completely restored the unity of our lives. Sabiha was to leave London for a few days, and promised to come again on her return. My wife said: "I have seen you again, and that is all I care about."

That night, she seemed to have gained a new strength, but when I went into her room at five o'clock in the morning, little Nan whispered to me that the end was near. Margaret was beside her bed. I took her hand as I had often promised to do, and spoke her name. Her eyes flickered and a smile of welcome was on her lips. Her breathing grew more and more gentle. Her hands were already cold.

Several times I thought her breathing stopped, and I spoke her name as I had promised. Each time a gentle breath returned. At last, it was over. For a long time, we sat in complete stillness. I spoke her name, and to my joy and amazement another breath came, a second and a third and then no more. She had given me a signal that she remained conscious through death, and wished me to know it.

As we sat with her, we could feel her presence in the room and a great joy. She was finally liberated from the personal attachment, and had found the union of the soul that neither death nor any other creature can dissolve. I have never felt separated from her since that time.

The Djamichunatra, with Pak Subuh and his group approaching, 1957

26: ELIZABETH

The unrelenting pressure of events since Subud came had left me with little time and no inclination to write. Concerning Subud had written itself with little conscious intention on my part. It was my duty to return to *The Dramatic Universe* and finish the task left in the air with the publication of the first volume. I looked upon this volume as little more than an introduction to the deeper notions that had slowly matured in me since my first vision in the Rue de Pera in 1920. From recognition of the need to go beyond dualism to the triad, the awareness had grown in me that every number is significant as the bearer of a quality that contributes to the total meaning of existence. The book I had first written in 1941 had, by 1956, been re-written at least eight times. As soon as each version was finished, I found that what I had written no longer expressed what I now understood. And yet, by 1956, I seemed to have the whole story in front of me. There was nothing more that I had to say, though I would have wished to be able to say it better.

Now, in August 1958, I took stock once more. With great reluctance I set myself to read what I had written at Franklin Farms and at Cae Crin, the cottage in Wales where I had taken refuge before the coming of Bapak. I expected to find a deep incompatibility between what I had written then and what I understood now. Beyond all doubt, I myself had changed. One year of Subud had done more for me than the previous thirty. One change that I was aware of had been a shift in the centre of gravity of my experience, from my head to my heart. All my life I had been led and dominated by my mind. Prince Sabaheddin's comment to my wife, when she was still Mrs. Beaumont: "Notre enfant genial a le coeur encore glace", had remained true through all the changes of the years. Subud had melted my frozen heart, and nothing could ever be the same again. So, when I set myself to read what I had written, I expected to find it uninteresting or even repugnant. I had revolted against my old researches and theories, against my tendency to live in abstractions and to ignore facts. I had been inclined to cast my manuscripts into the flames and write no more until I could write from the heart.

When I began to read, I was astonished. The book was not what I had pictured. Abstraction and theory were there in plenty, but in them and behind them was an understanding that wholly agreed with my experience of Subud. The second volume of *The Dramatic Universe* was quite unlike the first. That had been a mental construction, starting from insight. This second was insight embedded in and emerging from the mental construction. It was an important book, and had to be published.

With a shock of surprise, I saw that I had begun to trust my own judgment. I knew that all my life I had acted willfully, with little regard for the opinions of others, but I had never trusted myself. I had leaned upon Ouspensky and Gurdjieff, upon my wife, and indeed upon each last person who expressed an opinion as to what should or should not be done. My way of acting had always been exasperating to my best friends just because of this constant vacillation between self-will and self-efface-ment. Pak Subuh had done for me what no one else had been able to do. By refusing to allow himself to be used as a prop, he made me stand on my own feet.

I said: "Now I must marry Elizabeth." When I asked her, she replied by telling me a strange story. "When I was a child I used to see people round me. As you know, I was a sick child, and was ill from about eight till eighteen years old. My 'companions' used to come round my bed. I never spoke of them to my family, and I knew, I don't know how, that when 'real' people were in the room at the same time, I must not appear to notice the 'companions'. I could really see them in just the same way as I saw everyone else. As I grew older, certainly before I was fifteen, I ceased to see these companions, but I kept their memory as something strange but true." As she was speaking, I recalled her wartime experiences, when she had served in the W.A.A.F., as a plotter in Fighter Command, and had seen much of death and the horrors of war. She went on to speak of her meeting with me and later with Gurdjieff. The ten months she had spent in Paris, seeing Gurdjieff daily up to the end of his life, had made so prodigious an impact upon her that nothing had ever been the same again.

It was, therefore, quite unexpectedly that she found herself, in the summer of 1957, once again aware of the presence of a 'companion' somewhat in the manner she had known as a child. She was then living at Coombe Springs Lodge with her two boys. Eva Bartok had occupied a room there during the early days of her stay at Coombe, and Elizabeth had been the only woman who had shared with Ibu and Ismana the duty of exercising with her. I had remarked that Pak Subuh and Ibu looked upon her as having unusual spiritual gifts. When I said this to Elizabeth she said: "No, surely not," and continued her story.

"While Eva was staying at the Lodge, one night I could not sleep, being acutely aware of my own unworthiness and lack of faith. After an almost entirely sleepless night, at about five o'clock I got up and went to work in the garden, before the children woke. When the time came to go back to the house, I felt very calm and tired, but contented. It was a quiet, sunny summer morning. As I came to the house, I saw a tall woman in a blue dress leaning against the doorpost watching me. She was very much at ease; relaxed, with her arms folded across her chest. I could not see her face clearly, but I knew she was a stranger: I thought she was an early visitor, and felt ashamed to have kept her waiting. As I came forward to speak to her, she walked backwards into the house, quite unhurried, and when I followed her into the hall there was no one there. Not until I had looked into the other rooms did it occur to me that she did not exist in the flesh. While I was giving the children their breakfast and getting them ready for school, she appeared several times: usually in a doorway, and she never turned her back towards me. I took no notice of her, and as far as I know the children did not see her; anyway they said nothing about her. At about mid-day, when I was alone downstairs, she appeared again, walking towards me from the kitchen. This time I faced her and went to meet her, and at once she disappeared. She was friendly and quite unalarming. I could never see her face distinctly, but I had the impression that she was smiling faintly. I saw her once more, as the light was beginning to fade, about half past eight in the evening. She was once more leaning with folded arms in the kitchen doorway, watching me: I took no notice, and the next time I looked up, she was gone. I never saw her again, but I remember very clearly her tall figure and her way of moving, though I cannot recall having seen her face. I did not consider all this very important, and in any case we were then so busy and had so few opportunities of speaking privately with Bapak that I did not tell him about the blue woman till a month or six weeks later. When he heard the story, he asked: 'Why did you not tell Bapak before?'"

Ibu and Ismana had been present at her talk with Bapak, and all three had shown unusual interest in what she had to say. Ibu asked: "How was her hair done?" Elizabeth described with a gesture, and Ibu nodded saying: "Yes; that is quite right!" Bapak then gave an explanation of the occurrence, saying that the 'Woman in Blue' was the true wife of Mr. Bennett. She would enter into Elizabeth, and their souls would be united. When the time came, Mr. Bennett would marry Elizabeth and she would bear him children who would be true servants of God. When Elizabeth had replied: "But Mr. Bennett is already married, and he is united with his wife," Bapak had given her an enlightening account of the true relationship between man and woman. He had said that the mutual completion of the male and female natures can be realized between more than two souls. The work that Mr. Bennett still had to do in the world required that he should have a companion beside him, and Elizabeth was destined to be that companion.

Elizabeth had spoken to no one about this conversation, but now felt free to do so. We had long been aware that we were closely linked both in our earthly lives and in our spiritual hopes. When she had finished telling me the story, and had answered some questions I put to her about the 'Woman in Blue', I pointed out that what Bapak had said agreed exactly with what Sheikh Abdullah Daghestani had said to both of us three years earlier.

The 'Woman in Blue' has remained a mystery, but I was convinced that there was some element of truth in what Bapak had said, for Elizabeth had changed more profoundly since Subud than anyone else I knew. There was matter here to astound the psychologist. The Elizabeth I had known for fourteen years was still there, but there had been an unmistakable enrichment of quality. Where she had been reserved and unapproachable, making few friends, she now showed a deep insight into people, and could win their confidence so that the most varied characters would seek her out at the Lodge, and ask for help with their problems. She kept her incisive sense of humour, but no longer wounded. The change reflected itself in her children, who, formerly rough and unruly, now became gentle, self-possessed and wise beyond their years.

I realized that I not only admired her, but loved her in a way that was quite new to me. I had never before wished for the life of a family. Indeed, it had not occurred to me that I might find satisfaction in having a wife and children round me. I had never even wished to have a home of my own. In nearly forty years of married life, I had scarcely known what it meant to have a private life. I had travelled, moved from house to house, and when finally we settled at Coombe Springs, it was not to make a home but a centre for my work.

Now, to my astonishment, I found myself at the age of sixty-one wishing for the kind of life that a young man might look for at twenty-one. Elizabeth exactly fitted the picture, and I cannot tell which was cause and which effect: whether my love for her made family life attractive or the need for family life drew me towards her. Anyhow, we were married on 27th October, three days before her fortieth birthday. Between her and my late wife was a difference in age of forty-three years. Perhaps this contributed to my sense of rejuvenation, but it seems to me that the change lay deeper. I was becoming aware of the real meaning of harmony. I had long been convinced that nothing can maintain itself in isolation, and that the bonds that unite beings of different kinds are more important than the barriers that separate them. But the conviction that a proposition is true can fall far short of that immediate certainty that comes from its verification in our own experience. I disliked my own character; my own actions distressed me, but I was powerless to change them. I had struggled, had gained much and learned more, but the underlying character was unchanged. Now at last I was aware that, even beyond the 'character', a new self had been born.

Elizabeth Bennett at Coombe Springs, 1965

I suppose that the greatest test of our true condition is our attitude to fear. I had always been deeply afraid, because I was not living in my true self. It seems to me that this fear is almost universal among men and women, though usually hidden from their waking consciousness. We are afraid because we do not really live, and our fear is of having our unlivingness exposed to ourselves and to others. 'See, he has no clothes on,' is the denunciation that the Emperor in each of us dreads to hear from the innocent child - a child that is within us also.

Now, at length, I woke up to find that I was no longer quite naked. I had been the mere simulacrum of a man, and now I could be sure that, behind the false appearance, the real man, albeit still young and inexperienced, was taking his rightful place. Therefore I was ready and able to live with a wife as a husband and a father.

I had written in *The Dramatic Universe* about multi-term systems; about the progressive deepening of harmony as it develops from two to three, from three to four interdependent terms. I was now beginning to climb the ladder of harmony in my own experience. Elizabeth and I were quickly aware that, in a real sense, we shared one human soul. And yet we remained completely ourselves; a man and a woman as different as only a man and a woman can be.

In the language of Sufism, the condition of union of man and woman is called the Beit-ul-Muharrem, or the Secret Dwelling. Pak Subuh had often spoken of it, and described it as the first heaven which the human soul can enter. His attitude to marriage, as a most sacred state destined for man from his very conception, made a deep impression on us. It was not until my marriage with Elizabeth that I became aware of what the union of man and woman could mean. In a strange and wonderful way the perfect harmony that we recognized in ourselves did not separate me from my dead wife. On the contrary, I was certain that she shared with us the same Secret Dwelling. I saw that, though the harmony of man and woman is that of the dyad or two-term system, it does not lead to separateness or isolation. As our relationship grew closer, we felt ourselves more and more drawn towards others.

By this time, interest in Subud had spread all over the world. People in at least fifty countries had expressed the wish to receive the contact, and most of them wanted to see Bapak in person. The travelling expenses were obviously going to be far too heavy for us in England to bear. No other country except the United States could do even as much as we could. A small but active group had been started in New York. When I asked them for support they responded generously, but urged me to come myself to New York with Elizabeth, in order to prepare the ground.

The journey plans took shape. Pak Subuh went first to Singapore, Hong Kong and Japan, and then was to go by way of Australia and New Zealand to Mexico, where we would meet him. Elizabeth and I sailed on the Queen Elizabeth with two good friends, Pat Terry-Thomas and Karl Schaffer, both of whom in quite different ways were witnesses to the authenticity of Subud. Pat had been opened in June 1957. In the midst of the prevailing chaos, she had come to hear me speak of something the very name of which she had not heard before. By mistake, she was sent into the dining-room, where Ibu was opening fifteen or more women. She was given no explanation whatever, but was told: "Close your eyes.

There is only one God. Do what you like." She had been aware of a change of inner state, which was all the more convincing in that she had no idea what it was all about. Since then, two years had passed. She had persisted in the *latihan* through many vicissitudes, and had reached a point where she could no longer doubt its value for herself and others.

In March 1958, Karl Schaffer had written to me from Athens in a state of despair about himself. He had come to live at Coombe, and between October and February passed through a prolonged religious crisis. I had recognized his self-loathing as a condition that I knew only too well. He believed himself to be irretrievably lost and rejected by God. As often happens in such a state, his self-condemnation knew no limits. He was the arch-sinner; the cause of all the suffering in the world, condemned to eternal damnation. I took upon myself to sustain him through his crisis. Almost every day, sometimes several times a day, and even in the middle of the night, he would come to the Lodge, where Elizabeth and I lived after our marriage, and announce that he was irredeemably damned. I would read to him passages from Leo Tolstoi or John Bunyan; from the Dark Night of the Soul of St. John of the Cross, and from others who had passed through a similar crisis, assuring him that it was a purgative experience and not a state of damnation. He would go away comforted, only to return a few hours later, saying that I was surely mistaken and could not know how unforgivably he had sinned.

All this was happening at a time when I was enjoying such happiness as I had never before known in my life. Elizabeth, the two boys and I were living in perfect harmony. Our understanding was so complete that, again and again, I would have a thought and Elizabeth would speak of it before I opened my mouth. We could not believe that such happiness could be shared by two human beings. The effect upon us of Karl's anguish can be pictured. We remembered how we had suffered in Paris with Gurdjieff, and all the bitter disillusionments of our own gradual self-revelation. No trouble was too great to help someone who was still in the Slough of Despond, and we grew to love Karl as a brother.

When we set out for America he was much better, but the crisis had not passed. I knew that I was taking a risk, but I was certain that all would be well. He did in fact emerge from the dark night on the day before we berthed. During our stay in America, and ever since, he has been a tower of strength to Subud. After three strenuous weeks in New York, with visits to Montreal and Washington, giving lectures, opening men and women day after day, hearing of all the troubles and anxieties through which people were passing, Elizabeth, Pat and I went to Mexico on 9th March. Karl went to Florida, where there was an insistent demand for Subud.

The arrival of Subud had been well prepared by Stella Kent, a former student of Dr. Maurice Nicoll, and there was relatively little for me to do, except to give one or two lectures. I could not lecture in Spanish, but I could understand enough to verify the translation. By the time Pak Subuh arrived on 26th March, about fifty men and women had been opened. He brought with him Ibu, his eldest daughter, Mrs. Rochanawati Wirjohudojo, and as helpers Dr. and Mrs. Anwar. All went well, and the party left for South America on 31st March. So far as I personally was concerned, the strongest impression was made on me by an experience on Good Friday. I went to do the *latihan* with a man in a state of deep distress. Whether or not his presence was relevant I cannot say. In the midst of the *latihan* I became aware of Jesus on the Cross and was raised up and entered into His body, and looked through His eyes upon the maddened or uncomprehending crowd below. I became aware of the dreadful stench and of swarms of flies over the Body. Everything in me was outraged and disgusted. There was no mercy anywhere; nothing clean. And I knew that Jesus was aware of it all and infinitely more: of all human uncomprehendingness stretching away and away in time and place. I was aware also of the immensity of the love that could see all and forgive all. I noticed that my arms had been raised, and I could feel that I was involved in the Crucifixion. Then I fell into a kind of unconsciousness in which everything became remote, and out of the darkness a brilliant light emerged, growing brighter and more and more glorious. In this radiance I was aware of the Other Nature of Christ; the glorious Divine Nature, untouched by anything that exists. Gradually the radiance rose higher and higher above me, and I was left behind. I became myself again, wondering what might be the meaning of what I had lived through.

When the *latihan* was finished, I felt myself as weak as if I were about to die. I could not bear the presence of others, and went away and hid until my usual condition returned. As I sat in solitude, I understood that I must learn to live with the reality of the Christian beliefs, and to accept that there is here a mystery that the mind of man never can and never will penetrate.

While we were in Mexico together, Pak Subuh gave a talk to the group of helpers there that clarified one of the most difficult features of Subud. He was asked why he denied that he was a healer or Subud a way of healing. In reply he said: "There are many powers latent in man that can be developed by ascetic practices. These include the power of knowing the future, of telling people's thoughts, and also the power of healing. When a man develops such a power by his own efforts, he is able to use it as he wishes, like any of the ordinary powers that he can acquire by mental or physical training. In Subud it is quite otherwise. The powers that come to us are bestowed by God, and God can also withdraw them. If Bapak receives guidance and can show other people the way, it is not because Bapak has learned much or acquired supernormal powers. No, it is only because Bapak is wholly submissive to God's Will. If it is God's Will that someone should be healed, Bapak can be the means, but he cannot heal from himself. Therefore Bapak cannot be called a healer; only God is the healer. Nor is Subud a method of healing; it is only a method of surrendering one's own will to the Will of God. If Bapak asks a question and it is God's

Will, he receives the answer, even if the matter is quite outside Bapak's possible knowledge. But if it is not God's Will, Bapak is helpless; he can do nothing of himself. That is the difference between the way of self-development and the way of submission to the Will of God."

This explanation was deeply satisfying to me. I have often quoted it to those who suggest that Subud is a kind of magic, by which people can hope to acquire occult powers. It is also an answer to the assertion that Pak Subuh claims infallibility for his own utterances, or the possession of powers not given to ordinary men.

Several interesting people came to visit Pak Subuh in New York. Among them were Aldous Huxley and his Italian wife. I had first met Aldous in the thirties, when he and Gerald Heard used to come regularly to Ouspensky's meetings in Colet Gardens, say nothing, and go away. He had entered himself as a Subud probationer in Los Angeles, and was on a short visit to the East.

He put three questions to Bapak: "Who are you? Are you a prophet, or an Incarnation?" Bapak had replied that he made no such claim. He was one who showed the way. He had opened a door which people could go through if they wished. "But," said Aldous, "you cannot divest yourself of your own position. You are the founder of Subud, and its spiritual leader. How can your followers help being dependent on you?" "No, Bapak is not a leader. He does not go in front. At first people may misunderstand and think that Bapak will lead them. But later, if they practise the *latihan* sincerely, they learn that God alone is their leader and guide, and they do not depend upon Bapak." "Even if you are not their leader, you are at least the teacher. They must learn from you and to that extent be dependent on you." "No; there is no teaching in Subud and therefore no teacher. Bapak may give explanations, but they are provisional only. As time goes on, each one gains his own understanding, and no longer needs explanations." Aldous was clearly not fully satisfied, but said: "It would be wonderful if it could only be true. This world needs more than anything else people who can make their own independent judgments."

The Huxleys then put questions about the position of children, saying that if there was any hope for mankind, it must be in the new generations, still unspoiled by our mishandling of education. Bapak replied at length, explaining that children could not be helped directly, but only through their parents. Once again, I saw that the Huxleys were favourably impressed but not convinced. Aldous was opened the same day, and I was sure that he had really received the contact. But I was sad to see that the merciless pressure of his commitments was going to prevent him from practising the *latihan* regularly. As I was driving him back to his hotel, I said: "This is something that can be tested only by trying. There can be no evidence for or against the value of an inward spiritual action except one's own experience." He agreed, but did not commit himself. I said no more, fearing that perhaps I had already said too much.

While in Mexico, I received a letter from Father Bescond, a monk in the Benedictine monastery of St. Wandrille in France. Father Bescond had read my book on Subud, and wrote that he and other monks of his monastery would like to meet Pak Subuh. Realizing that the Subud experience could not be communicated in words, they wished to make trial of it for themselves. This letter, which was forwarded to me in Mexico, interested Pak Subuh more than any other. He said that he could not go, but that I should try to do so. I went in June 1959, and spent about seven days in the monastery. I was invited to speak about Subud to several of the monks, who put searching questions. It transpired that several statements made in my book on Subud were unacceptable from the Catholic standpoint. I pleaded ignorance, and the haste with which the book had been written. In the outcome, three of the fathers asked for the contact. They made it clear, in doing so, that their action in no way engaged the Magistracy of the Catholic Church which had not yet taken cognizance of Subud. They themselves were making an experiment which, I assured them, they were free at any time to abandon.

To share the *latihan* with men seeking only to do the Will of God, and untroubled by material cares that beset worldly men, was an immense happiness. During my stay in the monastery, I was aware, for the second time in my life, of the state of Love of God. I had known only too well that, although I believed in God and was obedient to His Will, I had never been able to love God. I ascribed this to my determination to keep free from anthropomorphism; that is, from picturing God as a Superman. It seemed easy enough to love an image, and this, no doubt, could be an immense help and comfort to those who were not assailed by intellectual scruples. But I was convinced that God is the Supreme Will that is beyond individuality, even in its purest and most perfect form. God was not for me the Absolute of the philosophers, nor the Brahman of the Vedanta. I was always on the watch to put away any tendencies I might find in myself either towards Pantheism or towards Monism. But if I were not to fall into the naive anthropomorphism of common religious beliefs, I must hold on to the notion of God as pure Will - Source of all Harmony. It seemed impossible for me to love a Will that I could never hope to comprehend.

Now the marvel had happened. I was aware that the Love of God could be experienced without any image or thought. To love God means to participate in God's Love. The awareness was delicate and fleeting. It was a ray of hope and not an attainment.

The true nature of harmony is to be neither active nor passive, but in a third state which embraces such diverse qualities as Love, Freedom and Order, Reconciliation and Truth. This third state is so unfamiliar to our modern thought that our languages lack a word for it. I recognized it in Pak Subuh's references to the Roh Illofi, or the Spirit of Reconciliation. I had known it as the Tao of the Chinese, as Sattva of the Hindus, as the Harmony of the Greeks, as the Holy Spirit of God of the Old and New Testaments, and as the Zat Ullah, the Divine Essence of Islam. All my life I had sought for this Third State. The need to understand and experience it lay at the very root of Gurdjieff's teaching, and all his exercises were directed towards its attainment. The qualities associated with the third state, in its various combinations with the active and passive conditions, had been one of my chief studies for years.

One of the main themes of my *The Dramatic Universe* is the distinction between Self-hood and Individuality. I had now complete and unshakeable evidence in my own experience that two selves could be combined with a single individuality. By Individuality, I understand a single undivided will that is independent of time and place. I had recognized my own Individuality in the twinkling of an eye in the restaurant car on the way to Paris. I had known it again when I could live through the days of purgative anguish in 1957, and yet remain outwardly unchanged. It was the bond that kept me in contact with my wife through death. Now I was aware that my Individuality had acquired its own vessel, and that within that vessel, Elizabeth and I could live forever as one. But the marvel was that this oneness had in it no exclusion. My

Polly was also there, and others too could enter. In that place, there was a single will. It was not 'my own' will and yet it was 'my' will. Those who have known the subordination of Self to Individuality can recognize what I mean.

For two thousand five hundred years mankind has held what could be called the 'atomic' theory of personality. We regard the soul, or self, if we believe in it at all, as something indivisible and permanent just as nineteenth century scientists used to regard the atoms of chemistry. Subud not only splits the psychic atom, but builds it up again into more complex forms. Just as the greatest source of physical energy known to man is derived from the 'fusion' of atomic nuclei, so we are finding that an immense spiritual power is generated by the 'fusion' of selves. The saying of Christ: "Where two or three are gathered together in My Name, I am among you", has acquired a concrete significance that was impossible so long as the two or three souls were conceived as separate atoms.

By demonstrating in our direct experience that the isolation of human selves is not due to an inherent atomism, but to the closing of the doors of perception, the *latihan* had opened the way to a new understanding of human destiny. We are moving slowly away from psychic and social atomism towards true human society. But this process will be painful as well as slow, for it will oblige us to abandon many notions built upon the assumption that the soul or self of man is atomic; that is, permanent and therefore immortal; self-sufficient and therefore God-like. Humanity of the future will live by values, and will search for realities, which we in our immaturity may vaguely feel but certainly cannot express.

Pak Subuh kept me very busy. He gave many talks which I had to translate; in Paris, in Wolfsburg, in Munich, Vienna, Geneva, Nice and finally in Athens. During these weeks I passed through an inner crisis different from those that had gone before. Revolt convulsed me. I wished to see Coombe Springs closed down and sold. I wanted to destroy all that I had written. While all these emotions were raging in me, I continued to act and even to think just as usual. It was as if a wild animal, mortally wounded, was lashing about in the depth of my soul, but my outer self was untouched by its agonies. I could not understand what it all meant, until, on 4th January, I was sitting next to Pak Subuh in the plane from Nice to Rome. I told him what I had been feeling. He said: "Yes. Bapak has been watching. It is true that you have a wounded animal in you. It is a very big animal." He paused, to let what he was about to say make the more impression. "It is an elephant. This is the last animal that must die in your soul. But you need not fear, for the soul of God's Messenger is already within you and will always guide and direct you in the future."

These words came to me as a revelation. I saw only too clearly the 'elephant' in myself; that is, the character that demands to be acknowledged as the lord of the beasts, that never forgets, and when angered does not destroy life but material things. By the time we reached Athens, the crisis was over. The elephant was not dead, but I was sure that it had been tamed. If this were true, it would mean that I should be free from the impulse to take upon myself, in season and out of season, every kind of burden, and also from the 'lord of the beasts' picture that I had always had and wished to eradicate.

While we were in Athens, I was drawn closer to Bapak and his daughter, Rochanawati, than ever before. She had always rather daunted me, with her combination of imperious exigence and undoubted sensitivity and clairvoyant powers. She was the mother of five children, whom we had seen in Djakarta, and at least two of whom were themselves uncannily percipient.

One day, in Athens, I had to drive Rochanawati to a women's *latihan*, Ibu being too tired to go. She spoke to me about myself, saying that she was very happy to have seen a great change in me since we had left London: "Now I see that all the time Mr. Bennett is worshipping God." Then she added unexpectedly: "For Mr. Bennett it is very bad to drink alcohol. It shortens his life. Mr. Bennett must not die young, because he is needed on the earth. So it will be better if he does not drink alcohol."

I was a little surprised at this, for since we had started the *latihan*, all of us, including myself, had found that we could not drink much wine, and spirits not at all. I only report this incident to illustrate the kind of advice we were given.

Soon after my return from Athens, I went again to the Benedictine monastery. This time, I felt the need to participate as fully as possible in the devotional exercises of the monks. Matins and Lauds at 5.20 a.m. last for an hour and a half or more, and the exercises end with Compline at 8.30 p.m. I felt truly at home. The benevolence of the Very Reverend Father Abbot and the kindliness of all the monks had become a treasure in my life. The monks who had been opened had practised the *latihan* faithfully and regularly since my last visit, and I was aware of the change it had worked in them. Our modern intellectual hypertrophy has penetrated into the monastic life. Even monks tend to think too much, and so to close the channel that leads to the deeper secret consciousness where worship of God is unmediated. The *latihan*, even if regarded as no more than a natural exercise for training ourselves in the attainment of the 'third state', must surely be of immense value to anyone who is called to the contemplative life.

One of the Fathers drew my attention to the analogy of the *latihan* state with diffuse contemplation, as it is described by the great Spanish mystics, especially St. John of the Cross. The marvel is that in former times contemplation was regarded as the fruit of long austerities and meditations, whereas through the practice of Subud it can be reached in the conditions of our ordinary life. The three stages of the mystic path: Purgation, Illumination and Union, had already become for me a reality, though I had only known the state of Union for brief moments.

During my stay in the monastery, I received several illuminating experiences in the *latihan*. Once I heard a voice within me saying: "Surrender to the Will of God is the foundation of all religion." Then I became aware of the Presence of Jesus, and saw that He is the manifestation of the Love of God. The thought entered my mind: "Then Christianity is the one true religion." At the same moment, I found myself intoning the opening chapter of the Koran: "*El hamd ul IllahRabb-el-alemeen er Rahman er Rahim*: Glory to God the Lord of the Worlds, the Compassionate, the Merciful." Then the same voice said: "It is my Will that my Church and Islam should be united." I said in astonishment: "Who can accomplish such a task?" and the reply came: "Mary." Soon after, the *latihan* ended.

This locution amazed me. Could I have invented it? I had never been able to understand the role of the Blessed Virgin. I had read ecclesiastical history and knew how the great doctors of the Church, such as St. Thomas Aquinas, had resisted the popular demand for the extension of the cult of the Theotokos. Nothing could have been more remote from my entire way of thinking than to associate the Blessed Virgin with a movement to bring together Christianity and Islam.

I told the reverend Fathers what I had experienced. The eldest of them, a most saintly man whose kindness had touched me deeply, said that he found nothing strange in the assertion that the Blessed Virgin should undertake to unite all who worship God in purity of heart. I have since come to understand the cosmic significance of the Marial presence.

At a later visit, I received an illumination concerning the 'Will of God'. For years I had wrestled with the problem: 'I cannot know God's Will. How can I submit to God, if I have no possibility of knowing what is required of me?' One day in the *latihan* with the monks, the words of Deuteronomy came to me: 'The Lord our God is one Lord; and thou shalt love the Lord thy God with all thine heart and with all thy soul and with all thy might. And these words which I command thee this day shall be in thine heart.' Then the words of Leviticus: 'Thou shalt love thy neighbour as thyself; I am the Lord.' As the words were repeated within me, I remembered how they were quoted with approval by Jesus and repeated again in the Koran. They were and are the Will of God for me and for each of us.

All these notions welded themselves together in my consciousness. I was overwhelmed with love. The love I felt towards Elizabeth transformed itself into a love of all humanity. Then everything human and personal vanished. I was aware that God's Love and my love were one and the same. I stood trembling, taking in deep breaths like sighs. I could no longer bear the love that flowed through and through me, and I fell to the ground. As I lay prostrate, I became aware that something more was being shown to me. There were no words, so I must interpret as well as I can. The effect was that I must be satisfied at present to know the Will of God in general. I was not yet ready to know it in any particular instance. But later, I would be shown more; very much more. For the time being, I must be satisfied.

These are lame words; they cannot convey the assurance that a promise had been made to me that would surely be kept. If I for my part could achieve the love of my neighbour, then I would be received into the Love of God.

27: SERVICE AND SACRIFICE

Fifteen years have passed since I wrote the first edition of Witness. Now in my seventy-seventh year I can look back with some degree of impartiality upon the man who was writing it. I can see my life as a succession of 'final revelations' all of which have carried me a step forward, but each of which has proved to be a false crest from which I have seen new peaks to climb. Many years ago, in a moment of disillusion, I said to Elizabeth: "All my geese are the Archangel Gabriel." I tend to look at what might be rather than what is and to convince myself that I am seeing a present reality. Fifty years ago, Ouspensky expressed the same idea differently when he said I reminded him of a Chinese fable in which the hero insisted on living in a graveyard because he believed that the dead were alive.

One of Gurdjieff's subtle insights into human nature was his doctrine of 'chief feature'. Each of us has a central characteristic that colours all our responses to the world process. It is our blind spot and although we may recognize its manifestations, we do not see where they originate. So long as it works in us mechanically or unconsciously, it is our chief weakness, but when we can separate from it and observe its action critically, it becomes our chief asset. I have recently studied the working of the feature in nearly a hundred students and I am more than ever convinced that it is the key to understanding some of the strangest characteristics of the human psyche.

As I look back to 1961, I can see how I persisted in believing that Pak Subuh was 'the Archangel Gabriel', long after I should have understood that Subud was far more limited in its action than he had led us to believe. I could not help seeing that I myself was losing my grip. Coombe Springs was in disorder. I had abdicated its direction and handed it over to others in order to devote myself to writing the final volume of *The Dramatic Universe*. I was not properly involved in the life at Coombe Springs nor was I free from it. There were constant dissensions, financial crises, distractions of visitors from all over the world, all of which took too much of my time to allow me to write in peace.

By the autumn of 1960, the realization came to me that I had ceased to work on myself and had relied upon the *latihan* to do what I should be doing by my own effort. Without telling anyone, I resumed the discipline and the exercises I had learned from Gurdjieff and almost at once I found that my state changed for the better. Some of my old friends and pupils came and told me that they felt that something was wrong and described symptoms similar to my own. I suggested that we should quietly resume our early morning exercises and especially set ourselves 'will tasks' that would require effort and sacrifice.

When we exchanged our observations, we became convinced that the *latihan*, though excellent as a means of opening the heart, did nothing for the will and that we must find a way to restore the balance. Within a few months forty or fifty were again working together as we had done before Subud came. When this became known to the Subud Brotherhood in London, many were terribly shocked and upset. Letters were sent to Pak Subuh telling him that I was breaking all the rules of Subud. Much 'testing' was undertaken and the results almost invariably confirmed that I had lost my way or even fallen 'under Satanic influences'. As had happened so often before in my life, events were misreported, rumours exaggerated, until Pak Subuh in Indonesia was led to believe that I was setting myself up as the voice of Subud in the West and defying his authority. Once again, I found myself cut off from old friends and compelled to ask myself if I were sunk in my own self-will or awakened to a new understanding.

I could not doubt that the *latihan* had worked wonders for me and for Elizabeth. I could see many others who had been changed for the better. We were freer, more open and above all more hopeful than we had been before Subud came. I could see clearly the harm done by the unnecessary pessimism and restrictiveness of the Gurdjieff groups. I could no longer believe in the pessimist's creed as formulated by F.H. Bradley in the Preface to Appearance and Reality: "When everything is rotten, it is a man's business to cry stinking fish", nor could I interpret Gurdjieff as many were doing in terms of Bradley's definition of the optimist who says: "This is the best of all possible worlds and everything in it is a necessary evil."

It was impossible to doubt that I had changed and that I could communicate with a source of wisdom that was within myself but beyond my consciousness. The cruel turn of Fate was that I saw myself obliged to break away from the very thing that had done so much for me. It was as clear as day to me that the 'testing' which was obsessing the Subud groups in London and indeed all over the world, was largely self-de-ception and wishful thinking. I had seen something of the development of the 'Oxford Group', initiated by Dr. Buchmann, which later became Moral Rearmament, and recognized the perils which surround the belief in 'guidance from the inner voice'. I was in the absurd position of rejecting in others what I had come to rely upon in myself. I was convinced that I could communicate with my own conscience, but not convinced when others told me that they could receive messages and guidance direct from God.

After many months of agonized self-questioning, I discovered the solution to the paradox. Whenever I deliberately 'tested', that is put myself quite passively into the *latihan* and asked specific questions, I got ambiguous answers or no answer at all. But if I allowed the slightest wish for a particular answer to colour my asking, that answer came, and did so often in a subtle and indirect way that made self-deception very easy. On the other hand, if I did not ask at all but prayed for guidance, the indication of what I should be doing came unexpectedly and unpredictably without the *latihan* and especially when I was not thinking about it. These indications were so sensible and usually so different from what I myself wanted to do or thought of doing, that I could not doubt their veracity. I tentatively formulated the following criteria for accepting the promptings of the 'inner voice':

1. They must not be contrary to common sense.

2. They must be surprising or at least unexpected.

3. They must be unprompted and unsolicited except in very general terms of 'asking for help'.

It also became evident to me that if one is to take the guidance of Conscience seriously, one must be prepared to follow it wherever it may lead. It is not an imperative command, but a 'still, small voice' that is easily silenced. It does not strive nor cry, but if we trust it, it begins to trust us and to come more and more into the open - that is into our mental awareness.

A remarkable instance occurred in January 1961. One day in January, when I was sitting in the Djamichunatra doing my morning exercise with fifteen or twenty of the group then living in the house, I heard the voice of the Shivapuri Baba saying to me "come soon or it will be too late." I had never seen him nor had I thought much about him during the twenty years since I first heard of him from Professor Ratnasuriya, a Ceylonese Buddhist who had become a devoted pupil of Ouspensky. His widow, Vajira, after his sudden death in 1950, had lived with us for a year at Coombe Springs. I knew that he was a great sage, over 130 years old, who lived in the Shivapuri hills below the Himalayas in Nepal. I had recently heard from Hugh Ripman, another pupil of Ouspensky, that the Shivapuri Baba was then living in Nepal near Katmandu and could be visited, but I did not seriously think I could make the journey, nor felt any particular urge to do so. Thus, the 'invitation' that came to me was both unexpected and unsolicited. On reflection, I saw that it made sense. I needed to consult someone who was both wise and impartial, and the

Shivapuri Baba was likely to be both.

A series of improbable coincidences made the journey possible and with Elizabeth and our close friend, Pat Terry-Thomas, I went to Katmandu during the Easter holiday in 1961. I have described this, and the second visit I made in 1962, in my book, *Long Pilgrimage.* The Shivapuri Baba himself suggested that I should write about his teachings, and his chief follower, Thakur Lal Manandhar, undertook to provide his own notes. I can see now that the task of writing about him was necessary for me, for it opened my mind again to Indian spirituality that I had neglected for nearly forty years since I studied Sanskrit with Dr. Kanhere. The Shivapuri Baba was universal. He had gone beyond the distinction of teachings and religions and had attained liberation from the conditions of personal existence, but he was a Yogi and took the *Bhagavad Gita* as his bible. To be with him was to be given the assurance that liberation is possible. Incidentally, he confirmed - at my second visit in 1962 - my conviction that although 'submission' in the Subud sense is needed, it will not work without self-discipline. Indeed, his entire teaching of Right Living can be summed up as the three-fold discipline of body, mind and spirit. Brief though my contacts with him were, the Shivapuri Baba was a decisive influence in my development. I can see, however, that the brevity of the encounter was a safeguard against my tendency to plunge unreservedly into an activity that offers a high potential for achievement.

The Shivapuri Baba planted in my mind the seeds of belief that I might be destined for reaching 'here in this very life', as the Buddha put it, the transformation of being that Gurdjieff had promised me in 1949 when he said: "Do not be satisfied with Paradise, but seek only to come to the Sun Absolute." For the first time, this audacious quest appeared to be something more than a distant vision.

As I returned home through Turkey and climbed again to the gallery of St. Sophia where, in 1919, I had first witnessed the Night of Power, I saw how my confidence had been shattered by successive blows. One after another of my props had been removed and I was once again face to face with my secret world. My repeated mistakes and misjudgments rose before my inner vision and I could see the wretched combination of weakness and arrogance, false humility and inward stubbornness that had led me from one disaster to another. But I could also see a sure guiding hand. Each disaster had been the death of part of myself, but in every case, it had been followed by resurrection. Outwardly my life had been a recurrence of promises unfulfilled; inwardly it had been a step-by-step liberation from a false belief in the outer and a growing confidence in the inner. The Shivapuri Baba had tipped the balance in my favour.

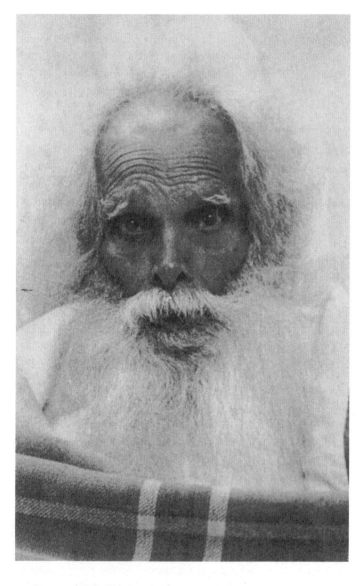

Shri Govindananda Bharati, known as the Shivapuri Baba, last day, Kathmandu, 1963

In one of my private talks with him, I asked about my growing conviction that I should join the Catholic Church. He had spoken of religion as the refuge of those whose minds were not strong enough to pursue knowledge of God to the exclusion of all else. So I was unprepared for his immediate assurance that this was the right way for me. I would find, he said, God-realization through Christ. In Chapter 26, I have described my first experience of the Benedictine rule at St. Wandrille. I was very happy to go as often as I could to spend days or even weeks with the monks there, but I was not yet clear as to my vocation.

Soon after my return from Nepal, I went to St. Wandrille and decided to pray for guidance. The sign came as usual in an unexpected but convincing form. One day I was at High Mass, sitting as a guest of the Monastery behind the choir, but in front of the rail at which communion was distributed to the laity. This means that the celebrant had to pass me as he brought the Sacrament. My thoughts were wandering, when I felt a shiver pass through my body. I became completely aware that Christ was coming towards me in the sacrament. I could feel Him go past and felt the deepest reverence and pure joy. As I knelt, I understood beyond doubt that God could be and was present in the host. I saw in a flash how the doctrine of the Real Presence is free from the anthropomorphism that so distressed me in most Christian theology. If God is pure Will, then He can manifest in and through any vehicle. I saw how the second Person of the Trinity must be manifested, and indeed is a person by reason of manifestation. All these and many other understandings poured into my mind, while I felt at the same time joy and gratitude that this should be shown to me. Above all, I was aware of the Love of God as beyond all the limitations of existence - of 'name and form' - in terms of which we think. I was sure that this omnipresent love was able to reach me as the small being kneeling unnoticed in the aisle of the chapel.

From that moment, I began to prepare myself and a few months later I was received into the church by my friend the Father Abbot. A year later my wife and children were received. At first, Elizabeth came in order to share her worship with me. It was not until much later that she also had a personal revelation that convinced her of the Real Presence and enabled her to accept much that she could not understand of the church and its dogmas. In spite of my belief in the validity of the sacraments of the Roman Church, and therefore of the validity of the Apostolic Succession, I could not help seeing how much human speculation and even human fantasy had entered the teaching of the Church. I am well aware how little resemblance the gospel story as we have it in the New Testament corresponds to the reality of the events that took place in Galilee and Jerusalem, and I can see how necessary it is to establish a new understanding of the Incarnation. The Church is equally astray in its conservative and in its modernist wings, nor is the centre any better. The Catholic Church is the custodian of a mystery that it does not understand, but the sacraments and their operation are no less real for that.

The combined effect of my visit to the Shivapuri Baba and my experiences at St. Wandrille was to liberate me from the depression into which I had fallen and to give me fresh hope that I would find the spiritual reality that I had failed to find in Subud. New ideas and new insights were opening for me, and I was resolved to do something with them.

One of the first fruits of my new confidence was the decision to organize a seminar at Coombe Springs for the summer of 1962, in which I would develop my own interpretation of Gurdjieff's psychology. I could see for myself that a great change had occurred. For the first time, I was daring to be myself. Only two years earlier, I had reached what I thought was the end of my search, when I became aware that, through Subud, my material self had died and that I was reborn with a real capacity for compassion and understanding of others. Now, I saw that so far from being the end, I was still a child or at most an adolescent. At the age of 65, I had to 'grow up'.

The seminar was an exciting experience for all who took part in it. I was helped by two old friends, Isabel Turnadge, a Quaker, and John Holland, whom Polly had renamed 'Dick', both of whom were then living at Coombe Springs. They had supported me in the painful extrication from Subud and encouraged me to go forward alone for the fourth or fifth time in my life.

The discussions at the seminar were preserved on that remarkable instrument, the tape recorder. At the time, I used to say that it was one of the very few inventions that seemed entirely beneficial to man. Since then it has been applied for 'bugging' private conversations with deplorable results, once again confirming the infinite stupidity of man. However, the tape recording in this instance allowed us to reconstruct the seminar and, with Isabel Turnadge's help, put it in book form. I sent it to Paul Hodder Williams to enquire if it could be made into a publishable work. To my surprise, he replied a few weeks later that his readers liked it and recommended him to publish it just as it was. It appeared in 1964 as A Spiritual Psychology, was sold out and has been reprinted three or four times. I would probably have continued to develop the psychological techniques and reestablish Coombe Springs as a centre of the Gurdjieff teaching, but for another unexpected development.

In June 1962, as I was preparing for the seminar, I received a letter from Reggie Hoare who had been one of Ouspensky's earliest pupils, having joined his group in 1924 on returning from Turkey. Reggie had shared with me the ups and downs of Ouspensky, Gurdjieff and Subud. He had quietly left Subud in 1960, having refused to involve himself in the dispute that followed the Subud Congress.

With his letter he enclosed a newspaper cutting describing a visit made by the author to a sanctuary in central Asia in which he had found a teaching that was unmistakably of the same origin as much that we had learned from Gurdjieff. This letter prepared the way for the announcement that Reggie, and three or four other old friends and fellow-pupils, had met Idries Shah, who had come to England to seek out followers of Gurdjieff's ideas, with the intention of transmitting to them knowledge and methods that were needed to complete their teaching.

At first, I was wary. I had just decided to go forward on my own and now another 'teacher' had appeared. One or two conversations with Reggie convinced me that I ought at least to see for myself. Elizabeth and I went to dinner with the Hoares to meet Shah, who turned out to be a young man in his early forties. He spoke impeccable English and, but for his beard and some of his gestures, might well have been taken for an English public school type. Our first impressions were unfavourable. He was restless, smoked incessantly, talked too much and seemed too intent on making a good impression. Half way through the evening our attitude completely changed. We recognized that he was not only an unusually gifted man, but that he had the indefinable something that marks the man who has worked seriously upon himself.

For several months, I did not follow up the contact. In the autumn Reggie Hoare persuaded me to see him again, assuring me that he had most thoroughly 'verified his credentials' and was convinced that he had been sent to the West by an esoteric school in Afghanistan, probably the very one which Gurdjieff describes in the last chapter of *Meetings With Remarkable Men*. Reggie attached special significance to what Shah had told him about the Enneagram symbol, and said that Shah had revealed secrets about it that went far beyond what we had heard from Ouspensky. Knowing Reggie to be a very cautious man, trained moreover in assessing information by many years in the Intelligence Service, I accepted his assurances and also his belief that Shah had a very important mission in the West that we ought to help him to accomplish.

This put me in front of a new kind of situation. Shah was not, and did not claim to be, a teacher, but he did claim that he had been sent by his own teacher, and that he had the support of the 'Guardians of the Tradition'. He gave me a document authorising me to make it known to my own pupils and anyone else I thought fit. I reproduce some of the key passages here, with Mr. Shah's permission.

DECLARATION OF THE PEOPLE OF THE TRADITION

(Copyright Octagon Press, 1966 & 1974)

Among all peoples, in all countries, there is a tradition about a secret, hidden, special, superior form of knowledge accessible to man after passing through circumstances of difficulty. This declaration is concerned with that subject. We declare that such knowledge exists; that at the present time and for the people to whom this material is addressed, there is a possibility of its being transmitted. Because this knowledge, and its operation, is of a nature other than that which is expected of knowledge, attempts to find it and make use of it generally fail. It will respond and operate fully only if approached in a certain manner. This is the first of the difficulties encountered in the 'path'. Few people have lifetimes long enough to discover, by trial and error, the necessary conditions of the 'search'. Specialised knowledge and technique are required. Mass endeavor cannot compensate for the incapacity or ignorance of the individual. This knowledge is concentrated, administered and presided over by three kinds of individuals, existing at any given time. They have been called an 'Invisible Hierarchy', because normally they are not in communication or contact with ordinary human beings, certainly not in two-way communication with them. In one sense, the way to the knowledge lies through a 'chain of succession' in which the perception of the ordinary man must have help in attaining a higher contact. Religion, folklore, etc. abound with disguised examples of this process. Many religious, magical, alchemical, psychological and other manifestations in reality form vestigial parts of the science about which we are speaking. Very often subjects which are considered to be 'Ways to Truth' and so on are nothing more or less than the traces of techniques which have been used in the past to attain the link referred to above. One of the great 'difficulties' in this quest for knowledge

of a higher kind is the very existence of, and misemploy-
ment of, these survivals. That which was the chrysalis for
a butterfly (as it were) becomes a prison for the caterpillar
which tries to use it to become a butterfly himself. He does
not generally realize that he has to make his own chrysalis.
Thus we have attachment to the form of rites, beliefs and
personalities which were of specific and high function. This
becomes a 'conditioning': a sentimental one, or an intellectual one. If the true greatness and importance of such institutions, individuals and procedures were in fact realized, instead
of pathetic attempted identifications with the externals
of them, paradoxically the votaries of these superseded
methodologies would then be able to understand the true
beauty, grandeur and greatness of the things which they
think are threatened by remarks such as the present ones.
Man, then, is generally out of alignment with the truth which
he knows in some way to be there. He has to get into alignment
with it. This he can do only by using a formulation of his quest
which is innocent of past associations. Here we have the reason
for the very many past formulations of the Path of Truth.
This is not to say that man must dissipate existing associations
or automatisms in order to build afresh; because now here and
now there is a possibility to slip through the veil of conditioning
to a perception with a part of the mind which is virtually unused.
It is this enterprise upon which we are at present engaged.
Conditions now exist in the community now being addressed in
which a work of this kind can take place. There is no advantage
at this point and level in discussing any 'reason' for the
existence of these conditions. Such discussions become mental
exercises - useless unless accompanied by parallel experience.
It is the task of the custodians of this Tradition to
communicate as best they can, in whatever language is
indicated, with those who may be able to benefit from what
is being said. They are concerned with capacity on the part
of the people addressed, and capacity alone. They have no
special interest in the nominal background, seniority or
superficial psychological tendencies of the people addressed.
If anything is consistent, it is the experience that suitable
candidates may be found in the members of any tradition.
Another of the 'difficulties' of the Path to Truth always has
been that the knowledge of which we are speaking exists in

places and with people who may not be expected to have it. Its appearance is therefore often contrary to expectation. What has been said about 'difficulties' will show that these are always more apparent than real. A difficulty is always great to one who cannot adjust himself to the real facts of a situation. In addition to making an announcement and feeding into certain fields of thought certain ideas, and pointing out some of the factors surrounding this work, the projectors of this declaration have a practical task. This task is to locate individuals who have capacity for obtaining the special knowledge of man which is available; to group them in a special, not haphazard, manner, so that each such group forms a harmonious organism; to do this in the right place at the right time, to provide an external and interior format with which to work, as well as a formulation of 'ideas' suitable to local conditions; to balance theory with practice.

This Declaration was read to the groups at Coombe Springs and in London. After so many years during which they had heard about the Tradition and the 'Inner Circle of Humanity', it was astonishing to learn that here in England was a man who was entitled to speak on behalf of the 'Invisible Hierarchy'. I had seen enough of Shah to know that he was no charlatan or idle boaster, and that he was intensely serious about the task he had been given. He always insisted that he was not acting on his own initiative but on the instructions of his Teacher, who had entrusted him with the mission described in the last paragraph of the Declaration.

It was early in 1963 that I asked myself if I did not have an obligation to put myself at Shah's disposal and do all that I could to help him. At that time I was visiting him in his flat in Notting Hill gate for weekly tête-a-tête meetings that lasted for hours. It is significant that, though thirty years my junior and at that time unknown and with few followers, he seldom visited me. It was I who made the tedious journey from Coombe Springs once a week and it was he who did all the talking. His avowed aim was to 'validate himself', that is, to convince me of the authenticity of his mission and the reality of the force behind him. He referred frequently to the Sufi doctrine of 'Baraka', which I recognized as the same 'Higher Emotional Energy' that Gurdjieff had referred to at the Prieuré in 1923, and that he called Hanbledzoin in Beelzebub's Tales and his conversations at the end of his life.

It seemed to me that I must determine for myself whether Idries Shah was indeed a messenger from the Guardians of the Tradition or

'Hidden Directorate' as I called them in *The Dramatic Universe*. In January 1965, I became convinced, in the unaccountable way that these things happen. One morning as I was praying, I asked to be given clear indication as to whether I should trust Shah completely. As I was driving up to London, the reply came: "For that you must pray together." When I met him, I told him what had happened. He replied: "That is quite right; the truth is revealed only in prayer." This answer satisfied me and I asked no more. Later I noticed that he had not in fact done what I asked: that is that we should pray together, and I asked myself if I had perhaps failed to go through with the indication I had received.

Soon that was forgotten in the growing interest aroused by Shah's unfolding of his plans for reaching people who occupied positions of authority and power and who were already half-consciously aware that the problems of mankind could no longer be solved by economic, political or social action. Such people were touched, he said, by the new forces moving in the world to help mankind to survive the coming crisis. This agreed with my own conclusions that I had expressed in a series of lectures and had given the year before with the title The Spiritual Revolution of Our Time. I could also fully agree with him that people attracted by overtly spiritual or esoteric movements seldom possessed the qualities needed to reach and occupy positions of authority. I also agreed that there were sufficient grounds for believing that throughout the world there were already people occupying important positions, who were capable of looking beyond the limitations of nationality and cultures, and who could see for themselves that the only hope for mankind lies in the intervention of a Higher Source.

As time went on, I saw that Shah was looking to me for a decision-commitment to help him to get his work going on a new and much larger scale. He made it clear that he wanted a place like Coombe Springs and that he needed to reach many more people. I made various suggestions, including that of putting Coombe Springs entirely at his service. He rejected them all and finally began to press me more strongly to decide what I could offer, saying that, "the time is short. The caravan is about to set out. Those who are not ready to join it will be left behind."

I saw that what he wanted was not the use of Coombe Springs, but the property itself; not only access to my pupils, but the right to take under his own wing any that could be useful to him. I also saw that this was an opportunity for me to liberate myself from my attachment to the place. I had lived there - but for one year - since 1941, and I had expected to die there and see my work continued, perhaps by my own sons. I loved the place dearly, and especially the Djamichunatra which was my own inspiration. It was the one monument that I could leave behind me. I could not bear the thought that it might be neglected. Nothing could be harder for me than to walk out and leave it all. The more these feelings grew in me, the more did I become convinced that I must make the sacrifice.

Shah insisted that if we were to give him Coombe Springs, the gift must be absolute, irrevocable and completely voluntary. If I wanted to do it, I, and not he, had to convince my Council and the members of the Institute that it was the right thing to do. By June 1965, my mind was made up. I set about the task. I saw that it would not be difficult. The majority of members were nearly ready to follow me without question. A few revolted and demanded assurances. I was grateful to them, for they obliged me to search my heart to be sure that I was not acting from impulse. That summer we held the last seminar at Coombe Springs. Shah came down and spoke to the students. Without attempting to persuade them or indeed to say anything at all that bore on the subject, he conveyed to them the importance of his mission and created a sense of urgency.

In October we held an Extraordinary General Meeting of Members, to give the Council the power to give away the Institute's most valuable asset. Experts told us that Coombe Springs would be worth more than £100,000 and several of our members argued that we should sell it and, if necessary, give half the money to Shah and keep the rest to buy a place in the country. I was sorely tempted to seek some compromise, but Shah continued to insist that it was all or nothing. Finally the decision was taken and we prepared to move out. Twenty years of occupation of a large house builds up a great accumulation of chattels. We sold what we could and destroyed all that we could not take away and use. We left for Shah all that he might want, including the Djamichunatra with its carpets and furniture.

By this time, he was urging us on, saying that his work would brook no delay. I did not know where to go. One day we heard of a house for sale in Kingston. Elizabeth and I went to see it the same morning, made an offer that was accepted, and got ready to move to 23 Brunswick Road. On 13th January 1966, we celebrated Gurdjieff's birthday with a great feast attended by more than 250 members and friends. For the last time, we gave a demonstration of Gurdjieff's movements in the Djamichunatra. I was deeply divided within myself. I had no positive evidence that Shah would establish a Sufi centre at Coombe Springs; he had insisted that his hands must be perfectly free. As I myself had said at the General Meeting: "Suppose that Shah sells up Coombe Springs and sails back to

Afghanistan with a hundred thousand pounds in his pocket. What is that to us? We are doing the right thing in giving his mission all possible help. To ask for guarantees would be to ruin the spirit of the action." In spite of these brave words, my misgivings remained. Where was my resolve to go ahead on my own? Where was my confidence in my own mission? I had allowed everything to be swamped by the conviction that it was all-important to make a big and decisive sacrifice. I wanted to prove to myself that I was free from attachment to any material situation or to the position I occupied with my pupils. I had done it all, and yet I was not sure if I had done the right thing.

The next few months were hard to bear. No sooner was Shah in possession, than he banned our people from visiting Coombe. He complained vehemently of any delays in vacating. He made me feel unwelcome, so I stopped going there. Some of my pupils, who went to see him to protest at his treatment of me, received short shrift. The only invitation I received was to the 'Midsummer Revels' that lasted two days and two nights and were primarily for the young people whom Shah was then attracting round him. Shah is a man of exquisite manners and delicate sensibilities. His behaviour could be accounted for if it was adopted deliberately to make sure that all bonds with Coombe Springs were severed. I was also well aware that I was not popular with some of his loyal supporters and could not see myself occupying any useful place in his organization. I had done my part, and there was no reason for pushing myself forward. I plunged into the Education Research project which could, if successful, make a very real contribution to the needs of the future. With my usual enthusiasm, I saw our method being used all over the world to transform education from a passive process, in which teacher dominates pupil, to an active self-directed learning available to all.

In 1966, we heard that Shah had decided to sell Coombe Springs. Our first knowledge came from a notice of intention to sell posted on the gates to satisfy the Charity Commissioner and the Department of Education and Science, who had reluctantly agreed to the transfer from our Institute to the Society for Understanding the Foundations of Ideas, i.e. SUFI, that had been set up as a trust and recognized as a charity. We heard several months later that the property had been sold for more than £100,000 ($300,000), to be developed by building twenty-eight luxury houses. Shah and his family moved to Langton House in Kent, a place undoubtedly more suitable for his purpose than Coombe Springs, and I felt no sadness that Coombe was to lose its identity. The only wrench was to see the Djarmichunatra destroyed. Some effort was made to save

Rosemary Rutherford's beautiful stained glass windows, but this proved impossible, and all went for scrap.

All this happened in 1966, at a time when I was fully absorbed in the education project. I had handed my groups over to Shah, who had undertaken to integrate all who were suitable into his own work. Of some three hundred people, about half found a place and the remainder were left in the air. I could do little for them, and this was one reason why I slowly began to work with groups again.

The period from 1960, when I began to withdraw from Subud, to 1967, when I was once again entirely on my own, was of the greatest value to me. I had learned to serve and to sacrifice and I knew that I was free from attachments. It happened about the end of this time that I went on business to America and met Madame de Salzmann in New York. She was very curious about Idries Shah and asked me what I had gained from my contact with him. I replied: "Freedom!" Until then I had always looked for some support - even the realization that I had been given both hope and faith did not set me free to follow my own destiny. By setting myself to do all in my power to further Shah's mission, in which I personally had no place, I had paid the debt I owed for the help I had received from other men. I could now turn myself to pay the debt I owe my Creator.

At that time, I was obsessed with the idea of self-effacement and withdrawal. My seventieth birthday was approaching, and many friends wished to mark it by a collective gift. A large sum of money was subscribed by more than a hundred people, and I was asked what I wanted. In a very boorish and unkind way, I refused everything, insisted that the money should be returned to the donors and said that I did not even want a birthday party. This uncivil behaviour was attributable to my inner turmoil.

In 1921, it had been predicted to me, in the experiences I describe in Chapter 7, that I would not find the true meaning of my life until I was seventy years old. The moment was approaching and I could not see what it could signify. There was no one in the world to whom I could turn for advice, and my inner voice had become silent. I had learned to look at my life in a new way. I saw that two things had profited me most. One was to undergo humiliation and the other was to serve and make sacrifices for a cause that was not my own. Not only had I gained freedom, but I had come to love people whom I could not understand. I was no longer l'enfant au coeur glacé, but I was still a child. Notwithstanding my seventy years, I still did not know the 'sense and purpose of my existence'. I only knew that it would be courting disaster to attempt any more without a clear vision not only of what had to be done, but also the time and place to do it.

28: LIFE BEGINS AT SEVENTY

For ten years, from 1960 to 1970, my outer life was mainly occupied with an attempt to apply what I had learned about human nature to the problems created by the changed tempo of modern life. Throughout the world, education is centuries behind the times. Our universities are mediaeval in origin and mediaeval in outlook. Our schools are only beginning to emerge from the teacher-pupil, rows of benches in a classroom, model that has existed for hundreds of years. We cram all our education into the years of childhood and adolescence, that is, before most people have any idea of what they want to do with their lives. In the majority of professions, what is learned at twenty is out-of-date at forty. The pace of change is accelerating and the need for continuous education throughout life is becoming more and more obvious. But the inertia of the present system, with its vast investment in buildings and people, makes rapid change impossible. More money is spent on education than on any other organized activity of man and we have little to show for it. We are not better people, nor better citizens, than those who receive little or no education. In the 'developed' countries, there is more dissatisfaction, more unhappiness and more downright madmen than in the so-called 'backward' countries. Civilization has ceased to be civilized.

At one time, I would have looked at all this and passed by on the other side, thanking my stars that I had other aims than to 'help mankind'. Now that I was well aware of my own inability to do anything, I saw that this was not the point. The scale of what we do must correspond to our forces, and to attempt more is to live in the dream world where nothing happens anyhow.

Among the many young men and women who came to Coombe Springs between 1957 and 1960 was Tony Hodgson, a research chemist who had devoured the first volume of *The Dramatic Universe* and was ready to try anything. He had been dreadfully injured in a climbing accident in Norway, and this had turned his mind to the question of the 'sense and purpose of our existence'. He moved to London and brought together a group named Integral Science Education Research Group - ISERG - which set itself to apply the integral ideas of *The Dramatic Universe* to the reform of science teaching. I saw great promise in this undertaking.

By chance, I was invited to serve on a committee of the Middlesex County Council with the intriguing terms of reference: "How to think?"

The object was to discover why young engineers, released by their employers to study for a year at technical colleges, were getting so little benefit. ISERG did some research and discovered that the technical courses were all closed-ended, that is, focused on predetermined precise operations and results. Real engineering problems are open-ended and require a totally different approach from that then being taught in schools. We tried the experiment of introducing a short deconditioning course at the end of the regular studies, and the first results were spectacular. The students, mostly of fairly low educational standard, suddenly 'saw what it was all about'.

Unfortunately the deconditioning required skilled and dedicated tutors, able to hold the balance between control and chaos required for deconditioning. Such tutors were unobtainable for, if they possessed the required qualities, they were needed for much more advanced work. Was it possible to mechanize the process; to use a computer, for example? By asking this question we became involved in a research that led to the invention, by our friend Bob Arbon of G.E.C, of a new kind of teaching machine, which we called the Systemaster. Karl Schaffer, whom I have already mentioned in connection with Subud, brought off a remarkable coup in getting the Systemaster exhibited at the Annual Convention of the American Management Association in New York in 1965. The lively interest aroused enabled us to get the support of the English General Electric Company. There is nothing unusual about the story of the development, which went through the usual vicissitudes of any such invention. By 1968, we had set up an educational trust, Centre for Structural Communication, and set about launching our technique. We had a useful medium in Systematics, the journal of our Institute, already well-established in academic circles.

Finding that it would take a long time to penetrate into the educational establishment, we turned our attention to industry. In 1969, we were able to launch a company, Structural Communication Systems Limited (S.C.S.), well supported by leading financial interests in the city of London. I found myself more and more involved in finance, adminis-tration and selling. It was a strange experience just twenty-five years since I had started with Delanium and Powell Duffryn. Once again, I could give no time to writing, and I lost touch with my groups. The only contact was with those working with me at S.C.S. and a few others living in Kingston, who took to coming regularly to our house early in the morning to exercise together and to receive a little instruction from me in the methods of the work. This group was the saving grace for all of us. I began to see that this was my real work and not industry and finance.

The company could perform a useful social service, but I was not the right man to administer it. My weaknesses, particularly my inability to say 'No', were still there and I could do little to overcome them.

In 1968, a new influence had entered my life. My first meeting with Hasan Shushud was in 1962, when I visited Turkey with Elizabeth and Pat Terry-Thomas. I was urged by a Turkish lady, a friend of my sister Winifred, to visit her teacher, an accomplished Sufi, living up the Bosphorus near Tarabya. At our first meeting, he gave me a copy of his book *Hacegan Hanedanı*, which was the story of the Masters of Wisdom of Central Asia, coupled with an account of the way of Absolute Liberation - *Itlak Yolu* - of which he was and is the leading exponent. I had not paid much attention, as I was still under the influence of my visit to the Shivapuri Baba. A few years later, when I was asking myself if I should give everything I could to help Idries Shah, I wrote to Hasan for an opinion. He replied, saying that I should be following my own path, and that the time had come for me to be free from all teachers and all schools. I did not listen to this advice although I recognized the message hidden in the words. It was not until three years later, when Hasan came to England to visit me, that I began to see that he was right.

He came and stayed with us, first at Brunswick Road, but moved restlessly from place to place. I felt ashamed that the pressure of business prevented me from seeing as much of him as he hoped. Nevertheless, he made his intention very clear; he had come to arouse me to the recognition of my own destiny and to restore my confidence in my ability to fulfill it. He insisted that I was a 'master' and that I had gone beyond all those whom I regarded as my teachers. He taught me and others the zikr-i-daim, or perpetual prayer of the heart, which has no words and spans all religions. Since then five years have passed and I have derived immense benefit from this exercise. It includes a method of breath control that is more effectual than anything I had previously encountered. I did not, at first, take to the zikr because I was suspicious of breath control exercises that worked differently from those I had learned from Gurdjieff. However, after a few weeks I became aware of a most reliable and beneficial action. The breath control transfers the action of the zikr from the physical body to the Kesdjan or Astral body, which becomes perceptibly stronger and more effectual.

Hasan assured me that the vision I described in Chapter 7 of this book - which he had read and evidently knew thoroughly - was authentic and was now being fulfilled. I was destined, he said, to go beyond anything I could hope for. I was to live to a great age, and the zikr would help to prolong not only my life, but my energy. I have to admit that these promises struck a responsive chord in me, for I myself felt that I was being prepared for a great step forward. There is a sense of bewilderment and foreboding that I have learned to interpret as a premonition of death and resurrection. Life around seventy loses its reality. One asks oneself if one has lost one's way or if one's powers are failing. The external life ceases to make sense and yet nothing ostensibly is going wrong. These states are, at least in my case, an indication that a crossroads is drawing near.

Hasan took immense trouble to convince me of my own importance. It would be unseemly to repeat all that he told me, but I have to refer to this because of its effect on my life. One result was to widen my horizon and make me attend seriously to the entire human predicament on the scale of centuries rather than decades. When one does so, it becomes obvious that no large-scale action is possible during the next twenty years. The inertia of the social systems of the world cannot be overcome without wholesale disruption. One of Ouspensky's striking dicta, uttered in about 1924, was that it is reformers who prevent change by providing safety valves that release dangerous tensions. Those who are in a hurry to change the world do more to obstruct true progress than all the conservatives.

I have always known that true changes have come by the power of ideas, but those that are really new are very slow-acting. The idea that all human lives are equally sacred was unknown before the sixth century B.C. It was launched in all parts of the inhabited world by Buddha and Confucius, the Hebrew prophets of the exile, Solon and Pythagoras, and, in the very centre of the world, by Zarathustra. Until these prophets proclaimed the message, the division of mankind into a small caste of superior beings and a shadowy proletariat, with no personal rights or significance, was universally accepted. The heroic or, as I called it in *The Dramatic Universe*, the Hemitheandric Epoch had created the city state, established trade and trade routes by land and sea, had discovered the art of writing and made great technical advances. But it had done nothing for the common man who could be massacred in tens of thousands at the whim of a conqueror without arousing moral indignation even from priests and poets. The new idea of the sanctity of human life, and the right of all men to seek their own salvation, was both powerful and appealing. It was desperately needed if mankind were to be saved from catastrophe. Yet we can see from history that centuries had to pass before the new set of values implied by this idea gained universal acceptance.

We are now entering a New Epoch in which naive individualism is no longer enough. The world has become so complicated, and human interests so interdependent, that concern for others must take precedence over concern for oneself. This was certainly a central theme of the Christian teaching: "Bear one another's burdens and so fulfill the law of Christ" (St. Paul, Gal. 6:2). Two thousand years of Christian culture have almost totally failed to gain acceptance for the obvious and necessary truth, that egoism is equally disastrous for ourselves and for others. We must accept the evidence that the means so far employed to induce people to 'love one another' have failed and will always fail. Something new is needed that will capture the imagination before it satisfies the intellect, and this 'something new' must enter unobtrusively on a small scale and prove itself before it seeks wider acceptance. The industrial revolution made the forms of society suitable for agricultural people obsolete, as they in their turn had made the nomadic life obsolete. Communism cannot work except on the basis of profound religious faith and discipline. History has shown not only recently in Russia, but on many earlier occasions, that atheistic communism cannot work without brutal oppression.

From where is the new idea to come which can give mankind a new lease on life? In *The Dramatic Universe* I said that the idea of cooperation with Higher Powers - Synergism - would be the key-note of the corning age. Even when I was writing this, I did not see the full force of it. I was still thinking of the 'Higher Powers' as somehow outside humanity. I put forward the hypothesis of a 'hidden directorate', composed of people who had attained objective reason and could therefore communicate with the Demiurgic Powers.

Now, in the course of talks with Hasan Shushud, and even more as a result of practicing the zikr, I began to see that the 'Higher Powers' cannot work except through man. They can do nothing without human instruments. Synergy is not cooperation with the Demiurgic Essence, but becoming oneself a demiurgic intelligence. I should have seen this long before, because as far back as 1960 I had, in *The Dramatic Universe* Vol. II, equated the Demiurgic Essence with the 'higher nature' of man. Until I began to experience for myself the reality of what I had accepted in theory, I could not understand how the 'inner circle' works. I was still unconvinced that this 'working' could take place in me. Hasan convinced me that this is in fact possible, though he expressed it in terms of his own Itlak Sufism. It was, after all, what Gurdjieff had taught from the beginning. It was a dogma that I had accepted without referring it to myself - as we so often do with dogma. Only now, after forty years, did I see myself recovering from the conditioning to which I had been subjected in the Ouspensky groups, where it was constantly emphasized that the higher levels of being were far away and that objective conscious-ness was no concern of ours.

It was impossible to disregard the changes that were occurring in my inner life. I could see for myself that I had spoken the truth when I had written fifteen years earlier, that 'the Will does not exist' and that 'God, being pure Will, does not exist'. The corollary of this was that, so far as my own real being was concerned, I did not exist either. To see quite clearly and objectively that one does not exist and that what does 'exist' is only a material object, a mechanism, in which a dreamlike awareness takes the place of true consciousness, was not so terrifying as it sounds, but rather the touchstone of reality and the one source of hope.

As my inner life awakened to new vistas, I began to ask myself if my way of life was making sense. All through my life, I had got myself into situations in which I had to carry a heavy burden. They all had an artificial, almost fictitious, element that prevented them from attracting enough external support. I had to work excessively hard merely to keep things going. It was as if I was always trying to create a real situation out of make-believe. At one time, I thought that Structural Communication would be different. Here was a really original and valuable technique with a great potential for improving the learning and communication processes on which modern life increasingly depends. I had the support of intelligent and devoted people, and we were adequately financed. Business consultants, who examined our plans, had given advice which we followed, and success seemed to be assured. And yet one after another, set-backs occurred. Events, unforeseeable or at least unforeseen, such as the drastic cut-back in research and development expenditure decided by Sir Arnold Weinstock, head of the General Electric Company, delayed the production of demonstration machines and lost us a very important contract with the U.S. Navy. We had splendid contacts at high level in I.B.M. and had convinced a group sent over to see our work that the Systemaster should be tried out as a possible key to computerized education. Then suddenly I.B.M. top management decided to cancel their ambitious programme in the educational field, and we were left with encouragement and some financial support, but no prospect of a major breakthrough. We were caught, like thousands of others, by the cut in social expenditure that followed Mr. Nixon's election as president. To keep going, I had to make repeated visits to the States, and give more and more time to the company. I was chairman of the board and should not have been concerned in running the company, but the pattern of my fate seemed to be repeating itself.

The intention had been that I should devote a few days a month to the company and spend the rest of my time in writing. I had contracts with my publishers. I wanted to develop the science of Systematics and follow up the researches begun when I was working on *The Dramatic Universe*. I also knew that I needed more time for my inner life.

Hasan Shushud had returned to Turkey, begging me to take more care of my health. I disregarded his advice. By December, I was not only exhausted, but seriously ill. By great good fortune, I had at that time renewed my contact with Dr. Chandra Sharma, whom I had known intermittently since 1948, when he was introduced to me by Ratnasuriya. Sharma is one of the really extraordinary men I have met. He had started life in a village in South India, became a temple attendant and waited on Sri Ramana Maharshi, who had sent him to Bombay to 'become a physician'. He has since become a fully qualified medical practitioner in the United Kingdom and one of the leading exponents of homeopathy and other forms of natural medicine. He is a diagnostician with uncanny, almost miraculous, insight into the total state of his patients. I have sent literally hundreds of my pupils and friends to him when orthodox medicine had failed to help them. His record of astonishing cures has brought him such a reputation - mainly in England, Northern Europe and the U.S.A. - that he is now one of the most sought-after specialists in the country.

This digression is to explain what happened to me in January 1969. The company S.C.S. Ltd. had just been formed and demanded all my attention, but I could scarcely drag myself to the office. Dr. Sharma had warned me that I would need a prostate operation, but he wanted first to build up my strength.

Then on January 28, I collapsed. My wife called Sharma to say that I was delirious and seemed to be in real danger. He came immediately and remained with me for sixteen hours until I was out of danger. I could not communicate with him or anyone else, for I was separated from my own body. Nothing that I was saying or doing had any connection with my consciousness. I was aware of Elizabeth's presence but I could do nothing to reassure her.

I then went through one of the most important and instructive experiences of my life. I was fully aware that my blood was full of poison and that if it reached a certain intensity, my brain would be destroyed and I would never again be able to communicate. I also knew that I would not die at once, but remain in a state of total imbecility so far as the outer world or the people in it could tell. Yet I was fully and directly aware that 'I' was, and would always be, exempt from it all. 'I myself' would remain free and there would be even moments when communication would be possible. I tried then and there to say something reassuring to my wife, but I was totally helpless. I was talking, but it was not 'I' who spoke. I was aware that Dr. Sharma was doing something to me, but I could not even open my mouth when he asked me to.

This state lasted many hours, probably twenty, and for much of it I was very close to irreparable damage. Nevertheless, I was filled with joy and confidence, for I knew for certain and forever that I could lose not only my 'body' but also my 'mind', and still remain 'myself'.

When I recovered from the immediate crisis, I had to wait six weeks for the operation. At that time we had just bought a cottage at Sparkford in Somerset, that for centuries had been part of the Bennetts' family estate and had been sold to strangers in 1919. We went there for my convalescence, also just fifty years since the last time I had a serious operation after being wounded in France. I could look at my life as having completed a great cycle. In March 1919, I had seen that I could be without my body; now I had seen that my mind was also expendable. It was possible to be in a state of consciousness consisting of pure 'seeing', without any mental process and without any external manifestation. This state of consciousness was not 'in' space and time; more exactly, it was free from the conditions of space and time. It was neither 'here' nor 'there', neither 'now' nor 'not-now'. After such a revelation it was strange to think of 'business'. Yet, thanks as always to Sharma, I recovered with astounding rapidity. All my powers returned and I was full of energy.

I went back to the company and for a year and a half struggled to get it firmly established. The details are interesting, on account of the contacts we made with some of the greatest corporations in the world. They are, however, not relevant to the main theme of my life, and I pass on to July 1970. At that time, I saw that I must either devote myself wholly to business for several years or hand it over to others. The opportunity to hand it over was there, thanks to the friendship of the chairman of a very successful company, which was prepared to buy us out and provide the management experience badly needed. If I withdrew, I could turn again to my writing, but the opportunity to use the techniques we had invented for the reform of education would be lost. This was because the intended purchasers were concerned with industrial relations and not with school or university education. As the very reason I had embarked on the project eight years earlier had been to find a way of introducing new life into the educational system, the move seemed to be a betrayal of our deeper purpose.

At that time, I was invited to America by Saul Kuchinsky, General Manager of the Electronics Components Division of the Burroughs

Corporation. He had hired a chateau in New Jersey, where I gave a seminar on Systematics, attended by several prominent businessmen and engineers including Warren Avis, the founder of American Behavioral Science Laboratories, in Ann Arbor, Michigan. The two days were too short and I failed to get over the full power of Systematics. In spite of this, real interest was shown. I found a technique of real value in Warren's 'Shared Participation', which I have since used in my own work. I returned to Europe more uncertain than ever as to what I should be doing next. There were, however, two very significant meetings with groups of very young American men and women. One group was of the 'hippy' type and the other, respectable college men and women from middle class New England. Both showed almost passionate interest in work ideas, and assured me that if I were to come and stay for a year in Boston or New York, I would have thousands of followers. Some of these later joined in a group working with Paul and Naomi Anderson.

The choice had to be made. I went to St. Wandrille in September to meditate in quiet and solitude on the situation and ask for guidance in prayer. The decision could not be taken on rational grounds, since there were no clear reasons for taking either course. The unexpected happened. I received the clearest possible indication from the voice that has always spoken to me in my breast at moments of crisis. I heard it say: "You are to found a school." This happened at a moment during Matins, when I was chanting Psalm 94, *Si vocem ejus audieritis, nolite obdurare corda vestra* ("If you will hear my voice harden not your hearts") and my attention was rather on my lack of gratitude for what I had received in the past, than on what I might be doing in the future. At first I thought it referred to the education project, but it quickly became clear that I was called to an entirely new undertaking. I spent all that day in prayer and meditation and remembered that Gurdjieff had told me, in 1923, that one day I would follow in his footsteps and take up the work he had started at Fontainebleau. I also lived again through those hours on the Saturday morning before he died when he had said to me: "You. Only you can repay for all my labours." I had consistently refused for twenty-one years to put myself forward as a leader or teacher. At Coombe Springs I had been the mouthpiece of Gurdjieff or Subud or the Shivapuri Baba. I had bolstered up my own authority by quoting theirs. I had known that this was not due simply to cowardice, but rather to the awareness that my time had not yet come.

Now the moment had arrived. My next task was to be neither a businessman nor a writer, but the founder of a school. Why a school? This question that Krishnamurti put to Ouspensky in 1932, now came again before me, demanding an immediate reply. "Because people must be prepared for the troubles ahead." Then there entered my awareness the significance of the 'Fourth Way'. There was a task for me to do and I had to prepare people who could help me in it. The school to be founded was a school of the Fourth Way.

I had much experience of teaching situations. I had seen continuing centres: the Prieuré, Gadsden, Lyne Place, Franklin Farms, Coombe Springs. I had followed for fifty years the different kinds of group work in which people met fortnightly, weekly or even more often, but did not live together or work continuously under a teacher. I had seen ways with natural capacity for expansion like Subud and Transcendental Meditation. I had seen the life and work of a Benedictine monastery at St. Wandrille. I had also seen something of dervish communities in Asia. None of these could give what was now required. If I was to do something useful, it had to be different from all these. I reflected that Gurdjieff had always worked with people for a limited time and then sent them away or even had driven them out. I was also well aware that even in its heyday in 1923, his Institute at Fontainebleau had been no more than an experiment. He had been too much involved in making money to keep it going, to be able to devote enough of his own time to the pupils. Apart from the movements, none of the methods used had been persisted in long enough to give lasting results, and even the movements had been geared to the visit to the States in 1924 - the visible manifestation had to take precedence over the inner work.

If I was to achieve a better result, I must be able to devote myself wholly to the task and for that I had to have the right people, a suitable place and enough money to relieve me of material anxieties. I had none of these things. I said to myself: "If the Higher Powers really want me to undertake this task, they must provide me with money, place and people."

I returned to England and spoke of the project to Michael Franklin, the Chairman of the Institute Council. With no visible hesitation, he assured me of his full support. He told me later that a similar idea had been germinating in his own mind. Soon after, in October, we had our Annual General Meeting and I spoke of the founding of a school. There were questions and reservations - particularly as regards my own three questions: Where is the money coming from? Where will you do it? How will you find people ready and able to give up a year of their lives to such an undertaking? I did not reveal my own state of mind, beyond saying that if this was what the Higher Powers intended, they would provide the means.

It happened that the twenty-fifth anniversary of the founding of the Institute would fall in April 1971. I suggested, and all agreed with enthusiasm, that we should have a jubilee celebration and at the same time launch the new school. I thought then of starting with twenty-four pupils at a house in Kingston, although I felt deeply that for a real school it was necessary to have closer contact with the earth than was possible in a city. By the date of the Jubilee dinner, I had six candidates and the offer from Lili Hellstenius, for twenty years a most loyal supporter, of her house in Kingston to be used or sold. I decided to give the school the name International Academy for Continuous Education, to indicate, on the one hand, its Platonic inspiration and, on the other, to emphasize that it was to offer a teaching for the whole life of the men and women who came to it.

My friend and publisher, Paul Hodder Williams, was the guest of honour, supported by H.E. Apa Pant, the High Commissioner for India. Nearly three hundred members and guests met in the ballroom of St. Ermin's Hotel. The dinner was preceded by an all-day Conference on 'The Whole Man'. I spoke briefly, announcing that the Academy was founded that day. The reception was wholly favorable. There was no publicity, no press notices and no stir. People, place and money were still wanting.

Then by a peculiar set of coincidences involving an extraordinary young man in the American youth movement and my own friends in the U.S.A., I was invited to give lectures at various centres. It was already May, the university year was ending. Without publicity, how would one get audiences? However, I decided to go and arrived in Boston to be met by my old friends, Paul and Naomi Anderson, with members of the group that had formed around them after my visit in 1970. Lectures were hastily improvised at the students' union at Harvard and at Clark University, in Worcester, Massachusetts. I severely criticised the educational systems of the world, saying that they offered nothing to prepare people for the devastating changes that were to occur in the world, and said that the Academy was an experiment with a totally new approach to the 'Whole Man'. I invited those who were prepared to commit themselves to come and work very hard for a year to come and talk with me after the lectures. The response took me by surprise. Within two days, I had thirty good candidates.

I called Elizabeth in England and said that we needed a very large house. She had been to see Sherborne House, which had been a school for one hundred forty boys and had beautiful gardens and meadows. It was in the heart of the Cotswold Hills, in one of the famous beauty spots of England. I told her to go ahead and see if we could buy it.

From Boston, I went to New Hampshire with Karl Schaffer to speak at Franconia State College, which brought two candidates. Then to San Francisco, Berkeley and Sonoma State. Before I left California, the Academy was fully booked with the seventy-two candidates I considered the maximum I could take. I went to St. Louis, at the request of Irving Kahan, and spoke at Washington University. By that time nearly all students had gone on vacation and yet several excellent candidates appeared. Finally, New York, where I spoke at the Gotham Book Mart under the benign auspices of the lovely Frances Steloff, younger than ever with all her eighty-five years.

When I returned to England, I found that I had enough money to buy Sherborne House and ninety candidates for the First Basic Course. The Higher Powers had played their part with a vengeance. Never in my life had anything comparable happened to me. Hitherto, the possible had been made difficult. This time, the impossible had been made easy.

The academy was inaugurated on 15th October 1971. I had planned nothing and prepared nothing. I had Elizabeth, who was completely confident that all would go well and has worked without pity for herself ever since. To help me, I invited a very old friend and colleague already mentioned, John (Dick) Holland. To teach movements, I had Anna Durco. To organize the place I had Gilbert Edwards, and that was all. We had occupied Sherborne House on 7th September, and in five weeks had had to repair and redecorate, reinstate the heating, renew the derelict kitchen, buy and install furniture and set up a secretariat. I myself did not even have a secretary to write my letters.

And yet everything went as if predestined. The course unfolded itself. The immense wealth of ideas and techniques that fifty years of search had given me was there to call on. I had the experience of twenty-five years at Coombe Springs and all the seminars and summer schools. Even so, it was a constant source of astonishment to me, and all of us, that so much should be happening so quickly. The very absurdity of the environment was a potent factor for creating a feeling of determination to succeed. At one time, before our big cooker was working, we were cooking for a hundred people on a broken down electric stove bought for a few pounds. We lived with the smell of paint in every room and corridor. The central heating was constantly breaking down and even hot water for washing was often lacking. The rooms were cold, damp and very sparsely furnished.

In these conditions we worked hard at the Gurdjieff movements, we cleared the kitchen gardens of weeds and planted vegetables - which were promptly eaten by pigeons and rabbits. A large proportion of the students combined their zeal for higher things with all kinds of prejudices connected with food and living conditions. My first talk was about 'like and dislike'. I said that unless one was free from one's own reactions of like and dislike, desire and aversion, one could not even start. All struggled manfully with these unaccustomed demands.

Sherborne House

As usual, I overdid it. Working in the garden to show the young men how to dig, I ruptured myself and was obliged to take two weeks off for a hernia operation. This gave me the leisure to search again within myself. I could see that my life had changed because I myself had changed. I was in communication with a Higher Wisdom and it was a real two-way communication. I could ask for help and guidance, and receive them. I could even argue and insist upon the message being clarified. I was never left in doubt as to what I should do. My own weaknesses and stupidities no longer mattered. In my delirium a year before, I had seen that I could be myself without my mind. I now discovered that I could be myself in spite of my mind. As the work no longer depended on my ability to do it, I could be confident that it would succeed.

By the New Year, I saw that we were really moving. We celebrated Gurdjieff's 95th anniversary on 13th January 1972 with a great feast, at which we drank the Toasts to the Idiots as we had done in Fontainebleau forty-nine years before. We began to have visiting Saturdays, at which we demonstrated the movements and learned to tell visitors what we thought we were doing.

In April 1971, Hasan Shushud came to stay at Sherborne. He was happy in the English countryside and he was pleased to see me, but he did not think much of the students, nor did he see any sense in what I was doing. He insisted that my role was far beyond that of teacher. "You have been chosen to be one of the rare ones," he said, "who are destined to go all the way to final liberation from the conditions of existence. Your only home is the Absolute Void." I remembered Gurdjieff's words to me in Vichy in August 1949, "You can now have Paradise, but you must not be satisfied until you have attained *Soleil Absolu.*"

I was able to talk daily with Hasan, which had not been possible two years earlier in Kingston. Within a few days I began to have visions and auditions. The latter were usually in English, but sometimes in Turkish. I was convinced that I had lived before in Central Asia, at the time of Khwaja Ubeydullah Ahrar, and asked Hasan how it had come about that I had been born so far away from my native land. I have always felt at home in Asia and a stranger in Europe. He said: "The wind can blow the seed across continents. The wind is blowing towards England now. That is why you were born here."

After a week, Hasan had met most of the students and talked privately with several of them. He took a better view of them and said that several would be helpers. He also began to see some sense in the way I was teaching. He had previously insisted that all we need for our perfecting is fasting and zikr, the latter including breath control. He now told me that he found my method ideal for our time and for Western people. He said that I must not be disappointed that so few of the students had any high potential. Such people are rare. In all his life, he had met only two who could go beyond the elementary stages. I was one and the other was a Turkish doctor living in Detroit, but even he was limited because he depended too much on bodily austerities.

Several of the students came to me and asked me to explain his dicta. He had told them that I was the first European since Meister Eckhart who had grasped the secret of Absolute Liberation. I laughed and said that they must only believe what they could verify. How did they imagine that they could understand the realities of non-existence? Hasan was strong meat for them, but his presence produced a deep sense of the reality of the Unconditioned World.

Meanwhile, entries for the following year were coming in steadily. We tried to buy the really magnificent Stable block, a gem of mid-Victorian architecture. Lord Sherborne would not sell, but leased us a large area, and also gardens and cottages, that greatly increased the available accommodation. The building work was undertaken by a group of students who had acquired astonishing skills in stone masonry and other building arts.

Outside Hasan Shushud's home, Levend Istanbul 1972

Photo: Nezih Uzel

In the final weeks of the course, I set all the students to teach one another what they had learned at Sherborne. I said that we can only truly possess what we share with others and that giving is the necessary completion of receiving. I wanted them to go back and collect round them small groups to whom they would transmit the ideas and methods they had learned. "So long as we remember," I said, "that we can do nothing and understand nothing in our conditioned nature, we shall be protected from the stupidity of thinking that we are better than those we teach."

As the course ended and I watched them go, I was astonished that so much had happened to so many. Some of those who looked least promising at the start had proved to be outstanding. Even so, I had to admit that they were still living in the conditioned world of material objects, sense perceptions and thoughts. None had seen more than a glimpse of the Unconditioned. I could also see my own mistakes. Much time had been wasted on lectures and other activities that feed the mind, but do not stir the heart.

The one sure method, the value of which became more vividly evident with each passing month, was the 'decision exercise'. This is my own adaptation of a technique I had learned almost casually from Gurdjieff, and to which he refers almost casually in the Third Series of his writings, Life is Real Only Then When 'I Am'. I will not describe it here, because I have found that it cannot be transmitted effectively except by personal contact between teacher and pupil.

When the course ended, I went with Elizabeth and the girls to Turkey, where I not only met Hasan, but also Hadji Muzaffer, the sheikh of a Halveti Dervish khalka, whose *tekke* is in Istanbul near the Aqueduct of Valens. I was delighted to see how Sufism has re-established itself in Turkey since the time of Menderes. It is now possible, not only to find, but to be accepted by real sheikhs. I could also see, for myself, how much more we have at Sherborne, where we have brought together ideas and methods from all parts of the world and so have a repertoire of techniques that allows much more rapid progress for those who are willing to work.

The Second Course is now coming to an end and the candidates for 1973-74 are coming in even faster than last year. This is happening without any publicity, mainly through the impression made by last year's students on their families and friends. I have said that I will give five such courses up to 1975-76. In 1976-77, I intend to invite those who have shown themselves capable of transmitting what they have learned, and are ready to make a step forward.

In June 1972, the pattern of my life disclosed one more facet, when I was asked by Valya Anastasieff, Gurdjieff's nephew, to help the family to resolve their dispute with the Editions Janus, a publishing agency to which Gurdjieff had entrusted the publication of his books and music. Gurdjieff's only surviving sister, Sophie Ivanovna, had died a few months previously and only four nieces and Valya himself remained. They were distressed at the failure of Janus to publish the Third Series of Gurdjieff's writings and to do more to spread his music and dances. I was happy to renew a closer connection with Gurdjieff's family, especially those who had been with him in Paris in 1948 and 1949. They all share a penetrating understanding of human nature and great versatility in a wide variety of skills. These characteristics, essential for survival in an alien environment, are the justification for the peculiar educational methods that Gurdjieff adopted for his own family. I have adapted them as well as I could for the students at Sherborne.

It transpired that the family's aim in coming to me was to secure my cooperation in getting *Life is Only Then, When 'I Am'* published in accordance with Gurdjieff's wishes, expressed in the prologue to the last book. This was a very delicate matter as I was not in the 'orthodox' group of Gurdjieff's followers who had set themselves to preserve his teaching 'without change or addition'. On the contrary, I had searched for myself, found new ideas, new methods and had served new masters. Some of Gurdjieff's followers were particularly shocked by my suggestion that Pak Subuh might be the 'one who is to come' that Gurdjieff had spoken of in 1949. I could blame no one for rejecting me and I did to make matters worse by taking the great responsibility of editing the Third Series. However, when I looked into the position closely and upon study and consultation with some of the older pupils in France and in the United States, I felt that I could help to heal the animosities that had been burning for so long. I had a strong feeling that Gurdjieff's family had been unfairly treated, but that they, for their part, did not appreciate the sincere wish of Gurdjieff's followers to do the right thing by them. The best course seemed to be that I should agree to edit the work and to find publishers.

The editing of the Third Series revealed to me some very subtle elements in Gurdjieff's teaching that have been a great help to me. I was asked by the family to include lectures given by Gurdjieff and perhaps intended by him to be worked into the Third Series, but never labeled as such. This raises the question of just what purpose Gurdjieff intended his writings to serve, which in turn makes us ask what Gurdjieff's life as a whole was about. I had been examining just these questions in the course of writing a biography and critical examination of Gurdjieff's work, commissioned by Turnstone Books. I had started to write this book just before the inauguration of the Academy. I regarded this task as a step towards fulfilling the promise I had made to Gurdjieff at the end of his life, that I would do all in my power to make his ideas known and understood.

I had reached the conclusion that Gurdjieff was more than a Teacher and less than a Prophet. He was a man with a true mission and he devoted his entire life to it. He needed people who could understand his message, and yet he was compelled to make the message obscure and hard to understand. Therefore, he had to look for those who could acquire the required perspicacity and also the singleness of purpose to carry his work forward. Today, twenty-four years after his death, there are thirty or forty people in different parts of the world who are capable of transmitting the teaching, but there are very few who can look beyond the man to his message. The time to go deeper and bring out the core of the message is now coming, and we must be prepared to make sacrifices of our own limited viewpoints to allow the greater image to emerge. This will take a number of years and there is no time to lose, for events are catching up on us.

I write as if I shall still be alive five, ten or twenty years hence. Who can say? The span of human life is a little understood subject. It is easy to observe that some people age more slowly than others, that there is no obvious reason why a healthy man or woman should not live to a hundred or more, and, in general, that we are beginning to learn something about the science of gerontology. None of this meets the question whether or not a self-realized man can live as long as he chooses. I knew the Shivapuri Baba, in full possession of his faculties at one hundred thirty-six. In 1919, I met a Turkish Hamal with authenticated papers showing that he was born in 1776, twelve years before the French Revolution. He was slow and deaf, but by no means senile. Gurdjieff asserts that longevity is the most important of all human problems. A man must be able to live as long as is necessary to fulfill his mission on this earth - to complete his higher being body and attain 'the requisite gradation of objective reason'.

For myself, I am aware that death is a phenomenon of the conditioned world. 'Survival' or 'life after death' is also a conditioned state and not a very desirable one, for it is a state of dreaming without awakening. One needs a body to wake up in and where is a body to come from!

The path of reality does not lead into the future, but out of time and space altogether. Once one realizes this simple truth, life and death go into a different perspective. Life and death, time and space do not cease to exist, but existence itself is seen as a mirage.

Meanwhile, there is this human world and its predicament. For mankind the future is real enough. We cannot turn our backs on the needs of the world, especially if we are convinced that they matter on a larger scale than that of this planet alone. 'Conscious labour and intentional suffering' are called for - more especially by those who have the possibility of sowing the seeds of the new age. The world needs, more than ever before, men and women who have achieved inner freedom and who can live and love impartially. It is my hope and intention that before I depart from this conditioned world, I shall have helped many to find their way.

More than seventy years have passed since I began to ask questions and remember the answers. I asked my mother: "Why can't we see God?" to which she replied, "I expect He doesn't want us to." This did not satisfy me then, but it satisfies me now. I can understand much better why some mysteries must remain mysteries and why others can be revealed. I am wholly convinced that there is a Providential Power at work in the world, but it cannot help us without our consent. I finish this new edition of *Witness*, as I did the first, by quoting Gurdjieff: "Two things have no limit: the stupidity of man and the mercy of God."

EPILOGUE

J. G. Bennett died on 13th December 1974, about 18 months after he had completed revisions to *Witness*, with the Fourth Basic Course at Sherborne only two months old.

His death was a massive shock to his students and friends all over the world, though with the benefit of hindsight, there were reasons to expect it. His wife Elizabeth's diaries refer to his health problems almost daily for a period of 18 months. Bennett suffered particularly from high blood pressure, and it's hard to resist the idea that simple overwork drove his body early into the grave. Of course, no one apart from his doctor, the legendary homeopath Chandra Sharma, and Elizabeth herself, were fully aware of his medical condition. The rest of the world, from Madame de Salzmann to his humblest student, continued to expect him to behave like superman.

Nevertheless, there were other signs that, at some level, Bennett himself knew that his physical death was imminent. He had introduced the fourth year students to advanced exercises and ideas that he had not shown until the end of the previous courses. And as the 'theme' for what turned out to be his - but not the Basic Course's - final week, Bennett chose 'Completion'.

Elizabeth and the other members of the small staff at Sherborne - including Pierre and Vivien Elliot, Anthony Blake, and Michael Sutton - decided to continue the Fourth Course and, subsequently, to run a complete Fifth Course, thereby completing Bennett's own commitment to run formal courses for five years. When the fourth-year students left for a Christmas break a few days after Bennett's funeral, Pierre Elliot offered them a full refund of their course fees should they not wish to return, since Bennett himself was no longer directing the course. None took up the offer, and all returned for the remainder of the course, which turned out to be particularly fruitful.

At the end of the Fifth Course, Elizabeth admitted that holding such an enterprise together, in the absence of a teacher of Bennett's stature, was virtually impossible, and once his original five-year commitment had been honoured, Sherborne House was sold to Beshara, a neighbouring Sufi group. Meanwhile, during a meeting of the Council of the Institute for Comparative Study (which owned Sherborne) on the day of Bennett's funeral, a decision had been made to go ahead with establishing an experimental community at Claymont Court near Charles Town, West Virginia, in the United States, based on the principles and techniques that Bennett had taught at Sherborne.

Thereafter, Claymont became the focus for much of the activity of the new American Society for Continuous Education. A community was inaugurated on the property, and a series of ten-month courses were offered until the mid-1980s. The enterprise was supported by visitors, residents and generous financial donations, but as a community it never reached the hundreds of residents that JGB envisaged. In retrospect, it is clear that this was a project on a scale that only someone of his magnetic power could have sustained, even though Bennett's nephew, Pierre Elliot, with his wife Vivien, devoted himself to Claymont for many years. Elsewhere in America, others of Bennett's students started groups and communities on a more modest scale, some of which continue to flourish.

With the ending of Sherborne in England, an attempt was made to set up a similar centre on a smaller scale at nearby Daglingworth, but that experiment was rapidly caught up in the sort of schism that almost invariably follows the death of a teacher. In this case, the appearance of a powerful new figure from America had the effect of splitting what remained of Bennett's Institute for Comparative Study, and several of his more prominent students aligned themselves as a group with this new man. Those remaining, including his wife Elizabeth, continued working on more traditional lines, giving support to the English and American groups and to the Claymont experiment.

It is now nearly forty years since Bennett's death. Many of the predictions he made about the collapse of contemporary society have yet to be fulfilled, since he expected widespread disruption by the end of the last century. However, this doesn't invalidate his analysis. He may have been wrong (or over-optimistic) about the speed at which change would come, but coming it certainly is, and on a scale that even he could not have foreseen. The way we people continue to put our own short-term convenience ahead of accelerating climate change is the most startling example of human cupidity - and stupidity - but it is by no means the only one. The fundamental problem facing humanity and the planet, is humanity itself, and Bennett stressed that is only by changing ourselves that we can hope to change the world.

Bennett hoped that the ideas and practices he taught students on his courses at Sherborne would give them the tools to take a step towards 'making a new world' (the title he chose for his seminal work on Gurdjieff, published the year before he died). The essence of the new world would be 'synergy', and 'Synergic Epoch' was the name he gave in *The Dramatic Universe* to the coming era. For Bennett, synergy meant cooperation not only between people, but between humanity and the Higher Powers, which were, for him, a present and practical reality, as he describes in the last chapter of this book.

In the aftermath of his death, many of Bennett's students proved too young and untested to sustain any great experiment, such as the grand plan at Claymont, but the challenge remains for all of us. What are we really prepared to give up in order to sow the seeds for a new world? It is clear from Witness that sacrifice is necessary; Bennett's life is full of examples of sacrifice, but his account also makes clear that sacrifice opens possibilities in a way nothing else can, both inwardly and outwardly. Bennett hoped that his students would actively pursue the task of sharing what they learned and later developed - it was not for nothing that he called his school the Academy for Continuous Education - but he also envisaged the establishment of communities which would be a model for a new way of living. Both are challenges that too few of his pupils have been ready to answer, but there are signs that this is changing.

As Bennett describes so vividly in this book, in his account of the aftermath of Gurdjieff's death, some of his students stuck more or less to the methods and practices he taught, while others - including Bennett himself - experimented more radically. The same has been true of Bennett's own students, but in recent years, there have been encouraging signs of increasing cross-fertilisation between these two necessary approaches. Bennett was convinced that a new world is in the process of being born and that we people living now have a part to play in sowing the seeds. Among his former students, even those who have diverged quite markedly, there is a growing realisation that all of us who aspire to work towards creating a new world - whether we be students of Bennett, Gurdjieff or any other teacher - need to cooperate with each other.

George Bennett
Massachusetts
13th December 2012

BIBLIOGRAPHY

J.G. Bennett:

The Crisis in Human Affairs, first published Hodder & Stoughton, London, 1946
The Dramatic Universe
Volume 1: The Foundations of natural Philosophy, first published Hodder & Stoughton, London, 1956
Volume 2: The Foundation of Moral Philosophy, first published Hodder & Stoughton, London, 1951
Volume 3: Man and His Nature, first published Hodder & Stoughton, London, 1966
Volume 4: History, first published Hodder & Stoughton, London, 1966
A Spiritual Psychology, first published Hodder & Stoughton, London, 1964
Long Pilgrimage, first published Hodder & Stoughton, London, 1965

G.I. Gurdjieff:

The Herald of Coming Good
All & Everything:

First Series: Beelzebub's Tales to His Grandson,
Second Series: Meetings with Remarkable Men, first published
Third Series: Life is Real Only Then, When "I AM"

P.D. Ouspensky:

Tertium Organum
A New Model of the Universe
In Search of the Miraculous

INDEX

A

Abbas Hilmi Pasha, ex-Khedive of Egypt 84, 345
Abdul Hamid, Sultan 33, 39, 46, 84, 88, 89, 99, 103, 111–113, 132, 135, 140, 144, 148, 159, 161, 306
Abdullah Daghestani, Sheikh 325, 328, 329, 332, 358
Abdul Medjid, Crown Prince of Turkey 71, 303
Accumulator, the Great 128, 130, 133
Adana 307, 316
Africa 33, 325
Africa, South 9, 183, 230, 238–244, 334, 350
Ahmad, Icksan and Ismana 346
Ahmad Tabrizi, Dervish 329–330
Ahmed Çelebi 33
Ahrar, Khwaja Ubeydullah 9, 399
Albania 83
Ali Riza Bey 11, 16, 19
All and Everything, Gurdjieff 198, 266, 276, 277, 323
Anastasieff, Valentin 401
Anderson, Paul and Naomi 396
Angels 327, 330
Anglo-Turkish relations 20, 73
Armenian atrocities 28
Ataturk, Mustafa Kemal Pasha 18, 19, 26, 305
Atesh Baz 35
Athenaeum Club 197
Athens 73, 142–153, 366
Atrocity stories 23
Australia 350
Aya Sofia 39

B

Babylon 311–312, 319
Baku 24

Baroda, Maharajah, Gaekwar of 107
Bartok, Eva 347
B.C.U.R.A. 186, 190, 191, 195, 204, 205, 207, 211, 214, 215, 217, 224
Being and Consciousness 225
Being and Knowledge 64, 105, 117, 133, 166, 177, 222, 254, 276
Beit-ul-Muharrem 360
Benedictines 364, 367
Bennett
    daughter. See Ubsdell, Ann, nee Bennett
    father. See Bennett, Basil Wilfred
    first wife. See McNeill, Evelyn, afterwards Mrs. Bennett
    mother. See Bennett, Annie Caroline, nee Craig
    second wife. See Beaumont, Winifred, afterwards Mrs. Bennett
    sister. See Udale, Winifred, nee Bennett
    third wife. See Mayall, Elizabeth, afterwards Mrs. Bennett
Bennett, Annie Caroline, nee Craig 38
    mother 15, 82, 97, 151, 154, 156, 225, 228, 261
Bennett, Basil Wilfred
    father 13
Bergson, Professor Henri 10
Beshara ii
Bissing, Ronimund von 325, 339
Born, Professor Max 207
Bradley, F.H. 371
British Coal Utilization Research Association 185
Brown, R.L. 207
Brunswick Road 382, 388
Buchmann, Dr. 371

76038458R00263

Made in the USA
San Bernardino, CA
08 May 2018